FIGHTING
FOR
FRANCO

FIGHTING
FOR
FRANCO

**International Volunteers in Nationalist Spain
during the Spanish Civil War, 1936–39**

JUDITH KEENE

Foreword by Professor Gabriel Jackson

Leicester University Press
London and New York

Leicester University Press
A Continuum imprint
The Tower Building, 11 York Road, London SE1 7NX
370 Lexington Avenue, New York, NY 10017-6503

First published 2001

British Library Cataloguing-in-Publication Data
A catalogue record for this book is available from the British Library.

ISBN 0-7185-0126-8 (hardback)

Library of Congress Cataloging-in-Publication Data
Keene, Judith, 1948–
    Fighting for Franco: international volunteers in nationalist Spain during the Spanish Civil War, 1936–1939 / Judith Keene; foreword by Gabriel Jackson.
        p. cm.
    Includes bibliographical references and index.
    ISBN 0-7185-0126-8 (hardbound)
    1. Spain—History—Civil War, 1936–1939—Participation, Foreign.   2. Fascists.
I. Title.

DP269.45 .K44 2001
946.081—dc21

                                                                        2001023395

Typeset by BookEns Ltd, Royston, Herts
Printed and bound in Great Britain by Biddles Ltd, Guildford and King's Lynn

Contents

Foreword

Let me start by indicating the unique character of this book. There have been dozens of studies published concerning the International Brigades, the approximately 40,000 volunteers from some fifty countries who came to Spain in 1936 and 1937 to fight in defence of the Spanish Republic. We know in great detail who they were, where they came from, what ideologies and what personal experiences motivated them to see in the struggle *against* Franco a cause worth the sacrifice of their lives. We also know in considerable detail, though with less in the way of individual biographies, the numbers and the motives of over 70,000 uniformed Italian troops and aviators, approximately 20,000 German military specialists and several thousand Portuguese soldiers who were sent by Mussolini, Hitler and Salazar to fight in the ranks of General Franco's army. And in the cases of both the International Brigades and the military units sent by the fascist dictators, we know pretty much what was their military importance to the side they were supporting, and what were their political roles in the course of the 32-month Civil War.

But the above paragraph does not account for another, much less numerous and less militarily significant, group of foreigners; namely, the perhaps 1000 to 1500 English, Irish, French, White Russian and Romanian volunteers who came to Spain to fight on the side of General Franco. There have been several important studies of the English and Irish groups, which studies are referred to in Professor Keene's notes and bibliography, but there has been no previous scholarly study of the pro-Franco foreign volunteers as a whole, and this is the unique characteristic of the present volume.

Franco's volunteers came from a wide variety of social and ideological backgrounds, but the common denominator of their motives for coming to Spain was the conviction that the Republic was Communist-dominated, and that it must be militarily destroyed in order to prevent the establishment of a Soviet-style Communist regime in Western Europe. Many were Roman

Catholics outraged by the fact that the Spanish Republic had disestablished the Church in one of Europe's historically most Catholic countries, and by the church burnings and lynchings of priests which occurred in the first few months of the Civil War. Others were fascists, convinced that Socialist, Communist and anarcho-syndicalist trade unions and propaganda organizations were destroying the patriotic traditions, the necessary discipline and social hierarchy of Western capitalist societies. As fascists they also shared the leadership principle, the glorification of militarism and the male bonding characteristic somewhat of Mussolini's, and very strongly of Hitler's, ruling parties. The White Russians and Romanians were mostly members of the Orthodox national churches in their homelands, but they were spiritually united with Western Catholics in the defence of 'Christian civilization' against the 'satanic hordes' of Marxists, agnostics, atheists and Freemasons. The great majority were also anti-Semitic and anti-Muslim.

In their hero-worship, their militarism, their anti-Communism and anti-Semitism, they were psychologically comfortable with the Falangist, Carlist, politically dogmatic and thoroughly conservative ideals of the military in Franco Spain. Protestants were occasionally offended by some of the things they heard said about their faith, but the anti-Communist and pro-fascist aspects of most conversations were much more important than religious differences within the Christian camp. Most of the volunteers were anti-Muslim on both religious and 'racial' grounds, but they had no difficulty in accepting the fact that General Franco was using tens of thousands of Moorish troops. The use of elite foreign mercenaries has been frequent in the history of many empires. In the present instance, General Franco's Moorish Guard and redoubtable Moroccan assault troops contributed to his prestige as a crusading warrior and effectively terrorized both the Republican troops and the civilian population. At the same time, their iron discipline and complete subordination were evidence, for all fascist supporters, domestic and foreign, that these Muslims were the obedient servants of a Christian ruler.

Two other factors have surely been important in the relative neglect of the subject of Franco's volunteers in the massive bibliography of the Spanish Civil War. For one thing, Franco always insisted that there were virtually no foreigners fighting on his side. All his propaganda efforts, co-ordinated with those of Mussolini and Hitler, were directed towards attributing the whole Republican military resistance to Communist, Bolshevik and Masonic influences. The Spanish officer corps had been generally sympathetic to Germany in the First World War, and Spanish neutrality in that war had meant that they had had practically no contact with their French and British peers. During the Civil War they felt great professional respect for the Germans, and felt mixed gratitude or scorn towards the Italians depending on the flow of military events. But, in any case, they were very loath to credit military victories to their German and Italian allies.

The second factor was the small numbers, the unknown languages and the truly minor military role of the 1000 to 1500 Irishmen, Anglo-Saxon Protestants, French and Belgian Catholics, White Russian Orthodox and Romanians. These were people of whose history and religion the franquista leadership knew absolutely nothing (and the same was true in reverse). Communication was severely limited by the fact that very few knew a word of each other's languages. Personal attitudes were inevitably based on ignorance of just about everything except the shared pro-fascist and anti-Communist sentiments expressed in the simplest forms. In addition, after the Second World War, both Franco Spain and its foreign supporters were busy adjusting their statements to the triumph of democracy and claiming that they had never been fascist or Nazi, only more consistently anti-Communist than the Western democracies had been in the 1930s.

For various reasons, the lives, motives and roles of Franco's real foreign volunteers have received very little attention in the historical literature. It is to the great credit of Professor Keene that she has undertaken a detailed, fully documented study of these volunteers as a group. She has evaluated their letters, their journalistic and autobiographical memoirs. She has placed them in the context both of their home countries and of the armed forces led by General Franco. She has combed the English-, French- and Spanish-language press for all references to the volunteers. She has seen them as human beings apart from their political roles and has reported their activities as thoroughly as possible without in any way exaggerating the measurable effects of those activities.

Gabriel Jackson

Map 1 The Iberian peninsula showing locations (annotations to GMT cartography by Sam Keene).

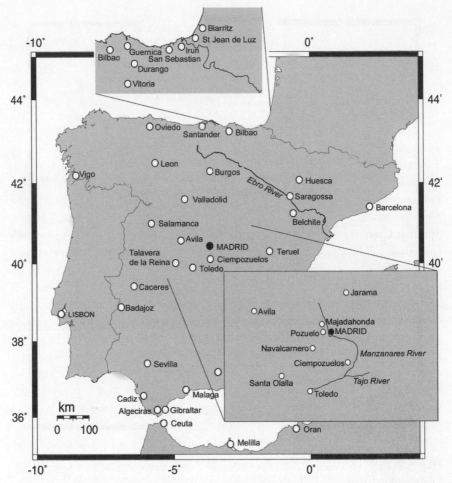

Map 2 The Iberian peninsula showing locations (annotations to GMT cartography by Sam Keene).

Introduction

❧

Towards the end of Pierre Drieu la Rochelle's autobiographical novel, *Gilles*,[1] the hero, Gilles Gambier, a Frenchman passing himself off as a Belgian Rexist, is picked up on the coast of Majorca by two men in a pleasure yacht. They have come south to support General Franco in the Spanish Civil War. The yacht's owner is Irish and stowed below are arms for Franco. The yachtsman tells Gilles that he is a 'Catholic who wants to defend Catholic civilization'. The other passenger is Polish, a 'Catholic fascist' committed to a fascist revolution from which, he says, the Church will benefit. The dangers and the exhilaration of battle kindle a spirit of camaraderie among the three, determined as they are to fight for Franco.

Gilles and his comrades powerfully evoke a large segment of Franco's foreign volunteers. The bravado, the eulogizing of action and their other clerico-fascist sentiments all ring true. Familiar, too, is the restlessness they exude and the desire for adventure coupled with an existence unbound by ties to home and hearth. Equally authentic is their extravagant commitment to a 'New Europe' and 'virile Catholicism' from which are excluded a good many citizens living in Europe. These volunteers for Franco robustly reject the League of Nations as effete and seek in its place a unity of 'genuine' Europeans who can hold the line against the anti-Europe of Communists, atheists, Freemasons and Jews. In the mid-1930s, with Rightist dictatorships in ebullient ascendancy, Drieu's characters and their swaggering presumption of success were perfectly plausible.

Gilles Gambier provides a fitting introduction to this study in another way. He is totally absorbed by the effort of coming to terms with his own place in the flawed world after the First World War. In each setting and every episode of his life, Gilles remains focused on himself. The landscapes he traverses and the individuals he meets never take precedence over the enterprise of his own self-examination. While Drieu's purpose may be to evoke the essential solipsism of all existence, the figure of Gilles recalls the mindset that motivated many of Franco's volunteers. The spur to enlist came from the individual's own circumstances, or from the exigencies of their particular national politics.

In almost all cases, Franco's volunteers spoke no Spanish and knew little about Spain before they arrived. The adventurers came for the action; and the ideologues perceived the Spanish Civil War, simply, as an extension of the political struggles in which they were engrossed at home. In consequence, more often than not, foreign volunteers were misapprised of the specificities and domestic dimension of the Spanish Civil War. The reality of Franco's Spain was that Spaniards, whether civilian or military, did not welcome foreigners with open arms, particularly those who had little to offer but themselves as footsloggers in Franco's crusade. In the end, many of Franco's foreign volunteers, when they finally managed to enlist, found life very harsh in Nationalist Spain.

One of the enduring myths of the Franco state was that the Nationalist forces that won the Spanish Civil War consisted of patriotic Spaniards, while the Republic was defended by a rag-tag army of foreign 'Reds'. During the Civil War, however, many groups on the European Right were galvanized by the Nationalist cause. Just as outside Spain the Republic appealed to the Left, so Franco and the Nationalists were a powerful symbol for pious Catholics, crypto-Nazis, aspiring fascists, old-style conservatives and anti-Semites of every stripe. As exemplified by Gilles Gambier or his real-life comrades in this study, Franco's 'Glorious Crusade' was often viewed as a single episode in a war that had begun in 1917. A number of Franco's foreign volunteers had fought against the Bolsheviks in the Russian Civil War. Others were with Mussolini in 1935 in the Italian invasion of Ethiopia. In 1939 some of Franco's foreign veterans fought against Soviet soldiers in the Russo-Finnish War; or in 1941 went on to enlist with Hitler on the Eastern Front. In this sense, for the European Right, the Spanish Civil War was an important step in a series of defining political events between the wars.

There is an enormous literature on the 35,000 to 40,000-strong International Brigade of foreign volunteers for the Spanish Republic.[2] Historians and participants have mapped the motivations of the volunteers, their politics and their stories, large and small. There is also a library of material tracing the political disputes between Spanish liberals, Socialists, Communists and the 'anti-authoritarian left', as well as the role of international volunteers in all these combinations. Similarly, almost from the start of the war, there was debate about the military contribution of the International Brigade: were its members better qualified as soldiers than their Spanish fellows; and was their arrival in Madrid in November 1936 critical in turning the tide against Franco in the first part of the war?

Whether as individuals, ideologues or soldiers, very little, by contrast, has been written about Franco's foreign volunteers. José Luis de Mesa[3] has produced a useful compilation of selected material from the Spanish Military Archives but uses few other sources and attempts no analysis of the whole. In a meticulous study of Latin Americans in the Spanish Civil War, Gerold Gino Baumann provides a great deal of information – names, nationalities and occupations – of them all, including the comparatively small number who fought for Franco.[4] Two recent scholarly works, by Robert A. Stradling and Feargal McGarry respectively, examine the Irish in Spain, both those who fought for the Republic and the much larger unit that comprised the Irish Brigade for Franco.[5]

The small number of studies is partly a function of the relatively few foreign volunteers for Franco; but it is not simply a matter of numbers. Franco's foreign volunteers have tended not to feature because their absence has served both Republican and Nationalist mythology. It has always been important to the legitimation of the Republican cause to show that non-Spaniards who came to fight in Spain were volunteers in the International Brigades. From a pro-Republican point of view, the foreigners who fought for Franco were not in Spain of their own volition, but there at the command of their totalitarian governments. Certainly, this is the case with the Italian, German and Portuguese soldiers, but it does not cover all foreigners on the Nationalist side. It is not surprising, however, that the difference in the motivations of the two sides has been emphasized by Republican supporters because it highlights the nobility and heroism of those who fought for the Spanish Republic.

The same components of the myth, albeit for a different objective, served the Franco state as well. The official Nationalist position was always that there were few foreigners in Nationalist Spain, in contrast with the 'hordes of Reds' on the other side.[6] In a broadcast from Burgos on 1 October 1937, to mark the anniversary of his becoming head of the Spanish state, General Franco laid out the position unequivocally. The Nationalists were 'fighting against international units: not against sons of Spain but against the sons of Russia and the offscourings of Europe in a magnificent undertaking for the re-conquest and the fight against Red Europe and Moscow.'[7]

Contemporaries frequently noted that, as a matter of course, franquista sources minimized the numbers of foreigners on their side.[8] Even when Franco conceded the presence of foreigners with the Nationalists, he always claimed that they were few and had come only after the arrival of 'all the detritus of the whole world that the Reds send to the Republic'.[9]

Apart from it suiting domestic consumption to claim that Spaniards were for Franco and foreigners were for the Republic, it also fitted franquista foreign policy from the end of the Second World War to play down the enthusiasm with which European fascists had embraced their cause. The high point of Spanish official pro-fascism coincided with the *apogée* of Ramón Serrano Suñer at the Spanish Foreign Ministry. Franco's brother-in-law and an active Falangist with close ties to Mussolini's circle, Serrano's removal from the Foreign Ministry by 1943 signalled the start of a change of direction in franquista foreign policy. Evidence of the official shift can be tracked in the changing volume of published pamphlet writings about European fascism that appeared in Spain in the decade after the war.[10] The high point of the record, in terms of numbers of pamphlets and the topics covered, was in the early 1940s, which was also at the height of German success in Europe. In the last years of the Second World War there was a marked falling away of publications with Madrid imprints eulogizing the governments and political systems of extreme-right European nations which were pro-Franco.[11] From late 1943, increasingly, it was apparent that the Axis countries would lose the war and therefore it was necessary for Franco to reposition Spain in the new Cold War configuration that would dominate international politics after the Second World War. Similarly, the cultural historian Paloma Aguilar Fernández identifies 1944 as marking a shift away from the 'heroic and Manichean' presentation of the Spanish Civil War in official news and documentaries (Nodo) in Spain.[12]

Aims of the study

The aim of this study of Franco's foreign volunteers is quite modest. I make no claim to comprehensiveness. Even if a full recording of Franco's foreign volunteers was the most pressing issue on the research agenda, the patchiness of the documentation and its dispersal across a great range of national archives probably preclude the possibility of a study of every single one of Franco's foreign volunteers.

This book is structured into seven essays, each of which deals with a set of Franco's foreign supporters or, as in the case of the second essay, with some of the travel narratives written by foreigners in Nationalist Spain. In each of the case studies of the volunteers – English-speakers, French, White Russians, Romanians and Franco's foreign women – I have tried to lay out the social and political contexts outside Spain from which they originated as well as what happened when they crossed the border. Since they came to assist the Nationalist war effort, I have attempted, as well, to weigh up their contribution in terms of the political and social benefit that accrued to themselves versus the military assistance they provided towards Franco's victory. Where possible, too, I give some indication of what happened to these characters after 1939. Because they were on the winning side, as it were, in Spain, many of them assumed the same outcome would prevail in the much bigger stakes of the European Civil War from 1939 to 1945. When this was not the case, many of Franco's foreign supporters – outright fascist, militant Catholics and anti-Semites – had to renegotiate their lives after the Second World War and disguise their pre-war politics. Some of them have seen the collapse of the Soviet Union as a vindication of their interwar political commitments and have begun to write about themselves and their experiences at that time. Where they are relevant I have used this new material.

The year 2000 is a good time for research on this topic. It is close enough to the event to benefit from the new memoirs and primary material that have become available, but far enough away to allow the historian to revisit without having to work within the divisions between Right and Left of the 1930s. In the study, I try to reconstruct the world-views of Franco's Nationalist volunteers, honestly and empathetically. This does not mean that I am less sympathetic to the Republicans or in any way denigrate their cause.

On these matters, it is impossible when researching this topic not to engage with the work of Herbert Rutledge Southworth. His robust deconstruction of whole swathes of franquista scholarship about the Civil War was based on meticulous bibliographical analysis and a deep knowledge of the issues from his own personal involvement defending the Spanish Republic during the war; and as an unshakeable critic of Franco's Spain ever since. Reading Le Mythe de la croisade de Franco (1964) or Guernica! Guernica!: A Study of Journalism, Diplomacy, Propaganda and History (1977) with their unassailable scholarship and strongly partisan authorial voice is as arresting today as it was when the books first appeared.

When Herbert Southworth was in San Diego in the late 1970s he was bemused but tolerant of the fascination that many graduate students like myself felt for anarchist communes and libertarian women in the Spanish Civil War. But unerringly he would remind us that it was important that people of the Left should work on topics on the Right. He talked to me about this exact topic in San Diego and later in France at Château Roche, and I was spurred on when I returned to Australia to make a small foray into the life of an Australian who fought for Franco in the Spanish Foreign Legion. Some years later I came back to Franco's foreign volunteers and began systematic work on the subject. At this time, too, Herbert Southworth made useful suggestions, his encouragement a sign of great generosity, because by then he was very frail and in fact approaching the end of his life which came in October 1999.

One of Southworth's great strengths was his ability to demolish false franquista claims about the Civil War by demonstrating from the literature that their version was not what, in fact, had happened. My interest is somewhat different. I do not so much wish to set the perceptions of Franco's foreign volunteers against some putative notion of what 'really happened'. Rather, I wish to reconstruct their own views of the enterprise on which they were engaged and the response it elicited in Nationalist Spain, in order to gain an insight into the Extreme Right during these years.

This study is, therefore, a mission of historical recovery, retrieving the stories of these 'disappeared' characters in the history of the Spanish Civil War. And, because their lives and the political impetus that brought them to Spain were so anchored in the politics of the decade, their experiences in Franco's Spain also provide a small but clear window into the political concerns of the extreme Right leading to the Second World War.

Who is in and who is out

The study excludes Germans, Italians and Portuguese, who, with a few exceptions, were not volunteers in the proper sense of the word. These three national groups were in Spain as part of military missions accredited to their respective governments, which were in close contact with Franco's headquarters. As well, the foreign soldiers received payment in some form or another from home governments. In the same way, their travel to Spain was arranged for them as part of an official plan between Nationalist Spain and their countries of origin.

Among the Germans in Spain, the most notable were the Condor Legion, which at its height comprised some 19,000 men with approximately 6500 personnel at any time.[13] It consisted of flyers and technical staff who maintained highly sophisticated communication facilities for more than a hundred aircraft of various types. The Condor Legion provided invaluable support to the Nationalist war effort while at the same time gaining experience that could be put to Germany's advantage in the Second World War.

German pilots and technicians were rotated every six months and the whole operation was carried out with great secrecy. Adolf Galand, one of the pilots, recalled the pattern. Between 1936 and 1939 a comrade who had dropped from sight would suddenly turn up again in Germany 'in high spirits, with a suntan and having bought himself a new car' and would proceed to tell his close friends, in confidence, the most remarkable stories about his adventures in Spain.[14]

Germans serving with Franco normally wore their own uniforms, or civilian clothes, and even when they wore combat clothes with a Spanish cut they displayed the swastika or the death's head on sleeve or lapel. All German ranks automatically moved up a grade in Spain. German salaries were paid at home with a special loading for Spanish expenses and in Spain were paid in Reichsmarks which were converted into local currency.[15]

Mussolini sent contingents to Spain from the regular army and the Blackshirts which became the *Corpo Truppe Volontarie* (CTV). In total they comprised some 80,000 men, of whom approximately 6000 were from the Italian air force, 45,000 from the regular Italian army and 29,000 in Blackshirt militias. At the height of the Italian commitment there were about 50,000 Italian soldiers in Spain at any one time.[16] Like the German contingent, Italians functioned as distinct units, often wearing their own uniforms or khakis cut in Spain but bearing identifying insignia. The families of these Italian soldiers in Spain were paid at home by the Italian government. Even after Italians were integrated into the Nationalist army to serve under Nationalist command overall, there were Italian officers and adjutants functioning as intermediaries.[17]

The estimates of the numbers of Portuguese in Spain vary between 1000 soldiers and 20,000, though the latter figure is undoubtedly too high.[18] Ricardo de la Cierva estimates 2000 Portuguese and Charles Esdaile offers the figure in between of 15,000 soldiers. Neither author indicates the basis of his estimate.[19] Portuguese soldiers wore no distinguishing insignia and were therefore impossible to identify. The muster of foreign volunteers in the Spanish Foreign Legion in August 1938 indicates that Portuguese comprised the largest number of foreigners at 869 enlistments. The figure refers only to those who registered in the Legion.[20] As well there were Portuguese in the regular army and the Requetés as well as in Falangist units.

At the first news of the Generals' uprising in Spain, the leader of the coporatist Portuguese state, Antonio de Oliveira de Salazar, offered soldiers to Mola.[21] There were also volunteers from the Portuguese Legion, the militia of the Salazarist movement. Equally importantly, throughout the war, Nationalist army representatives were allowed to come and go freely across the Portuguese border. From 1936 to 1939, Salazar favoured Franco, and a great many Portuguese soldiers who fought in Spain arrived in groups organized by the Portuguese government. Typical of them were the 56 army officers who arrived at the end of March 1938. The Portuguese army had called them up from regular infantry regiments to serve in the Nationalist army. They were guaranteed full pay and promised quick promotion.[22] Although a signatory, if reluctantly, to the Treaty of Non-Intervention in Spain, Salazar had no compunction in aiding Franco wherever he could. Throughout the war there was a good deal of cordial visiting between official groups and good wishes sent between Lisbon and Salamanca. Portuguese veterans' organizations sent delegations to greet Moscardó in Toledo and Mola in Talavera de la Reina. Similarly, Portuguese and Spanish Falangists enjoyed sports competitions and fostered fraternal cultural visits between the youth groups in both countries.[23] At the same time Portuguese officials turned back to Francoist Spain pro-Republicans at the border and cracked down on pro-Spanish Republican groups in Lisbon.

The numbers

There are difficulties in estimating precisely how many foreign volunteers were with Franco. According to Hugh Thomas there were not more than 1000.[24] According to the Nationalists' own figures, before the Civil War there were 67 foreigners from 13 countries enlisted in the Spanish Foreign Legion. By August 1938 the numbers had grown to 1248 foreigners from 37 countries.[25] These figures, too, are most likely understated. At least at the start of the war, there were foreign volunteers serving with the Carlist

Requetés and, though fewer in number, with the regular Spanish army. According to the French consul, who as we shall see expended great amounts of effort in tracking down French volunteers desiring repatriation, it was easy for men to use fake identity papers. In the Foreign Legion no identity papers were required and it was common for recruits to register under assumed names and false nationalities. For example, in the muster of foreigners in the Spanish Foreign Legion in 1938, referred to above, there is a French volunteer registered as 'Mauricio Chevalier' and another with the unlikely moniker of 'Francisco Ferrer Illich'. Perhaps, though, it was less likely for recruits to assume another nationality if they did not speak that language, though there was no official prohibition on such self-designation. Probably, too, Spanish recruiters faced with difficult foreign names simply Hispanicized them into 'Josés' and 'Juans' and did likewise with unfamiliar places of birth. In the broad picture, none of these details matters very much except that they preclude obtaining figures that are totally accurate.

The sources

The sources on which this study is based are widely dispersed. They include material in the Biblioteca Nacional in Madrid and in the Archivo General Militar at Ávila and in the repositories of the Spanish Foreign Legion in Ceuta and Melilla. There are also relevant series of government records in Franco's Spain in other national repositories. The Public Record Office at Kew, in London, contains a wealth of material from British diplomatic and consular officials. The Sound Archive of the Imperial War Museum has collected oral testimonies on Britishers in Spain. Also in London, the archives of Reuters, The Times and the Marx Memorial Library contain useful material. In France, the Archives of the Ministère des Affaires Étrangères at Quai d'Orsay and the Centre des Archives Diplomatiques in Nantes contain French ambassadorial and consular correspondence from Nationalist Spain as well as comments on Nationalist Spain sent from Portugal, Romania and the Irish Free State. In Washington, the National Archives provided ambassadorial and consular correspondence from Spain and from the series of German Captured War Materials. As well, the Archives of the FBI have material relating to various individuals in Spain during the Civil War. The Southworth Collection on the Spanish Civil War in the Mandeville Collections at the Geisel Library at the University of California, San Diego, holds valuable material on Nationalist Spain, as does the Library of the Hoover Institution on War, Revolution and Peace at Stanford University.

Romanian autobiographies in exile publishing houses provide sources for Romanian volunteers, as does the series *Cuardernos Hispanico Romano*, which until 1944 was published in Spain. Since 1989 in Romania, after the Ceauşescus were swept from office, it has been possible to revisit the history of the Iron Guard and the febrile decade of the 1930s which was quarantined during half a century of official censorship.

Exile material on White Russians with Franco is contained in exile journals, such as *Chasovoi*, published in Paris and Brussels. The Hoover Archives hold large collections of papers of White exiles, including the remarkable diaries of General Shinkarenko, a leader of Franco's Russians in Spain.

An unlikely source on the French Jeanne d'Arc battalion is contained in the family papers of the Australian Nugent Bull, whose schoolboy French landed him in a battalion of French volunteers in the Spanish Foreign Legion. And equally fortuitously, the family papers of Vincent Patriarca in Naples contain information about this Italo-American enthusiast for Mussolini, who began his flying training in upstate New York.

The structure

The study is arranged in a series of seven essays. The first lays out the historical context of the Spanish Civil War and looks thematically at some of the issues that are important in understanding the contextualization of the foreign volunteers for Franco within Spain. The second chapter examines English-speaking travellers in Nationalist Spain, setting out first the travelling amateurs who were mightily impressed with Franco and his circle and took as their own interpretations that came from Franco's men, particularly those in the press corps. The second part of the essay examines the narratives of the foreign correspondents written after they had left Spain. This experienced body of men, and two women, with considerable previous war service, created public opinion on international affairs in the 1930s.

The third essay examines Franco's Anglo-Saxon volunteers. The first part of the essay looks at four men from different parts of the English-speaking world who joined the Spanish Foreign Legion. Their experiences are set against the troubled history of the Irish Brigade brought to Nationalist Spain by Eoin O'Duffy to form a separate battalion in the Foreign Legion.

The fourth chapter traces the political background and motivation of the French volunteers in the Jeanne d'Arc battalion. Strongly influenced by Maurras and the newer forms of the French Right, these volunteers saw their engagement against the Spanish Popular Front as the symbolic prelude to the real conflict which they hoped to foment with Blum and his political allies on the French Left. The majority of the ordinary Frenchmen in Franco's Spain was treated very harshly and bore the brunt of deeply held anti-French prejudices that were whipped up by the Nationalist Command against the French and Spanish Popular Fronts.

The fifth essay pieces together the experiences of the contingent of White Russians. With strong support from their fractions of the exile community in France and Belgium, they hoped in Nationalist Spain to regroup the exiled White armies to defeat the 'Godless no-gooders' of Bolshevism on the Iberian Peninsula and return to Mother Russia to restage – and this time win – the Russian Civil War. As individual ex-Tsarist officers were humiliated to discover, Nationalist command cared little for the White Russian's view of war and even less for Russian military tradition and experience.

The penultimate chapter examines the Romanian Iron Guard who exemplify, in a striking form, one set of the major features of Franco's foreign volunteers. The Romanians in Spain perceived Franco and themselves to be launched on the same crusade against 'Satan and his Judeo-Masonic henchmen', to use the Iron Guard's graphic parlance. They eulogized the man of action who was ready to sacrifice himself in a Christian cause. When confronted with real battle at the front, however, they suffered disastrous consequences. It was only back in Bucharest that the true impact of the expedition to Spain became apparent and provided a muscular display of the Iron Guard's following.

The final essay looks at a remarkable group of foreign women who lent their efforts to Franco's victory as nurses, journalists and publicists for Franco. They were all anti-Communist, whether as monarchists, Catholics or outright admirers of the interwar dictators. Between the political doctrines they espoused and their own actions in Spain, however, there was considerable dissonance. In coming to Spain, alone and in wartime, they demonstrated that they were independent and uncon-strained by traditional Spanish notions about the proper behaviour of respectable women. In their demeanour they resembled nothing so much as the interwar New Woman, who in Nationalist Spain was associated strongly with the much despised modern women of the Spanish Republic.

Franco's foreign women volunteers embodied the paradox facing many women active in right-wing movements, in that they were working to create a society in which independent women like themselves would have no place.

Foreign volunteers in Spain who had fought in the First World War were often supercilious about the lack of military experience of their Spanish comrades. For example, the White Russian officers were part of an imperial military caste and considered that they warranted respect because they had shown their mettle in the First World War and the Russian Civil War. These presumptions by foreigners that they were entitled to respect for experience garnered elsewhere were disregarded in Franco's Spain. Far more frequently, the Spaniards in Nationalist Spain viewed foreign volunteers with a decided lack of enthusiasm and were suspicious of the motives that had brought them to the Iberian Peninsula. Nor were Spaniards at Franco's headquarters sanguine about the political reliability or the military capacities of these foreign volunteers. It is true that, in the case of military prowess, the franquista assessments were often correct. Franco's foreign volunteers in Spain, with the possible exception of some of the foreign women – particularly those in front-line medical service – made no significant contribution to Franco's military victory.

Franco's foreign volunteers were a diverse group. They shared a visceral hatred of Communists and a perception that in Spain the Republic was synonymous with Communism. But, as well, there were variations in motives and gradations of belief on a variety of issues. Because the volunteers provide a snapshot of the aspirations and mentality of some of the very extreme Right in the decade leading to the Second World War it is useful to map the ideological world that they inhabited: the commonalities they shared as well as the specificities of their differences.

Overall, what I conclude is that these foreigners were motivated by personal and political agendas that were rarely tied to the specifics of Spanish politics. In some cases, they saw in Spain what they imagined that they would see, though it may not always have been what was actually happening. On balance, their military contribution to Franco's victory was not overwhelming. Within Nationalist Spain foreigners were often treated according to national stereotypes and Spaniards were suspicious of the politics of Franco's foreign volunteers and indifferent to their experience outside Spain.

Acknowledgements

Before I began working on this subject I could not believe that it had not already been covered. It struck me as a fascinating area, peopled with intriguing characters and part of an important strand of the interwar Right. When I started serious research, however, I realized that the topic had not been worked over because it bordered on the unmanageable: sources widely dispersed and in a range of languages. As I continued the research my interest in this segment of the interwar Right has grown, though I now know that the study will never be completely finished. Without a doubt, though, I have had much pleasure writing this book. It has taken me into a series of national histories in order to contextualize the origins of the various groups of volunteers for Franco. In this I have received help from historians and scholars in a whole range of fields. Because the archives have been far-flung I have also enjoyed hospitality from scholars and friends in a great many places. While it is not possible to acknowledge it all, every bit of help has been appreciated.

To paraphrase Eric Hobsbawm, archivists and librarians are to historians what the opium grower is to the addict. This project would have been impossible without the scholarly assistance of librarians and archivists. Lynda Corey Claassen, the Head of the Mandeville Collections at the University of California, San Diego, has been unstintingly helpful. She also suggested the image that is on the cover. Many other archivists have been generous with their expertise: Francisco J. Bellido Andréu at the Archivo General Militar de Avila; and Miguel Ballenilla in the Tercio Gran Capitan 10 de la Legion in Melilla. I particularly thank the colonel of the Tercio Duque de Alba of the Foreign Legion in Ceuta, Juan Miguel Mateo Castañeyra, for providing searches and allowing me to use internal *Tercio* documents. Among much assistance at the Library and Archive of the Hoover Institution on War, Revolution and Peace, I thank Linda Wheeler, Helan Solanum, Carole Leadenham and Mollie Molloy. As always, the staff at the Ministère des Affaires Étrangères at Quai d'Orsay and now in the new repository at Nantes were helpful, skilful and expeditious. In London the staff at the Public Record Office have been endlessly helpful, face to face and by e-mail, as has Rosemary Tudge at the Imperial War Museum Sound Archive. John Entwisle at Reuters Archive started off my thinking about the press in Spain and Professor Donald Read, the historian of Reuters, was generous in making suggestions, as was Amon Dyas, archivist for *The Times*, Tish Newland at Marx Memorial Library, and Victor Berch at ALBA at Brandeis and Sr Marie Foales at the Adelaide Diocesan Archive. Perhaps my greatest debt is to Marian de Saxe and the inter-library loan staff at the Fisher Library, the University of Sydney, who are unfazed and efficient whether dealing with a request for a book in Romanian, an obscure Russian exile journal or an update on the latest edition from a Spanish press. They have provided the lifeline of this project.

I am glad to acknowledge financial support from the Australian Research Council, 1995 to 1998; the Hoover Institution on War, Revolution and Peace; the Research Institute of Humanities and Social Sciences at Sydney University; and the Friends of the Mandeville Collection at the University of California, San Diego.

For friendship and hospitality I thank: in Romania, Georgel, Peetee and Horea Mihut and the *bonikas* in Cluj as well as Marian Ivan in Bucharest; in Paris and Cassis Edith and Yves Vincent-Lancelot, and the Millers and M. Blanc in Caune Minervois; in Palo Alto, Jim and Catherine Gardiner; and Lynne Moran in San Diego. As well, I am grateful for assistance from the Patriarca family in Naples; Enzo Pan in Sydney; Nigel Stokes and Ann Herriman in Adelaide; and the family of W. N. Bull in Newtown.

A great many colleagues have talked to me about this project or read parts of it. They include José Alvarez, Gino Baumann, Martin Blinkhorn, Richard Bosworth, Iain Cameron, John Carver Edwards, Patrizia Dogliani, Nick Doumanis; Victoria Enders, Sheila Fitzpatrick, Kay Fraser; Bruce Fulton, Ignacio García, Amirah Inglis, Gabriel Jackson, Roger Markwick, Paul Preston, Isabel Perez Molina, Karen Offen, Vlad Protopopescu, Pamela Radcliff, Liz Rechniewski, David and Kathy Ringrose, Michael Seidman, Yavor Siderov, Glenda Sluga and especially Grahame Harrison and Tony Cahill. Research assistance has been provided by the very able Yavor Siderov, Kira Raif, Eve Setch and Pat Fenech. Janet Joyce, Valerie Hall and Elizabeth Leroy at Continuum have been excellent editors. Most of all I relied on the support of the four *compañeros*: Trudi Valeau at home and Jock, Emma and Sam, who were patient during my long hours in the back room sorting out the fascists.

Notes

1 Pierre Drieu la Rochelle, *Gilles* (Paris: Gallimard, 1939), pp. 657–80.
2 Hugh Thomas, *The Spanish Civil War* (New York: Touchstone Books, 1986), p. 982.

3 José Luis de Mesa's *Los otros internacionales voluntarios extranjeros desconocidos en el Bando Nacional durante la guerra civil (1936–1939)* (Madrid: Ediciones Barbarroja, 1998).

4 Gerold Gino Baumann's *Los voluntarios Latinamericanos en la Guerra Civil Española: en las Brigadas Internacionales, las milicias, la retaguardia y en el Ejército Popular* (San José, Costa Rica: Editorial Guayacán Centroamericana, 1997). Baumann has also collected much material on the Swiss on both sides in Spain.

5 Robert A. Stradling, *The Irish and the Spanish Civil War 1936–39: Crusades in Conflict* (Manchester: Mandolin, 1999); and Fearghal McGarry, *Irish Politics and the Spanish Civil War* (Cork: Cork University Press, 1999).

6 See, for example, the report by Radio Salamanca in March 1938 denying the 'campaign of calumny' by the foreign press and the declaration that there was 'not a single foreigner in the last year who had passed the frontier', transcribed in Ministère des Affaires Étrangères (MAE), Centre des Archives Diplomatiques de Nantes (CAD), Direction des Affaires Politiques et Commerciales, Guerre Civile, Volontaires, Nov. 1937–June 1938, V 238, p. 107, St-Jean-de-Luz, 18 March 1938.

7 Reprinted in the *Advocate*, 4 November 1937.

8 See the observation by Swiss journalist, Georges Oudard, *Chemises noires, brunes, vertes en Espagne* (Paris: Librairie Plon, 1938), pp. 64–7. For a recent franquista statement on foreign volunteers see Ricardo de la Cierva, *Historia esencial de la Guerra Civil Española: todos los problemas resueltos, sesenta años después* (Madridejos: Editorial Fénix, 1996), pp. 377–89. Alberto Reig Tapia argues that if the Italian, German and Portuguese are added into Franco's army it was more 'internationalized' than the Republic and the International Brigades. See his *Franco 'Caudillo': mito y realidad* (Madrid: Tecnos, 1966), 2nd edn., p. 111.

9 Interview *ABC*, November 1936.

10 For example, the published catalogue of the Southworth Collection provides a useful field to assay for dates.

11 See the imprints in the printed guide to the Catalogue to the Southworth Collection, Mandeville Library, *Spanish Civil War Collection* (Woodbridge, CT: Research Publications, 1987).

12 Paloma Aguilar Fernández, *La memoria histórica de la Guerra Civil Española (1936–1939): un proceso de aprendizaje político* (Madrid: Centro de Estudios Avanzados en Ciencias Sociales, 1995), p. 93.

13 See Karl Ries and Hans Ring, *The Legion Condor: A History of the Luftwaffe in the Spanish Civil War 1936–1939*, trans. by David Johnston (West Chester: Schiffer Military History, 1992), pp. 44–5. Raymond Proctor's figure is 19,000 men in total in *Historical Dictionary of the Spanish Civil War 1936–1939* (Westport: Greenwood Press, 1982), p. 145. Thomas notes that probably 10,000 Germans were in Spain at maximum numbers, and 14,000 veterans attended the Condor Legion parade in Berlin in May 1939, *The Spanish Civil War*, p. 977.

14   Quoted in Peter Monteath, *Writing the Good Fight. Political Commitment in the International Literature of the Spanish Civil War* (Westport, CT: Greenwood Press, 1994), p. 24. See as well, Alfred Lent, 'The Blond Moors are coming: German flak gunners in Spain–the Condor Legion story,' in Philip Toynbee (ed.), *The Distant Drum: Reflections on the Spanish Civil War* (London: Sidgwick & Jackson, 1976), pp. 95–104; and Herbert Rutledge Southworth's survey of the first person accounts by German flyers, in *Le Mythe de la croisade de Franco* (Paris: Ruedo Ibérico, 1964), pp. 41–2.

15   Ries and Ring, *Legion Condor*, pp. 44–5.

16   Thomas, *The Spanish Civil War*, pp. 978–9.

17   See Patrizia Dogliani, *L'Italia Fascista 1922–1940* (Rome: Sansoni, 1999), pp. 407–18; Brian R. Sullivan, 'Fascist Italy's military involvement in the Spanish Civil War', *Journal of Military History*, 59 (October 1993), pp. 697–727; John Coverdale, *Italian Intervention in the Spanish Civil War* (Princeton: Princeton University Press, 1975); and José Luis Alcofar Nassaes, *C.T.V. Los legionarios italianos en la Guerra Civil Española 1936–1939* (Barcelona: DOPESA, 1972), pp. 62–3.

18   Herbert Southworth cites the higher figure, in his *Le Mythe de la croisade de Franco*, p. 253. The pamphlet from anti-Salazar sergeants in training in Oporto states 20,000 volunteers, cited in MAE, Nantes, Vol. 238, Lisbon, 29 March 1938, pp. 130–1. Hugh Thomas scales back his estimate to 'several thousand' in *The Spanish Civil War*, p. 979.

19   Ricardo de la Cierva, *La leyenda de las brigadas internacionales* (Madrid: El Alcázar, 1969), pp. 58–9; and Charles Esdaile, 'Hombres y armas: la ayuda extranjera', in Octavio Ruiz-Manjón Cabeza and Miguel Gómez Oliver, *Los nuevos historiadores ante la Guerra Civil Española*, Vol. 1 (Granada: Diputación Provincial de Granada, 1999), p. 146.

20   Servicio Histórico Militar, Ávila, 2/168/30/5, Cuartel General del Generalisimo-Estado Mayor, Sección 1. 'Secreto. Despacho número 15.773 Relacionado con el número de extranjeros alistados a la Legión antes y después de iniciado el Glorioso Movimiento Nacional 29-8-38'. 2/168/31/27 Cuartel General del Generalísimo-Estado Mayor Sección 1.29 Div. 10. 'Relativo a que remita con urgencia relacionados por bandera los legionarios extranjeros que existen en ese Cuerpo', Desp. 13331, 21–8–1938'.

21   See António Costa Pinto, *Salazar's Dictatorship and European Fascism: Problems of Interpretation* (New York: Columbia University Press, 1995), p. 73; and César Vidal, *La Guerra de Franco: historia militar de la Guerra Civil Española* (Barcelona: Planeta, 1996), p. 121.

22   MAE, Nantes, Vol. 238, Lisbon, 29 March 1938, pp. 128–9.

23   MAE, Série B 566–1 Guerre Civile espagnole. Les Puissances, Lisbon 12 Feb. 1938; St-Jean-de-Luz, 14 Dec. 1937; 21 Jan. 1938; Lisbon, 12 Feb. 1938. The French Legations abroad kept an eagle eye out for involvement of countries which were signatories to the Non-Intervention Treaty.

24 Ricardo de la Cierva discusses the foreigners for Franco in 'Las Brigadas
    Internacionales de Franco', in *La leyenda de las Brigadas Internacionales* (Madrid:
    El Alcazar, [1969]), pp. 57–60; and for Herbert Southworth's assessment see *Le
    Mythe de la croisade de Franco*, pp. 33–48. Hugh Thomas provides updated figures
    overall of about 1000 in *The Spanish Civil War*, pp. 974–85.
25 See note 20.

CHAPTER 1

The historical context of the
Spanish Civil War

෨

This chapter briefly sketches the historical context of the Spanish Republic and the Civil War which provided the backdrop to the endeavours of Franco's foreign supporters in Nationalist Spain. The central development which led to the Civil War was the failure of the Second Republic to manage the transition from the old monarchical regime to a modern democracy. Between 1931 and 1936, strikes, demonstrations and street disorder provided a noisy backdrop to the Second Republic's efforts to raise the scaffolding of a new Spanish state. Demonstrations and strikes are not fatal to a working democracy, provided they remain within the bounds of the political system. During the Second Republic, various groups perceived themselves disadvantaged by the reforms of the new government. Each attempt at change produced a burst of anti-Republican protest that hardened into a knot of opposition because the changes were either too radical or they were not radical enough. Much more lethal, however, for the future of the Second Spanish Republic, and highly relevant to this study, was the response of the Spanish armed forces to attempts at reform by the government.

Municipal elections in Spain which took place in April 1931 revealed a groundswell towards Republican parties, not in every electorate but in the urban areas where the voting system operated more freely. King Alfonso XIII certainly read the election results as a vote of no confidence and a few days after the polls he left for Alicante, from where a warship took him to France and exile. Queen Ena travelled by train. In a vignette that encapsulated the changeover, her train was shunted into a siding near the French border to make way for a trainload of jubilant Republican exiles coming back to Spain to begin the work of establishing the Second Republic.[1]

In the first national elections a coalition of Left-Centre parties won a majority of seats in the Cortes and Socialists, Left Republicans and regional Republican parties shared out seats in the cabinet. There was broad enthusiasm for the new state, '*la Niña Bonita*' (the beautiful girl), as it was affectionately called. Most Spaniards felt that the time was ripe in Spain to bring the nation's political structure and the rights of citizens into line with modern liberal democracies in the rest of Western Europe.

The new Cortes, conscious of the historic moment, held its first session of parliament on Bastille Day, 14 July 1931. A new Constitution was promulgated which, among other things, provided women with the vote, separated Church and state and abolished aristocratic titles. The Republican government began a broad programme of social reform. A statute giving autonomy to Catalonia was drawn up and another promised for the Basque regions. Land surveys that presaged widespread land reform were begun and an arbitration commission was established to set wages and mediate disputes between industrial and rural employers and employees.

Manuel Azaña, Minister of War and later Prime Minister, had long seen the 'military ambition and interference' of the Spanish army as a 'major institutional obstacle to the development of a civil spirit in Spain' and wished to improve the standard of operations and cut costs.[2] Spain, which had not participated in the First World War, was saddled with one of the most top-heavy armies in the world, boasting a ratio of one officer to every six enlisted men. There were some 566 generals and 22,000 officers on the books.[3] Azaña offered voluntary retirement on full pay, halving the number of officers, and began to democratize recruitment structures, while raising the general level of education and training.[4]

The Spanish officer corps resented any interference from civilian politicians. In consequence, the Azaña reforms during 1931 and 1932 sowed a deep antagonism within sectors of the officer ranks, creating an environment congenial to anti-Republican conspirators.

Ostensibly in response to the Catalan autonomy statute, in August 1932, General José Sanjurjo, the head of the Civil Guard, who was being backed by a group of aristocratic southern landowners, staged an abortive uprising against Azaña's government. It was the upheavals over agrarian policy at the end of 1932, however, that brought down the first Republican government. The specific, and final, incident took place at Casa Viejas, a small village in southern Spain, where a group of anarchist peasants proclaimed their commune for libertarian Communism and were brutally repressed by the Guardia Civil and the newly created Republican Guardias de Asalto.[5]

The next elections, before which the united front of the Left had disintegrated, were won by a Rightist coalition. Between November 1933 and the elections which brought in the Popular Front, in February 1936, a coalition of the Catholic parties, the Radicals and the Right dismantled or let lapse most of the reforming legislation of the first two years. In the 'two Black Years', as they were sometimes called, the Spanish Falange, which had been formed in 1933, became an increasingly vocal, though still very small, presence on the Spanish Right.

The simmering political tensions boiled over in October. Once in office, the second administration of the Republic had granted an amnesty to those implicated in the Sanjurjo rising and returned the land that had been confiscated from the Grandees convicted of rebellion the year before. In October 1934, Gil Robles, the leader of the Catholic coalition, insisted on taking a cabinet post. Though he was legally entitled to it, the Left feared that the position of Catholic 'accidentalism' that he had publicly expounded meant in reality that he would use his office to bring in a political system like Mussolini's fascist state or Salazar's corporate model next door in Portugal. Robles had visited Nazi Germany and been impressed in Vienna by Dollfuss's authoritarian regime. When Gil Robles entered the cabinet on 4 October, the Left called a general strike. It succeeded in the Asturias where the miners' union, under Socialist leadership with strong support from the anarchists, shut down the city. The strikers dug in for a long siege. After three weeks the government declared martial law and brought across the Army of Africa and units of Moors in the *Regulares Indigenas*. Commanded by General Francisco Franco, the troops put down the strike with unremitting violence which left more than 1000 dead and 3000 wounded.[6] Among the crowds of arrested was the unlikely figure of Manuel Azaña, the ex-Prime Minister, who was a died-in-the-wool liberal for whom revolution Right or Left was anathema. The sheer volume of prisoners and the capriciousness of many of their arrests united the Left in a way that it had not been since before the institution of the Second Republic.

In the elections of February 1936, the last Republican elections to be held in Spain, the Popular Front on the Left and the National Front on the Right faced each other almost equally matched. In many districts the voting was as close as 1 or 2 per cent. Overall, the Popular Front defeated the National Front by a small majority and formed government. Spanish electoral law gave a majority of seats to whichever side won outright on votes.[7] Between 19 February, when the Popular Front took office, and 18

July, when the members of the military conspirators made their move, town and countryside in Spain were battered by riots, civil disorder and violence. In this period the constituencies of centre groups, for both Right and Left, disappeared as the extremes of both wings of politics attracted more and more followers. The Spanish Falangists, who had not obtained a single seat in the 1936 elections, found their numbers swollen by previous Catholic Action types who perceived that the Catholic parties had been routed, leaving them with the Falange as the only place remaining to go.[8] Similarly on the Left, individuals and some groups, for example the Young Socialist movement, moved towards the Spanish Communist Party. The PCE, with a single deputy in 1936, hitherto had not been able to attract large numbers of the working class which was loyal to the Socialists or to the even larger anarchist movement.

On 17 July, the Spanish generals who were caught up in the military conspiracy made a *pronunciamiento*. The form of these military uprisings had been honed in nineteenth-century Spanish politics and exported to Latin America. The conventional form was that several senior generals would call out the army, in effect in a military form of general strike. A proclamation against the incumbent government would be read out on the parade ground and possibly a few shots would be fired. In the normal sequence, the politicians, realizing that their time had come, would resign to make way for a new government which would be sworn in. Immediately this was achieved, soldiers and commanders withdrew to the barracks. By July 1936, however, this means of government change was outmoded. Its previous success relied on a population that was disenfranchised and politically apathetic. By contrast, in 1936, Spaniards, male and female, were full citizens and habituated to being part of an active, if volatile, political system. When the generals 'pronounced', the citizens formed up in militias and prepared to defend the Republic that had enfranchised them.

The Spanish generals and the National Movement

The uprising consisted of several disparate political strands. Labelled by its adherents as *El Movimiento Nacional*, the name papered over the division between the groups within the National Movement. While they were all united in the belief that the parliamentary form of government of the Republic must be replaced by an authoritarian hierarchical state, there was no agreement about its exact form.

The most important element was the army. Among the conspirators who led the uprising in July 1936 were four senior generals. Mola was the director of the conspiracy. A bespectacled 59-year-old, he 'looked more like a professor than a soldier'[9] and, at six-feet tall, towered over his fellow Spanish generals. Stationed in Pamplona in 1936, he led the Navarrese garrison in a successful insurrection in July and commanded what was to become the army of the north. Mola's reputation had been made in Morocco commanding Moorish *Regulares*. His leanings, too, were Republican and though he was the moving force in the creation of the Junta of National Defence in Burgos, in which Franco was named Commander-in-Chief, Mola had opposed Franco's being made, simultaneously, Head of State. On his way to confer with Franco in Burgos on 3 June 1937, his plane crashed in the fog and Mola was killed.

General José Sanjurjo Sacanell, 64 years old, a Republican and a veteran conspirator, was the second important instigator of the *pronunciamiento* from exile in Portugal. Sanjurjo, like his fellow conspirators, had served with distinction in the colonial wars in Morocco where he had earned the sobriquet of 'Lion of the Rif'. Under the Second Republic, until he led an abortive coup against the government in 1932, he had headed the Guardia Civil. Undoubtedly fortuitous for Franco, on 20 July Sanjurjo was killed in a plane crash in Portugal, when the monoplane that was to take him back to Spain failed to clear the runway in take-off and burst into flames.

Gonzalo Quiepo de Llano y Serra, the 61-year-old general of the army of the south, whose swashbuckling cavalry exploits in Morocco had brought him fame, was a Republican who at first after 1931 had enjoyed great distinction. He had resisted the downgrading of the army's independence, however, and by 1936 had been sidelined to head the *Carabineros* who oversaw Spanish Customs. In the generals' uprising, Quiepo de Llano seized Seville by a mixture of daring and ruthlessness and until the end of 1938 ran the southern command as an independent fiefdom. During the Civil War, his nightly broadcasts over Radio Seville were famous: hour-long harangues in which he made vulgar boasts about the grisly end that was in store for the Republicans and the officers in their army and the fate that awaited their wives.

Francisco Franco became Supreme Commander in October 1936 and indeed the head of Spain under a military dictatorship that lasted until his death in November 1975. From the perspective of the later dictatorship, inconceivable without Franco, it may be hard to believe that, at the start of July 1936, there were several other more likely figures for overall command. Even setting aside the civilian politicians, Calvo Sotelo or Gil Robles, leaders of the monarchist and Catholic parties respectively, among the dissident generals a far more likely bet in 1936 would have been Mola or the dashing Lion of the Rif.

Franco had been favoured with exceptionally rapid promotion in a brilliant military career: a general at 34, he was the youngest ever in Spanish military history and, at 44 in 1936, he was the youngest of the conspirators. In the colonial wars in Morocco, Franco had shown great courage and leadership and, purportedly, a flair for military strategy. He was also reputed to be a serious student of military history, tactics and cartography and with little taste for the lusty pursuits favoured by full-blooded soldiers on bivouac. It is worth noting, in all of this, that recent scholarship on Franco by Alberto Reig Tapia and Paul Preston has shown that the Caudillo's military prowess has been greatly exaggerated.[10] His reputation as a military scholar was carefully constructed by Franco himself. Further, Preston argues that his conduct of civil war was driven more by the primacy of a personal, political agenda to cement his own position as leader of the new state than by the military objective of a swift rebel victory.[11]

Franco, not much over five feet and always portly, did not cut a striking figure. He was born in 1892 into a Galician family whose sons for generations had entered the army and the navy. His older brother Nicolás became Spain's ambassador to Portugal and the younger brother Ramón, wildly Republican before the Civil War, was a dashing aviator and later the Caudillo's confidant. During the six years of the Second Republic, Franco kept his authoritarian and anti-Republican cards close to his chest, though his career waxed and waned according to the political complexion of the Republican government in power. He was on a downswing, relatively speaking, in the first years of the Republic when the reforming Azaña headed the Ministry of War and later was Prime Minister. Again, under the Popular Front, Franco was shunted sideways to Tenerife. He achieved the height of favour under the Rightist government coalition of Radicals and Catholic Action from 1933 to the end of 1935. In October 1934, in the Asturian miners' strike, when Franco was called in to put down the uprising, he did so with great ferocity using units from the Army of Africa stiffened with Moorish *Regulares*, the first time they had been used on the mainland against Spanish citizens. Ruthlessly, he gave no quarter to strikers in house-to-house fighting. As a consequence of his effectiveness in the Asturias, Franco was promoted in May 1935 to be Chief of General Staff.

Franco believed all his life in an international Masonic conspiracy powered by sinister Freemasons, Jews and Bolsheviks, who wished to weaken Catholic Spain. In the franquista world-view, liberal democracy and the paraphernalia of political parties, elections, women's rights and so forth, always and inevitably degenerated into Communism and disorder. The grab bag term of 'Reds' encompassed all the above, including the subcategory of Basque and Catalan separatists whose 'anti-Spanishness' was a solvent to the nation, 'one, united and great', and therefore to be extirpated.

More than a creature of his caste, however, Franco, in Preston's depiction, is a complex character: puritanical, ruthless and secretive, driven by a 'personality in which instinctive caution coexisted with almost unlimited ambition.'[12] Franco repudiated his father, whose dissolute womanizing and drunkenness, perhaps not untypical of the sailor's life, evinced a deep revulsion in his son. Instead, from an early age Franco forged an intense, almost neurotic, identification with his mother. These deep insecurities within Franco's character were, perhaps, the root of a shyness and prudery that was manifested in face-to-face relations and which some who met him thought bordered on effeminacy.[13] And it was, perhaps, this diffidence that caused him to shrink from intimate fellowship and was the basis of Franco's reputation as a man who preferred over anything else, the company of his wife and child.

Despite the display of public piety and a polemic to promote Catholic religiosity, it was the army that Franco saw as the saviour of Spain. And indeed, under his dictatorship society functioned on a military model. The Caudillo at the head oversaw his generals and administrators and, at the bottom, like obedient conscripts, ordinary citizens carried out the orders from above. Spaniards who were undisciplined or marched out of step could expect immediate and unequivocal punishment.

Among a gaggle of military figures, other important people in the cohort around Franco included Lieutenant Colonel Juan Yagüe Blanco, a Falangist, who in 1936 led the uprising in Ceuta and took over the Foreign Legion. Once on the mainland, Yagüe was Franco's field commander as the Army of Africa advanced north, from Seville along the western strip that bordered Portugal. Yagüe's troops captured Mérida and Badajoz and by early September turned eastward to take Talavera de la Reina. Proceeding through the terrain as though it was a colonial war, Yagüe's troops treated Republican militia and the citizens they came across with unrelenting ferocity. In Badajoz, Yagüe's troops on 14 August took the city in bloody house-to-house fighting with heavy casualties on both sides. On several succeeding days, Republican soldiers and suspects were rounded up in the bullring and systematically executed. There were reportedly around 2000 military and civilian prisoners dealt with in this way, some of them refugees who had fled the fighting into Portugal and been turned back by Portuguese customs guards. Franco's headquarters always vehemently denied the stories of a massacre at Badajoz, as equally did his supporters outside Spain.[14]

Among other generals, José Enrique Varela Iglesias in southern Spain took Ronda and Cordoba in August 1936 and, at the end of September, led into Toledo the column that relieved the siege of the Alcázar. Alfredo Kindelán y Duany, one of the founders of the Spanish air force, was close to Franco as the commander of the Nationalist air force during the war. As well, he was a core figure in the monarchist group at Nationalist headquarters.

The monarchists divided into two distinct groups. The aristocrats and nobility of the Alfonsine monarchists, from the owners of large estates, filled the upper echelons of the military and civil administration in Franco's camp. Under the Second Republic the monarchist *Renovación Española* had fomented discontent within the military and the agrarian elite and fostered ideas about an uprising against the Republic.[15] They favoured a restoration of Alfonso XIII. When the ex-king renounced his rights before his death in 1941, and the eldest son was killed in a car accident, monarchists looked to the second son. Violently anti-Republican as most were, they rallied to the insurgents from the outset but, equally, always, almost to a man, were committed to a monarchical restoration. After the victory, the differences between Franco and the monarchists, that had simmered below the surface during the war, openly flared when it became clear that Franco had no intention of an early royal restoration. The Caudillo sent several of them, like the Infantes de Orléans, the ex-king's cousin and his wife, the granddaughter of Queen Victoria, under house arrest to remain on their estates.

The other strand of monarchism was the Carlists who, since 1833, had followed an alternative Pretender to the Bourbon throne in Spain.[16] During the Second Republic Carlism flourished as a rallying movement for ultra-traditional Catholics opposed to Republican secularism. The traditional ground for Carlism was Navarre and parts of the Basque country but between 1931 and 1936 it grew from small seeds in parts of Andalusia. During the Civil War, Carlist Requetés, with their distinctive red berets and carrying a large cross aloft as a standard, were some of Franco's most disciplined and reliable regiments.

Members of the Catholic Action parties comprised the third strand. During the Republic they fielded the largest political coalition on the Right and were led by the subtle and skilful politician José María Gil Robles.[17] He favoured a Spain run on Catholic corporative principles, much like Salazar's Portugal or the Dollfuss regime in Austria. While Minister of War, from 1935 until the Popular Front elections, Gil Robles encouraged anti-Republican dissidents in the military but, after the generals' uprising, he was less welcome around Franco and was eventually squeezed out to live in forced exile in Portugal.

The last strand within the National Movement, and with quite different aspirations from all of the above, were the Falangists.[18] The Spanish Falange had close connections with the Italian fascists from whom they received funds and shared a noisy polemic about the need for a new, invigorated modern state based on national renovation, with the old forms of privilege of wealth, land ownership and aristocratic birth abolished. The Spanish Falange, however, eschewed the polemics of paganism of Italian fascism: in the Falangist new state, the Spanish Church would provide a central pillar. Much of the violence behind Nationalist lines during the Civil War was caused by Falangist militia.

The founder of the Falange, José Antonio Primo de Rivera, the son of the former dictator, had been arrested in Alicante just before the uprising for illegal possession of firearms. After a summary trial, he was executed towards the end of November 1936. In death, José Antonio became the first national martyr in Franco Spain, officially mourned in place names and public rituals. For example, his name was always read out in roll call at important military gatherings to which the orchestrated response was 'Presente'. José Antonio's demise removed a charismatic leader who would have been the obvious contender to head the civilian state in a New Spain, with Franco commanding the armed forces. When Franco summarily dissolved all political organizations in April 1937 and formed them under his own command into the single 'Glorious National Movement', *Falange Española Tradicionalista y de las Juntas de Ofensiva Nacional-Sindicalista*, he arrested Manuel Hedilla, José Antonio's successor, and kept him under sentence of death until 1946, when he was released.

The Nationalist army

In July 1936 the Spanish army consisted of two parts, the Peninsular Army and the Army of Africa. The former, totalling some 66,000 men and, except for the officers, under strength at all levels, drew on poorly disciplined and badly trained conscripts. The officers of the territorial army tended not to have gained their promotion through service in the colonial wars. At the time of the *pronunciamiento*, the divisions of the Peninsular Army were spread roughly equally between government and insurgents.[19] When the uprising took place, local volunteers and militias joined up too. They provided a larger proportion of the Republican forces, approximately half, compared with roughly a quarter in Franco's forces. The Army of Africa, solidly behind the insurgents, was a professional force of some 30,000 trained men who had been disciplined and toughened in the Rif Wars in Morocco.

Charles Esdaile has argued with common sense that if quality, discipline and equipment are taken into account as well, the Nationalists were far better off. For example, they were organized into operational fighting units from the start in a way that only much later was adopted by the Republicans. The International Brigades, despite the mystique of their fighting prowess, were often no better than the Peninsular Army because the command was improvised and at lower levels was based on Communist Party loyalty rather than on military expertise.[20] As well, there were the paramilitary arms of the Civil Guards, commanded by officers in the regular Spanish army, the Assault Guards created by the Second Republic in 1931 and the carabineers who oversaw Customs.

The Spanish Foreign Legion

The most prestigious unit of the Spanish army was the Foreign Legion which, in 1936, consisted of about four and a half thousand fighting men, well led and in peak condition. Created in 1920 by José Millán Astray, with Franco as his deputy, the *Tercio*, as it was known, constituted a separate army within the Spanish army.[21] It had been formed at the height of the Spanish colonial wars in Morocco, when Spain's military forces were demoralized, poorly trained and equipped with antiquated technology. The military caste in Spain had never recovered from the resounding defeat in the Spanish–American War. The major problem with the Spanish army was that it was poorly led, badly organized and riddled with corruption, especially in Morocco. Spain's isolation in the First World War meant that the army had been isolated from many modern developments in structure which the war had brought to combatant nations. The organization of the Spanish Legion replicated the French Foreign Legion, though foreigners in the Spanish Legion never numbered more than 10 per cent. The Legion's credo was based on Millán Astray's own personal philosophy which, according to José Alvarez, was an amalgam of the 'Japanese code of Bushido, fervent Catholicism, and most importantly an overriding belief in honourable death on the battlefield'.[22]

The legionnaires were elite forces whose mystique and training set them apart from the rest of the army. Each individual legionnaire's name was, and still is, preceded by the initials 'C. L.', standing for the honorific 'Caballero Legionario' (Gentleman Legionnaire). Members of the Legion wore a distinctive uniform of breeches, a green open-necked shirt turned back over the tunic, a cloak that covered all and a garrison cap with a long red tassel. They were better housed and better fed than regular troops; at their home base in Morocco well-cooked food was properly served on china plates by waiters, and officers and the men dined on the same fare. Above all else, the Legion valued loyalty to comrades and courage on the battlefield. Traditionally, the legionnaire's call of 'To Me the Legion' obliged all legionnaires nearby to come to his assistance. Units of the Foreign Legion never fell back in battle or abandoned comrades in the field. Their cult of death eulogized heroic death in combat. As they called themselves, and sang in their marching song, 'Somos los Novios de la Muerte' (We are the Bridegrooms of Death). The last stanza of the Legion's credo stated 'death in battle is the greatest honour: One does not die more than once. Death comes without pain and dying is not so terrible as it seems; what is truly terrible is to live like a coward'. In this necromantic ethos, Millán Astray was a fitting symbol: a 'mutilated' figure sporting a black eyepatch that covered the sightless socket of one eye, he had lost an arm and walked with a severe limp, all injuries 'won' in combat.

Discipline in the *Tercio* was harsh and unremitting. Officers used *fustos* (pliant leather whips) to train recruits and severe beatings even for small infractions of the rules were the order of the day. But conditions and pay were far better than for soldiers in the regular army. For example, the latter were not paid while out sick or wounded in hospital, presumably in order to give the least encouragement to shirking, self-wounding or malingering. By contrast, soldiers in the Foreign Legion were paid on full rates while ill or injured in hospital, because it was assumed that no legionnaire would be so cowardly as to mutilate himself; and injury in battle was proof of an heroic and fearless demeanour under fire. At enlistment, recruits were asked for no identification; the use of pseudonyms was common and entirely acceptable, suggesting that recruits on joining the Legion began a new life and assumed a new identity.[23] As an all-volunteer army, the Foreign Legion was living proof of the old soldiers' adage that a single volunteer is worth a dozen conscripts.

The Legion often worked closely at the front with units of Moroccan mercenaries. A professional force led by Spanish officers, the Moroccan mercenaries had been formed in 1911 and seasoned subsequently in the colonial wars. They were used to great military effect by Franco in the Asturias in 1934 and on the Iberian Peninsula during the whole Civil War. In July 1936 they numbered 17,000 and consisted of *Regulares, Mehallas* and groups of the former Native Civil Guard. By the end of the war the numbers of Moroccan mercenaries had been increased by conscription and enlistment to between 60,000 and 70,000.[24]

During the Spanish Civil War, as at other times, the battalions (*banderas*) of the Foreign Legion were used as shock troops sent in first to carry out the hard combat of flattening the opposing army. Afterwards, the Spanish regular soldiers and the conscripts would mop up. Given the Foreign Legion's training, prowess and ferocious reputation, it is little wonder that the sight of the *Tercio* bearing down on a village was often enough to disperse the townspeople and the local Republican militias in terror. At the beginning of the war, the Legion consisted of six *banderas*, each roughly the size of a battalion. By 1939 there were twenty, which had included the French Joan of Arc and the 15th Bandera of the Irish Battalion. Each of these units is discussed in later chapters.

The foreign soldiers who served on the Republican side consisted of the International Brigade comprising some 35,000 individuals and another 10,000 in medical and support services. It is probably not surprising that the largest group among them came from France, with about 10,000 people and, in descending order, there were Germans and Austrians, Poles and Ukrainians, Italians, Americans, British, Canadians, Yugoslavs, Hungarians, Swedes and other smaller groups. As well, probably a hundred Russian pilots served for the Republic.

The course of the war

Leading figures in the Spanish military had been disaffected with the Second Republic almost from the start. They were resentful of efforts in the first years to prune the officer corps and bring the whole military enterprise under civilian cabinet control with a civilian Minister of War. Well before the victory of the Popular Front in February 1936, there had been rumours that a military rebellion simmered in the wings. The Popular Front government, as anxious to forestall a challenge from the Left as from the Right, ran a non-confrontational course between the two. The cabinet responded to reports of disloyalty within military ranks by shuffling dissident generals at the top and filling the vacated places with officers thought to be loyal to the Republic. Franco was posted to Tenerife to command the Canary Islands' garrison; Mola was recalled from Morocco and despatched to Pamplona; and another potential conspirator, Goded, removed from his desk in Madrid at the War Ministry, was hustled off to the Balearic Islands.

Raw conflict, also, sawed away between Right and Left within the lower ranks of the officer corps as the secret organizations the Rightist UME, the Spanish Military Union, and the Anti-Fascist Republican Military Union, the UMRA, faced each other off. The new government, unwilling and in fact unable to do much about it, simply hoped that the Republican officers would cancel out the machinations of the anti-Republicans. And, when the UME attempted a *pronunciamiento* when Azaña became President in April 1936, the government treated the rebels very leniently in order not to stir further military turmoil. Despite this softly-softly policy, Mola in Pamplona and the others from their dispersed commands were in touch with Sanjurjo in Portugal and Rightist politicians in Madrid who saw their constituencies disappearing in the polarizing groundswell to the extreme Left and Right.

In all these dealings, General Franco was cautious, and it was not until early July that he signalled a definite commitment to the conspirators. By this time plans were well under way: anti-Republicans abroad, for example, the monarchists around Luis Bolín and the Duke of Alba in London, had already begun arrangements to purchase weapons and charter an aeroplane and pilot ready to bring the conspirators together.

Against a backdrop of rising disorder two incidents clinched the date. On the evening of 12 July, a lieutenant in the Assault Guards and an UMRA member who trained a militia of Socialist youth, José Castillo, was assassinated by a rightist gunman. At four o'clock the next morning, in retaliation, a group of comrades in the Assault Guards pulled José Calvo Sotelo, the monarchist leader, out of his bed, took him away in a car and murdered him. His body was found the next day in the morgue at the Almudena cemetery on the outskirts of Madrid. Calvo Sotelo enjoyed a high profile as a correspondent on the monarchist daily *ABC* and was the outstanding spokesman for the Right on the parliamentary floor. The two killings spurred the military uprising five days later, which in turn triggered the Civil War.

On 17 July most of the military garrisons in Spain rose. The rising had been planned for 18 July, but some units of the Army of Africa rose late on 17 July, and amidst great confusion, with conflicting press and radio reports, many garrisons followed on 18 July and others over the next few days. During that critical week, the authority and administrative structure of the Spanish state was shattered. General Franco in the Canary Islands flew to Morocco to take over from the dissident generals who had already called out the Army of Africa. In the major cities on the mainland, Madrid, Barcelona, Valencia, Málaga, Bilbao, where by and large the Guardia Civil and the Assault Guards remained loyal to the government, the insurrection failed. However, in the north Mola had successfully taken Navarre, Burgos and Salamanca.

By the end of July, the rebel generals held approximately a third of Spain. It was in the predominantly agricultural areas but some of them, for example in the south, contained islands of population, such as the agro-towns of Andalusia, which had voted solidly for the Popular Front. In general, the urban centres with the largest populations remained loyal to the government. In these places, while the Republican government was immobilized by developments, political parties, trade unionists and locals rushed to form militias to fight the rebels. It was ironic, perhaps, that the generals who had made a *pronunciamiento* in order to 'save Spain' from an imminent social revolution, by calling out the troops produced exactly the conditions which promoted it.

The most complete transformation took place in Catalonia, the historic heart of anarcho-syndicalism in Spain. In a great many areas, factories and work places were seized by workers' councils, and trade union committees and peasants shot, or drove off, their landowners. In the Republican zones, the first months of the war were a period of chaos, but one of exhilaration and revolutionary fervour for those who welcomed the change.

In the administration of the Republican army it was inevitable that the government would take over the militias and centralize military administration as soon as it was able. As well intentioned as many of the militias were, and in many cases movingly so, it was unlikely that the Republican army based on decentralized militias could match the professionals of the Army of Africa, the Spanish Foreign Legion and the units of the Moroccan regulars who comprised the Nationalist armed forces, not to mention the Falangist, Carlist and CEDA militias. On the battlefield, and in logistics and supply, Nationalist Spain functioned as a system geared to the military. The Republic, too, was totally submerged by the war but it remained a state with a civilian government that was in command of the armed forces, though for the first few months government authority was displaced by local committees, militias and trade unions.

In Madrid the government brought the militias under central control from December 1936; the bitterness of the policy was aggravated by its being part of Stalinist efforts to eradicate the non-Stalinist Left.[25] As the Soviet Union and, less important in arms acquisition, Mexico, were the only countries to sell supplies and military hardware to the Second Spanish Republic, the prestige and power of the Communist Party in Spain and its Soviet advisers was enormously enhanced. Just as Hitler's contribution strengthened Franco's hand, Soviet arms were earmarked for the government's forces that were under the command of the central army with strong Communist Party backing. The International Brigades, whose volunteers were from some 60 countries, also strengthened the centralizing hand of the Republican government. By mid-1937 the revolutionary impulse in Spain had ebbed, or been quashed, and the Republican army was functioning as a conventional military institution.

Within the rebel zone, by the end of July 1936, the insurgent bases consisted of widely separated beachheads in the north-east and in western Andalusia in the south. In the north they held an area centred around Burgos and extending from the Portuguese border to the Galician coast but within which, with the exception of Navarre, the Basque Provinces remained firmly with the Republican government. In the north-east the insurgent zone was bordered by western Aragon, where the front settled in a line running roughly from Teruel in the south through Saragossa and to Huesca in the north. These towns were in rebel hands. The Aragon front remained in this broad configuration until early 1938, when the Nationalists began a steady push eastwards to the Mediterranean Coast.

The government retained the central plain of Castile that swept around Madrid and to the eastern seaboard and Catalonia. The rebel holdings studded parts of south-western Andalusia: Cadiz and the coast around Gibraltar, Cordoba and Seville. The insurrection in the latter was led by General Quiepo de Llano, who outwitted the Republican opposition in the city and then ruthlessly suppressed the militias and the resistance in working-class areas.

Some of the Spanish navy remained loyal to the government. In the Mediterranean, the under officers and sailors mutinied on the warships when commanding officers declared for the insurgents. This was an important factor in the military progress of the war because, without naval transportation across the straits, the Army of Africa was stranded in Morocco.

It was at this point that foreign intervention by Italy and Germany was critical. With central direction among the insurgents uncertain and rebel chiefs running their zones more or less independently, it empowered Franco in the leadership stakes that delegates from his headquarters managed to persuade first Mussolini and then Hitler to send air transport that would carry the troops to the mainland.

By the end of July, two dozen Italian aeroplanes were on the wing to Spanish Morocco.[26] Two machines came down in French territory in Morocco and were identified by the French air attaché as Italian military planes with their markings painted over. Both pilots were Italian and carried military papers. By mid-August, German Junker 52s were also ferrying load after load of Spanish soldiers and Moorish regulars to the mainland.[27] Without the airlift, Mola would have remained cooped up in the north and Franco and the African troops cut off across the straits in Morocco with only Queipo in Andalusia.

The international Non-Intervention Committee

In September 1936, at Britain's instigation, and with French backing, a Non-Intervention Committee was established with the aim of preventing foreign involvement of all sorts in the Spanish Civil War.[28] It was hoped that blocking the departure of soldiers, sale of armaments and assistance to either side would isolate the war within the Iberian Peninsula. The committee met in London and consisted of 25 nations, excluding Spain. The main players were Britain, France, Germany, Italy and the Soviet Union. Despite the paraphernalia of non-intervention, signed diplomatic agreements, the establishment of naval and air observation patrols around Spain, the committee's work was entirely ineffective. Even more so, in taking responsibility for international negotiations in relation to the Civil War in Spain, the Non-Intervention Committee drained power away from the League of Nations in whose assembly conventionally such issues would have been aired. It is likely that at the League the Spanish Republic would have received a more sympathetic hearing as the Second Spanish Republic had been a stout and conscientious member and an active participant in committees and associations. Even though all nations from 1937 were supposed to prevent their own citizens from going to Spain or trading, there were massive violations. Because the Non-Intervention Committee had no powers to bind its members to any of its agreements, it functioned as an empty front that enabled Western Europeans to be seen to be doing something while in effect doing nothing. Behind the façade, Italy, Germany and Portugal aided Franco and the Soviet Union sent arms to the Republic.

The siege of the Alcázar in Toledo

Before surveying the stages of the military campaign, it will be useful to look separately at the incident in Toledo that took place at the start of the war and became a rallying symbol for Nationalist supporters. To a remarkable degree, Moscardó and the 'heroic cadets of the Alcázar' captured the imagination of people outside Spain who were backing Franco's victory.

At the end of September the Army of Africa, on an undefeated sweep south to north through western Spain, was diverted in order to take Toledo. Strategically, this side campaign made little sense when the fall of Talavera de la Reina had cleared the road for a direct push into Madrid.[29] As well, the Toledo campaign arrested the momentum that would have brought the insurgent troops up to Madrid before Republican defences were organized and before the *madrileños*, the inhabitants of the city, had settled into the stoic habits of endurance that came to characterize their indomitable behaviour throughout the wearing years of war. The taking of Toledo, however, and the raising of the siege of the Alcázar, provided a boost to Nationalist morale at home. It was also tremendously important to propaganda abroad.

In July 1936, Colonel José Moscardó, the military governor of Toledo, declared for the insurgents. When the city of Toledo remained with the government, Moscardó and about 1300 like-minded supporters withdrew into the Alcázar, the huge grey fortress with four towers that looms over Toledo. At that time it housed the Infantry Academy. Despite the fact that the accounts often refer to 'Moscardó and the cadets of the Alcázar', in reality there was only a handful of cadets in residence at the time. The besieged comprised about 800 members of the Guardia Civil from the surrounding region and their families; some one hundred military officers; and various local right-wing figures and their families, though not including Moscardó's own wife and children. There were also some Republicans and families who had been taken hostage and at least some of them spent the siege shackled underground.[30]

The besieged sat it out within the catacombs and corridors deep within the thick walls of the fortress. There was water in an underground cistern that had been used as a swimming pool and grain to make bread in the stores, replenished with several forays to the outside. The horses and mules from the Military Riding School provided meat for a daily stew.

Women numbered about 500 and there were 50 children as well.[31] Two babies were born during the siege. It is perhaps a revelation of the deeply ingrained ideas about gender and the proper place of Spanish women that, even in the extraordinary conditions which prevailed in the Alcázar, Spanish females were expected to be pious and retiring, with prayer their only public outlet. Because it was a military operation, women were not permitted to participate in the pressing tasks of building barricades, or even in such female-specific activities as cooking and nursing the wounded (pp. 85–8). This may be the reason, as well, that many franquista accounts emphasize that the women in the Alcázar were at pains to maintain their femininity. Narratives of the siege often repeat the example of women using plaster off the walls as face powder, even though it seems extremely unlikely that women would have squandered their energies for such a fruitless outcome when they were living in semi-darkness with only the shadowy illumination from horse-fat candles.[32] Similarly, some franquista accounts, anxious to present the besieged as saintly, emphasize that husbands and wives abstained from sexual relations throughout.[33] Geoffrey McNeill Moss's informants, though, told him that in the first weeks, young men and women in the evening would bring a gramophone out into the courtyard and dance in the twilight, but such activities lapsed as the siege dragged on.

A good portion of the stone and masonry of the Alcázar, parts of which dated from the time of Charles V, had been rebuilt after a fire in 1886 when beams were strengthened with steel girders and concrete reinfor-cing. Despite aerial bombardment and heavy shelling from across the Tagus, which reduced the structure to enormous ruins, the besieged remained sealed inside. Republican attempts to storm the fortress were unsuccessful; the military and the Guardia Civil had brought a huge supply of ammunition with them and were able to repel all advances. The government sent sappers to blast a way from underneath the fortress and, though the explosions from below blew huge craters and eventually brought down the towers and much of the external walls, the perimeter of the defence was never penetrated. After two months, the corner towers and the external walls of the huge complex had been reduced to great mountains of rubble strewn over the ground.

The Republican government sent several emissaries to Toledo to urge Moscardó to give up. A priest was admitted and heard Mass and baptized the children, but Moscardó refused to surrender. Similarly unavailing were the efforts of the Chilean ambassador, the dean of the consular community in Madrid, who pleaded through a loud hailer.

General Moscardó, the senior military figure in the Alcázar, was 58 and until the siege had pursued an undistinguished military career. In 1936 he was 'on the shelf' and living in 'semi-retirement' in Toledo.[34] Tall and taciturn, and a stickler for detail rather than the big picture, Moscardó was fortunate during the siege to have an energetic second in command, Lieutenant Colonel Pedro Romero Basart. Head of the Toledo Guardia Civil, he was probably responsible for the day-to-day organization of guard duty and maintaining the barricades. The incident that clinched Moscardó's reputation was reported to have taken place on 23 July, when the head of the Toledo militia telephoned to say that Moscardó's son, Luis, had been arrested, and unless the Alcázar surrendered immediately the youth would be shot. In various forms in its retelling, Luis was brought to the phone, whereupon Moscardó's advice was simple and austere: his son should commit his soul to God and die for Spain, like a man.[35]

In a robust deconstruction, Herbert Southworth draws on a deep knowledge of the literature in order to show the inconsistencies in the reporting of the incident: the uncertainties about Luis Moscardó's whereabouts; the ambiguities in the detail and dates of his execution; and even his reported age at the time.[36] More recently, Isabelo Herreros has expanded Southworth's critique to challenge further the Nationalist version.[37] According to Herreros, Luis Moscardó's political sympathies were liberal and there was tension between father and son. Also, Herreros backs Southworth's claim that the exchange between father and son and Luis's subsequent execution – core incidents in the heroic version – were probably a fabrication. Citing entries in the Toledo cemetery records, Herreros claims that Luis' body was brought there much later, and the register back-dated. In Herreros's view, the entry was probably made in April 1956 at the time when Luis' body was placed in the crypt in the Toledo Alcázar to lie beside his father who had recently died (pp. 38–41).

It mattered little whether the details of the story were embellished or not. To his devoted followers in Sydney, London or Bucharest, 'General Moscardó and the heroic cadets of the Alcázar' were martyrs who had suffered for their convictions and, against all the odds, had prevailed. For many people, Moscardó's name became a code word that evoked all the nostalgically recalled, positive values that had supposedly predominated before 1914. Similarly, the relationship between Moscardó and his son was a leitmotif to those who felt that they, too, were upholding Old World morality and Christian virtue in a heartless modern and amoral world. In this sense, the event encapsulated archetypal interwar anxieties, which is probably why the narrative of the Toledo siege was retold in many languages and enjoyed such currency before the Second World War.[38] It highlighted two interconnected elements which engendered popular dread. These were the fear of innocence overwhelmed by new forms of evil and the interconnected image of new technology, particularly air attacks, wiping out defenceless populations.[39] In the Toledo siege both fears were powerfully and visually represented. Although the walls of the Alcázar were enormously thick, buttressed by massive towers to withstand attack over the centuries, the stark pictures of the siege showed that the fortress had been reduced to rubble. It had been subjected to relentless battering by big cannon at long distance and from aerial bombardment. All the while the besieged were huddled together, defenceless except for the spiritual protection of prayer and the diversions of the pious routines of Christian life. And, as if that were not enough, the unguarded innocents faced a further assault coming from below as dynamiters, the famous 'Red' explosive experts from the Asturias, tunnelled towards them deep through the earth to lay, like poisonous eggs, the explosives that would blow up the fortress from underneath. The most satisfying part of this hellish narrative was of course that, despite all the horror and the apparent odds against them, the besieged had survived.

The news that Franco had relieved the Toledo Alcázar was greeted with jubilation by his supporters everywhere. And as we shall see, it was often the event that spurred foreign volunteers to head off to Spain and attempt to enlist with Franco. Certainly, in the narratives of foreign visitors to Nationalist Spain, meeting the 'Hero of the Alcázar' was often as memorable as setting eyes on the great Caudillo himself.

Stages of the military campaign

The military campaign fell into three stages, after the first decisive month of July 1936. After taking Toledo, the Nationalists waged a full-scale attack on Madrid in November. It was repulsed, though the city was subject to four weeks of aerial bombardment which killed about 1000 people and began the terror that was intermittently the *madrileños'* lot for the next three years. The trenches, dug by both sides on the western outskirts of the capital and through University City, became a permanent fixture of the war.

During 1937, the Nationalists again sought to cut off Madrid by driving a wedge through government territory and cutting the Madrid–Valencia communications. The offensive failed. In March 1937, a large Italian force was roundly defeated at Guadalajara. By contrast, the month before an Italian and Spanish force had taken Málaga, forcing streams of terrified refugees out of the city and along the coast towards Almería, being shelled from offshore by a German battleship as they fled.

A Republican effort to draw Nationalists away from the northern coast into eastern Aragon failed, largely because the Republicans were dogged by internal fighting between militias and the central army. In particularly heavy combat the Basque regions fell to Franco. In April 1937, the Basque capital Guernica was razed by aerial bombing by the Condor Legion, as successive waves swept over the town. It was market day so the town's population was augmented with farmers from around about who had come to sell their produce. Many of those who died were immolated in the fierce firestorm that followed the bombing, while Franco's headquarters maintained that the Basques had burnt the town themselves.[40] In June, after a long blockade and ferocious fighting, the Republican port of Bilbao collapsed.

In 1938, the superiority of Nationalist sources of armaments began to tell while the Republic was faced with increasing shortages of supplies. Teruel had been in Nationalist hands but was retaken by Republican forces in a punishing effort in December 1937. The fighting took place in appalling conditions with many soldiers freezing to death as temperatures fell to −20°C. Franco retook Teruel in February 1938 and by August his troops had pushed across Aragon to reach the coast above Valencia. Republican Spain was cut in two.

The Nationalists then pushed south towards Valencia but were thwarted at the Ebro River by a counter-offensive from the Republicans which, at three and a half months, was the longest and most punishing battle in the Civil War. Some 27 brigades of the Republican army were marshalled, about 80,000 men, including all five International Brigades, and supported by air power. They crossed the Ebro in early August and faced a massive build-up of Nationalist forces supported overhead by the Nationalist air force and the Condor Legion. The last decisive battle in the Civil War lasted from early August until mid-November with a tremendous loss of life, perhaps 60,000 in total and almost that number again wounded. By early November the Republican defence had disintegrated and by mid-November the Nationalists were victorious. In the midst of the battle for the Ebro, the Prime Minister of the Republic, Juan Negrín, agreed to the repatriation of the International Brigades overseen by the League of Nations. It was hoped that this gesture might kick-start international disapprobation against Nationalist Spain. The battered men who marched through Barcelona on 15 November were bidden farewell by the Prime Minister and the foremost Communist woman deputy La Pasionaria, who referred to them as 'crusaders of freedom' who had given everything for progress and democracy in Spain.

By Christmas 1938, the Catalan front had broken and, at the end of January 1939, Franco's troops entered Barcelona, pushing ahead of them to the French border a flood of terrified refugees. The Spanish capital surrendered at the end of March, the last days caught up in a sordid mini civil war in which the military commander of Madrid, Segismundo Casado, attempted to negotiate a separate settlement with Franco in return for eliminating leading Communists in the capital. Holding absolute victory in his hand, the Caudillo was interested only in unconditional surrender. With the fall of Madrid, the quintessential symbol of Republican resistance was extinguished. On 19 May 1939 there was a huge victory parade. Franco, flanked by Italian, German and Portuguese dignitaries, took the salute as the Nationalist army, the Foreign Legion and the Requeté columns, as well as German and Italian units, marched past in their full colours.

Notes

1 There are a great many excellent books on the Spanish Republic and the Civil War. See Paul Preston and Ann L. Mackenzie (eds), *The Republic Besieged: Civil War in Spain 1936–1939* (Edinburgh: Edinburgh University Press, 1996); George Eisenwein and Adrian Shubert, *Spain at War: The Spanish Civil War in Context 1931–1939* (London: Longman, 1995); Stanley G. Payne, *Spain's First Democracy: The Second Republic, 1931–1936* (Madison: University of Wisconsin Press, 1993); Manuel Tuñón de Lara, *Historia de España Tomo IX. La crisis del estado: dictadura, república, guerra (1923–1939)*, Tercera Parte: Tuñón de Lara y María Carmen García-Nieto, *La Guerra Civil* (Barcelona: Editorial Labor, 1993), pp. 241–545; Paul Preston, *The Spanish Civil War* (London: Weidenfeld & Nicolson, 1986); Hugh Thomas, *The Spanish Civil War* (New York: Touchstone, 1986); Manuel Tuñón de Lara, *La guerra civil española: 50 años después* (Madrid: Labor, 1985); Gabriel Jackson, *The Spanish Republic and the Civil War 1931–1939* (Princeton: Princeton University Press, 1971); Pierre Broué and Emile Témime, *The Revolution and the Civil War in Spain* (Cambridge, MA: MIT Press, 1970); and, for a clear text and superb photographs of daily life during the war, see Javier Tusell, *Vivir en guerra: España 1936–1939* (Madrid: Sílex, 1996).

2 Stanley Payne, *Politics and the Military in Modern Spain* (Stanford: Stanford University Press, 1967), p. 267.

3 *Ibid*.

4 Payne, *Politics and the Military*, pp. 266–76; see also John Whitaker, *Fear Came on Europe*, preface by John Gunther (London: Hamish Hamilton, 1937).

5 See the study based on oral testimony by Jerome Mintz, *The Anarchists of Casas Viejas* (Bloomington: Indiana University Press, 1994).

6 See Payne, *Spain's First Democracy*, p. 220; and Adrian Shubert, *The Road to Revolution in Spain: The Coal Miners of Asturias, 1860–1934* (Champagne-Urbana: University of Illinois Press, 1987).

7 Franco's publicists outside Spain during the Civil War made much of this electoral outcome under which each electoral district disposed of a block of seats; the first party, or coalition of parties, past the post took the bulk of the seats. The system had been introduced through the Cortes in 1931 in order to avoid a situation, which was common in the Italian Assembly and the French Third Republic, whereby a close vote could produce a plethora of splinter parties often unable to govern.

8 For a close analysis of the impact of the Popular Front victory on the Catholic parties in Salamanca see Mary Vincent, *Catholicism in the Second Spanish Republic: Religion and Politics in Salamanca 1930–1936* (New York: Clarendon Press, 1996), pp. 236–56.

9 Francis McCullagh, *In Franco's Spain: Being the Experiences of an Irish War-Correspondent during the Great Civil War Which Began in 1936* (London: Burns, Oates & Washbourne, 1937), p. xix.

10 See Alberto Reig Tapia, *Franco 'Caudillo': mito y realidad* (2nd edn., Madrid: Tecnos, 1996); and Paul Preston, *Franco: A Biography* (London: Fontana Press, 1995). See also Carlos Blanco Escolá, *La incompetencia militar de Franco* (2nd edn., Madrid: Alianza Editorial, 2000).

11 Preston, for example, has pointed out that there was no library at the Pardo, Franco's residence, in 'The discreet charm of a dictator', *Times Literary Supplement*, 15 March 1993, p. 13. For a short but dense overview of Franco's strategy see Preston, 'General Franco as military leader', *Transactions of the Royal Historical Society*, Sixth Series, IV (London: Royal Historical Society, 1994), pp. 21–41.

12 Preston, 'Franco as military leader', p. 23.

13 See, for example, René Benjamin, 'Avec Franco, général et chef d'état', *Candide*, No. 697 (22 July 1938); and John T. Whitaker, *We Cannot Escape History* (New York: Macmillan, 1943), p. 105.

14 See Herbert R. Southworth, *El mito de la cruzada de Franco* (Barcelona: Plaza & Janés, 1986), pp. 217–32; and Thomas, *Spanish Civil War*, pp. 374–5. For a recent denial of the 'legend of Badajoz' promoted by the 'stubborn American propagandist Herbert Southworth', see Ricardo de la Cierva, *Historia esencial de la Guerra Civil Española: todos los problemas resueltos, sesenta años después* (Madridejos: Editorial Fénix, 1996), pp. 224–6.

15 Paul Preston, 'Alfonsine monarchism and the coming of the Spanish Civil War', in Martin Blinkhorn (ed.), *Spain in Conflict 1931–1939: Democracy and Its Enemies* (London: Sage Publications, 1986), pp. 103–32.

16 See Martin Blinkhorn, *Carlism and Crisis in Spain 1931–1939* (Cambridge: Cambridge University Press, 1975); and for the relations between Carlism and Alfonsine monarchism see Martin Blinkhorn, 'Conservatives, traditionalism and fascism in Spain 1898–1937', in his *Fascists and Conservatives: The Radical Right and the Establishment in Twentieth-Century Europe* (London: Unwin Hyman, 1990), pp. 118–37.

17 See José María Gil Robles, *No fué posible la paz* (Barcelona: Ediciones Ariel, 1968); and Frances Lannon, *Privilege, Persecution and Prophecy: The Catholic Church in Spain 1875–1975* (Oxford: Oxford University Press, 1987).

18 For an analysis of the Falange which places the movement within overlapping connections with the rest of the Spanish Right in the 1930s, see Paul Preston, *The Politics of Revenge: Fascism and the Military in Twentieth-Century Spain* (London: Routledge, 1995), pp. 3–29; Herbert Southworth, 'The Falange: an analysis of Spain's fascist heritage', in Paul Preston (ed.), *Spain in Crisis: Evolution and Decline of the Franco Regime* (Hassocks: Harvester Press, 1976), pp. 1–22; and Stanley Payne, *Falange: A History of Spanish Fascism* (Stanford: Stanford University Press, 1961).

19 See Thomas, *The Spanish Civil War*, pp. 328–33; Ramón Salas Larrazábal arranges the formations differently to provide figures of the same order but with higher

totals, in 'Las fuerzas militares', in Edward Malefakis (ed.), *La Guerra de España (1936–1939)* (Madrid: Taurus, 1996), pp. 231–62; and for an attempt to estimate the sides chosen by the military with a rather triumphalist history of the unification of Franco's army, see Ricardo de la Cierva y de Hoces, 'The Nationalist Army in the Spanish Civil War' in Raymond Carr (ed.), *The Republic and the Civil War in Spain* (London: Macmillan, 1971), pp. 188–212. Both Salas Larrazábal and de la Cierva argue that the Republican army was stronger at the start of the war; however, the assessment is based on heads counted, not on the quality and discipline of the troops. See also Ricardo de la Cierva, *Historia esencial de la Guerra Civil Española: todos los problemas resueltos, sesenta años después* (Madridejos: Editorial Fénix, 1996), pp. 169–76.

20 Charles Esdaile, 'Hombres y armas: la ayuda extranjera', in Octavio Ruiz-Manjón Cabeza and Miguel Gómez Oliver, *Los nuevos historiadores ante la Guerra Civil española*, Vol. 1 (Granada: Diputación Provincial de Granada, 1999), pp. 145–54.

21 John H. Galey, 'Bridegrooms of Death: a profile study of the Spanish Foreign Legion', *Journal of Contemporary History*, 4(2) (April 1969), pp. 47–64; R. Geoffrey Jensen, 'José Millán-Astray and the Nationalist "crusade" in Spain', *Journal of Contemporary History*, 27 (July 1992); and José E. Alvarez, *The Betrothed of Death: The Spanish Foreign Legion During the Rif Rebellion, 1920–1927* (Westport, CT: Greenwood Press, 2001), *Contributions in Comparative Colonial Studies*, 40.

22 See Alvarez, *Betrothed of Death*, p. 28, note 12, and Jensen, 'José Millán-Astray and the Nationalist "crusade" in Spain'.

23 See Alvarez, *Betrothed of Death*, p. 31, note 22, for the short shrift that was given to a new recruit who wished to use the pseudonym of 'Millán Astray'.

24 María Rosa de Madariaga, 'The intervention of Moroccan troops in the Spanish Civil War: a reconsideration', *European History Quarterly*, 22 (1992), p. 77; p. 80.

25 There is a large and highly partisan literature on this question and two recent popular films: Ken Loach, *Land and Freedom* (1995), and Vicente Arandas, *Libertarias* (1995). See also my 'Nor more than brothers and sisters: women in front line combat in the Spanish Civil War', in Peter Monteath and Frederic Zuckerman (eds), *Modern Europe: Histories and Identities* (Adelaide: Australian Humanities Press, 1998), pp. 121–33.

26 For his own part in the operation, see Luis Bolín, *Spain: The Vital Years* (London: Cassell, 1967), pp. 9–54; and for a detailed analysis of the negotiations between Mussolini and the Nationalists, see Paul Preston, 'Mussolini's Spanish adventure: from limited risk to war', in Paul Preston and Ann L. Mackenzie (eds), *The Republic Besieged: Civil War in Spain 1936–1939* (Edinburgh: Edinburgh University Press, 1996), pp. 21–51.

27 See Angel Viñas, *La Alemania nazi y el 18 de julio: antecedentes de la intervención alemana en la guerra civil española* (Madrid: Alianza, 1974); and for the role of key individuals, Christian Leitz, 'Nazi Germany's intervention in the Spanish Civil War

and the foundation of HISMA/ROWAK', in Preston and MacKen
Republic Besieged, pp. 53–85.

28 For a recent assessment of non-intervention set against A. J. P. Ta   ...sic
statement of the Civil War as a domestic Spanish affair, see Mary Habeck, 'The
Spanish Civil War and the origins of the Second World War', in Gordon Martel
(ed.), *The Origins of the Second World War Reconsidered: Second Edition: A. J. P.
Taylor and the Historians* (London: Routledge, 1999), pp. 204–24. For a clear
analysis of the larger international picture and the Spanish Civil War, see Enrique
Moradiellos, 'The Allies and the Spanish Civil War', in *Spain and the Great
Powers*; and David Carlton, 'Eden, Blum and the origins of non-intervention',
Journal of Contemporary History, 6(3) (1971), pp. 40–5. For the ramifications of
Britain's malevolent neutrality see Moradiellos, *La perfidia de Albión: el gobierno
británico y la Guerra Civil Española* (Madrid: Siglo Veintiuno, 1996); and for
France, M. D. Gallagher, 'Leon Blum and the Spanish Civil War', *Journal of
Contemporary History*, 6 (1971), pp. 56–64.

29 Toledo is a key piece in Preston's argument that it was the primacy of Franco's
political agenda that drove the course of the war. The kudos that accrued to Franco
in saving the Alcázar strengthened his hand at a time that the Nationalist high
command was deciding who would be sole commander. As well, Franco harboured
a 'colonial' rather than a military objective, to annihilate all opposition rather than
bring the conflict to a quick end. See 'Franco as military dictator', *Transactions of
the Royal Historical Society*, Sixth Series, **IV** (London: Royal Historical Society,
1994), and the discussion of the Alcázar in *Franco: A Biography* (London: Fontana
1995), pp. 173–84.

30 Webb Miller, with the first journalists to enter the Alcázar when the siege was
lifted, saw 'four militiamen with legs chained behind a railing'. See his 'Little world
war in Spain', in Eugene Lyons (ed.), *We Cover the World, by Sixteen Foreign
Correspondents* (London: George G. Harrap, 1937), p. 424.

31 Major Geoffrey McNeill Moss, *The Siege of the Alcázar: A History of the Siege of
the Toledo Alcázar, 1936* (New York: Alfred A. Knopf, 1937). McNeill Moss
arrived in Toledo three weeks after the lifting of the siege and stayed three months,
interviewing survivors and having access to Moscardó's daily record and the
newspaper that was produced inside the Alcázar. The book, which recreates, day
by day, the events that took place, was enormously popular and reprinted into a
number of languages and editions. Apart from consistently referring to government
forces as 'the enemy' and greatly admiring the heroism of the survivors, McNeill
Moss is careful to indicate what is his surmise, what is based on rumour and what
is oral testimony. McNeill Moss's narrative is the basis of most of the English-
language versions of the siege, though many of them are not as careful with the
facts as was their original source.

32 See, for example, Luis Bolín, *Spain: The Vital Years* (London: Cassell, 1967), p.
195; and Arnold Lunn, *Spanish Rehearsal: An Eyewitness in Spain during the Civil*

War (1936–1939), with a foreword by William F. Buckley Jr. (Old Greenwich, CT: Devin-Adair, 1974, reprinting 1937 edn.).

33 For example, see Arnold Lunn, *Spanish Rehearsal*, p. 150.

34 McNeill Moss, *The Siege of the Alcázar*, p. 28.

35 The story of Moscardó and his son is told in various degrees of elaborate detail in a string of narratives and even today in the museum of the Alcázar tourists hear two scratchy voices that are supposed to be Moscardó and his son.

36 Herbert R. Southworth, *El mito de la cruzada de Franco* (Barcelona: Plaza & Janés Editores, 1986), pp. 92–120. Southworth points out that, in the 1939 edition of the Brasillach and Massis volume, with Moscardó's own introduction, Luis's age is incorrect. See Brasillach and Massis, *Les Cadets de l'Alcázar* (Paris: Plon, 1936), p. 100. See also the reply to Southworth's earlier French edition by Rafael Casas de la Vega, *El Alcázar* (Madrid: G. del Tro, 1976).

37 Isabelo Herreros, *Mitología de la Cruz de Franco: El Alcázar de Toledo* (Madrid: Vosa, 1995).

38 It may be that the impact of the incident was greater outside Spain. For example, in Paloma Aguilar Fernández's analysis of historical memory in postwar Spain, the siege of the Alcázar hardly features. When the Toledo Alcázar was mentioned in official Spanish Film News and Documentaries (Nodo) seven times between 1943 and 1975, five of them were in relation to official visits by foreigners (Argentinian military and President; Portuguese President and military and the British Foreign Minister); see her table in *La memoria histórica de la guerra civil española (1936–1939): un proceso de aprendizaje político* (Madrid: Centro de Estudios Avanzados en Ciencias Sociales, Instituto Juan March de Estudios e Investigaciones, 1995), pp. 515–75.

39 For the enthusiasm and unease that went with 'air mindedness' in the 1930s and its effect on the Spanish Civil War, see Gerald Howson, *Arms for Spain: The Untold Story of the Spanish Civil War* (London: John Murray, 1998), pp. 14–15. Eugen Weber discusses the growing fear of devastation by air bombardment on civilians in *The Hollow Years: France in the 1930s* (New York: W. W. Norton, 1994), pp. 240–3.

40 See Thomas, *Spanish Civil War*, pp. 623–31; and Herbert Southworth, *Guernica! Guernica! A Study of Journalism, Diplomacy, Propaganda and History* (Berkeley: University of California Press, 1977).

CHAPTER 2

English narratives about Franco's Spain

Introduction

Within Nationalist Spain there was a good deal of mistrust of foreigners. Visas for travel were hard to come by and, once across the border, foreigners were carefully monitored. First-person accounts by non-Spaniards during the Civil War came from amateur commentators and professional journalists and the different tenor of each group of writings reflects the contrasting treatment they received at the hands of franquista officials. Amateur travellers, carefully vetted and usually arriving with recommendations from pro-Franco groups abroad, were more welcome than were the professionals in the foreign press corps. Ostensibly, the narratives by travellers from the first group describe the writer's individual experience in Spain. Most usually, though, they repeat the opinions of the franquista officials who ferried them about and who were at pains to show 'New Spain' as it was proclaimed: 'united, great and free'.

Working journalists received a much more chilly reception. Franquista officials held no truck with freedom of the press and begrudged journalists access to any information about the war except what was officially provided by the Nationalist Propaganda and Press Bureau. The narratives by journalists, discussed in the second part of this essay, catalogue the frustration they experienced as they attempted to collect material for stories that would meet editorial standards and deadlines of newspapers abroad. Seasoned in previous wars, members of the press corps were not easily deterred from their vocation. The accounts that a number of them produced about Spain, once they were free of franquista censorship, offer a fascinating insight into the war on Franco's side; and into the important role that independent journalists played as observers and participants in international affairs.

It is worth pointing out that there was another category of foreigners who came later to Nationalist Spain. Though they published no commentaries, Franco had already garnered their goodwill. In mid 1938, when the scales of war had tipped more decisively towards the Nationalists, their Propaganda and Press Corps began running wartime package tours around the battle sites.[1] The brainchild of Luis Bolín, the aim was to build support abroad for Franco's cause while gaining precious foreign currency.[2] These most desirable foreign visitors were, as Bolín described them, 'friends of ours', nuns, Catholic teachers and clerics (Bolín, p. 304). The tour groups travelled in a fleet of new American school buses, each vehicle named after an important Nationalist victory, Alcázar in Toledo, Teruel, Alfambra. An official guide travelled with them explaining what it was that the visitors were seeing as they followed a well-established itinerary. The first tour left from Irún in July 1938 and for nine days motored around the 'War Routes of the North'. Staying in first-class hotels and making expeditions 'in Wartime to the battlefields', they took in San Sebastian, Oviedo and Bilbao.

For the equivalent of £8 sterling, paid in any foreign currency, such pious travellers could see 'history in the making among unsurpassed beauty'. At the same time, they could 'make [their] own judgement about the real situation in National Spain today'. By the end of the war there was a similar circuit operating through the south from Cadiz to Málaga, Seville and Granada.[3]

The narratives that do exist of English travellers in Nationalist Spain were written for a readership in Britain, the Dominions and the United States. Like the authors themselves, the readers were right wing, mainly Catholic and already pro-Franco. Many of the writers had come to Spain to collect material to promote Franco's cause at home and were already high-profile members of pro-Franco committees in English-speaking circles. A subcategory of the English pro-Franco travellers were the observers with a military bent. Mostly retired British army, they had sniffed the wind of the future in war and weaponry and decided that it was blowing from across the Pyrenees.

In Britain throughout the three years of the Spanish Civil War, the polls of the British Institute of Public Opinion showed little variation in an overwhelming popular preference for the Spanish Republic. In January 1937, 86 per cent of those polled considered the Republic to be the legitimate government of Spain while only 14 per cent favoured General Franco. In January 1939, by which time the Republican cause was lost, support for the Republic had fallen to 71 per cent but Franco's backing had also dropped to 10 per cent. The loss in both categories was taken up by an increase in the number of Britons undecided for either side.[4] As these figures suggest, Franco's supporters in the broad English population constituted a small proportion. Their political impact, however, was far from insignificant.

The conservative National government that was in power in Britain throughout the Civil War, led until 1937 by Stanley Baldwin and afterwards by Neville Chamberlain, favoured Franco's victory.[5] It was at pains to keep Britain out of any foreign entanglements that might upset the international balance of power.[6] Spain always had had the potential to impinge on a British policy that was geared to the maintenance of unimpeded sea lanes to the Empire and, therefore, in which it was essential that Gibraltar stayed in British hands to ensure free access across the Mediterranean.

The British government's response to the Iberian crisis was to promote a policy of international non-intervention. The Non-Intervention Committee, which began in September 1936, met in London under the auspices of the Foreign Office, with the permanent delegates consisting of the ambassadors to the Court of St James of the 27 member states.[7]

Sir Henry Chilton was Britain's ambassador to Spain between 1935 and 1938. Like many foreign embassies in Madrid, the British staff were on summer vacation in San Sebastian in mid-July 1936 and, rather than return to the capital in wartime, the ambassador set up residence in a fine house overlooking the sea at Saint-Jean-de-Luz, a pleasant seaside town a few miles along the French coast.[8] Embassy business was carried out from a small shopfront in an old grocery store on the French side of the border at Hendaye, very close to the international bridge over the Bidassoa River that divides France from Spain.

Chilton's contacts with Franco's headquarters went well beyond the conventional cordiality of foreign representatives abroad. He was intransigently opposed to the loyalists, whom he habitually referred to as 'Reds'.[9] Several of the British consuls in Nationalist Spain, also, openly advocated the insurgent cause.[10] Such partisan behaviour was inappropriate when Britain's diplomatic relations were with the Spanish government and official British policy was for non-involvement in the Civil War.

At the end of November 1937, Sir Robert Hodgson had been appointed British Commercial Agent to Nationalist Spain and set up office with a staff of three in the Grand Hotel in Salamanca. At the same time the Duke of Alba became Spanish Agent in London.[11] This exchange of officials, though without formal diplomatic relations, constituted a de facto recognition of Franco's regime. Hodgson, whose wife was White Russian, had been a British consular official in Omsk in 1918 with General Kolchak's White Army and had been forced to flee when Kolchak's troops were routed by the Bolsheviks.[12] He saw the Spanish conflict quite simply as an extension of the Russian Civil War, with the Republicans standing in for the Bolsheviks. Until 1939 he looked with favour on Hitler and Mussolini as bulwarks against Communist expansion. Hodgson was greatly irritated by the British press referring to Franco's side as 'Insurgents' (though he himself always referred to the Republicans as 'Reds'). In his view, the Nationalists were engaged in the noble enterprise of 'pouring out their lives in thousands to save their country from absorption by Communist-controlled hordes inspired by the Comintern and supported by the human scum, largely alien, from which the Republican forces are recruited.'[13]

Long before the war had begun, however, the Spanish Republic could marshal few advocates within the British Establishment. Republican rhetoric about reforming the Spanish economy and the taxation system found little favour among British investors, who at the time provided 20 per cent of the total foreign capital in Spain.[14] British owners and their managers in Spanish mining and heavy mineral export industries in north-west and southern Spain were unaccommodating towards the Republican government's attempts after 1931 to improve the conditions and wages of Spanish workers.[15]

The 'Friends of Spain' was created in London in 1932 in order to counter what its members perceived to be the unwarrantedly favourable coverage of the Spanish Republic in the British press. They lamented the 'apostasy' of the English, wrong-headedly 'fair-minded' and perfect dupes to receive 'anti-clerical envoys from Moscow'.[16] In the words of a moving spirit in the group, Luis Bolín, 'England was separated from Spain by the Reformation'.[17] The group consisted of two important Spanish monarchists, the Duke of Alba, the head of the Spanish Academy of History, who spent much time in England and later became Franco's ambassador to Britain, and Bolín himself, the London correspondent for the monarchist Madrid daily, the *ABC*. The English contingent comprised Sir Charles Petrie, political historian and committed monarchist and in 1931 working on his *History of Spain 711 to 1931*; the Tory MP Victor Raikes; and, probably the most active for Franco of the Englishmen, Douglas Jerrold, director of Eyre and Spottiswoode publishers, who, in 1931, had become editor of the High Tory *English Review*.[18] Others involved were the Marqués del Moral, Juan de la Cierva, an engineer, whose father had been a minister under Alfonso XIII, and the Marqués Merry del Val, Alfonso's ex-ambassador to Britain.

In 1933, Jerrold, Bolín and the Marqués del Moral reworked a pamphlet by Calvo Sotelo, which appeared anonymously as *The Spanish Republic*. It catalogued the anticlerical 'horrors' of the Republic, the deaths, disturbances and church burnings that it claimed were fully sanctioned by the new government in Spain. It is hard to tell that it made much difference to English attitudes: the *Daily Mail*, predictably, applauded the 'lifting of the veil on a "Reign of terror" in Spain'; the (then) more measured *Times Literary Supplement* saw paranoia in the author's suggestion that 'Evil Spirits' were behind the new Republic.[19]

Jerrold played an important role in England in the early days of the uprising. Early in July, Bolín had introduced Jerrold to a mysterious Spanish visitor who asked the Englishman to find 50 machine-guns and a quantity of ammunition for the planned insurrection.[20] Jerrold agreed, though the equipment was never shipped. The next time Jerrold saw the arms dealer was in the Grand Hotel in Salamanca, a year into the Civil War (*ibid.*, p. 369). In addition, the Englishman stepped into the breach when Franco needed a plane. Jerrold made the arrangements to charter the Dragon Rapide and the English pilot and they left Croydon airport on 11 July to collect Franco in the Canaries and transport him to Morocco to take command of the Army of Africa. The outcome was deadly serious though the description of the venture smacks of farce: Bolín and de la Cierva, with much conspicuous cloak-and-dagger antics – hiding behind pillars in restaurants and unable to find their way to Surrey on the map – rustled up the retired English major, Hugh Pollard. He in turn produced the travel cover of a vacation trip with 'two blondes', one of whom, as Jerrold tells it, 'kept her cigarettes in her knickers' (Jerrold, p. 373).[21]

Equally important to Franco's cause, Jerrold was responsible for disseminating evidence which purported to demonstrate that the Communists had detailed plans for an imminent take-over in Spain. Referred to as ' the Confidential Reports', it contained details of alleged meetings of the Third International in Spain on behalf of the Central Body of the Russian Revolutionary Committee, ready to hook Spain into a combined French–Spanish–Russian Revolution. The precise source of these reports and their whereabouts were never specified. The so-called proof about them was most important to the Nationalists because it enabled them and their supporters to sidestep the awkward fact that

Franco and his fellow conspirators had rebelled against a legally elected civilian government.[22]

Like many of his compatriots who made the trek to Franco's Spain, Jerrold believed that the 'Apostles of militant communism meant to establish control in the West as well as the East'. And in their master plan, Spain was a central piece. It mattered not that the Spanish Communist Party was miniscule until 1936, because Jerrold made no distinction between Communists, the Left and Liberals. In his view, the generals' uprising was not a military revolt ('that was propaganda'), but the Spanish army was the only force able to put down the 'reign of murder and sacrilege' (Jerrold, p. 374) in which Calvo Sotelo's murder presaged the long-prepared Communist coup.

The original Friends of Spain became Friends of National Spain, in early 1937, chaired by Lord Phillimore. Members included Conservative MPs Alfred Denville, Captain Victor Cazalet, Sir Henry Page Croft, Sir Nairne Stewart-Sandemann and Labour MP A. T. Lennox-Boyd. There was also the Methodist founder of the Christian Unity Movement against Atheism and the father of mass travel in Britain, Sir Henry Lunn. With his son, Arnold Lunn, they were among the most tireless publicists for Franco and prominent figures at English pro-Franco events.

In Britain several organizations, with varying success and considerable overlap in membership, supported Nationalist Spain. The Spanish Infanta, Princess Beatrice of Orléans, attempted unsuccessfully to launch a non-sectarian General Relief Fund for the Distressed Women and Children of Spain.[23] No more successful was Brigadier General Sir Edward Bellingham, in October 1936. The Spanish Relief Fund for Sufferers from Red Atrocities planned to carry supplies to Spanish ports controlled by Franco. Although boasting an impressive list of patrons, and with rooms in Grosvenor Place, the committee's intemperate language frightened off the Admiralty.[24] Without official backing it was impossible to navigate around the warring Spanish ships and the international vessels observing non-intervention.

The very successful Bishops' Committee for the Relief of Distress in Spain was established in mid-1936 and is discussed in Chapter 7 along with Gabriel Herbert, the young woman who ran its medical service in Spain. Another organization that shared membership with those already listed was the Duke of Wellington's Committee for the Repatriation of the Basque Children. Its members agitated tirelessly for the return to Spain of the Basque children who had been evacuated and billeted with sympathetic families in May 1937, just before Bilbao fell to the Nationalists.

Devoutly Catholic and pro-Republic, the Basques were a fly in the ointment of franquista propaganda, which depicted all Republicans as atheists and Communists. The children's repatriation would be proof that not all Basques were anti-Franco and that the Caudillo himself was a humanitarian leader. As a result of the committee's efforts, on 12 November 1937, the first of two expeditions left to take the 650 children from Britain back to Spain.

An Australian journalist, Paul McGuire, travelled with the first 130 children. A devout Catholic from Adelaide, he was in Britain to observe the Catholic Life Movement. At the Spanish border the papal nuncio for Spain, Monsignor Antoniutti, joined the train, which was given a public welcome at each station on the way to Bilbao. McGuire was greatly moved by the experience, perhaps as much by the honour of rubbing shoulders with a papal nuncio and a crowd of Spanish generals.

His articles, syndicated worldwide in the Catholic weeklies, traced the trip from Southampton through 'Red France' until the jubilant arrival in 'peaceful, industrious and Catholic Spain'. There he found 'the cry of Christ the King on everyone's lips' and 'the Christian Thing is reborn'. While in Franco's Spain McGuire wished that he 'might see in Australian cities so many laughing children.[25]

There were historic ties between the Catholic Church in Britain and the Spanish Catholic hierarchy that had been fostered at the Irish College in Salamanca and in Valladolid at the Scotch College and St Alban's, where for centuries British priests had been trained.[26] In Britain, Franco drew his most active supporters from the Catholic hierarchy and the extreme wing of the Conservative Party, many peers among them. Although few, their wealth and membership of elite circles gave them an impact far beyond their numbers.

The pivotal figure in the pro-Franco movement within Britain was the Archbishop of Westminster, after December 1937 Cardinal Arthur Hinsley, head of the Catholic Bishops' Conference for England and Wales. Hinsley, who all his life kept a photo of General Franco framed on his desk, saw the Spanish Civil War as a straightforward struggle between Christ and the anti-Christ. And, within the bounds of legality and energy, Hinsley was devoted to Franco's victory.[27] Almost all the English Catholic pro-Franco groups operated under Hinsley's aegis. He wrote letters, spoke to church bodies, facilitated fund-raising and maintained a constant and vigilant eye promoting Franco's side.[28]

The Catholic press in the main reflected Hinsley's views, which were also those of the episcopal hierarchy. This was the case with the three Catholic popular weeklies, in descending order of circulation, *Universe*, *Catholic Herald* and *Catholic Times* and the Jesuit-controlled *Month*. The weekly *The Tablet*, under the new editorship of Douglas Woodruff, also pushed an intransigently pro-Franco line.[29] Reports from Nationalist Spain, the most frequent by correspondents from *The Tablet*, were syndicated through the whole range of Catholic papers and journals.

During the war, Arnold Lunn, whose *Spanish Rehearsal* is discussed in detail below, and Douglas Jerrold, F. Britten Austen, Tom Burns, Hilaire Belloc and Douglas Woodruff, among others, travelled to Spain to collect material for stories about 'Red Horrors'.[30] Like the English military tourists in Spain, none ever visited the government side, though they invariably contrasted Republican violence with the orderly Christian spirit that prevailed in Franco's Catholic state.[31]

These pro-Franco travellers, military and civilian, shared a view of the world anchored by several certainties. The most fundamental was that the 'Reds' in Russia were interchangeable with the Republicans in Spain. And the Civil War was the latest episode in a long-running crusade by Russian Communists bent on world domination. The converse was that Nationalist Spain was standing against the 'Red Tide' and, if General Franco faltered, France would go next and inexorably Britain would follow. As utterly implausible as the last idea was, there were a number of reasons for English Catholics to believe it.

James Flint has argued that, from the early 1920s, English Catholics regarded the Soviet Union as an 'almost unique repository of evil'.[32] As well, between the wars, a conjunction of factors drew a strong element of English Catholics inexorably to embrace the New Right. According to Adrian Hastings, the Catholic Revival in the second half of the 1930s shone with an intellectual brilliance that came from a 'spate of glittering converts'. At the same time, the lustre was 'partially tainted' by an ultramontanism that shaded into anti-Semitism and was under the sway of the dictatorships that had found roots in the Catholic countries.[33] In the 'country-house fascism' that many English Catholics expounded, the corporative state became the ideal because it appeared to combine Catholic social doctrine and a robust anti-capitalism with a populist rhetoric about national renovation.

Douglas Jerrold is a good example of the phenomenon. In *Georgian Adventure*, he recalls the 1920s and 1930s as the 'years of disillusion'. In this era, Victorian civic virtue gave way before an upper class obsessed with job seeking and 'stunting' and an enfranchised mass that had become the 'hysterical Public crowding popular spectacles and mobbing film stars'. Real political leadership was no more; by the 1930s it was the prerogative of 'ennobled cads and ruffianly millionaires' (p. 246). In this dismal scenario, Mussolini's corporatism and the Glorious Crusade of General Franco offered the only future that incorporated the spirit of Catholicism.

Among many English narratives of travellers in Spain there is a sense that what they found in Nationalist Spain reminded them of a time in England when life and values were purer and freer.[34] The other side of this coin of course was that the observer looked at the Spanish surroundings through English values and English eyes which occluded Spain and the Iberian landscape.

Douglas Jerrold, again, provides a particularly clear example. Travelling in Spain with two English ex-military men in March 1937, he revelled in the atmosphere, seeing everywhere sights that 'tugged at the heart strings'. A man who longed to bring back 'the clean and simple past' (Jerrold, p. 237), he felt that in Spain he had 'found England again': the England of 1914 and 'of [his] youth' (*ibid*., p. 378). Everywhere men were in uniform and drilling for a greater purpose than their own. Taken to the look-out near Madrid, the three Englishmen were forced to cross in the line of sight of a sniper. Jerrold was exhilarated to realize that the three represented the arms of British military tradition. Major-General Fuller, the infantryman, walked unhurriedly across; their second companion, the author of *The Bengal Tiger*, next stepped gracefully into the trench. In his turn, Jerrold, upholding the tradition of naval common sense, kept his cool as he heard the 'once familiar ping' of a bullet hitting a nearby surface. All the while in Spain, Jerrold had to remind himself that he had not gone to Spain to 'recapture old memories', but was there to 'get the wherewithal to kill new and foul lies' (*ibid*., p. 379).

His lack of observation of the specifics of the Spain around him was perhaps the consequence of an overwhelming nostalgia that his Spanish experience evoked. In any event, Jerrold's lack of perspicacity is breathtaking. For example, he declared that 'Nationalist Spain is nothing if not democratic'. And, if the government 'errs it is on the side of informality, clemency and casualness to friend and foe'. It is a regime in which you can 'Go where you like, say what you like' and 'no one asks you who you are and what is your business' (p. 380).

Much like Jerrold, the other narrators, too, were overwhelmed by the orderliness of Nationalist Spain. From their first greeting across the border until the last farewell at the end of the three to ten days which it took to sweep north to south through the western zone, visitors were dazzled by the discipline and militarism they observed everywhere.

Catholic travellers revelled in the public display of the faith. Flags flew everywhere, carrying the image of the Virgin superimposed on the red and yellow of traditional Spain. Pictures of Nationalist leaders, Franco most commonly, were on windows and hoardings, often with the image of the Sacred Heart above and the words 'I will reign in Spain' in a scroll underneath. Carlist Requetés marched to the front with medals and rosaries around their necks, the badges of the Sacred Heart sewn to their tunics, and their cloaks embroidered with large white crosses. Church dignitaries were prominent at all official events and public celebrations of Mass were common. Morning and evening, men and women thronged the churches.[35]

Visitors were equally thrilled by the buzz of life behind the lines in wartime. Men in uniform crowded bars and restaurants. In the Grand Hotel in Salamanca, always packed and deafeningly noisy, high-spirited young officers from the Foreign Legion, with their collars turned back to reveal their smooth brown throats, jostled for tables with Falangists, whose blue shirts sported the insignia of the yoke and the red-tipped five black arrows. Fair-haired German aviators, the backs of their necks bright red from the sun, sat earnestly drinking cocktails.[36] And among the throngs of uniformed men were a small sprinkling of women, whether in the uniform of the Falangist women's organization or in their best clothes, most wearing a medal or a badge on their breast attached by a red and yellow ribbon.

The trappings of the new totalitarianism were also on display. Shopfronts and hoardings carried huge portraits of Mussolini and Hitler flanking Franco. The Roman salute – in Franco's Spain 'el saludo nacional' – was declared the official greeting in May 1937 and practised everywhere with gusto. Though English travellers grumbled that their food grew cold on the table with all the standing and saluting, more often than not they admired the fervour and unity around them. Whenever the Italian, the German or the Spanish anthems were played over the radio, which happened frequently, the listeners rose to their feet and raised their arms. The journalists Karl Robson and Alexander Clifford were thrown out of a fashionable hotel in San Sebastian for merely standing at attention with arms by their sides during the Spanish anthem.[37] In the dining room of the Grand Hotel, where a long central table was permanently reserved for German personnel, Nazi saluting was de rigueur. As superior officers hove into view, subordinates leapt to their feet, their rights arms snapping upwards in greeting.

The standard stops on the visitors' itinerary took in Burgos, the centre of the Nationalist uprising in the north in July 1936 and Franco's headquarters after August 1937. There the visitor could marvel at the tomb of El Cid and the Gothic vastness of the cathedral. In Salamanca, Franco's base in the first year, they sauntered around the deep colonnades of the Plaza Mayor and gazed at the architecture of the university and the detail of the Casa de las Conchas. If they were lucky, they could obtain a bed or a meal in the bustling Grand Hotel. Next was Talavera de la Reina, the recruiting centre for the Spanish Foreign Legion, and if the visitor was Catholic, and especially in Holy Week, there would be a couple of days in sunny Seville.

All made the obligatory side trip to stand on the flat roof of a house on the outskirts of Madrid, purportedly belonging to General Cabanellas, to take in a panoramic view of the capital. The spike of the Telephone Exchange permanently visible, on a clear day through field glasses travellers could count the pillars on the façade of the Royal Palace, glistening white across the brown gash of the Manzanares.

As well, everyone, always, was taken on a day excursion to Toledo to gaze in awe at the ruins of the Alcázar. And, if status warranted, there might be a meeting face to face with Moscardó, the sad-eyed taciturn hero of the siege. Or, if the visitor was less important, a few words could be exchanged through an interpreter with one of the thousand survivors. Later, when the propaganda value of the Alcázar was fully exploited, a young soldier would lead visitors gravely through the rubble pointing out the sights and retelling the story of the siege which, in any event, all travellers knew beforehand.

By 1938, when the Nationalist army was pushing eastwards across Aragon, visiting foreigners were taken to Saragossa, first to kiss the Virgin of the Pillar, the patron saint of Franco's army, miraculously saved when a Republican bomb had scored a direct hit on the basilica but failed to explode. Then they would motor up in convoy to stand on a hilltop a mile or so away from the battle line and experience the vicarious frisson as real soldiers exchanged real fire. The high point of the expedition, achieved only by those with political clout outside Spain, was a meeting with

Franco. Invariably foreigners, face to face with the Caudillo, were struck by his shy demeanour: the soft voice, the small hands and feet and the moist brown eyes which he was in the habit of modestly lowering as he spoke. These qualities, as well as his standard imprecautions against the 'Marxist Hydra', were what the amateur writers recalled when they later put pen to paper.

In the tales the same anecdotes appear over and over. Partly this was because foreigners without Spanish used the previous narratives of their compatriots as travel guides which created a self-referential loop of information. For example, from December 1936, when Major McNeill Moss's epic of the Alcázar[38] appeared, visitors to Toledo pored over his detailed diagrams as they clambered over the ruins. In the same way, French travellers brought Henri Massis and Robert Brasillach's *Les Cadets de l'Alcázar*[39] under their arms.

The repetitions in the tales were also because most of the travellers spoke no Spanish and were therefore reliant on the explanations of the Spaniards who accompanied them. The Nationalist Press Bureau kept junior press officers on a very short leash. Most were reluctant to offer any opinions on the state of the war that in any way could be attributed to them later. Instead, press officers trotted out a stock of stories, mostly about the hideous atrocities carried out by the Reds in the other zone. As we shall see, hard-bitten foreign correspondents were less easily fobbed off. Enthusiastic lay travellers, however, were attentive listeners. Their own beliefs about the behaviour of 'Reds' were affirmed by franquista accounts and, later, when writing up the trip, foreign writers reproduced the anecdotes in their entirety. The fact that they were told and retold in a number of narratives simply added to their authenticity. Their readers, already pro-Franco and sharing the writer's assumptions, found the details of the atrocities entirely credible.

As well, within the British Catholic elite, there was a long-standing connection to an 'Anglophile nucleus'[40] in the Spanish aristocracy. Many of them were educated in English Catholic public schools such as Beaumont, Downside, Ampleforth and Stonyhurst. As Tom Burns discovered, in Spain in the summer of 1937 to drive an ambulance for English medical aid, most Spanish aristocrats spoke fluent English.[41] For example, Pablo Merry del Val, Chief Liaison Officer with the Foreign Press, had been a contemporary of Burns at Stonyhurst when Merry del Val senior had been the Spanish ambassador to Britain.

Anglophiles, like the Duke of Alba, the Duke of Sanlúcar la Mayor and

Pablo Merry del Val, had been key figures in the Spanish foreign service during the monarchy. After July 1936 they became solid franquistas and during the Civil War served as spokesmen, go-betweens and chaperones to English-speaking visitors to Nationalist Spain. In mediating the experiences of the British visitors, these Anglophile aristocrats were powerful publicists for Franco. They understood what would impress the English and fed them the sort of information they could use back home. The Spaniards' upper-class credentials and their familiarity with the markers of English upper-class life gave credence in English ears.[42] For example, Arnold Lunn ran into an old boy from Stonyhurst at Mérida in April 1937. The Spaniard first regaled him with grisly stories about what the 'Reds' had done to various members of his family and then abruptly questioned the Englishman about Oxford's chances in the Boat Race.[43]

As a consequence of the generosity and helpfulness of Franco's publicists, they appear over and over in English accounts. The Spaniards the English travellers most often encountered were Merry del Val, father and son, Luis Bolín, the Duke of Alba and Captain Aguilera, the Conde de Alba y Yeltes, the Filipino Ignacio Rosales, Juan de la Barcenas and the diplomats the Marques de Manzanedo and the Duke of Lécera.

Foreigners who were not within the charmed circle were treated quite differently.[44] Captain Aguilera, one of the senior press officers, was a polo-playing ex-cavalry officer and friend of Alfonso XIII, with a Scottish mother to boot. His fluent English, urbane manners and ready information impressed all English Catholic visitors, but he was surly and menacing towards the American journalist, Virginia Cowles. Strongly disapproving of her sex and what he presumed were her pro-Republican sensibilities, he brusquely told her that he hated 'sob-sisters for the Reds' and would 'like to see them all impaled and wriggling on poles'.[45] Fearful that he would have her arrested, Cowles fled back to France. Merry del Val greeted the American Quaker, Howard A. Kershaw, in Nationalist Spain for the American Friends' Service Committee, with the 'condescending graciousness of a haughty aristocrat'.[46] He was contemptuous of Kershaw's ideas of democracy, 'old fashioned and naïve and no longer functional in the modern world' which, the Spaniard declared, needed a 'dominant aristocracy in control' (Kershaw, Quaker Service, p. 43). Peter Kemp, a young British volunteer just down from Cambridge, found Merry del Val 'retained the austere manner' of his English public school education and Kemp always felt that any moment he 'might tell him to bend over and take six of the best'.[47]

Reading together the narratives of these travelling amateurs, with their formatted characters and stock anecdotes, is reminiscent of gazing at a tableau or watching a diorama turn through its rotation. The figures of good and evil are instantly recognizable and, as the scenes are cranked, the characters move on a fixed and predictable trajectory. The evil figures – Communists, Jews, atheists or hideously unfeminine females – attempt to ensnare the virtuous characters – Catholic, disciplined and part of an organic hierarchy. The audience knows that the virtuous will eventually be victorious because they have God on their side, but it will be achieved only after they have passed through a series of trials.

John Corbin's elegant explanation of the discrepancies between local testimony and the historians' version of events in Ronda during the Spanish Civil War can be applied equally to foreign pro-Franco narratives.[48] Drawing on Lévi-Strauss's notion of 'intellectual bricolage', Corbin reconciled the wild disparities in the narratives of these emotionally charged events. Their narration, functioning as 'myth' rather than fact, 'mapped the event of their telling, [not the detail of] the event they recounted'.[49] In Lévi-Strauss's conception, 'intellectual bricolage', as opposed to concrete knowledge, relies on blocks of information whose meanings are 'finite, closed and fixed'.[50] In using this sort of knowledge to explain an event, a narrator may rearrange the pieces into a new configuration but the new assemblages will not, in any way, alter the constituent meanings of the pieces or the original meaning of the incident which it signifies. This exactly encapsulates the narrative process in many of the atrocity stories that foreigners in Spain relate.

Keeping all of this in mind, it is worth beginning by looking at some of the travellers' commentaries from Nationalist Spain sent by ex-members of the British military. They constitute almost a genre of their own and, in the lead up to what many people saw as a possibility of war, the reports of these men, who were accepted as experts on military matters, received public attention. And they were the object of more notice than was warranted by the quality of the information they presented.

Major-General Fuller, advocate of the new tank warfare, made several trips to Spain to record his impressions of Franco's military strategy. By this time, Fuller had moved from the 'fascist political fringe' to become a full-blown anti-Semite and activist in the British Union of Fascists.[51] Writing in uncharacteristically flat prose, he discussed the 'Soviet strategy of the Reds' in warfare, though without ever visiting the government side. He digressed at large on the 'unmitigated curse' of parliamentary democracy, which in Spain had 'opened the door to class hatred and foreign intrigue'.[52] As well, based on his October trip with Lunn, he produced a commentary on the possible methods to protect troops from air attack by low-flying aircraft, which in Spain were being carried out by the Nationalist air force.[53]

Major Francis Yeats-Brown, the founder of the crypto-fascist journal *Everyman*, had written several books based on his experiences in the Indian army.[54] The *Bengal Lancer* was enormously popular when it appeared in 1930. In Nationalist Spain with Fuller and Jerrold in March 1937, he wrote an enthusiastic report to Whitehall that predicted Franco's certain victory. It came with a fulsome covering note from Ambassador Chilton who gushed that Yeats-Brown had 'received a very friendly welcome from the Generalisimo' and that as Franco previously had complained about a lack of visits from 'prominent British subjects', Chilton hoped that in the future 'more gentlemen of Yeats-Brown's calibre' would visit Franco. A handwritten comment in the margin crisply noted, 'Major Yeats-Brown is a Fascist'.[55]

Charles Grey, founder and editor of the *Aeroplane*, shared the politics of the men above. He toured Nationalist flying bases accompanied by the flying ace, the Duke of Lerma.[56] There were also visits from serving military atachés keen to see whether new armaments were being used in Spain. For example Group Captain D. Colyer, on an official visit to Portugal for the RAAF, took the opportunity to cross to Vigo in order to see first-hand the Spanish Falangists about whom he had heard a great deal. He found them in the flesh to be 'clean and of good type'.[57]

Perhaps the most dotty, but not atypical all the same, was the 36-page rambling commentary by the retired Major-General Sir Maxwell Scott. It was based on a fast fortnight's run around the battlefields at the end of March 1937. Scott had met Franco when both were visiting foreign military observers at a French officers' course at Versailles in October 1930. In Spain he was accompanied by the English-educated 'John' de la Barcenas.[58] His purpose in coming to Spain was ostensibly to get to the bottom of the 'persistent rumours' that Protestant pastors were mistreated in Nationalist territory.[59] Once there, he discovered that a number had been shot, but was told that it was not their Protestantism that had caused Spaniards offence but that they had allowed 'their conventicles to be used for red propaganda' and were front organizations for Protestant missionizing.

Maxwell Scott had his eye on other matters as well. These included the state of health of the hound pack in the Royal Gibraltar Calpe Hunt, all thriving and being exercised near Algeciras, he was glad to report. On foreign involvement in Spain, he saw Germans in military uniform but his hosts had reassured him that there were no German troops, and in fact, those he had seen were not military but ordinary Germans come to 'instil proper ideas of discipline into Falange youth'. And given the state of youth in the world, the Major-General could only applaud. On the vexed matter of British naval strength, Scott was chagrined that the military governor in Málaga had 'kissed his fingers in the air' when asked what he thought of the present state of the British navy.

In Salamanca, Scott had managed a ten-minute interview with Franco, the Caudillo presumably having more pressing matters on his mind. Franco, however, had taken the time to explain that the military uprising had been necessary because the Republican government had 'intentionally' given petty officers 'swelled heads' in order to undermine military discipline.

Nigel Tangye, as air correspondent for the *Evening News* was technically speaking a journalist; his narrative, however, fits more properly with the 'amateurs' than the foreign press corps.[60] In Spain for a couple of weeks, he came away knowing little more than when he arrived. Because in London his 'sympathies with the New Germany' were well known, he arrived in Spain with letters of warm recommendation from the German embassy in London to General Faupel, Franco's German ambassador. A curiously introverted character, he was ex-navy but was 'physically sick at the sight of blood' and had to screw up his courage to enter the hospital in Talavera de la Reina to look around. He spoke no Spanish and was a teetotaller, both qualities that did not bode well in Spain. In Paris, on the way, he 'carried out an experiment' with red wine and champagne, because he had heard that drinking in Spain was expected and he wished to be sure he could 'retain possession of his faculties' (Tangye, *Red, White and Spain*, p. 19). The language problem, however, was unfixable.

On the strength of the German contacts, Luis Bolín gave Tangye permission to travel alone, a most unusual occurrence, and provided him with a car and driver. With them he trailed around on the periphery of the war for two disconsolate weeks. At one stop, he was relieved to exchange some words with Irish volunteers and, by a stroke of luck, in Seville he ran into an English nanny from the redoubtable Norlands Agency for English children's nurses. Most of the time, however, he was mute and miserable.

Horrified at the reckless abandon with which his chauffeur drove the car, Tangye spent fraught hours searching through his *All You Want in Spain*, trying to master the phonetic forms with which to tell the driver to slow down (*ibid.*, p. 82).

Sir Arnold Wilson, a Conservative MP and the editor of the *Nineteenth Century and After*, was also a Friend of National Spain. In the mid-1930s, Wilson wrote a popular series entitled *Walks and Talks*, in which he recorded his impressions. In August 1937 he travelled home from the Nuremberg rally via Nationalist Spain, where Peter Kemp accompanied him to visit the Alcázar in Toledo and the Basque countries. Predictably he noted Franco's good government in contrast with the 'infections', 'poisons' and 'diseases' that had spread from Russia into Republican Spain.[61]

Sir Arnold Lunn, Catholic convert, Christian apologist and the person who introduced slalom skiing into the 1936 Olympics, was one of Franco's most indefatigable supporters. In fact, the Spanish Civil War remained the touchstone in Lunn's long career as publicist for right-wing Catholicism.[62] Even though he spoke not a word of Spanish and never visited the Republican side, his first-person account of Franco Spain, *Spanish Rehearsal*, became a handbook for Franco's supporters in the English-speaking world.[63] During the Civil War he travelled in Nationalist Spain twice, for two weeks each time, just before Easter in 1937 and again in 1938. On both trips he was chauffeured about in a convoy of foreign visitors by Franco's chief press officer, Captain Aguilera. On the first occasion, among his travelling companions, writing for the *Daily Mail*, was the bumptious young Randolph Churchill, whose overbearing bluster was tolerated because he was Winston's son (Lunn, *Spanish Rehearsal*, pp. 219–25). The following year, Major-General J. F. C. Fuller and Austen Britten made up Lunn's party as they trailed the Nationalist army eastwards across Aragon. In each case Lunn managed to spend Holy Week with the Infante de Orléans's family, whom he knew from the Swiss ski slopes and whose three sons were pilots attached to the Condor Legion.

Unable to speak, his bag gone astray and without lodgings arranged, Lunn found his initial introduction in Irún to Nationalist Spain inauspicious. At Burgos, the trip picked up. He ran into Gabriel Herbert, a young English woman working in front-line medical services for Franco, and passed an enjoyable evening with two young English aristocrats. They shared his assessment that the 'Gangsters on the Spanish Left', the Popular

Front, were interested only in 'assassination, arson and loot' (*Spanish Rehearsal*, p. 11). In Salamanca, where Lunn was delighted to spend a few days in the 'cloistered calm' of the Irish College, Luis Bolín took over the arrangements. An old friend from a luncheon club in London at the *English Review*, Bolín was back in Spain with the 'thankless task' of dealing with foreign journalists.

For the next three days Lunn sped south in a Propaganda and Press Bureau car, chauffeured by the English-speaking Captain Aguilera. Lunn faithfully repeated Bolín and Aguilera's opinions on the Civil War. For example, Nationalist sensitivity to any mention of Irish and Italian volunteers was the fault of the Non-Intervention Committee. And, if French journalists insisted on snooping about when the Germans were testing out their latest anti-aircraft guns, then they could only expect to find trouble (*ibid.*, p. 18). Also echoing franquista propaganda, Lunn made a distinction between the 'inevitable casualties of modern warfare' (those caused by the Nationalists) and the 'deliberate massacre of innocent women and children' (carried out by the Republicans) (*ibid.*, p. 10). His Nationalist friends assured him that the Russians had started the war, long before Franco had stepped in. He accepted as well Douglas Jerrold's details of the so-called 'Confidential Reports', the secret documents that proved that a Red Revolution was imminent when the insurrection took place. In any event, Lunn himself was not convinced that democracy would work in Spain. In England, it was possible because the English play cricket and carry into practice the philosophy of the game (*ibid.*, p. 79). But in 1937, even in the home of the MCC, Lunn was not sanguine about democracy 'if the sort of intellectuals favoured by the Left Book Club' ever achieved power (*ibid.*, p. 80).

As they drove about, Aguilera expounded his philosophy of race, Spanish life and nature. Lunn approvingly repeated Aguilera's distinction within the Spanish race between the 'conquering, Franco-Norman types' like Quixote, 'tall, fair and with blue eyes'. By his 'appearance, breeding and philosophy' Aguilera was himself part of this group. The other half of the Iberian race were the Sancho Panzas: 'sturdy, thick set,' 'hard working and without ideas'; and with whom there had been no problems until the 'Reds got hold of them' (ibid., p. 37).

In Toledo, McNeill Moss's book in hand, Lunn tramped over the Alcázar and was enchanted to meet one of the survivors. Doña Carmen Aragones, 'as beautiful as all heroines should be', throughout her ordeal had taken great care to maintain her femininity by 'ingeniously substituting plaster from the walls for face powder'. Aguilera and the English party lunched with the vivacious survivor though, to Lunn's chagrin, the party divided into the 'happy hilarious minority who spoke Spanish' and the 'disconsolate majority' who did not. And though Lunn did what he could 'with a phrase book and a mixture of French, Italian and Latin, it was a poor best' (*ibid.*, p. 51) He promised himself to return to Toledo, ever the travel agent on the look out for future destinations, but he swore to learn Spanish before then.

What is notable about Lunn's narrative is how little of it in fact relates to Spain. Wherever he went, he was reminded of other places and other conflicts, and it is these on which he expounds. These in turn had more to do with the intellectual baggage of an Englishman with a classical education than with the Spanish landscape he was traversing.

First of all, Franco's colours were the same as those of the MCC: the sight of the fluttering red and yellow standard evoked languid summer afternoons idled away at Lord's (*ibid.*, p. 22). Burgos was like England in 1914, 'when Englishmen had stormed the recruiting offices' (*ibid.*, p. 8), a curious recollection in itself, since Lunn did not serve in the First World War but spent the years in Switzerland.[64] Near Badajoz, where the Nationalists' massacre of Republican troops and civilians in the first month of the war was hotly denied by Nationalist officials, Lunn recalled Wellington's English troops in 1812, massacring the Spanish garrison. But it was the classical heroes that teemed in his head. In Pozuelo near Madrid, he recalled Achilles' threatening words to Priam (*Spanish Rehearsal*, p. 44); at the Aragon front, as he watched troops march by he was reminded of the noble Socrates fighting as a hoplite at Potidaea, and in battle saving Alcibiades; and Aeschylus at Marathon; and Thucydides with his seven ships coming to the rescue when Antipolis fell (*ibid.*, p. 26). In April 1938, when he learnt that the Nationalists troops had reached the east coast, he heard inside his head the cry 'Thalassa! Thalassa!' that had sprung from the lips of Xenophon's army when it reached the sea in the expedition of Cyrus (*ibid.*, p. 218).

And everywhere, as well, he heard about the 'Reds' and their unspeakable atrocities. Quoting McNeill Moss, Lunn explained to the reader that 'they are called Reds because they fight in red shirts, wear red badges and scrawl "Up the Reds" behind the loopholes they defend' (*ibid.*, p. 15). His stories, many of which were told over and over again in English narratives, encompass all the elements of the genre of the Red atrocity story. There is mindless cruelty, not directed at the utilitarian objective of wiping out the enemy, but in order to prolong the victim's travail in this life. Frequently added is sexual transgression, wanton theft and a glimpse of the hand of the Moscow puppet-master.

In the south, for example, Lunn met a man who presided over courts martial. With an English education and having spent a lot of time in England, he was, in Lunn's eyes, an impeccable source. The story the man told was of a village in which the richest person, in effect the 'capitalist in the village', was a woman who was an 'ardent Communist'. This, a transgressive state of affairs in itself, was not the only odd thing. She used her funds to pay workmen to dig up the bodies of buried nuns and priests. When she had collected these, one by one, she threw them into the fire, the same one on which the local priest was roasted. The woman also advocated Free Love in the village. Despite being so wanton with her funds on other projects, she had never been able to find a man and, in fact, she 'died a maid'. Lunn's informant explained that it was her sexual desperation that had produced her anticlericalism: she was enraged that the priest had willingly chosen the state of celibacy that she had been so keen to abandon. Eventually, when the Nationalists had driven out the Reds, the woman had been brought before a tribunal but had 'gloried in her crime'. She was tried and executed and, as she lay dying, her last words were 'Long Live Russia' (*ibid*., p. 23).

This highly improbable story is a textbook example of Lévi-Strauss's 'intellectual bricolage'. Each part of the narrative has been added to the succeeding part but without transforming the meaning of the story as a whole. Instead, each part of the narrative sequence retains its original significance. The horror of the story comes from each separate incident, not from the build-up each part produces towards a climax of the whole.

Lunn related another atrocity story which was told over and over in narratives from Nationalist Spain, and which he attributed to the Catholic Bishop of Gibraltar. In it, a priest was facing an execution squad and asked to have his hands unbound so that he could bless the executioners. They promptly cut off his hands and, with the bleeding stumps, the priest made the sign of the cross over the gunmen as he was killed (*ibid*., p. 178).

There are many other stories like these. While it would be foolish at the end of the twentieth century to pretend that atrocities do not happen, or that they did not in the Spanish Civil War, many of these stories are unconvincing. Lunn himself never observed the events he described but claimed that he could vouchsafe their truth by the 'look in the eye' of the person who had told them to him (*ibid*., p. 210).

Partly, Lunn and the travellers like him were on unfamiliar territory. When he, Fuller and Britten Austin were in Aragon in 1938, they came in the van of the Nationalist troops that took Huesca. The town had been encircled by local anarchists from almost the first day of the uprising. The militias, holed up in the cemetery outside the city walls, had turned the area into a rabbit warren of hides and trenches. Soldiers had dossed down in funeral vaults and set up bivouac among the coffins. When routed, they left behind the litter and detritus of the occupation: coffins broken open, bones disinterred and walls and headstones scarred with pro-Republican and anticlerical graffiti.

Britten Austen, in Spain for the first time to gather material for *The Tablet*, and unaccustomed to Spanish anticlericalism, was shocked beyond measure. Appalled that the so-called 'fighters in the cause of democracy had torn off coffin lids' and interfered with the remains, he attributed this 'sadistic Satanism' to the followers of the anarchist leader Durruti, who, he had been told, was 'a notorious character in the White Slave underground'. An equally horrified Major-General Fuller claimed that 'it would be an insult to beasts to describe this as bestial'.[65] By contrast, the young English woman, Pip Scott-Ellis, nursing at the front for more than a year, noted in a matter-of-fact tone in her diary that her unit in the same region had come across cemeteries and chapels that were 'scribbled all over with rude remarks and filthy pictures', left by the Red soldiers who had been camped there.[66]

Despite the catalogue of gruesome 'Red Horrors'[67] and the harrowing fact that Spain was tearing itself apart in Civil War, Lunn undertook his travels with gusto and robust enjoyment. As he noted, 'few experiences can be more exhilarating than to follow the day-by-day advance of a victorious army' (*Spanish Rehearsal*, p. 221). In April 1938 near Morella on the east coast, Lunn described the excitement of watching through glasses from a hilltop as the Nationalists half a mile away took out a Republican artillery unit. Above, 30 bombers swept across the sky, like 'eagles with angry wings', diving 'disdainfully through the puffs of white cloudlets' thrown up by the anti-aircraft fire. With his companions he spent 'three lazy hours watching the dying battle. The air was fragrant with spring and the ground where they lay was graced by April flowers' (*ibid.*, p. 219). At sunset they regained their cars and, as they drove away, they passed a lorry full of sombre, hooded Moors, in silhouette against the last glow of the evening sky. It was, as Lunn observed, a 'vivid memory of a memorable day'. Back in the village, their press officer had found them beds in a private house for the night and, despite the cold, Lunn slept deeply and awoke refreshed.

For a man who loved the outdoors, Spain at war offered an appealing life. It provided him with a couple of intense weeks in invigorating activity that was shared with admirable comrades who returned his respect. The vicarious excitement of a wartime adventure provided grist for the writer's mill for years to come. It is no wonder, then, that the Spanish Civil War remained the high point of Lunn's political and intellectual life.

Foreign correspondents in Franco's Spain

The decade of the 1930s was the heyday of the foreign correspondent. Dashing figures with portable typewriter at the ready, they were, like the famed Reuters man, 'hard-working and healthy, good at languages, ready to travel' and wholeheartedly committed to reporting the news around the world.[68] An increasingly literate public was avid for news and attuned to international events in a way that had never been before. According to Noel Monks, a correspondent for the London *Express*, many people could vividly remember the First World War and, those of the generation that could not, were fascinated by everything about it. In the 1930s, readers were riveted particularly by what Monks called 'I stories', in which journalists related their own experiences in international events.[69] Many were included in the popular collections of first-person accounts and autobiographies by famous newspapermen reporting world events.[70]

Mass-circulation dailies sent their own correspondents on mission or used syndicated stories from the British, American and European news agencies. All were in cut-throat competition for a news scoop. There were foreign correspondents on location cabling stories back from the major international crises between the wars. Many of the journalists in Spain, for example, had already covered the Russian Civil War from Vladivostock and the Baltic, or had followed Mussolini's forces across the baking deserts and the sparse highlands to Addis Ababa. After Madrid and Burgos, they went on to Vienna, Munich, Prague and Warsaw as they reported the sequence of crises that led to the Second World War.

Foreign reporting, without a doubt, was a strenuous business. Much ingenuity was required to beat the competitors to a breaking story. But it was also an exciting and satisfying occupation. According to the Irish correspondent, Francis McCullagh, who was present at the major interwar conflicts and twice taken prisoner to boot, newspaper men returned from a foreign posting, 'boisterous, bursting with good health, sunburnt, a stone heavier, and with two inches more around the chest'.[71]

War reporting in Nationalist Spain was different.[72] First of all, it was a Civil War and, again in McCullagh's estimation, journalists in Nationalist Spain were made as welcome as an 'inquisitive stranger in a house where a domestic squabble was in full blast' (p. viii). The Nationalist Press Bureau distrusted the foreign press corps and maintained strict controls over foreign reporters and what they could see and say.[73] Luis Bolín, appointed by Franco to head the Press Bureau, was arrogant and unhelpful to working journalists even though he himself had been a correspondent in London. The appeals by journalists to him, that they needed first-hand information and their cables were expected to meet the publication deadlines set by home editors, fell on deaf ears.

McCullagh, a devout Catholic and committed to Franco, was scathing about Bolín, who strode about in a Foreign Legion uniform with Sam Browne belt, high boots and 'Saville row jodhpurs'. When he appeared at the press office, invariably very late, Bolín would 'cleave his way' through the crowd with an 'imperial eye that made contact with no one to right or left' (*Franco's Spain*, p. 104). Even the crypto-Nazi, Nigel Tangye, with his pockets stuffed with letters of recommendation and initially welcomed by Bolín, was filled with 'fury, livid fury', which made his 'nerves tense, teeth clenched and muscles taut', as he waited for days on end to receive the travel pass that had been readily promised.[74]

No travel was permitted without such a pass and all articles were scanned by the Official Censor. The Press Bureau in Salamanca occupied several rooms on the ground floor in the Bishop's Palace, where Franco had his headquarters. There were press offices, as well, in Burgos, Ávila, Talavera de la Reina and Seville. In all these places, at any time of the day and night, foreign correspondents, particularly British, American and French, milled about waiting for permission to travel; or for their stories to be checked by the censor so that they could be cabled to the editors at home.

The Official Censor even checked stories published in newspapers outside Spain. Correspondents of the paper that contained reports that were considered derogatory to Franco would find themselves threatened with expulsion or, at the worst, under arrest. This meant that journalists and editors had to be very careful. Karl Robson, for example, was excluded from Spain on the strength of a leader page in his paper, *The Daily Telegraph*, that referred to the Nationalists as rebels.[75]

Between thirty and fifty foreign correspondents were expelled from
Franco's Spain and a dozen more arrested for a range of infractions.[76] The
first journalists in Spain, Edmond Taylor, Harold Cardoza and Bertrand
de Jouvenal, were briefly arrested by nervous Falangists when they
camped out at the front in the first weeks of the war. Sefton Delmer, *Daily
Express*, was expelled almost immediately, even though his paper was
looked on with favour.[77] Denis Weaver from *News Chronicle* and James
Minifie of the *New York Herald Tribune*, visiting the front from Madrid,
were thrown into prison in October 1936 when they strayed into the
Nationalist Zone. Their driver and guide were shot and, after spending a
very uncomfortable week, they and another journalist, Hank Gorrell,
arrested previously, were expelled across the border. Webb Miller was
briefly imprisoned because United Press in London sent him a cryptic
telegram which the censor interpreted as threatening General Mola.[78]

Among the arrests in 1937 was the unlikely figure of H. R.
Knickerbocker, an American correspondent for the Hearst Universal
News Service. He had been favoured by the Press Bureau initially,
probably because his *Siege of Alcázar*[79] recorded enthusiastic support for
Franco during the first months of the war. Although he mentioned the
Italians and Germans he came across, Knickerbocker was wholeheartedly
identified with the 'Whites against the Reds' and filled with admiration
for the foreign legionnaires, 'decent soldiers' and hospitable. Knickerbocker was particularly taken by Captain Aguilera, a virile soldier who 'is
fifty-two, looks forty and acts like thirty'. As they travelled around the
battlefields the two shared a great camaraderie (*Siege of Alcázar*, pp. 136–
7). Predictably, the high point of Knockerbocker's narrative is in Toledo
where in the Alcázar he met 'the heroes of all history' (*ibid.*, p. 186).

Unfortunately, in his enthusiasm for a Nationalist victory, Knickerbocker overreached himself, tarnishing his own reputation. In November
1936, Franco announced over Lisbon radio that he was poised to enter
Madrid and Knickerbocker wrote a vivid description of the Caudillo's
victorious march into the capital. He graphically described the cheering
crowds, and even that an enthusiastic small dog had followed the
procession, barking jubilantly. The Republican Press Service was quick to
point out the fraud.[80]

In April 1937, Knickerbocker was denounced by an unnamed person
and abruptly arrested. He spent 36 very unpleasant hours being threatened
and interrogated and only Randolph Churchill's persistent enquiries
ensured that he was released. Finally, franquista officials expelled him

across the international bridge at Hendaye, never to be permitted back into Spain.[81]

A Law of the Press was passed in 1938, declaring that foreign journalists arrested in Nationalist Spain would be treated as spies. Ostensibly directed at journalists from the Republican side caught by the Nationalists, the law was a threat also to every foreign working journalist in Franco's Spain.[82]

Certain topics were absolutely forbidden and any mention would incur immediate censorship. There was to be no word at all of the presence of foreign soldiers with Franco; or of the execution of prisoners; or of terror behind Nationalist lines. Similarly, Moors, whose exotic figures had raised considerable interest outside Spain, were to be described always as devoted God-fearing soldiers. Nor could there be any suggestion that the conflict had begun as anything but a 'rebellion to prevent a revolution'; or that those living in Nationalist territory were other than happy, well fed and overwhelmingly in favour of General Franco.

Despite the strictures, experienced reporters managed to get uncensored stories out of Spain, by hiding the evidence.[83] Journalists crossed into France in order to send stories, if they wished to avoid the censor, or used a courier. Frances Davis obtained her break with Cardoza and the *Daily Mail* by starting off as a deft and quick-witted courier, carrying stories from Spain to be telephoned to London from France. Those with the Official Censor's stamp of approval she carried openly in her pocketbook and those that did not she carefully placed sheet by sheet flat against her skin beneath her girdle. When she was leaving Majorca, she hid her notebook in the deep inside pocket in the man's coat she was wearing and, by a stroke of luck, the police woman who carried out the full body search missed it (*My Shadow in the Sun*, p. 271).

Foreign journalists telephoned their stories through from the Bar Basque at Saint-Jean-de-Luz. It was a popular watering hole for foreign correspondents and, in Peter Kemp's view, also for 'Play-boys and play-girls, black marketeers and conspirators of every nationality and political complexion'.[84] Noel Monks claimed that the Mittel-European barman, Otto, spied not only for both sides in Spain and for various factotums from Italy and Germany, but probably for many foreign journalists as well.[85] In all the narratives written about Spain, foreign journalists were scathing about franquista censorship.[86]

Travel to the front was strictly controlled by the Press Bureau. The routine was that, when it happened at all, members of the press, usually in their own cars, travelled in convoy with a Press Office vehicle at the head and tail, like bookends, to prevent stragglers going off on their own. Correspondents were strongly discouraged from speaking to soldiers and were not allowed to snoop about by themselves or move away from the group. Guardia Civil checked press papers every few miles. Lunches, packed by the hotel beforehand, were brought and eaten on the side of the road at the time and place chosen by the press officer. Without permission it was not possible to travel near the front. Captain Rosales, the press officer, took a tremendous set against an American news photographer, referring to his 'disgusting name' – it was Cohen – and ruined his professional survival in Spain by not permitting him to join the news convoys to the front and insisting on viewing all rolls of film he shot in Spain. Davis recalled that the German correspondent was equally disdainful of the Jewish American (*My Shadow in the Sun*, pp. 129–30).

Virginia Cowles, an American correspondent for the Hearst stable, who came under suspicion in both Republican and Nationalist Spain, found these 'mad tea party trips to the front'[87] unnerving. She was in Franco Spain for three months from the middle of 1937, during which time she travelled widely north to south. In Bilbao, just after the collapse, she also saw first-hand the fall of Santander and Oviedo. On a particular trip she went to León with fifteen or so English-speaking journalists, she riding with a very bad-tempered Captain Aguilera in his yellow Mercedes. Among the journalists were Dick Sheepshanks from Reuters, Reynolds Packard from United Press, William Carney of the *New York Times*, Harold Cardoza of the *Daily Mail*, and Kim Philby of the London *Times*. The press officer marshalled them all in convoy before they took off. Behind the front line, the press corps took lunch on a hillside – Spanish tortillas, bread and wine – while the Nationalist guns on a nearby mountain pounded a Republican position a couple of miles distant. Cowles felt revulsion at what she saw as the hypocrisy of their situation, that in the midst of destruction the press corps could laugh and make jokes about what they planned do in Paris when they were out of Spain (*Looking for Trouble*, p. 91).

By no stretch of the imagination could Cowles be called left wing. She was a close friend of the Churchills, in fact the godmother of one of Randolph Churchill's children, and in Republican Spain her perceived conservatism had caused her colleagues to suspect she was a Franco spy. In Nationalist Spain, however, she had grown more and more uneasy with the level of mistrust everywhere. For example, the accompanying press officer had been menacing towards her when she had seen Moors looting a village (Cowles, p. 73), and when an old man at Guernica had said that the town was bombed by German and Italian planes. The irrational, 'constant vilification of the enemy' (Cowles, p. 77) had driven her to despair, as had statements such as that of a handsome young officer that the 'only way to treat Reds is to shoot them' (*ibid*., p. 75). She had been shocked by the constant focus on the 'fight against Bolshevism' and the way in which 'Bolshevism had become an elastic word' to cover all kinds of patently non-Communist groups and activities. She was also taken aback by the widespread involvement of Italian troops. At Santander, she watched the Nationalists' victory parade, complete with high-stepping, black-plumed Italian soldiers and Black Shirts as motor cycle outriders. In captured Spanish cities, huge posters of the Duce and the Führer shared the walls with those of the Caudillo. All of this filled her with dread and the premonition that the Spanish war was the curtain-raiser to a larger and more dreadful international conflict.

Frances Davis, who worked with Cardoza for the *Daily Mail*, was the only officially accredited female reporter in Nationalist Spain. From a very early age she had been fired with a passion for journalism and arrived alone in Paris in mid-1936 with an introduction to Edward Mowrer, the correspondent for the *Chicago Daily News*. As well, she had a handful of promises, which she had rustled up herself, from provincial newspapers in America to take her columns about European events. In the hope of joining up with a famous reporter, she went by herself to the French frontier and, by a serious of fortuitous accidents, but mostly through her persistence, she managed to chum up with H. R. Knickerbocker, Harold Cardoza and Ed Taylor. She made herself indispensable as their courier carrying stories out of Spain. The *Daily Mail* took some of her stories and eventually, with Cardoza and Paul Bewsher, she became an accredited *Daily Mail* correspondent in Nationalist Spain.

The *Daily Mail* was extremely pro-Franco and Davis framed her stories as the editors wanted them. As well, she greeted everyone with a loud 'Arriba España', a salutation which many journalists who felt ambivalent about Franco could not bring themselves to make. As Davis became more established, however, she became increasingly unhappy about her situation. Although she loved the work and 'the Major' as everyone called Cardoza, less and less she 'liked the stuff the *Daily Mail* likes' (*My Shadow in the Sun*, p. 131). The paper's editorial policy was always to refer to Franco's army as the 'Patriots' and the Republic as the 'reds'. This naturally pleased Franco's press officers and, because she was a *Mail* person, she was very popular among Nationalist functionaries. Captain Rosales, the press officer with whom she dealt, a Filipino with an exaggeratedly 'English toff's accent', showed her great favour but he 'filled her with fear'. When he explained that 'the masses' need a 'touch of the whip for they are like dogs and will only mind the whip', she remained impassive but thought about her father, who was a union organizer in Boston, and her friends and teachers, who throughout their lives had 'worked and fought for labour' (Davis, pp. 136–7). When Rosales pointed out that Spain must be cleansed of the industrial proletariat and that the streets in Madrid would run with their blood, it turned her blood to ice. When the press officers forbade her to travel about alone, warning that the 'Reds' would rape her if they caught her, she thought to herself that, if she ever met any of them, she would explain that Emma Goldman and her mother had been friends in the old days in New York (Davis, p. 139). Unable to manage the strain of the dissonance between her professional position and her personal beliefs, Davis quit the *Daily Mail* and struck out on her own. She obtained a contract as an independent working for Mowrer and the *Chicago Daily News*, whose liberal politics echoed her own. She was extremely courageous, going alone to the front and spending time by herself in the sinister atmosphere of Majorca. Her story has a poignant end. The career which showed such promise was cut off almost before it had begun. In Talavera de la Reina Davis contracted a serious throat disorder, not diphtheria but something similar, that robbed her voice and caused her throat to constrict in asthma-like attacks that necessitated a tracheotomy. It could not be cured. Eventually, Davis was forced to return to New York to spend three years desperately ill in hospital, mute and pining for the camaraderie and excitement of her lost life as a foreign correspondent. From her bed she heard her close friend, possibly her lover, John Whitaker, in Europe broadcasting the declaration of the Second World War.

  John Whitaker, a very experienced American correspondent on the *New York Herald Tribune*, had at first been welcomed warmly when he arrived in Nationalist Spain at the end of 1936. Decorated by Mussolini for his positive reporting on the Italian troops in Ethiopia,[88] Whitaker had been immediately taken into Captain Aguilera's confidence. He turned a blind eye to Whitaker's travelling unaccompanied to the front. As the months went by, however, the press officer began to suspect that Whitaker was 'no fascist' (*We Cannot Escape History*, p. 109). Finally, in

Talavera de le Reina, where Whitaker had made his base, Aguilera and a German agent burst into his room very late one night and threatened that if he went again to the front unescorted they would shoot him.

It was true, Whitaker had observed many forbiddden things. In the main square at Santa Olalla, on the way to Toledo, he had watched the mass execution of a large group of 'beaten and listless republican militiamen' as they were mown down by Moors behind machine-guns (*ibid.*, p. 112).[89] Outside Navalcarnero, he had been horrified when two young Spanish women, arrested and presumed Republican sympathizers because one had a trade union card in her pocket, were handed over to 40 Moorish troops camped in a small schoolhouse nearby. Whitaker's blood turned to ice as he heard the 'ululating cry' of the Moors as they caught sight of the women (*ibid.*, p. 114). He also talked to Falangists in Toledo about executions behind the lines (*ibid.*, p. 111); how Colonel Yagüe had readily boasted that they had shot hundreds of prisoners in Badajoz (*ibid.*, p. 113); and how wounded Republicans in the Toledo hospital had been killed with hand grenades thrown into the wards after the Alcázar siege was raised (*ibid.*, p. 113).

Whitaker was repelled by franquistas who 'talked knowingly of death, fondling the word as if it were a woman, repellent yet seductive' (*ibid.*, p. 114). In the early days, Aguilera had expounded to Whitaker his own theory of history and philosophy of the world. According to it, the French Enlightenment had disseminated the dangerous doctrine of the Rights of Man ('does a pig have rights?'); and Britain and America were going 'howling red' like France. One of the problems according to Aguilera's assessment was that 'modern sewage disposal' had wiped out the 'plague and pestilence' that had previously kept down the numbers of the masses. And in the face of what was happening in Republican Spain, once Franco was victorious, it would be necessary to purge the country of 'one third of the male population' in order to be rid of the proletariat and fix unemployment for good (*ibid.*, p. 108).[90]

No matter where the correspondents were located, the Press Bureau always took them to the outskirts of Madrid to the flat-roofed villa that was supposed to belong to General Cabanellas. McCullagh, like other experienced journalists, chafed under the Press Bureau's restrictions, claiming that 'a correspondent's initiative is sapped by that monotonous ride to the villa' (McCullagh, *In Franco's Spain*, p. 162). Sir Percival Phillips, a senior foreign correspondent for *The Daily Telegraph*, which was favourable to Franco, left Salamanca for Lisbon in disgust after a

short time, complaining that the foreign press corps in Nationalist Spain
was treated like 'fancy Cook's tourists dragged around by a guide, or a
bunch of school girls under the guidance of a school mistress' (quoted in
McCullagh, *Franco's Spain*, p. 113). He could no longer work in a
situation in which the only stories that were officially sanctioned were the
'edifying but monotonous stories of Falangist valour which everyday fill
Spanish newspapers' (*ibid.*, p. 112).

Sir Percival claimed that in all his war reporting he had never
experienced such 'chilliness' from military officers, who in Spain 'dislike
the press and want them banned'. Even officers to whom he had been
introduced socially might shake the correspondent's hand but would then
'immediately turn their backs' in order to show their disdain. As well, to
Sir Percival's chagrin, when he had interviewed Franco for *The Daily
Telegraph*, he had been searched before he was admitted into the
Caudillo's presence.[91]

Other correspondents, too, noted the air of official suspicion with
which foreign reporters were observed. The restrictions of the press added
to the strenuous conditions of the work in wartime. Richard Sheepshanks,
in a long letter to his editor-in-chief, set out the hardships the press corps
faced: the lack of facilities for the press; the absence of despatch riders to
bring stories back. Because journalists were never permitted to remain at
the front overnight, he was forced to drive 150 miles each evening in order
to catch the censor to file his reports if he was to have any hope of getting
them away the next morning. He warned the editor that any mention of
Italians would bring down wrath on his head, despite the fact that Franco
himself had congratulated the Italian divisions for their good work at
Santander.

Sheepshanks, with a couple of other 'real journalists', had threatened
that they would send no more cables unless the Press Bureau became more
professional in the arrangements for travel at the front. In the 'normal'
expeditions they were 'herded together and sent off on a glorified picnic
tour with a miscellaneous rabble of photographers, amateur writers and
tourists under the charge of an incompetent officer whose knowledge was
non-existent and from which they returned exhausted and exasperated
and too late to send out the cables'.[92]

The danger of the life of a journalist was brought home on New Year's
Eve 1937, when three journalists were killed on their way to the Teruel
front. There were about a dozen of them in a five-car convoy that had
stopped to eat lunch in the square of the village of Caude. Because the

weather was freezing – the Teruel campaign was fought in blizzard conditions in heavy snow – the journalists ate in their cars while the drivers went to a nearby cafe. In the row of vehicles, Kim Philby of *The Times* and Edward J. Neil of Associated Press went back to join Richard Sheepshanks and Bradish Johnson, sitting in the car behind. Almost immediately a shell landed between the cars, instantly killing Johnson, who was in the front seat, and mortally wounding Sheepshanks. Sitting in the back seat, Edward J. Neil, a New Yorker, was badly wounded in the legs and body. A second shell hit the square, killing five Spanish soldiers and several mules that were hauling water. Neil and Sheepshanks were taken to the Saragossa hospital where Sheepshanks never regained consciousness and Neil died of his wounds the following day.[93]

'Dickie' Sheepshanks was a very able and popular Reuters man. Educated at Charterhouse and Trinity College, Cambridge, he had joined the agency in 1933 and was considered Sir Roderick Jones's blue-eyed boy. The chief editor's recommendations and the eulogies on Sheepshank's death suggest that it was his prowess on the cricket pitch that had first brought him to Jones's attention. He was an outstanding batsman, had captained the Eton Eleven and played county competitions for Yorkshire. In October 1935, Reuters sent him to cover the Italian invasion of Ethiopia. While there, he met the 37-year-old American, Edward J. Neil, and the two had become fast friends.

Neil was a distinguished foreign commentator. He arrived in Spain in March 1937 and had covered the Nationalist drive through the north. In Bilbao, during the advance, he had made a name for himself as an intrepid reporter who was so intent on getting his cables out that he had used the ex-Republican cable head to send his story while the bullets from both sides whistled past him. The third fatality was Bradish Johnson, a 23-year-old Harvard graduate with a promising career ahead. He worked out of Paris for *Newsweek* and the *New York Herald Tribune* and had been in Spain for just three weeks.

The Nationalist High Command pulled out all stops for the dead journalists. They were given a High Mass in Saragossa Cathedral and the bodies were shipped home in state. Pablo Merry del Val accompanied the three flower-laden hearses to the border. It was, perhaps, an indication of the signal tribute that Franco bestowed upon the men that he sent General Moscardó to lead the cortège on foot to the frontier at the Bidassoa.

The fourth injured passenger was Kim Philby, later of course of greater fame when his identity was revealed as a double agent for Moscow.[94]

Philby, already deeply immersed in Soviet espionage, had come to Franco's Spain in May 1937 as second correspondent for the London *Times*. The Nationalist Press Office knew that he was the son of a gentleman and assumed that he shared the conservative prejudices of his newspaper. Philby gave no indication otherwise.[95]

Philby's cover in Spain was strengthened by the female companion with whom he lived in Saragossa. The Canadian divorcée, Lady 'Bunny' Lindsay-Hogg, ten years older than himself and previously a minor actress on the London stage, was an ardent monarchist and 'wildly pro-German'. She had been in Spain in the 1920s and fallen in love with the place. During the war, she came back through Portugal to join the social circle around the foreign press corps; and became Philby's lover.[96]

In *My Secret Life*, Philby notes a couple of times in Spain that his cover was in danger. For example, he was arrested in Córdoba by the Guardia Civil when he had travelled there without a pass to see a bull fight. At the time, he had an incriminating slip of paper in his pocket containing a key to a Russian intelligence code, which, in the best James Bond fashion, he swallowed.[97]

Given the era and the international sensitivities, it was not considered surprising that Philby showed an interest in troop movements and hardware. As well, exactly like the other English-speaking correspondents, when he wished to send uncensored information, he did so from Saint-Jean-de-Luz or Biarritz.[98]

In the incident at Caude at the end of December 1937, Philby received only a mild scalp wound. At the time, John Degandt, the *New York Enquirer*'s correspondent (2 January 1938) on the spot, noted that it was odd that only a single press car had been hit when it appeared that the shell had fallen between two cars, and that it had exploded only in one direction. More than fifty years later, an Englishman, who had been involved at the time, offered a more sinister interpretation. Tom Duprée was an honorary consul with the English embassy in Saint-Jean-de-Luz and made the arrangements for transporting the coffins to the families. He claimed that he had always believed that Philby had planted the bomb in the boot of the car in which he was riding in order to kill Sheepshanks who was sitting in the car behind.[99] By getting into the back seat of the vehicle in which were Sheepshanks and Neil, Philby had been able to protect himself and escape unhurt. According to Duprée, Sheepshanks had discovered that Philby was a Comintern agent and was about to blow his cover and therefore Philby had had to arrange his death. The truth or otherwise of this story will probably never be known.[100] In any event, Franco awarded the Distinguished Military Medal to all four correspondents, Philby included. He remained in Spain and continued to write for *The Times* until August 1939.

Two events in Spain in which the role of the foreign press was highly contentious were the Nationalists taking Badajoz in August 1936 and the razing of the Basque capital of Guernica in April 1937. Both, already described in the previous chapter, have been extensively analysed and, therefore, only a brief overview is required here.

In the fall of Badajoz in August 1936, two French journalists, Marcel Dany and Jacques Berthet, and the Portuguese, Mario Neves, covered the event, including the massacre of Republican prisoners that had taken place. Part of their story was used in the United Press syndicated service under the name of Reynolds Packard, who was in insurgent territory, but not at Badajoz until some days later. The French journalists were arrested and held for several months and Packard was placed under serious suspicion.

In the longer run, almost as important as the arrests, was the fact that the misattribution of authorship, though the facts contained were correct, fuelled a sense of grievance among right-wing commentators that the press outside Spain was biased against Franco's side. This in turn greatly strengthened the credibility of those who argued the patently silly position that in the Civil War all atrocities were perpetrated by Republicans.[101]

At Guernica, George Steer from the London *Times* had raced to the city just after the bombing and verified that it had been flattened by planes. His colleague James Holburn, from the same paper, reported later, however, that the damage appeared to him to have been caused by exploding mines, and therefore was probably the work of the retreating Basques themselves.[102] Noel Monks, in Bilbao to write a story about the effect of the blockade on British shipping to Spain, visited bustling Guernica on market day, and while driving back to Bilbao in the afternoon, was strafed by a wave of bombers going towards Guernica. On hearing that the town had been bombed, he had gone back immediately and reported that the destruction was caused by aircraft.[103] The incident had enormous repercussions. It drove a wedge between Catholics abroad and left a legacy of acrimony in the arguments that have persisted until today, even though there is now no doubt that Steer's and Monks's version was what in fact had happened. The full detail of the evidence and the fascinating ramification of the press coverage have been rigorously analysed by Herbert Southworth.[104]

By contrast, the ambiguities that fuelled the controversy surrounding Arthur Koestler's arrest in 1936 have become perhaps less clear-cut as the years have gone by.[105] A Hungarian in exile when the Spanish Civil War began, Koestler was 32 years of age and working in France for the Comintern's West European Department under Willi Münzenberg. From July 1936, Münzenberg turned his formidable organization to campaign for the Spanish Republic.[106]

Koestler went to Spain at the end of August 1936, ostensibly as a correspondent for a conservative Hungarian paper and the London *News Chronicle* but in reality in order to collect evidence of German and Italian intervention on Franco's side. In Lisbon, by a stroke of luck, he met some members of the franquista exile community who took him for a fascist. Armed with a safe conduct and letters of recommendation from Nicolás Franco, he headed off to Seville where he found plenty of evidence of German intervention in the form of German pilots, planes and technicians. He was even able to interview Queipo de Llano, who assumed that his interlocutor was a good Hungarian fascist and talked at length about Italian and German involvement with Franco. By ill luck, Koestler was recognized by a German correspondent for a Nazi paper. Threatened by a warrant out for his arrest, issued by Luis Bolín from the Press Bureau, Koestler fled to Gibraltar.

Next, Willi Münzenberg sent Koestler to Madrid to search the papers of franquistas who had been seized in the capital. The aim was to find evidence of a collaboration with Hitler or Mussolini before the war in order to counteract the 'Confidential Reports' that Franco's side were touting as proof that the generals' uprising had been to head off an imminent Communist revolution. Although Keostler found such papers in Madrid, and Münzenberg used them in propaganda against Franco and the Nazis, they had little effect in the long run.

The Comintern sent Koestler to Spain a third time. In January 1937, he travelled south to collect material for a series of articles about the strength of anti-fascism in Málaga. As before, he travelled with the identification papers of an accredited correspondent with the *News Chronicle*. Just before he left he had finished a book for the Comintern on Spanish history which forcefully explained why the Second Republic was democratic and its cause just. The book was published by Victor Gollancz.[107]

When Málaga fell to the Nationalists on 8 February 1937, Koestler was trapped there and hid in the house of an English expatriate, Sir Peter Chalmers Mitchell, an eccentric English zoologist who had retired to southern Spain.[108] By an extraordinary coincidence, Sir Peter's next door neighbour was Tomás Bolín, the uncle of Luis Bolín, the Chief Press Officer who had attempted to arrest Koestler in Seville. When the war in Spain had begun, Sir Peter hid the Bolíns, reactionary monarchists in danger of reprisal at the hands of militiamen. Finally, Sir Peter helped the family escape from Málaga. In Febrary 1937, however, when the Nationalists arrived, Luis Bolín arrested Chalmers Mitchell and Koestler, whom he discovered in the house.

Transferred to prison in Seville, Koestler spent three months on death row, much of it in solitary confinement. His diary of this time, published as *Dialogue with Death*, describes with great power the suffering that he witnessed around him: the beatings and executions of the anarchist and Communist prisoners. First and foremost, however, Koestler's writing traces his own profound 'psychological introspection' as he faced execution.[109] Outside Spain, orchestrated by the Comintern and the Spanish Republican movement, there was a very effective public campaign for Koestler's release. In the end, an exchange of prisoners was arranged, through Dr Marcel Junod and the International Committee of the Red Cross. Koestler was traded for the wife of a Nationalist flying ace and allowed to leave Spain.[110]

Writing a decade and a half after the event, by which time he had abandoned Communism and repudiated his Comintern past, Koestler identified the stint in solitary confinement in Seville as enabling his tergiversation. At this date, he experienced the spiritual shift that took him into the next epoch of his life in which he became a leading anti-Communist intellectual with a profound interest in spirituality and the human psyche. Koestler, henceforth, distanced himself from the fervent support he had felt between 1936 and 1939 for the Spanish Republic, writing about it almost with an air of embarrassed regret.[111]

By contrast, it is interesting to look at the highly ideological writings of journalists on the Right. Knickerbocker of the Hearst group has already been discussed. Several *Daily Mail* correspondents produced narratives that were widely read by Franco's English-speaking supporters. Henry Cadoza, who habitually went about in the scarlet beret of the Requetés, was a good Catholic and had a 'romantic and religious attachment' to the Carlists. His *March of a Nation* records his travels as he followed Franco's troops as they 'cleared out the Reds' in the first year.[112] Edmond Taylor described Cardoza as a 'cool hand and a cheerful travelling companion, apart from his politics' (in Hanigen, *Nothing but Danger*,

p. 53). Predictably, the high point of the narrative is Toledo where he met the garrison of the Alcázar looking 'like figures taken from some mystic picture by El Greco' (*ibid.*, p. 129).

By far the most overtly ideological narrative was that of William Foss and Cecil Gerahty's *Spanish Arena*, which laid out the franquista history of the Republic and the Civil War, including a full reprinting of the 'Confidential Documents'. In a chapter entitled 'Fiction Factory', the authors claimed that there was a Jewish conspiracy behind the 'pro-Red' journalists. Among them they included Reuters and their correspondent Christopher Holmes. Reuters' lawyers declared it defamatory and, along with Noel Monks who had also been libelled, threatened to sue. The publisher Robert Hale withdrew the edition altogether. The book appeared a month or so later, with the offending passages excised, under the imprint of the Right Book Club and with an introduction by the Duke of Alba. The narrative is cast in the most exaggerated language. For example, Franco is described as a 'Western David standing against the Eastern Goliath of the hydra-headed monster of International Communism'.[113]

Much more interesting is the commentary by Irish war correspondent Francis McCullagh.[114] Ulster born, a devout Catholic and enthusiastic for Franco's crusade, he was also hard-boiled from long experience of reporting in foreign places.[115] He was a freelance journalist in Spain for almost a year from August 1936. Part of the foreign press corps, he therefore suffered the disapprobation of the Nationalists, and, with no press service behind him outside the country, was a soft target for official disdain. As well, the pesetas he had brought with him were seized by Spanish Customs at the Portuguese border so that he was forced to squander large amounts of time doing the rounds with unhelpful bureaucrats as he attempted to retrieve his impounded funds. Extremely hard up for most of his time in Spain, McCullagh saw the workings of the Franco state in a way that the better-off journalists and the more welcome amateur travellers never did.

McCullagh's narrative is curiously bifurcated. His close reporting of daily events is clear-eyed and unsentimental about the 'petty-minded tyranny and incivility of franquista officials'. At the same time, a broad-brush polemic runs throughout about the 'riff-raff of Europe led by the demagogues from Moscow' that were to be found on the Republican side, though McCullagh himself was never there (*Franco's Spain*, p. 5).

In January 1920 he had been imprisoned for four months in the Soviet

Union and in 1923 had returned as a correspondent for the *New York Herald*, despite the Soviet government's opposition. For the next few years he wrote highly critical reports of Bolshevik anti-religious policies, such as the trial of Archbishop Cieplak. These pieces, and those he wrote about government anticlericalism in Mexico some years later, were collected into several volumes that were much quoted in Catholic circles.[116]

His experience in the Soviet Union was the referent and the yardstick of everything that he saw in Nationalist Spain. McCullagh had never got over the shock of the 'flabbiness' of Imperial Russia and the 'scandal and disgrace' that in the White Army there were 'many magnificent physical specimens' but they had let 'all sorts of weedy Bolshevick wastrels cut their throats'.[117] As a consequence, McCullagh looked to Catholic Spain and the Church militant to stop the Bolsheviks this time; just as Spain in the past had 'barred the road to Napoleon, to Luther and to Islam' (*ibid.*, pp. 11–12).

McCullagh likened General Franco's position in Spain to Mount Fuji in Japan, where to see the mountain's pristine beauty it was necessary to 'look very high above the mundane horizon'. Even when obscured by dingy clouds, it was sufficient to know that unparalleled perfection existed. In Spain, even when unseen behind the 'disorganization, laziness, muddle and confusion on the part of officialdom', like the 'inscrutable face of Mt Fuji, was Franco and the Last Great Crusade' (*ibid.*, pp. xx–xxi). Although McCullagh was a well-trained observer and discounted as 'silly' the suggestion that the small Communist Party of Spain could lead the revolution, in his bigger picture, Stalin was prepared.

There is a particular 'Britishness' in McCullagh's comments on Spain that he shared with other Anglo-Saxons travellers. In addition to the unnerving recklessness of Spaniards behind the wheel, the English-speakers were all put out by the 'Latin hours' that Spaniards kept. Breakfasts that were advertised at 8 o'clock were never served before 9. At night ravenous Anglo-Saxons champed outside closed dining room doors where 'desultory suppers' never began before 10 and finished at all hours of the morning (*ibid.*, p. 254). Even the most sympathetic English person found it hard to believe that the Caudillo and the Falange could condone such indolence in the life of the country. In McCullagh's estimation it was not the servants that were to blame but the 'Quality', who kept them out of their beds till all hours. He was sure that, if encouraged by the example of their betters, ordinary Spaniards would 'rise early and eat a hearty breakfast' (*Ibid.*, p. 255). McCullagh left Nationalist Spain in mid-1937, having managed to wrest back his pesetas, though their value was considerably less. He was greatly chagrined to find, once outside Spain, that the few stories which he had managed to get through the censor had been impounded at the cable head and never sent.

Conclusion

These two sets of commentaries, produced by the amateur travellers and the professional journalists, could hardly be more different. The travellers who came as official visitors to support Franco saw 'New Spain' evolving under strong leadership and based on authoritarian values of which they greatly approved. The visitors enjoyed the official welcomes they received and the carefully planned trips as they were escorted around the war zone. In turn, their English-speaking hosts in the Nationalist press corps found an avid and uncritical audience for franquista propaganda. The anecdotes with which the press officers regaled the visitors appeared over and over again in the subsequent commentaries on their travels in Nationalist Spain.

The professional journalists were in Spain because they were sent there to do a job. They responded differently to franquista control. Censorship is anathema to most journalists and even those who were not unsympathetic to General Franco chafed under its restrictions. In Nationalist Spain the censorship was draconian. Contemporaries always commented on the difference in the effort that the Republicans put into good relations with foreign journalists compared with Franco's press corps.

A related and broader issue that English narratives raise in Nationalist Spain is how public opinion is formed and how people who are not present at international events find out about them. The readers of the narratives written by the first group, the pro-Franco travellers were, probably, pro-Franco before they ever took up the books containing the pro-Franco travel narratives. It is fairly unlikely that many pro-Republicans in the English-speaking world read Arnold Lunn's work, and, if they had, would have had their minds changed. Perhaps military buffs read the military commentaries by the ex-British army men who trawled through Franco's Spain, though one hopes that British military opinion would have been formed on a more substantial basis than what is revealed in the reports by these military commentators.

As in most cases, the public reading the daily press received information that was filtered first by the politics of the paper, for example, the difference in the reporting of the *Daily Mail* versus the *Chicago Daily News*, but in Nationalist Spain all journalism had to fit within the narrow frame of what was allowed by the Official Censor. Much more freewheeling and informative, in fact, are the narratives that journalists wrote about their experiences in Franco's Spain once they had left. Their stories are fascinating, not just because they speak about the Civil War that they observed, but because their own lives became interwoven with the tapestry of the war itself. In any event, the public opinion polls in Britain, and elsewhere, suggest that there was not a great shift during the war in the way that people outside Spain saw the war and therefore the reporting in the daily press probably simply consolidated beliefs that had already been formed.

Notes

1 See, for example, the National Spanish State Tourist Department's pamphlet, *National Spain Invites You to Visit the War Routes of the North* [1938] (Southworth Collection, UCSD).

2 Luis Bolín, *The Vital Years* (London: Cassell, 1967), pp. 302–7.

3 Bolín, *The Vital Years*, p. 305.

4 D. P. F. Lancien, 'British left-wing attitudes to the Spanish Civil War', BLitt thesis, University of Oxford, 1965, Appendix 1, quoted in Tom Buchanan, *Britain and the Spanish Civil War* (Cambridge: Cambridge University Press, 1997), p. 23.

5 Pablo de Azcárate, Spain's Republican ambassador to Britain, found it galling that the Prime Minister avoided being introduced to him even though it was part of the regular protocols of office. Similarly, British government officials and members of the City declined invitations to Spanish embassy functions; see Azcárate, *Mi embajada en Londres durante la Guerra Civil Española* (Barcelona: Editorial Ariel, 1976). At the same time, British officials readily visited Franco's agent, the Duke of Alba. When the Republic was defeated, he used all his influence to hound the ex-Spanish government leaders living in exile in Britain. See Rafael Rodríguez-Moñino Soriano, *La misión diplomática de Don Jacobo Stuart Fitz James y Falcó, XVII Duque de Alba, en la embajada de España en Londres (1937–1945)* (Valencia: Editorial Castalia, 1971).

6 Buchanan, *Britain and the Spanish Civil War*; Jill Edwards, *The British Government and the Spanish Civil War 1936–1939* (London: Macmillan 1979); and K. W. Watkins, *Britain Divided: The Effect of the Spanish Civil War on British Political Opinion* (London: Thomas Nelson, 1963).

7 The workings of the Non-Intervention Committee are discussed in more detail in Chapter 4.

8 Sir Geoffrey Thompson, a member of the diplomatic staff, evokes the atmosphere at the British embassy in his *Front-Line Diplomat* (London: Hutchinson, 1959), pp. 129–43.

9 The American ambassador, Claude G. Bowers, critical of the pro-Franco partisanship of diplomatic staff from the democracies, singled out Chilton in particular as 'showing himself from the first days to be violently against the Spanish Republic', in his *My Mission to Spain: Watching the Rehearsal for World War II* (New York: Simon & Schuster, 1954), p. 291.

10 Many British consular officials were pro-Franco: for example, Oxley in Vigo, Coultas in Seville, Clissold in Málaga and the British consuls in Jerez: PRO FO 371/ 20532, pp. 146–56; FO 371/ 21287 /47815, pp. 3–5. Bowers cites the British consul in Vigo's activities for the insurgents when the uprising took place, in *My Mission to Spain*, pp. 265–6; Arthur Pack, the British Commercial Secretary, was moved to Warsaw in April 1937 because his enthusiastic advocacy of Franco's cause had become an embarrassment: PRO FO 371/ 20546, pp. 301–18. The British journalist, Henry Buckley, was surprised to find that a friend of his with a passport issued by Franco's office in Berlin had no trouble in obtaining a visa to travel to Britain from the British embassy in Berlin or on her arrival in Britain, even though her papers were not legal, as Britain had no official diplomatic contact with Franco. See his *Life and Death of the Spanish Republic* (London: Hamish Hamilton, 1940), p. 209.

11 See Rodríguez-Moñino Soriano, *La misión diplomática de Don Jacobo Stuart Fitz James y Falcó, XVII Duque de Alba, en la embajada de España en Londres (1937–1945)*.

12 Sir Robert Hodgson, *Spain Resurgent* (London: Hutchinson, 1953), p. 91.

13 Hodgson, *Spain Resurgent*, p. 84. Sir Geoffrey Thompson, on the embassy staff at Hendaye, 'did not see eye to eye' with Hodgson's intransigent anti-Republicanism, in *Front-Line Diplomat* (London: Hutchinson, 1959), p. 135. Enrique Moradiellos points out that the official British view was that, in its latter stages, the Spanish Republic was in a pre-revolutionary crisis that replicated Russia just before October 1917; see his 'The origins of British non-intervention in the Spanish Civil War: Anglo-Spanish relations in early 1936', *European History Quarterly*, **XXI** (3) (1991), pp. 339–64. Moradiellos also shows that officials in the British Foreign Office saw Franco as a decent patriot who would respect British interests, in 'The gentle General: the official British perception of General Franco during the Spanish Civil War', in Paul Preston and Ann L. Mckenzie (eds), *The Republic Besieged: Civil War in Spain* (Edinburgh: Edinburgh University Press, 1996), pp. 1–19.

14 K. W. Watkins, *Britain Divided: The Effect of the Spanish Civil War on British Political Opinion* (London: Thomas Nelson, 1963), p. 8.

15 A number of British companies in Spain made contributions to an insurgents' 'war chest'. See PRO FO371/21394/ 47217, British Embassy Hendaye, 27 January 1937, 'Confidential', H. Chilton to R. H. Anthony Eden, pp. 21–2.

16 Douglas Jerrold, *Georgian Adventure: The Autobiography of Douglas Jerrold* (London: Right Book Club, 1938), p. 362.

17 Quoted in Jerrold, *Georgian Adventure*, p. 363.

18 In *Spain: The Vital Years*, pp. 122–3, Bolín claimed that he founded the committee. Douglas Jerrold attributes its origin to Sir Charles Petrie, in *Georgian Adventure*, p. 362.

19 Jerrold claims shared authorship in *Georgian Adventure*, pp. 361–2; and Bolín asserts that he wrote it himself, *Vital Years*, pp. 123–4.

20 Jerrold, *Georgian Adventure*, pp. 369–74.

21 For Bolín's recollections of the expedition, see *Spain: The Vital Years*, pp. 16–23.

22 Jerrold's detailed documents of the Communist plot were quoted and requoted in other sources, including those from Nationalist Spain. None indicate where the original documents were found. See *Georgian Adventure*, pp. 375–6; and quoted again in Jerrold's 'Spain: impressions and reflections', *Nineteenth Century and After* (April 1937), pp. 471–3 and reprinted in New York in the *American Review* (April 1937); and the references to Jerrold's article in many Nationalist pamphlets, e.g., Constantino Bayle, *Qué pasa en España?: a los católicos del mundo* (Salamanca: Delegación del Estado para Prensa y Propaganda, 1937), p. 12, p. 64 and pp. 18–20. The cited documents were reproduced in William Foss and Cecil Gerahty, *The Spanish Arena* (London: Right Book Club, 1939), pp. 268–70, and reproduced later in Arthur Loveday, *World War in Spain* (London: J. Murray, 1939); in *Spain: The Vital Years*, written after the war, Luis Bolín claimed that, in August 1936, the documents 'came to light near Seville'. See Herbert Southworth, *El mito de la cruzada de Franco* (Barcelona: Plaza & Janés Editores, 1986), pp. 196–213, for a detailed analysis of each of the secret documents and the variations between the national versions of them and the uses that subsequent historians have made of them. For present purposes it is sufficient to know that Jerrold was a crucial disseminator of the information.

23 Henry Robinson, an associate of the Infanta's committee, was jailed in Irún in January 1937 when he tried to make arrangements for the committee to operate in Nationalist Spain, in PRO FO 371/21283 47217, pp. 270–3, H. Chilton, 26 January 1937.

24 Their prospectus announced that in the Civil War 'the noble, chivalrous, and tradition-loving' Spaniards were fighting the 'unbridled rabble whipped on by Moscou to wanton "sans-culotism" by the officially countenanced prospect of wholesale murder, expoliation, loot and rapine' [*sic*]: PRO FO 371/ 20543/ 47185, 8 October 1936, pp. 7–13.

25 See, for example, *Advocate*, 16 December 1937; 24 December 1937; and *Southern Cross*, 16 December 1937; 24 December 1937; and 30 December 1937.

26 Maurice Taylor, *The Scots College in Spain* (Valladolid: Gráficas Andrés Martin, 1971); Michael E. Williams, *St Alban's College Valladolid: Four Centuries of English Catholic Presence in Spain* (New York: St Martin's Press, 1986).

27 Thomas Moloney, *Westminster, Whitehall and the Vatican: The Role of Cardinal Hinsley, 1935–43* (Tunbridge Wells: Burns & Oates, 1985), pp. 13–102.

28 For his role in the fund-raising for the rehabilitation of church property in Spain, see PRO FO 371/20536, 27 August 1937, p. 229.

29 The exceptions were the Dominican magazine, *Blackfriars* and the *Christian Democrat*, of the Oxford Catholic Social Guild, which favoured neutrality, Moloney, *Westminster, Whitehall and the Vatican*, p. 71.

30 The expression comes from Pip Scott-Ellis, a young English nurse in Franco's medical services. She had dinner at the Grand Hotel in Saragossa in April 1938 with Arnold Lunn, 'out here writing articles about "Red Horrors" and collecting material for speeches'. See Priscilla Scott-Ellis *The Chances of Death: A Diary of the Spanish Civil War*, edited by Raymond Carr (London: Michael Russell, 1995), p. 69.

31 See *Letters from Hilaire Belloc*, selected and edited by Robert Speaight (London: Hollis and Carter, 1958), p. 265; and a rambling discursion on Burgos in Hilaire Belloc, *Places* (London: Cassell, 1942), pp. 189–95.

32 James Flint, 'English Catholics and the proposed Soviet alliance, 1939', *Journal of Ecclesiastical History*, **48** (3) (July 1997), p. 468; and his 'English Catholics and the Bolshevik Revolution: the origins of Catholic anti-Communism', *American Benedictine Review*, **42** (1) (March 1991), pp. 4–21.

33 Adrian Hastings, 'Some reflections on the English Catholicism of the late 1930s', in his *Bishops and Writers: Aspects of the Evolution of English Catholicism* (Wheathampstead, Herts: Anthony Clarke, 1977), pp. 107–25. See also the discussion of Jerrold's 'romantic Catholicism in the Chestertonian tradition' and the attraction to Mussolini, in Richard Griffiths, *Fellow Travellers of the Right: British Enthusiasts for Nazi Germany 1933–39*, (London: Constable, 1980), pp. 13–31.

34 Tom Buchanan has noted that, for both the British Right and Left, Spain seemed to offer a society that was more desirable than Britain. See his *Britain and the Spanish Civil War* (Cambridge: Cambridge University Press, 1997).

35 See Francis McCullagh, *In Franco's Spain: Being the Experiences of an Irish War-Correspondent during the Great Civil War Which Began in 1936* (London: Burns, Oates & Washbourne, 1937); Paul McGuire, *Catholic Times* and *Advocate*, 7 October 1937; Thompson, *Front-Line Diplomat*, pp. 129–42; and Peter Kemp, *Mine Were of Trouble* (London: Cassell, 1957).

36 This was the tell-tale sign of Germans in Spain according to Georges Oudard in *Chemises noires, brunes, vertes en Espagne* (Paris: Librairie Plon, 1938), p. 15.

37 Karl Robson, 'With Franco in Spain', in Wilfrid Hindle (ed.), *Foreign Correspondent: Personal Adventures Abroad in Search of the News by Twelve British Journalists* (London: George Harrap, 1939), pp. 263–4. Sir Geoffrey Thompson remarked that the 'people in Salamanca seemed to be suffering from St Vitus's Dance with the incessant exchanging of salutes' (*Front-Line Diplomat*, p. 134).

38 Major Geoffrey McNeill Moss, *The Siege of the Alcázar: A History of the Siege of the Toledo Alcázar, 1936* (New York: Alfred A. Knopf, 1937). The book was issued in many editions and translations.

39 Robert Brasillach and Henri Massis, *Les Cadets de l'Alcázar* (Paris: Plon, 1936), or one of the many reprints of the work.

40 The term comes from Sir Robert Hodgson, *Spain Resurgent*, pp. 89–90.

41 Tom Burns, *The Use of Memory: Publishing and Further Pursuits* (London: Sheed & Ward, 1993), p. 80. The Marquis of Larios is typical: he was sent to English prep school at 9 and then to Ampleforth, in Lerma, *Combat over Spain: Memoirs of a Nationalist Fighter Pilot: 1936–1939* (New York: Macmillan, 1966), p. 1.

42 Juan de las Barcenas, father and son, were educated in England; the younger accompanied Major-General Sir Walter Maxwell Scott on his tour of western Spain in February 1937, in PRO FO 371/21287/5720–5744, p. 14; he was helpful in Salamanca to Sir Robert Hodgson. See Hodgson, *Spain Resurgent*, p. 81.

43 Arnold Lunn, 'The shadow of evil darkens Spain', *Advocate*, 15 July 1937, p. 4; and *Spanish Rehearsal: An Eyewitness in Spain during the Civil War (1936–1939)*, with a foreword by William F. Buckley, Jr. (Old Greenwich, CT: Devin-Adair Company, 1974), p. 83.

44 See Herbert Southworth, *Guernica! Guernica!* (Berkeley: University of California Press, 1977).

45 Virginia Cowles, *Looking for Trouble* (London: Hamish Hamilton, 1941), p. 90.

46 Howard A. Kershaw, *Quaker Service in Modern War* (New York: Prentice Hall, 1950), p. 41, and the similar reception which the Red Cross representative, Marcel Junod, received; see his *Warrior Without Weapons* (London: Jonathan Cape, 1951), pp. 87–126.

47 Peter Kemp, *Mine Were of Trouble* (London: Cassell, 1957), p. 67.

48 John Corbin, 'Truth and myth in history: an example from the Spanish Civil War', *Journal of Interdisciplinary History*, **XXV** (4) (Spring 1995), pp. 609–25.

49 'Truth and myth', p. 609. Gamel, the wife of Gerald Brenan and living outside Málaga at the start of the war, claimed that there was a pornographic element in the atrocity stories that ex-Spaniards and English expats recounted in Gibraltar. She cites the example that was much in currency of naked nuns being laid out in the square and run over by a bulldozer.

50 Claude Lévi-Strauss, *The Savage Mind (La Pensée sauvage)* (London: Weidenfeld & Nicolson, 1962), pp. 16–27.

51 Richard Thurlow, *Fascism in Britain: A History, 1918–1985* (Oxford: Basil Blackwell, 1987), p. 80, p. 158. See also Anthony John Trythall, *'Boney' Fuller: The Intellectual General 1878–1966* (London: Cassell, 1977), pp. 195–6.

52 Major-General J. F. C. Fuller, *The Conquest of Red Spain* (London: Burns, Oates & Washbourne, 1937). In *The First of the League Wars; Its Lessons and Omens* (London: Eyre & Spottiswoode, 1936), Fuller describes his travels accompanying the Italian invasion of Abyssinia. He combines graphic military commentary with

virulent anti-Semitism and wildly exaggerated denunciations of the 'crooks and cranks' (p. 10) who support the League of Nations. Azar Gat argues that Fuller's fascism was integral to his intellectual and military interests; see, *Fascist and Liberal Visions of War: Fuller, Liddell Hart, Douhet, and Other Modernists* (Oxford: Clarendon Press, 1998), pp. 13–42.

53 On the basis of this report, Liddell Hart recommended unsuccessfully that Fuller's fascist leanings aside, he should be reintegrated into the research arm of the War Office; Trythall, *'Boney' Fuller*, pp. 200–1.

54 Richard Griffiths, *Fellow Travellers of the Right: British Enthusiasts for Nazi Germany 1933–39* (London: Constable, 1980), pp. 17–18.

55 PRO FO 371/ 21287/ 47815, 17 March 1937, pp. 204–6.

56 Lerma, *Combat over Spain* (New York: Macmillan, 1966), pp. 162–4.

57 PRO FO 372/ 20537, 4 September 1936, pp. 64–75.

58 PRO FO 371/ 21287/ 47815, 19 March 1937, pp. 73–90. A handwritten annotation notes wearily that 'it would be impossible to discuss this report without writing a minute of approximately the same length'. For Scott's connection to the BUF see Thurlow, *Fascism in Britain*, p. 100 and p. 181.

59 British Protestants, like Dean Inge of Westminster, whose anti-Communism made him a Franco supporter, were concerned about Protestants in Catholic Spain.

60 Nigel Tangye, *Red, White and Spain* (London: Rich & Cowan, 1937).

61 Sir Arnold Wilson, *Thoughts and Talks, 1935–7. The Diary of a Member of Parliament* (London: Right Book Club, 1938), pp. 362–80; Griffiths, *Fellow Travellers of the Right*, pp. 158–63; and Kemp, *Mine Were of Trouble*, pp. 108–9.

62 See William F. Buckley Jr.'s foreword to the 1974 reprint of the 1937 edition of Lunn, *Spanish Rehearsal: An Eyewitness in Spain during the Civil War* (Old Greenwich, CT: Devin-Adair Company, 1974), pp. v–vii.

63 Lunn, *Spanish Rehearsal: An Eyewitness in Spain during the Civil War (1936–1939)* (London: Sheed & Ward, 1939). Lunn reused the material in this volume to provide a huge number of lectures and pamphlet reprints. See, for example, his *Spain the Unpopular Front* (London: Catholic Truth Society, 1937); *Spain and the Christian Front* (New York: Paulist Press, 1939). He also produced a series of autobiographies which rework the same incidents. For the most detailed material on Spain, see his *Come What May: An Autobiography* (London: Eyre & Spottiswoode, 1940). See also his *Memory to Memory* (London: Hollis & Carter, 1956); and his *Unkilled for So Long* (London: George Allen & Unwin, 1968).

64 See Lunn, *Unkilled for So Long*, p. 53.

65 Lunn, *Unkilled for So Long*, p. 71.

66 Pip Scott-Ellis, *The Chances of Death: A Diary of the Spanish Civil War*, edited by Raymond Carr (London: Michael Russell, 1995), p. 132.

67 The expression comes from Pip Scott-Ellis, who had dinner with him at the Grand Hotel in Saragossa while he was in Spain to 'write articles about "Red Horrors" and collect material for speeches'; *Chances of Death*, p. 69.

68 The qualities of a foreign correspondent according to the Chief Editor of Reuters, Sir Roderick Jones, in Donald Read, *The Power of News: The History of Reuters 1849–1989* (Oxford: Oxford University Press, 1992), p. 151. The discussion of foreign correspondents in Spain has benefited greatly by access to the Reuters Archive and the expertise and generosity of John Entwisle, Reuters Archivist, and his efficient staff. I am also grateful to Henry Stokes, of Adelaide, for sharing with me his memories of being 'Reuters' man in Franco's Spain'.

69 Noel Monks, *Eyewitness* (London: Frederick Muller, 1955), p. 96. According to Eugene Lyons, before the First World War, 'foreign news was of interest to the high brow and the specialist' but, by the 1930s, everyone was concerned because international events had implications for them all. See *We Cover the World by Sixteen Foreign Correspondents* (London: George G. Harrap, 1937), p. 15.

70 See for example: *Nothing but Danger: Thrilling Adventures of Ten Newspaper Correspondents in the Civil War*, edited by Frank C. Hanigen (London: George G. Harrap, 1939); and as well *We Cover the World by Sixteen Foreign Correspondents*, edited by Eugene Lyons (London: George G. Harrap, 1937); *Foreign Correspondent: Personal Adventures Abroad in Search of the News by Twelve British Journalists*, edited by Wilfrid Hindle (London: George G. Harrap, 1939); *The News Behind the News That's Fit to Print*, by thirteen correspondents of the *New York Times*, edited by Hanson Baldwin and Stone Shepard (New York: Simon & Schuster, 1939); and John Gunther's comments on the proliferation of journalists' autobiographical reporting in the preface to John T. Whitaker's *Fear Came on Europe* (London: Hamish Hamilton, 1937).

71 Francis McCullagh, *In Franco's Spain*, p. vii.

72 Among correspondents in Nationalist Spain associated with newspapers in English were: Paul Bewsher (*Daily Mail*); Ray Brock, Harold G. Cardoza (*Daily Mail*); W. P. Carney (*New York Times*); W. E. Casey (*The Times*); Randolph Churchill (*Daily Mail*); Alexander Clifford (Reuters); Virginia Cowles (Hearst Press); Frances Davis (*Daily Mail*); Sefton Delmer (*Daily Express*); Alan Dick (*The Daily Telegraph*); Walter Duranty, John Elliot (*New York Herald Tribune*); Charles Foltz (Associated Press); O. D. Gallagher (*Daily Express*); Cecil Gerahty (*Daily Mail*); John Gunther (*Daily News*); 'Binky' Hartin (*Daily Mail*); James Holburn (*The Times*); Christopher Holmes (Reuters); Bradish Johnson (*News Week*); H. R. Knickerbocker (*Washington Times*); Arthur Koestler (*News Chronicle*); Webb Miller, James M. Minifie (*New York Herald Tribune*); Noel Monks (*Daily Express*); Alan Moorehead (*Daily Express*); Edward Mowrer (*Chicago Daily News*); Edward J. Neil (Associated Press); Reynolds Packard (United Press); Kim Philby (*The Times*); Sir Percival Phillips (*The Daily Telegraph*); Samuel Pope-Brewer, Karl Robson (*The Daily Telegraph*); F. T. Rogers, Richard Sheepshanks (Reuters); George Steer (*The Times*); Pembroke Stevens (*The Daily Telegraph*); Henry Stokes (Reuters); William Studdard (*The Times*); Edmond Taylor (*Chicago Tribune*); Denis

Weaver and John Whitaker (*New York Herald Tribune*); Roland Winn (*The Daily Telegraph*).

73 See José María Armero, 'Corresponsales extranjeros en el bando nacional', in Jesús Manuel Martínez (ed.), *Periodismo y periodistas en la guerra civil* (Madrid: Fundacíon, Seminarios y Cursos, 1987), pp. 47–57; and Gabriel Jackson, 'El papel de los corresponsales extranjeros en la guerra civil', in Martínez, *Periodismo y periodistas*, pp. 39–43; and Southworth, *Guernica! Guernica! A Study of Journalism. Diplomacy, Propaganda and History*, pp. 45–59.

74 Tangye, *Red, White and Spain*, pp. 75–6.

75 Alexander Clifford to AGC at Reuters, 4 October 1938, Alexander Clifford Personal File, Reuters Archive.

76 Monks, *Eyewitness*, p. 69. Monks himself was arrested and threatened with shooting because his name was inadvertently attached to a story that was published and mentioned the existence of foreign troops in Nationalist Spain (pp. 79–84).

77 Sefton Delmer, not well disposed to the Republic ('a stooge for left wing groups'), claims that Germans who knew him as an anti-Nazi in Berlin insisted he be expelled from Franco's Spain. See *Trail Sinister: An Autobiography* (London: Secker and Warburg, 1961), pp. 259–78.

78 See Edmond Taylor, 'Assignment in hell,' in Haniger, *Nothing But Danger*, pp. 53–6; Denis Weaver, *Front Page Europe* (London: Cresset Press, 1943), and 'Through enemy lines', in *Nothing But Trouble*; Webb Miller, 'The little world war in Spain', in Lyons, *We Cover the World*.

79 H. R. Knickerbocker, *The Siege of Alcázar: A War-Log of the Spanish Revolution* (London: Hutchinson, October 1936).

80 Claude Bowers, *My Mission to Spain* (New York: Simon & Schuster, 1954), p. 320. Frances Davis, unintentionally, provides a possible explanation. Reporters, facing great difficulty in getting their reports out of Spain, would often write a dummy story ready to go if the opportunity arose. She cites Cardoza writing the story of the fall of Madrid in November 1936 'with blank spaces to be filled in with the details'. Frequently, correspondents also gave carbon copies of their stories to the colleagues they worked closely with, and any of them would post or cable the others' stories if the opportunity arose. See Frances Davis, *My Shadow in the Sun* (New York: Carrick & Evans, 1940), p. 163.

81 H. R. Knickerbocker, *Is Tomorrow Hitler's?* (Harmondsworth: Penguin Books, 1942), p. 29.

82 Amero, 'Corresponsales extranjero en el bando nacional', p. 49.

83 For example, the *Times* correspondent in Spain used a hollow container disguised as a mint lolly roll to hide censored information. I am grateful to Amon Dyas, the archivist at *The Times* for showing me this device.

84 Kemp, *Mine Were of Trouble*, p. 187.

85 Monks, *Eyewitness*, p. 69. There are references to the Bar Basque, the Café de

Paris and Sonny's Bar in Biarritz in almost all writing by contemporaries who came this way into Nationalist Spain.

86 See, for example, John T. Whitaker, *We Cannot Escape History* (New York: Macmillan, 1943), pp. 95–122; Taylor, 'Assignment in hell', in Hanigen (ed.), *Nothing But Danger*, pp. 63–5; Monks, *Eyewitness*, p. 68.

87 Virginia Cowles, *Looking for Trouble* (London: Hamish Hamilton, 1941), p. 90.

88 John T. Whitaker, *We Cannot Escape History* (London: Hamish Hamilton, 1943), pp. 95–122.

89 Other correspondents remarked on the 'sinister stretch of road' from Santa Olalla to Maqueda which was strewn with rotting bodies lying beside the road so that cars had to drive carefully to avoid them. See Edmond Taylor, 'Assignment in hell', in Hanigen (ed.), *Nothing But Danger*, p. 69.

90 Aguilera gave the same explanation to Peter Kemp and also that he had lined up his labourers at the start of the war and shot six of them to show the rest that he was still the boss; Kemp, *Mine Were of Trouble*, p. 50. He explained the causes of the war to Edmond Taylor from an 'original racist point of view', that it was a second Christian Reconquista between the Nordic Christian types and the Orientals, the Reds, whose ideas were brought to Spain by the Moors. See Taylor, 'Assignment in hell', p. 62. Aguilera similarly expounded the detrimental effect of progress on the 'slave stock' of the proletariat to Charles Foltz, in *The Masquerade in Spain* (Boston: Houghton Mifflin, 1948), p. 116.

91 H. R. Knickerbocker was also searched when he interviewed Franco in August 1936 in Seville; see his *Siege of the Alcázar*, p. 41.

92 E. R. Sheepshanks to Editor-in-Chief, Hotel Maria Christina, San Sebastian, Personal, 29 August 1937, Sheepshanks Personal File, Reuters Archive.

93 I have used the voluminous file on the incident from the Reuters Archive and am grateful to John Entwisle for drawing it to my attention.

94 See Phillip Knightley, *Philby: The Life and Views of the KGB Masterspy* (London: André Deutsch, 1988).

95 The Spanish Republic's ambassador in London complained to *The Times* that Philby's reporting was blatantly pro-Franco, *Times* Archive, HAR (Kim) Philby File, Memo from Foreign News Editor to the Editor, 1 February 1939.

96 See Bruce Page, David Leitch and Phillip Knightley, *Philby: The Spy Who Betrayed a Generation* (London: Sphere Books, 1968), p. 113; Hodgson, *Spain Resurgent*, p. 81.

97 Kim Philby, *My Silent War* (London: MacGibbon & Kee, 1968), p. xxv.

98 It may be that the tiny capsule disguised as a mint container was used by Philby. See note 9. Sir Geoffrey Thompson recalled that Philby, along with a number of other senior correspondents, was knowledgeable about German, Italian and Russian involvement in the war; see his *Front-Line Diplomat*, pp. 131–2.

99 *Londoner's Diary*, 21 October 1991. Virginia Cowles described Duprée as the fiancé of Sir Henry Chilton's daughter, Anne. See her *Looking for Trouble*, p. 63.

100 Professor Donald Read, who has a wealth of knowledge on interwar newspaper

correspondents and the press in general, considered the story highly unlikely (personal communication, London, April 1998).

101 In a huge literature, see, for example, the pro-Franco account by Joseph F. Thorning, *Why the Press Failed on Spain* (Brooklyn, NY: International Catholic Truth Society, 1938); and for the anti-franquista position, see Herbert Southworth, *El mito de la cruzada de Franco*, pp. 217–32; and his *Guernica!, Guernica!*, pp. 47–8. For a recent denial of the 'legend of Badajoz' as a myth 'promoted by the stubborn American propagandist' Herbert Southworth, see Ricardo de la Cierva, *Historia esencial de la Guerra Civil Española: todos los problemas resueltos, sesenta años después* (Madrid: Editorial Fénix, 1996), pp. 224–6, and for Guernica, pp. 547–63.

102 According to Phillip Knightley, after Philby defected many people assumed incorrectly that he wrote the piece. See his *Philby: The Life and Views of the KGB Masterspy* (London: André Deutsch, 1988), p. 62.

103 Noel Monks, 'I hate war', in Hanigen (ed.), *Nothing But Danger*, pp. 75–90.

104 Southworth, *Guernica! Guernica!*

105 David Cesarani has revealed the darker side of Koestler's character and sexual obsessions in *Arthur Koestler: The Homeless Mind* (London: Vintage, 1998).

106 Stephen Koch argues that the Spanish Republican campaign provided Münzenberg with protection against Stalin and the KGB who had him in their sights after purging his mentor Karl Radek. See 'The Spanish stratagem' in his *Double Lives: Stalin, Willi Münzenberg and the Seduction of the Intellectuals* (London: HarperCollins, 1995), pp. 265–97. See also Murray A. Sperber, 'Looking back on Koestler's Spanish War', in Sperber (ed.), *Arthur Koestler: A Collection of Critical Essays* (Englewood Cliff, NJ: Prentice Hall, 1977).

107 *Spanish Testament* (London: Victor Gollancz, 1937). 'Dialogue with death', based on Koestler's prison diaries, is reprinted in the second part of the book. Koestler reflects on the Spanish Civil War and his imprisonment in *The Invisible Writing: The Second Volume of an Autobiography: 1932–40* (New York: Stein & Day, 1984 [1954]), pp. 381–509. Sheila Grant Duff, sent undercover by Edgar Mowrer from the *Chicago Daily News* with the unlikely objective of contacting Koestler in prison, was menaced by Nationalist officers and fled Málaga after a single day. See her 'A very brief visit', in Philip Toynbee (ed.), *The Distant Dream: Reflections on the Spanish Civil War* (London: Sidgwick & Jackson, 1976). For the importance of the Spanish Civil War in the era of the Popular Front, see David Caute, *The Fellow Traveller: A Postscript to the Enlightenment* (London: Quartet Books, 1977), pp. 169–84.

108 See Sir Peter Chalmers Mitchell, *My House in Málaga* (London: Faber & Faber, 1937), pp. 246–315.

109 For a thoughtful analysis of the books which Koestler read on death row and their possible effect on his change of mind, see Richard Critchfield, 'Arthur Koestler's *Ein spanisches Testament*: crisis and autobiography', in Luis Costa *et al.* (eds),

German and International Perspectives on the Spanish Civil War: The Aesthetics of Partisanship (Columbia: Camden House, 1992), pp. 56–63.

110 Marcel Junod, *Warrior Without Weapons*, pp. 124–5.

111 See Koestler, *The Invisible Writing*.

112 Harold Cardoza, *The March of a Nation: My Year of Spain's Civil War* (New York: Robert M. McBride, 1937), p. 129.

113 See Christopher Holmes, Personal File, Reuters Archives; and William Foss and Cecil Gerahty, *The Spanish Arena*, with a foreword by the Duke of Alba and Berwick (London: Right Book Club, 1939), p. 7.

114 Captain Francis McCullagh, *In Franco's Spain: Being the Experiences of an Irish War-Correspondent During the Great Civil War Which Began in 1936* (London: Burns, Oates & Washbourne, 1937).

115 See Francis McCullagh, *With the Cossacks: Being the Story of an Irishman Who Rode with the Cossacks throughout the Russo-Japanese War* (London: Eveleigh Nash, 1906); *Italy's War for a Desert: Being Some Experiences of a War-Correspondent with the Italians in Tripoli* (London: Herbert & Daniel, 1912): the Futurist Marinetti challenged him to a duel for his criticisms of the Italians in Libya, pp. xxii–xxiv; and *Red Mexico: A Reign of Terror in America* (New York: Louis Carrier, 1928).

116 Captain Francis McCullagh, *The Bolshevik Persecution of Christianity* (London: John Murray, 1924); and *A Prisoner of the Reds: The Story of a British Officer Captured in Siberia* (London: John Murray, 1922).

117 McCullagh, *In Franco's Spain*, p. 11.

CHAPTER 3

Not quite king and country: Franco's English-speaking volunteers

❧

Introduction

According to José Alvarez, the historian of the early years of the Spanish Foreign Legion, the reasons that individuals joined the Legion were as 'varied as the backgrounds' from which they came.[1] In general, recruits shared the common characteristic that they were men who could not manage civilian life: some knew only the soldiers' way; others were destitute, or criminal or on the run; some were prisoners freed on the proviso that they joined the Legion. There was also a smattering of genuine patriots and a great many more adventurers in search of goods and glory.

The Welsh Protestant volunteer, Frank Thomas, whose own enlistment in the Spanish Foreign Legion arose from a combination of Fascist sentiment and adventure, identified three main categories of foreign volunteers in Spain.[2] First among them were those he tagged as 'philosophical religious crusaders' who tended to be well-educated, practising Catholics and often with considerable linguistic accomplishments. As well there were the 'Fascist types' and, as always, the individuals in search of adventure. In 1936 these made up the most common categories of non-Spanish volunteers. Thomas pointed out as well that for local Spaniards there was the additional incentive to enlist during the Civil War because a family member in the Legion gave protection to the rest of the family against government harassment (p. 53). And finally, Thomas concluded, many Spaniards joined up as well 'simply in order to be on the winning side' (p. 53).

For the four foreign volunteers discussed in this chapter, each from a different part of the English-speaking world, the motivations were a combination of ideology and adventure. As critical as these factors were in pointing to a general propensity to volunteer, it is also important to understand the specific conditions that drove each individual to break out of the daily routine and set off. As Edwin Rolfe pointed out in relation to the International Brigaders, a veritable 'no-man's land' separated those with the 'convictions' of the justice of their cause from those who actually took the concrete step and headed to Spain.[3]

The four English-speakers for Franco shared a restlessness and a dissatisfaction with their immediate futures. This is not unusual. Many individuals during their lives experience a sense of aimlessness, but most have no opportunity to change their circumstances. These four, two Catholics and two Protestants, were at a stage in their lives when they could cast off home ties and seek out new fields. The ideological component – whether to 'save the Church', defeat Communism, rally to the New Right or a combination of all three – meant that between 1936 and 1939 they made their way to Franco's Spain.

The individual experiences of these men, an Italo-American flyer, an Australian undertaker, a Welsh travelling salesman and a young Englishman straight from Cambridge, provide a fascinating foil for the short and troubled history of Franco's Irish volunteers. This contingent of some seven hundred men was raised in Ireland by General Eion O'Duffy. After much initial fanfare, they finally arrived in Spain and served as a separate *bandera* in the Foreign Legion. After a very short tour of duty at the front, they opted to return to Ireland.

Vincent Patriarca

The first of the four individuals to arrive in Spain was the American, Vincent Patriarca. He enlisted in August 1936 as a volunteer in the Nationalist air force.[4] A good deal is known about this young man, probably more than he or Franco might have wished, as he was the first foreign Nationalist pilot to be arrested after he had bailed out over Republican territory on 13 September 1936. Subsequently, the Spanish government used his testimony in the first of a series of documents that was presented to the League of Nations to prove the presence of foreigners with Franco's forces, in violation of the Non-Intervention Pact.[5]

Patriarca was, in his own words, 'nuts about flying'.[6] Without a doubt it was the series of contingencies that were tied to his passion for wings – particularly stunting – rather than an ideological commitment, which brought him to Nationalist Spain. Patriarca waxed lyrical on the pilot's exhilaration at the 'kick of a barrel roll or a falling leaf', especially when performed high in the sky at dawn when the air is free of 'bumps' and the 'ship handles perfectly' (Patriarca, 'Two Wars', p. 9). Between the wars the figure of the stunt pilot embodied a new sort of masculinity. Much as the flapper personified the femininity of the New Woman, the free-wheeling pilot in his tiny plane personified bravado and derring-do. A common sight at country fairs, the stunt pilot would take up passengers who dared to loop the loop high above the craning heads on the ground below.[7]

There were a number of these flying afficionados in Spain. Rupert Bellville was a Biggles-like young Englishman with an equal passion for the bullfight and the excitement of aerial high jinks. The beginning of the war found Bellville in Andalusia where he immediately joined up with a Falangist unit only to be disillusioned very quickly by the atrocities on both sides. He found it repugnant to take part in the execution of prisoners, one of the 'ugliest sides' of the Civil War,[8] and extricated himself from the Falange whose ranks were more porous than those of the regular armed forces. Bellville spent the next year knocking about in Nationalist Spain or at Biarritz on the edges of the war. English visitors who ran into him invariably responded to his swashbuckling charm and upper-class good manners.[9] His most notorious feat was when he and an old school friend, the son of a Cadiz wine merchant, flew into Santander with a load of cognac and sherry to present to Franco in order to celebrate the Nationalist victory. At Santander airport they stepped from the plane and greeted the waiting officials with loud 'Arriba Españas' and 'Viva Francos' only to discover that Santander was still in Republican hands. Promptly arrested, they both claimed to be English nationals. The Spaniard spoke perfect English from his public school days and, after several weeks in prison, they were exchanged for two Republican officers. With the flamboyance and luck that seemed part of his lifestyle, Bellville was paid £500 by the *Evening Standard* for his exclusive story when he touched down in France. Virginia Cowles records that he lost all the money the same night in the casino in Biarritz (*Looking for Trouble*, p. 100).

Gordon Selfridge, the son of the American owner of the London department store, flew his sister and brother-in-law, Viscount and Viscountess Jacques de Sibour, in his single-engine plane across the Channel in early August 1936 to spend an afternoon as tourists 'watching the shooting'. They landed at Burgos in time to join a party of journalists bound for the front, where they saw 'about 150 dead on the hillside' and counted 'sixty-two prisoners being herded by and jibbering with fright because they knew what happens to prisoners in the Civil War', After five hours of battlefield tourism, they regained their plane and flew back to England.[10]

An American stunt pilot, though on the Republican side, had also come to Spain from a flying career around fairgrounds in the American states. Alan Dick covered his trial in Salamanca for *The Daily Telegraph* when the American was shot down at the end of 1937.[11]

Franco's American pilot was the son of Italian immigrants. Patriarca's father was a barber in the Bronx and had helped Vincent scrape up the funds in 1933 for flying lessons at an aerodrome in upstate New York. At 17, and with 20 hours solo on the books, Patriarca was on the verge of a pilot's licence when the government raised the requirements to 50 hours in the air. In Patriarca's words, it was a 'terrible blow', as there was no possibility that the family could find the money for the extra lessons. At the time he had been 'filled with a sort of fury at the poverty which kept [him] grounded' (Patriarca, 'Two Wars', p. 9). The young man contemplated joining the US air force but, as he said, a 'buck private' without a college education had 'no chance of getting off the ground' (*ibid.*, p. 8). And though 'some fellows may be satisfied to gas up the planes and sit at the controls while the engines warm up', or 'to pull the chocks from the wheels only to watch someone else zoom off', he could not contemplate 'that sort of heartbreak' (*ibid.*, p. 8). By a stroke of luck, while disconsolately thumbing through an aviation magazine at Long Island Airport, Patriarca came across a notice inviting the sons of Italians living abroad to come to Rome for free training in an Italian air school. Part of fascist irredentism, Mussolini's policy was geared to restoring to the Italian nation the families lost through emigration. The next morning, Patriarca, 'so excited [he] could hardly speak', was outside the Italian consulate as soon as the doors opened. And, by November 1933, he was the first American to enlist in Rome in the Air Ministry Aviation School. His heart was in stunting and aerobatics and very soon he was admitted to the air school at Gorizia, near Trieste. Associated with the flamboyant D'Annunzio, the school was renowned for daredevil pilots who could pull off astonishing feats of precision flying.

In October 1935, Patriarca volunteered to fly in a squadron with Mussolini's forces in Ethiopia. He remained a year, based in Massawa on the Red Sea. The pilots endured tough conditions, flying sorties in tremendous heat, engaged in the most notorious part of Mussolini's invasion whereby poorly armed Ethiopian soldiers were subjected to aerial bombardment, often with canisters of poison gas. In the end, Patriarca achieved the grade of sergeant and suffered only stomach ulcers, rather than the dire fate of being 'skinned alive with their hearts cut out' (p. 11) that Italian pilots had been told awaited them if they were shot down in Ethiopian territory. Back in Rome, the American contemplated returning to New York: however, an Italian Air Force recruiter offered him a contract at a very good salary of $200 per month to fly Fiats in rebel Spain. He accepted and left by ship with the planes from Genoa on 14 August 1936. A little over a week later, he was in Melilla in Morocco and had enlisted under the *nom de guerre* of Cesar Bocalari.

The young American flew Italian planes in convoy with German Junker 52s to bring Spanish soldiers and Moorish mercenaries to the Spanish mainland. He was delighted when the opportunity arose to arrange his posting so that he was stationed in Cáceres under the command of officers with whom he had flown in Ethiopia. At about this time, an admiring Alan Dick, from *The Daily Telegraph*, watched some of these 'happy-go-lucky youngsters', at dusk in single-seater pursuit planes, 'stunting with sheer exuberance' as they returned to the Cáceres airfield, 'rolling and diving and side-slipping' in the darkening sky.[12]

On 13 September, somewhere between Olalla and Talavera de la Reina, Patriarca, while in a dogfight with a Republican air ace, clipped the wing of the other plane and brought down both machines. He parachuted into Republican territory and was picked up and taken to Madrid for interrogation. It was a terror-filled interlude for a young American, who expected at any moment to be tried and executed. Correspondents who saw him in prison reported that he was very fearful, 'despondent and weeping'.[13]

The American journalists, Jay Allen and Louis Fischer, who had discovered Patriarca's whereabouts, alerted the United States embassy. There were articles in the New York papers and a groundswell of public support whipped up by a 'Committee of One Thousand Mothers' who raised a petition to the United States government, demanding Patriarca's release.[14] After a great many diplomatic intercessions by the American ambassador, Claude Bowers, and the consul, Eric Wendelin, Patriarca was swapped for a Yugoslav pilot captured by the Nationalists.[15] Eventually the Spanish Minister of Air handed him over to Wendelin to spirit out of Spain. H. Edward Knoblaugh,[16] an American journalist who was living in the US consulate in Madrid at the time, remembered Patriarca as a 'pitiful figure' who gradually 'recovered something of his bravado' to become one of the most 'animated of the embassy's guests'. Despite Patriarca's recent trauma in the air, Knoblaugh noted that the young American remained passionately interested in flying and would 'run out into the embassy garden each time a "dog-fight" was staged overhead' and 'excitedly point out what were the faults in the manoeuvring'; and that if he were up there 'By God [he'd] show them' (Knoblaugh, p. 114). The consul eventually arranged for Patriarca to be taken incognito to Valencia. The foreign correspondents obligingly withheld his name from the list of departing Americans until he was safely aboard the USS *Raleigh* and on the high sea to the United States.

Back in New York, Patriarca denounced the treatment he had received while a prisoner of the Republic. He loudly praised General Franco and insisted that the Rebels would win because they were 'for the real Spanish people' while the Loyalists were 'only for Russia'. With fine under-statement Patriarca declared that he had 'not yet had enough adventure', and, as 'barbering was no longer in his character', he would not be heading back to pick up the scissors in his father's shop in the Bronx.[17]

Back in the United States, however, Patriarca found himself once again 'grounded', unable to fly without a licence from an American pilots' school.[18] Probably predictably, within a very short time he had returned to Italy, where he made his life and career as a pilot. During the Second World War he flew with the Italian air force and eventually became part of a crack aerobatic unit that put on displays at national airshows. After retirement from the Italian forces, he worked for NATO and the US government. Vincent Patriarca died in Naples in December 1994.

Frank Thomas

The next volunteer in this group of English-speakers, Frank Thomas, was not unlike Patriarca in that he left his home in South Wales because of a sense of restlessness and the lack of opportunity he faced in 1936.[19] Twenty-two years of age and the son of a well-off Welsh food wholesaler, Thomas had completed grammar school in Cardiff in 1931 and spent a couple of unsuccessful years poultry farming. When this failed outright, he joined his father's business in Pontypridd, South Wales, as a travelling salesman. The region provided the heartland of the South Wales Miners Federation and, incidentally, was the place of origin of some 150 miners who went to Republican Spain to enlist in the International Brigades.[20]

For Thomas, the two and a half years as a salesman were 'two years too long' during which his 'mental outlook was stationary' (Thomas, p. 39). In his words, he 'craved fresh fields to conquer' and saw the outbreak of the Civil War in Spain 'as a welcome relief' (*ibid.*, p. 39). It was not the 'sacredness of Franco's cause', however, which drew him to Spain, but the opportunity to try the 'professional soldier's life.' Again, in his own estimation, 'the die was cast, and on General Franco's behalf by virtue of his possessing a picturesque Foreign Legion' (*ibid.*, p. 39). Robert Stradling, the editor of Thomas's diary from Nationalist Spain, pointed out that the young man was an avid reader of the genre of *Boy's Own* stories of the British Empire.[21] Among his greatest favourites was W. C. Wren's *Beau Geste*, which provided a model for many young men in the late 1920s and 1930s who pined for the challenge of a valiant life of adventure. The novel traces the many heroic and manly escapades of three English brothers who join the French Foreign Legion.

Thomas's father's explanation for his son's enlistment, however, is more prosaic and political.[22] As he saw it, Frank had 'always been interested in Fascist political beliefs but more than that he has been restless, unable to suit himself to everyday life' (*ibid.*, p. 5). Despite this, Thomas had given his parents no sign of the 'turmoil in his mind' until he had set off. The family's last news had been from Burgos, where he had sent a letter stating that he would 'make a name for himself as great as any of his heroes'. His father added that he hoped that his son's adventure in Spain would 'make him a man' (*ibid.*, p. 5).

Thomas entered Spain at Badajoz on 12 October 1936, having come from Liverpool to Lisbon by ship. Managing 'the curse of Babel' by 'hand signals', a 'sixpenny dictionary' and the 'magic password *Inglés*' (*ibid.*, p. 44), he travelled by train to Burgos, where he found that they were only taking Spanish recruits for the regular army. Therefore he backtracked to Valladolid to join up with the Spanish Foreign Legion. Finally, he was sent on to the Legion's base in Talavera de La Reina.

He was admitted as a legionnaire second class for the duration of the conflict and was paid six pesetas a day, five of which were taken for his board and lodging and the remainder set aside to be recouped on demobilization. The quartermaster issued him with the uniform of the legionnaire: a khaki *chapiri*, the distinctive garrison cap with a long red tassle, light green jodhpurs, a shirt and vest and a khaki cloak that buttoned down both sides and, when unbuttoned, ingeniously converted into an overblanket. The rest of his kit he was expected to scrounge for himself. In the next few weeks, Thomas added a gunbelt, an overcoat, some eating utensils and several warm blankets, which he managed to pick up around the fronts or helped himself to in the houses of the villages the Nationalists occupied.

After a cursory day and a half of initiation into the Legion's commands and drill, Thomas was shipped up to the front. His experiences were probably fairly typical of an English-speaking foreigner in the Legion. Discipline was harsh, though he found himself as a foreigner exempt from some of the more barbaric forms. The corporal in the first unit to which he was assigned was quite proud to have him in the unit and took him under his wing, passing some of the more onerous duties onto his Spanish peers.

Beatings for indiscipline were common and officers of the Legion drilled new recruits with long pliant riding whips. Infractions of Legion rules would earn a good thrashing on the spot: a left turn when a right turn was ordered would bring down a sharp cut of the whip, as would a request made to a superior without observing the correct form of salute and respectful address. More serious infractions, such as slacking on duty or being drunk and disorderly, would earn a stint of hard labour on a punishment squad. Legionnaires in the latter served as 'beasts of burden' for their *bandera* or were required to carry out exhausting and humiliating duties, such as the occasion when Thomas saw prisoners on punishment detail using their hands as shovels in the meaningless task of clearing horse manure from the road. Soldiers who were deemed seriously insubordinate were shot. No wonder that the Foreign Legion was renowned for its discipline under fire and that the *banderas* of legionnaires were always sent ahead as shock troops on the battlefield.

Most foreigners, with the exception of the Portuguese, were exempt from the whips, Thomas noted, though their status did not protect two English-speaking sailors, a Canadian and a Britisher, who had swum ashore in Spain from a British ship in Gibraltar in order to join the Foreign Legion. They had received a 'frightful beating' at the hands of a drunken sergeant who suspected that foreigners were poisoning Spanish wells (*ibid.*, p. 52). The two English-speakers had enlisted at the same time as Thomas. When he saw them after their draconian treatment, which conjured up the Middle Ages not the 1930s, they were in very bad shape and 'determined to clear off as soon as possible' (*ibid.*, p. 52). In the final event, in June 1937, when Thomas deserted from the Foreign Legion, one of the two went with him.

In his descriptions of the Legion, Thomas's close comrades were other foreigners: an Hungarian ex-Catholic missionary, several Frenchmen, a Czechoslovak and a White Russian veteran from Wrangel's army, whose integrity and courage in the field Thomas greatly admired. Although his fluency in Spanish improved, it was French that was the lingua franca in communication with his foreign comrades. By way of contrast, the Portuguese, who provided a large number of foreigners in the forces in Nationalist Spain, were treated the least well among foreigners and Spaniards. Derided by everyone, Portuguese recruits were the butt of jokes and bullying.

Like other English travellers in Spain, it took time for Thomas to become accustomed to Spanish food: everything cooked in 'too much olive oil' and a two-meal-a-day regimen that included only black coffee at breakfast. Hard tack, on the days when the cookhouse could not bring hot rations up to the front, consisted of bread and sardines or sausage 'as hard as a board with slivers of bone enclosed with a meat in a tough skin container' (ibid., p. 54).

Between the end of October 1936 and mid-June 1937, when Thomas was smuggled out of Spain, he fought at most of the major battles on the fronts around Madrid. The rhythm of the soldier's day was set by the flux of military operations: intense periods of engagement with the enemy were followed by long periods of idleness, drilling, drinking and playing endless games of cards, mostly forms of poker for high stakes.[23] Certainly, at least at the beginning, the Welshman enjoyed the camaraderie and élan of being a 'caballero legionario' in the elite fighting group, respected, feared and never shirking combat.

In the diary, Thomas notes matter of factly that Republican prisoners were routinely executed, though he is at pains to claim that militia women were not among them. In early January, when a young female soldier was captured near Toledo, 'wounded in the posterior' (ibid., p. 84), she was given first aid and sent back behind the lines under armed guard. If she arrived safely, her treatment was in strong contrast with the treatment of her male comrades who were shot on the spot. Despite his first-hand knowledge of atrocities on both sides, Thomas stoutly maintained that only government troops mutilated prisoners and that 'Franco put many captured members of the International Brigade safely over the French frontier with a new suit of clothes and five pounds in their pockets' (ibid., p. 129).

Membership of the Foreign Legion cured Thomas of any illusions he may have had about fascists when he arrived in Spain. During his eight-month sojourn, he came to share the historic enmity that the other units harboured towards Falangists, who were seen as slackers and spongers who 'boast how they will rule Spain' (ibid., p. 119) but were reluctant to fight for their principles in real combat.

Like the legionnaires and the Moors around him, Thomas took part in the right of 'permitted looting' whereby it was accepted that the Foreign Legion and the Moors within the first 24 hours of victory could help themselves to anything they could find in the houses and buildings of the defeated.[24] Rapacious looting by the Moors had been noted by many foreign journalists at the front, as these mercenary soldiers carried off anything that could be traded or taken home. In comparison, Thomas's efforts were modest. He improved his kit as he went and, while his unit was bivouacked in the Casa de Velázquez in the University City, he helped himself to some valuable antique coins on display, which he later lost in the peripatetic soldier's life.

At Navalcarnero, some thirty kilometres outside Madrid at the junction of the road from Talavera to Escorial and Madrid, Thomas experienced his first taste of real combat. And, at the start of November, he was part of the Nationalists' full-scale advance on Madrid, during which his unit was caught up in fierce fighting as they pushed into the Casa de Campo on the western side of the Manzanares River and from where the centre of the capital beckoned tantalizingly, a short mile away. There was ferocious fighting that produced escalating casualties as troops fought under air attack from both sides. When the Nationalists pushed into the University City, Thomas's unit occupied first the Casa de Velázquez and later an annex of the Medical School. Both had been constructed in the university expansion that had taken place in the late 1920s. The Casa de Velázquez was provided by the French state and, during the military occupation, the priceless library and well-appointed apartments were ransacked. The books were used for barricades at the windows and items of any value were looted and carried off.

At the end of three weeks, the remnant of Thomas's battalion, having taken heavy losses, was withdrawn to Talavera, where the bandera collectively was awarded a Military Medal. They paraded before General Yagüe in the full battalion formation in which the empty spaces underlined the heavy losses they had incurred. Very soon replenished by new recruits – and as a consequence Thomas now enjoyed the privileged status of 'veteran' – the bandera moved up to Toledo.

On recreation and rest days, Thomas tramped over the ancient city of Toledo, marvelling at the 'miracle' of the Alcázar. On Christmas Day he visited a monastery nearby where a group of newly arrived Romanians and Germans were billeted. In early January, his unit was engaged in fighting along the Corunna Road from Las Rozas and Majadahonda and, in February, he was promoted to lance corporal, a legionnaire first class. For a few comfortable weeks subsequently, he served as batman to the captain of the company, from which more easy vantage he watched the Nationalists' unsuccessful advance along the Jarama front to cut the Madrid–Valencia Road. Both sides suffered horrendous losses.[25]

In April, promoted again, this time to full corporal, Thomas went back to the front to lead his own squad. In the last skirmish in which he was involved in the Spanish Civil War, Thomas was ordered to take his squad to attack up the steep slopes to the westerly heights above Toledo. Almost the last man left firing, suddenly he was struck by a bullet that passed under his right nostril and out beside his right ear (Thomas, p. 116). It was followed almost immediately by another bullet that struck his leg. Badly wounded and with blood gushing everywhere, he eventually managed to crawl to safety through the barbed wire and back across a clear fire zone to be taken to a front-line medical unit. From there he was carried down to Toledo, slumped in the packsaddle of a mule that had brought ammunition up the mountain. After Toledo, he was transferred to a field hospital in Griñon and later to Talavera de la Reina. Finally he was taken, still on crutches, to recuperate at a hospital near the Portuguese frontier at Cáceres.

While recuperating there, he ran into members of the Irish Legion who were awaiting repatriation after their abortive experiences in front-line combat. Their commander, Eoin O'Duffy, to whose mercy Thomas successfully appealed, promised to help smuggle the young Welshman out when the Irish unit returned home.

Thomas's reasons for quitting Spain are not entirely clear. Probably it was the combination of a whole series of factors. First, he was feeling the strain of the war and combat, undoubtedly exacerbated by his injury and what he called the 'depressing atmosphere of the military hospitals' (*ibid.*, p. 121), in which there was no 'regular nursing staff' of the sort that a Welshman would expect. Legion doctors and orderlies came in mid-morning and departed, leaving 'girl-volunteers' to deal with the beds and the patients. A precipitating factor was that Thomas had become increasingly fed up with the official anti-Britishness of Nationalist Spain, in which the press harped on British perfidy over non-intervention which supposedly aided the Republic. Similarly, he was infuriated by scurrilous Spanish reports on Edward VIII's abdication and a lack of respect in the coverage of the new king's coronation. At the same time, Thomas refers to his 'personal grievance' (*ibid.*, p. 119) that no one had helped him when his unit had been decimated above Toledo. He claimed that the Foreign Legion was no longer as it had been when he joined: it would have been 'inconceivable' in the 'old *Tercio*' that a wounded comrade would be left. On the traditional cry of 'the legion to me' all legionnaires must come to the wounded man's assistance. While this was the tradition, Thomas's claim that its loss caused his own disillusionment is unconvincing. After all, he had only been a legionnaire for a few months and his own loyalty to the Legion was such that he had no hesitation in deserting when a suitable opportunity presented itself. More striking are his ruminations while in hospital, in which his 'romantic fatalism became realism'. At that time he began to ask himself why should he, 'a mercenary adventurer' (*ibid.*, p. 119), risk certain death when 'hundreds of local dandies infest the cafes without attempting to fight for their cause' (*ibid.*, p. 128); and 'Fascists and hundreds of others in civilian jobs were hanging about risking nothing' (*ibid.*, p. 119). Presumably his being injured sharpened a recognition that, if he continued as a *legionario*, he must face 'certain death' (*ibid.*, p. 120). In his own summation, though he might be willing to manage this for 'national or strong political motives', it was not worth it for only 'love of adventure and four pesetas a day' (*ibid.*, p. 120). Probably, too, he was homesick and worn out. Certainly, the decision to go AWOL was 'consolidated' by the relief of meeting English-speaking Irishmen after a long period of not having used the language.

Consequently, on 17 June 1937, when the wounded Irish were taken by ambulance to join the train with their countrymen, Thomas, in borrowed civvies and hobbling on a walking stick, was with them. He and one of the two Britishers who had deserted from Gibraltar were hidden by their Irish comrades on the train that took them across the border into Portugal and finally to Lisbon from where they embarked for home.

Subsequently, Thomas wrote his memoirs and attempted to get them published. When the Second World War broke out, he set aside everything to enlist in what effectively was his own Second World War. With the British Eighth Army, he fought in North Africa and was wounded at Tobruk. Robert Stradling reported that in 1997 Frank Thomas was living quietly in retirement with his wife. The fact that he was an official deserter from the Spanish Foreign Legion meant that he had never returned to the Iberian Peninsula.

Nugent Bull

In October 1937, not long after Thomas had left, an Australian, Nugent Bull, a tall and fit 29-year-old, joined the Spanish Foreign Legion at Talavera de la Reina. He fulfilled the terms of his enlistment, first with the Sixth Bandera and later with the Seventeenth of the Second Tercio, for the duration of the conflict.

Bull spoke a smattering of schoolboy French but not a word of Spanish. The military recruiters, uncertain about his nationality, placed him in the French-speaking Joan of Arc company.[26] When he arrived in Spain, Bull knew a little about Spanish politics but next to nothing of Léon Blum and the French Popular Front, both of which constituted the overriding obsession of his French comrades. A robust Catholic, Bull had enlisted with Franco because he wished to 'defend the Catholic Church against Communism'.[27] The son of a prosperous family of Sydney undertakers, Bull had been educated at a prominent Marist boys school, where he had been strongly influenced by a teacher, Brother Gerard, an intellectual in the Sydney circles of Catholic Action.[28] From him and sources like the Australasian Catholic Truth Society pamphlets, available in the entrance of every parish church in the country, Bull had learnt that the Church was under challenge everywhere. Beginning with the Russian and Mexican Revolutions, the same pattern was now unfolding in Spain. The Vatican Osservatore Romano, syndicated in the Australian Catholic weeklies, provided regular and highly alarmist commentaries on the anticlericalism of the Second Republic in attempting to separate Church and state. At a time when Catholics in Australia were engaged in a political struggle for Catholic schooling, and many parishes were attempting to raise money to build schools, the laic education policy of the Second Republic and the destruction of church property reverberated with a particular Antipodean resonance.[29]

An extrovert and good at sports, Bull enjoyed a weekend stoush with Commmunist speakers at the Sydney Domain as much as a pick-up game of rugby or cricket. He was also fascinated by Taylorism and the new theories about how to raise productivity by the social organization of labour.[30] In the early 1930s, after his father had a stroke, Nugent took over the family's funeral parlour and, during a flamboyant stint at the helm, made a mark on the Sydney funeral industry. He purchased several powerful Rolls Royce cars which he painted white and converted into glamorous hearses. He also patented a new design for a more efficient funeral bier and, for a while, until the family put a stop to it, he replaced the subdued black outfits of the funeral attendants with dazzling white woollen suits.[31] In June 1937 his older brother returned from abroad and took over the business. Nugent was at a loose end, at a stage in life when many of his school contemporaries were launched into careers and settling into family life.[32]

In July 1937, Bull, supported by regular financial assistance from his family, set sail to Rome from where he made arrangements to enlist in Franco's army. There is an irony, clearer with hindsight, in the scion of an inner-city funeral parlour family becoming a 'Bridegroom of Death' in the Spanish Foreign Legion.[33] In the Joan of Arc battalion, his schoolboy French was useful, though in letters home he bemoaned his ignorance of the 'tu' form, the informal usage strictly out of bounds in Australian schools.[34]

With the Juana de Arco (Joan of Arc), Bull was part of the Nationalist counter-offensive to retake Teruel at the end of 1937. The city fell to Franco in February 1938 after a wearing campaign during which both sides slogged through heavy snow. While managing to avoid the 'red bullet', about which Brother Gerard's letters constantly warned, Bull contracted a fever in early 1938 and was seriously ill for several weeks in a military hospital at Calatayud. When the Nationalists cleared front-line hospitals in readiness for casualties in the advance on Teruel at the end of February, Bull was moved to a provincial clinic in Valladolid. In March he was convalescing at Peñafiel. A month later he continued to suffer painful swelling in the joints and hands, which aggravated a football knee injury, and was deemed unfit for active duty and was reassigned to the *bandera's* Transport Division. Henceforth he was part of the organization which arranged rail and road transport taking food, munitions and petrol up to the front. They also made much use of mule convoys; the animals, surefooted on narrow mountain tracks, were stoic under fire. The greater part of Bull's time, however, was spent chauffeuring the *bandera's* officers and shuttling vehicles from the front to the garages at the rear for petrol and repairs. In this job, presumably, his passion for powerful cars and his experience in arranging funeral cortèges stood him in good stead.

He was with the Joan of Arc *bandera* at Tremp in Catalonia in December 1938 and entered the Catalan capital when the Republican defences finally collapsed in February 1939. After the great victory parade in Madrid in May, he travelled with his *bandera* to Dar Riffien in Morocco where he was demobbed on 15 June 1939 with an honourable discharge and an accrued sum of 101 pesetas and 30 centivos.[35]

Bull's letters home are filled with commentary on French affairs. Like his comrades in the Juana de Arco, he read the proto-fascist *Gringoire* regularly, savouring the weekly's lively mix of scurrilous observations on French politics and the regular columns of leisure and fiction serials. According to Bull, the Frenchmen he was with were 'young fellows who are in Spain because they don't like communism'. Unlike the other English-speaking volunteers examined in this essay, Bull sympathized strongly with the Frenchmen's distrust of Freemasonry and shared the broad Nationalists' belief that Jews and Masons were a powerful force behind the British government. In a letter to Brother Gerard, Bull noted that 'England has never been a Friend of Catholic countries' and was a society in which 'the stamp of the governing classes is pronouncedly Jewish'. He believed that 'the English are burdened with a government of a masonic-plutocratic calibre'.[36] This attitude, at least in relation to Freemasonry and anti-Britishness, was not unusual among Australian Catholics, whose religion was influenced by a strong Irish Republican strand.

From his French *compañeros* Bull had learnt that, in Paris, 'masonic Jewry is certainly running the country' and the leader Blum, 'whose real name is Finkelstein', was 'doing his best for the Communist Party in Spain'.[37] The letters chronicle the growing power of the Communists in France, where 'every town now has its red centre' and the 'war against Atheistic Communism now being waged in Spain will certainly engulf France within two years'. As well, 'everyone' that Bull knew said that M. Daladier, the leader of the Radicals whose party took over from Blum's Socialists, was a 'Freemason first and a Frenchman second'.[38]

The analyses of Spanish domestic politics which Bull repeats are standard Nationalist polemic: Republicans are 'Reds' who act at the behest of 'their Masters in Moscow'; Franco is an 'overly modest man' of the sort of which the 'best leaders are made'. As well, the letters are peppered with hideously graphic descriptions of attacks on the clergy, particularly the Marist Order, presumably for the particular predilection of Brother Gerard and the College's Old Boys, in whose newsletter a number of the letters were reprinted. From the end of 1937, Bull predicted the imminent defeat of the 'Reds' because of the cowardice of the

International Brigades under fire and the preoccupations of their 'government's owners with the affairs in the East'.

Bull was perplexed as to how the 'tools of Atheistic Communism' had taken hold in 'Spain the most Catholic of countries'. He puzzled, too, over why the war dragged on so long. He discussed with Brother Gerard the theory he had heard, familiar in Maurrasian circles, that the de-Christianization of Spain had begun with the French Revolution of 1789. Another theory, put forward by the American priest, Owen McGuire, rather worried him, as it proposed that the Spanish monarchists' own intransigence was to blame because they had prevented an 'Anti-Red' coalition at the start of the Republic. In the end, Bull settled for the most simplistic explanation that was current among the French volunteers, which was that, because Spaniards had not been in the First World War, they had not been exposed to the 'super propaganda' which other nations had experienced and were therefore inured to. Innocent Spaniards, by contrast, were easily captivated by Communist propaganda. In a similar vein, the war dragged on because the International Brigaders, the 'riff raff of Europe', were enlisted to fight for 'red Democracy' in Spain.[39]

It is perhaps an indication of Bull's total identification with the Nationalist cause that, eight months after his own enlistment, he could expostulate against Republican claims that Germans and Italians were with Franco, because 'not a single European has enlisted with Franco in the last year while the French government has allowed hordes of reds to pour into the Republic'.[40]

Bull's colleagues predicted that, in the political configuration after the war, France and England would be isolated in a Europe already dominated by Mussolini and, as he observed, 'who can prove that it is a bad domination'. Germany and Italy would be 'determined to exclude Communism from Europe' and would not forget that Britain and France had turned a blind eye to the 'Red Spanish Peninsula'. Bull forecast that Spain under Franco would be strong, leaving 'France weakened with three frontiers to defend and this would be Spain's best method of repayment to her allies in the Civil War'. In a hope shared by many French and Spanish fascists, Bull anticipated that the political structure of the new Spanish state would replicate the corporative structure of Portugal, where the Church's position was central and its dominance shared by a strong army.[41]

The end of the Spanish Civil War found Bull footloose and looking for a job. He travelled to England, via Lourdes, at the end of August 1939 and

was in London when the Second World War was declared. The uproar in
the city under air-raid warnings took Bull back to the stoicism of the
people during the Civil War in 'my poor uncivilised Spain'.[42] In October
1939, after the intercession of a friend in Australia House, Bull was
accepted for an air gunnery course in the RAF and was posted to an
operational squadron of Bomber Command. On 3 September 1940, he
wrote home exuberantly about the 'cracker bombing raids' they were
making over Berlin during which they 'plastered the Siemens factory and
rang their bell with one and a half ton of bombs'.[43] There was some irony
in Bull's exhilaration in that he was bombing German factories which a
little more than a year previously had been churning out arms for Franco.
On the evening of 8 September 1940, Bull's Wellington bomber went
down over the English Channel and he was declared missing in action,
presumed dead.[44]

Peter Kemp

The last of the four English-speakers is the 20-year-old Peter Kemp, who
had just finished a degree in Classics and Law at Trinity College,
Cambridge, when the Spanish Civil War began. In his memoir, *Mine Were
of Trouble*, he reflects on Spain with the understanding of hindsight, two
decades after the event.[45]

In Kemp's assessment of his own motives, he states that, though he was
strongly monarchist and a Tory, on the far right of Cambridge Toryism,
his politics were important only in so far as they determined on which side
he joined up. As he saw it, the war had broken out at a 'particularly
opportune time' in his own life when he was burdened 'with a restless
temperament' and a decided resistance to entering a barrister's career.[46]
Not unlike Nancy Cunard's observation that she and her friends needed
the Spanish Republic more than it needed them, Kemp found that the war
in Spain came as 'a relief': it provided him with a 'splendid chance' to go
out on his own; to go to Spain and get to know its people and their
language; and learn something about warfare and adventure. And all in a
short time because he assumed, like everyone else, that the war would last
no more than six months.

Exactly like the three young men already discussed, Kemp was at a
crossroads in his life and had been something of a disappointment to his
family. Kemp's university career had fallen far below the academic and
sporting success that his father, an ex-High Court judge in the Indian

Colonial Service, had expected. His father also strongly disapproved of his son's wild lifestyle in London and Cambridge. Peter had barely scraped a third in his finals. A few days before the Tripos exams, he had lost control of a friend's Bentley roadster at high speed on a bend and smashed into a brick wall, bringing down a telegraph pole that cut the phone line between London and Cambridge for 24 hours. His father had written a stinging letter about 'this deplorable termination' to Peter's Cambridge career, observing tartly to his son that when he reflected on him he 'sometimes thought that God must have made you for a bet' (*ibid.*, p. 7).

Kemp assumed that his father would strongly disapprove of his intention to go to Spain, but was pleasantly surprised that, when he told his father, he welcomed the news. Perhaps, echoing the sentiments of Frank Thomas's father, Judge Kemp hoped that Franco's army would make a man out of his son. In any event, Kemp *père* opened a bank account for his son in Burgos and paid in a regular monthly allowance. His father also came up to London and took Peter to the Army and Navy Stores to purchase 'the right equipment for this sort of thing': stout walking clothes, boots and a 'bulky medicine chest'. Kemp also bought himself *Spanish in Three Months without a Master* to try and learn something of the language (*ibid.*, p. 6).

Never having been to Spain and knowing no one on the Nationalist side, Kemp was unsure how to go about getting there until an acquaintance introduced him to the Marqués del Moral. One of the British Friends of Nationalist Spain, del Moral provided an introduction in Biarritz to the Conde de los Andes, who ran a regular courier service across the French border to Nationalist headquarters in Burgos. Del Moral also encouraged Kemp to obtain a journalist's accreditation before he left. Several weeks later, when he motored over the International Bridge, a passenger in los Andes's large black saloon, Kemp had a letter of identification from the *Sunday Dispatch*. It was one of the papers in Lord Rothermere's stable, all of which were pro-Franco.

In Burgos these introductions from London gave Kemp entrée into the aristocratic circles with Anglophile members at Franco's headquarters. They strongly advised him against enlisting in the Spanish Foreign Legion 'as a private soldier' and instead introduced him to the Carlist command of the Requetés. In a short time, in November 1936, aided by the certificates that proved that he had been in the Cambridge Officer Training Corps, Kemp had joined a Carlist cavalry regiment based in Ávila.[47]

Carlist volunteers were provided with keep and equipment: recruits supplied their own uniforms and fended for themselves for extra comforts. Bolstered by his father's allowance arriving regularly, none of this was a problem. From November, Kemp enjoyed a fairly uneventful month riding out with the cavalry to guard a stretch of road between Toledo and Talavera de la Reina. His comrades were mostly Andalusian peasants. They sang plaintive Andalusian flamenco songs in the evening and, until he became accustomed to it, kept Kemp awake at night with the 'thunderous sounds of their breaking wind' in sleep. Needless to say, the meals provided a solid diet of beans and more beans (*Mine Were of Trouble*, p. 43).

The lieutenant colonel in the Requetés was a White Russian who had little time for England, which he believed had abandoned his motherland to the Bolsheviks (*ibid.*, p. 43). Among other foreigners, Kemp also served with a Polish count, who claimed that he had trained previously with a Polish cavalry regiment, as well as various individual Germans and a number of Portuguese.

Among Kemp's other companions was a 42-year-old Finnish aristocrat, 'Goggi' von Haartman, a flamboyant figure with a scarred face and a monocle who 'clicked his heels in the best Potsdam manner'.[48] His sometime adjutant, a Bostonian, Joe Sarallach, was reportedly a graduate of MIT.[49] As von Haartman told Robson, he could do nothing else, as soldiering was the only life he knew. Before Spain, von Haartman had fought in the First World War and the Finnish Civil War in 1918 as well as joining Mussolini's invading forces in Ethiopia in 1935. Between wars, in the 1930s, he was in Hollywood drilling extras who appeared as soldiers in war movies. He had come to Spain to fight 'Reds' but his hatred of them was 'outdone' by his 'passion for war'. He began with a Falangist cavalry unit near Santander but was mixed up with the Hedilla affair and arrested by Franco. Released later, he joined the Foreign Legion and, in mid-1938, shared a hospital ward with Peter Kemp in San Sebastian. As Kemp describes him in *Mine Were of Trouble*, despite an incapacitated arm, the Finn stayed out most evenings and drank himself into intoxication in the bars and brawled with other soldiers and legionnaires (pp. 198–9).

After a promotion to second lieutenant, Kemp left the cavalry in mid-December 1936 and transferred to a Carlist infantry platoon outside Madrid. They held a small group of houses in a salient in the front-line under constant fire and mortar attack. In February Kemp was part of the battle of Jarama in which many of his adversaries were members of the International Brigades.

Kemp hankered to join the Foreign Legion. He had come to see that the Civil War would be a long haul best endured with professionals and proper leadership. The Requetés were brave but badly supplied and often disorganized. Pablo Merry del Val introduced Kemp to Millán Astray in the Hotel Continental in San Sebastian, and it was arranged that Kemp could transfer into the Spanish Foreign Legion. Just as the Anglophone Merry del Val had helped him, the press officer, Gonzalo de Aguilera, also part of the Anglophile circle around Franco, assisted the young Englishman at various stages in Spain. Kemp admired Aguilera, whose extensive vocabulary of expletives earned him the sobriquet of 'El Capitán Veneno' (Captain Poison) (*Mine Were of Trouble*, p. 50).[50]

Kemp transferred into the Spanish Forcign Legion at the end of October 1937, and was attached to a machine-gun company of the 14th Bandera. With them he slogged through Teruel in February 1938 in temperatures that at times fell to $-20°$ Centigrade. The unit took heavy casualties at Calpe when they were accidentally bombed by their own planes.

The soldiering in the Foreign Legion was first class and Kemp was 'thrilled' to be with such 'superb soldiers', though in the early months he was forced to ride out a good deal of hostility because of his English nationality. His first commander told him bluntly, 'I shit on Englishmen' (*ibid.*, p. 112), and another, ostensibly friendly, blurted out his resentment at foreigners in Spain who were meddling in a war that was none of their business (*ibid.*, p. 169). Also, Kemp was a Protestant and found it hard to convince his fellows that he was not a Freemason. Only two other Englishmen had achieved officer status in the Foreign Legion and one of them, Lieutenant Noel Fitzpatrick, found that his career was finished in the Legion when he had admitted during an argument that he was a Mason.

Discipline in the Requetés had been no picnic. Kemp had seen men beaten for drunkenness by their officers using bare fists and the leather *fustas*. However, the Legion employed an order of savagery above that again. Insubordination was punishable by death. Indeed, Kemp himself was severely chastised by his commanding officer for having a man court-martialled for insubordination, rather than shooting him on the spot. The legionnaire had spoken back to a bullying officer. Prisoners taken in battle were routinely executed, and Kemp encountered 'one of the most horrible experiences' of his life when he was ordered to shoot an Irish deserter from the International Brigades who had crossed over to give himself up in Nationalist lines (*ibid.*, p. 170).

Exactly as in the other unit, however, Kemp and his comrades in the Foreign Legion spent inordinate amounts of time cooling their heels, waiting for orders. As well, during various stages in his assignment, in the Requetés and the Foreign Legion, Kemp set off for Burgos and Salamanca to lobby various members of the command so that he could make the transfer he sought. For example, he waited out his assignment to the Foreign Legion not back with the Requetés but in Vitoria in an apartment with two journalists from the English-speaking press.

Over the course of his full-time soldiering career in Nationalist Spain, Kemp was in two very heavy attacks, and in both he was seriously injured. At Caspe, just before the Battle of Belchite, and confronting an enemy composed of the British Battalion of the International Brigades, he was injured in the throat and an arm. On this occasion, he was taken by hospital train to Saragossa and eventually to Oviedo. In May 1938 he returned to the front which was just inside the border of Catalonia. By this time he had managed to transfer, as a lieutenant, into an infantry rifle unit which very soon was caught up in the first stages of the Battle of the Ebro. Kemp's squad came under mortar attack, and his dugout took a direct hit which shattered his jaw and deeply lacerated his hands. At a field hospital near the front at Fraga, Kemp had the very good fortune to be operated on by a skilful Spanish surgeon, trained in a London hospital, who succeeded in reconstructing the smashed jaw. When he could be moved he was transported across Aragon to the General Mola hospital in San Sebastian where, again fortuitously, Eastman Sheean, the Irish-American plastic surgeon, carried out further surgical reconstructions. On the ward, he received kindly care from the staff of Spanish nuns, but whose 'indifference to the principles of asepsis drove Sheean crazy' (*ibid.*, p. 197). Kent went home to England to convalesce for several months and, as much as he was able, to proselytize for Franco and the Nationalists. By the time he returned to Spain in July 1939 to receive his decommission, the war was over.

As a signal honour, General Franco invited Kemp for a private audience in Burgos on his final departure from Spain. Kemp found a 'small tubby figure dwarfed by the broad scarlet sash and the pendulant gold tassels of a full general' (*ibid.*, p. 200), but what struck him most was the Caudillo's 'very high, almost feminine voice'.[51] Speaking informally, Franco told Kemp that he feared that the British were unaware of the Communist threat and especially in the universities paid too little attention to the spread of 'subversive influences among British young people'. He also dismissed Kemp's fear that there would be another world war (*Mine Were of Trouble*, pp. 200–1).

Over the years, Kemp returned to Spain and kept in touch with his comrades from the Legion. During the Second World War, he joined the British Special Operation Organization and was parachuted into France and later dropped behind the lines to organize anti-fascist partisans in Albania. He also fought with the Polish Home Army, was arrested by the NKVD and held prisoner for a month and, when the war ended, had been in Thailand and Laos fighting the Japanese. Subsequently, he fought with the Vietminh against the Vietnamese nationalists, was in Budapest in 1956 and bobbed up in the independence struggles in Rhodesia, where he supported the strongman tactics of Robert Mugabe. His last sighting was in Nicaragua as an adviser to the Contras.[52]

The Irish Brigade

Probably, the most well-known group of foreign volunteers in Nationalist Spain was the Irish Brigade, some 700 men who came from Ireland with Eoin O'Duffy to fight for the 'faith of their fathers' in Franco's Spain. There is a substantial secondary literature on the group because their Spanish sojourn overlaps with a larger and, perhaps, more important question about the significance of the Blueshirt movement in contemporary Irish history.[53] O'Duffy was a core Blueshirt character, a leader almost from foundation, and a central rallying figure for the movement.[54] A fair number of the Irish Brigaders were recruited for Spain through membership or associations of some sort with Blueshirt networks.

In the existing literature, until recently, the Irish in Spain echo the sobriquet of the 'Gasoline Brigade' coined at the time by the British consul because of the 'rapidity with which the Irish transferred themselves from place to place'.[55] In a similar vein, a Swiss journalist who knew O'Duffy in Spain in 1937 described him as 'marionette-like' because after 'two or three turns on the stage he dropped entirely from view'.[56] Subsequent historians have shared the negative assessment made by O'Duffy's contemporaries. Hugh Thomas has referred to 'O'Duffy's ill-fated blue shirts' (*Spanish Civil War*, p. 768) and Mark Cronin described the Irish volunteers undertaking a 'comical excursion' to Franco's Spain.[57] By contrast, Fearghal McGarry and Robert Stradling have held these ideas up to new examination.[58] Stradling attempts to rehabilitate O'Duffy and his men from the denigration they have suffered from 'sixty years of unsympathetic public comment' and 'taproom ridicule'.[59] In his analysis he labels it a 'paradox' that the far fewer, and not popular, Irish International Brigaders are remembered with pride, while O'Duffy's name is 'virtually unspeakable in Irish historical discourse'. Because he fought on the 'wrong side', he was seen as a 'miserable running dog of reaction' and 'firmly displaced' from popular memory.[60] Fearghal McGarry shows most convincingly that the public memory of O'Donnell's Irish Brigade has been shaped less by Spanish events than by the way that Irish political culture developed in response broadly to European politics.[61]

As valid and interesting as are these new approaches, it is still the case that the Irish in Spain had a troubled history, despite the fact that they were treated far more leniently by the Nationalist command than were the equivalent foreign volunteers with Franco.

The Irish government was a signatory to the Non-Intervention Agreement and in February 1937 the Irish Dail reaffirmed the government's opposition to Irish citizens volunteering on either side in Spain. Citizens in the Irish Free State, from the beginning, however, supported the insurgents because they appeared to be pro-Catholic and anti-Communist. The Spanish Republicans, by contrast, were tainted with anticlerical violence, the destruction of churches and the harassment of priests and nuns which was attributed to the Republic's having fallen under the sway of Russian Communism. McGarry points out that, in Ireland, the 1930s was a decade of 'unprecedented anti-communist fervour' (*Irish Politics*, p. 35). As well, a popular perception in both countries was that Catholic Ireland and Spain shared historic links. Spain in the past had served as a haven for Irish intellectuals and priests fleeing the perfidy of Protestant England. In O'Duffy's memoirs, and in the recollections of Irish volunteers, the shared faith of the two countries was drummed up whenever there were rumblings of discontent among the Irish volunteers in Spain.[62]

Eoin O'Duffy was described in 1936, when he was 44 years of age, as a 'big benevolent-looking man with a red, clean-shaven face, like that of a parish priest'. And his weaknesses were an 'extreme irascibility and an absolute incapacity for working with anyone at all'.[63] In the Irish Civil War he had been a commander in the Irish Republican army. Later, until he was sacked by de Valéra in 1935, when the latter's United Irishmen took power, O'Duffy had been police commissioner in the Irish Free State and, for a short while, simultaneously, the commander of the Irish army and an activist in the Blueshirt movement. While the latter's greeting of

'Hoch O'Duffy' had not the assonance of 'Heil Hitler', and not all Blueshirts were believers, O'Duffy himself was a clerical fascist, as was the smaller Greenshirt movement he led away from the main movement in mid-1935. In December 1934 at Montreux, O'Duffy was part of the Secretariat of the Fascist International, rubbing shoulders with the leaders of the Italian-backed European fascist movements. At the same gathering he supported the motion of the Romanian delegate and future volunteer for Franco, Ion Motza, to attempt to bind all the movements into a core policy of anti-Semitism.[64]

In *Crusade in Spain*, O'Duffy claims he undertook to organize the volunteers for Franco after a member of the Carlist command approached him on the suggestion of the Cardinal Primate of Ireland. His original contacts were made through Juan de la Cierva from the London group of the Friends of Nationalist Spain. A letter he sent to the Dublin papers suggesting a brigade to defend the faith in Spain, according to O'Duffy, produced an avalanche of replies: 'every post brought hundreds of letters from Irishmen all over the country and in Britain and other countries' (*Crusade in Spain*, p. 14).

O'Duffy's first step in setting up the brigade was typical of the peripatetics that marked his Spanish adventure. On 20 September 1936, he set off by plane to Burgos and for the next ten months crossed back and forth from Ireland to Spain, making arrangements and enjoying the official attention that came with his position as Inspector General of the Irish Brigade.

The first three-week trip sealed the pattern of the Irishman's future relations with Franco's Spain. Without question, O'Duffy was flattered by the military pomp which Franco laid on for those foreigners who could help the Nationalist cause abroad. In the same way as other visitors, the erstwhile Irish commander basked in the official attention. His memoirs record carefully all the honours which were extended to him in Rebel Spain.

In September 1936, a guard of honour presented arms as he crossed the International Bridge, from where on the Spanish side a full military escort took him to Pamplona. On the way they stopped to visit sacred relics held by the Capuchins in a monastery in the Pyrenees, where 'many of the fathers wept with joy on hearing that Ireland wished to help the cause of the Faith in Spain' (*ibid.*, p. 16). The head of the Navarre Junta greeted O'Duffy, who was a guest in the palace of the provincial parliament. The next day, General Cabanellas, the acting president of the Burgos Junta, received him. It took a week of sightseeing to reach Valladolid, and he was with Mola when the siege of the Alcázar was raised. Despite the fact that Mola was 'in charge of the entire army' and, as they talked, 'couriers arrived with messages from various fronts', O'Duffy was charmed because the Spaniard spoke as though Irish business 'was the only business' (*ibid.*, p. 17). When news of the Alcázar came through, Mola purportedly 'rushed towards [the Irishman] and embraced him in an ecstasy of joy' (*ibid.*, p. 17). Before returning to Dublin, O'Duffy broadcast a stirring message over the radio promising in the name of 'Irishmen in every part of the world that Ireland will leave nothing undone to help her historic friend and ally' (*ibid.*, p. 24).

In London, de la Cierva had promised to provide the Irish with first-class transport to Spain. He would charter them one of 'Spain's best ships, fitted out with cabins and sleeping accommodation for one thousand men'. As a sign of official esteem, Franco's brother, Nicolás, would be in charge of arrangements, which included a Spanish admiral on board and an English-speaking staff of stewards. When the ship arrived in Vigo, a 'fleet of planes' would salute the Irish overhead and the Cardinal Primate of Spain would welcome them on the dock. A 'special train' would then carry them all in triumph to Burgos where 'convent schools and grounds' were already placed at their disposal (*ibid.*, pp. 58–9). It is impossible to know whether and to what degree O'Duffy embellished these details, perhaps abetted by de la Cierva's propensity to elaborate conspiracies. Douglas Jerrold in London had already experienced this when the Friends of National Spain were making preparations for the military uprising. In any event, none of the plans for O'Duffy's Irish eventuated.

On 14 October, as the 'keymen' in the expedition were shepherding Irish recruits by car to a secret point of departure near Waterford, and O'Duffy was packing his bags and shutting up his house, a courier from Franco arrived, calling off the operation. O'Duffy was devastated. He contacted those 'keymen' that he could and set off immediately to Nationalist Spain. In Salamanca he met Franco for the first time and found de la Cierva had already arrived. Franco was apologetic and blamed the Russians on the Non-Intervention Committee for the cancellation. O'Duffy was reassured to hear that despite everything 'after Spain, Ireland was still next in [Franco's] esteem' (*ibid.*, p. 65). The Caudillo invited O'Duffy to remain for a while in Spain as 'guest of the nation', accommodated in a 'special suite at the Grand Hotel' (*ibid.*, p. 67). Franco also placed a car and driver at the Irishman's disposal and appointed the Duke of Algeciras and the Count of Esteban from his own staff to accompany O'Duffy on a sweep through the western zone. After touring a few battlefields, they arrived finally at Toledo, where a miliary guard of honour presented arms to the Irish visitor in the 'grim ruins of the Alcázar' (ibid., p. 67). The Cardinal Primate of Spain was on hand as well and took O'Duffy on a private tour over the Cardinal's mansion and to view the priceless treasures of Toledo Cathedral. They then proceeded to the front near Madrid from where, even without glasses, O'Duffy could see the capital. After much flattering attention, O'Duffy returned to Salamanca where he, Franco and de la Cierva reinstituted plans for Irish volunteers to join the Nationalist forces.

The Irish battalion was constituted as the 15th Bandera in the Foreign Legion, with Irish officers and cooks and Spanish adjutants and interpreters as liaison. Initially O'Duffy made it clear that he did not wish his men to be placed on any front where they could be expected to fight their 'Catholic brothers among the Basques', though once in Spain he came to share the Nationalist view of the Basques as straightforward 'Reds'.

Six hundred and seventy Irishmen volunteered for Nationalist Spain. According to McGarry (Irish Politics, pp. 30–7) and Stradling,[65] the volunteers came predominantly from rural Ireland rather than Dublin and the larger towns but not necessarily exactly in the pattern of Blueshirt membership. In rural areas, the Church was the main institution and religious affairs provided the glue of social existence. In addition, the Catholic community of Ulster, in particular West Belfast, sent a strong contingent, probably a function of the solidarity among Ulster Catholics confronted with the Protestant majority. In addition, of course, O'Duffy was an Ulsterman. The majority of survivors that Stradling interviewed nominated religion as their main reason for enlistment with adventure a poor second.

Seamus MacKee, one of the Irish Brigade, divided the volunteers he met between a 'conscious' group who were ex-Blueshirts and the rest who, like himself, were 'ordinary decent young Irishmen deeply affected by Catholic teaching'.[66] Nineteen years of age when he went to Spain, MacKee grew up in a poor but hardworking Republican family and had been educated by the Christian Brothers at Ballyfinn. At the end of his schooling, he 'hung around doing odd jobs' and then headed to Dublin to stay with an uncle to look for work. A recruiter, one of O'Duffy's key-men, approached him about going to Spain and, as he was wanting to leave his uncle's house, he decided to 'take a chance with O'Duffy's outfit' (*I Was a Franco Soldier*, p. 9). McKee was part of a contingent of about 400 volunteers who had left Galway for El Ferrol, a naval base on the Spanish Galician coast. The voyage was extremely rough and many of the volunteers were miserably seasick.

O'Duffy had travelled with an earlier group which came via Liverpool and Lisbon. In his descriptions the trip had been immensely successful, with Spanish lessons during the day and Irish sing-songs at night. In Lisbon they had been greeted by three Irish priests and the entire Irish community and had spent a day sightseeing and visiting sacred relics. The next day, after lunch and having been blessed at Mass in the Irish Church in Lisbon, the group had taken the train to Badajoz where they were 'relieved finally to put their feet down on Spanish soil' (*ibid.*, p. 93). Francis McCullagh, a war correspondent and an Ulsterman, ran into the contingent at this time. Many wore the green shirts which O'Duffy had issued them before departure and they went about the town of Badajoz, in twos and threes. They were in very good spirits though 'intercourse with the locals was impossible' owing to the language. Later that night, the recruits got very drunk and broke out of the barracks and had to be 'quelled' by their officers.[67]

McCullagh was in Lisbon when the next group arrived and went to the dock with the Irish officer who had come from Spain to meet them. As the ship pulled into the harbour their voices rang out with 'Faith of our Fathers' and above the bulwarks were row after row of Irish faces. The Portuguese officials insisted that the men stay on board while their papers were processed and, although the ship pushed off from shore in order to prevent disembarkation, by evening the 'more reckless ones had jumped ashore, got drunk, fought the police and caused an awful scandal along the whole waterfront' (*ibid.*, p. 237). Finally Spanish lorries arrived and they were all loaded up for the drive to Spain.

MacKee's contingent in El Ferrol had made a difficult passage, crammed below decks on a German ship with Nazi-saluting German officers and flying a Nazi ensign. After disembarkation, the Irishmen travelled to Salamanca, where there was a civil reception with speeches and much reciprocal toasting in Spanish wine. Nigel Tangye, the air correspondent to the *Evening News*, watched with a 'lump in his throat' as the train with the Fighting Irish on board steamed into the station: 'lads bunched at every open window, with their arms outstretched in the fascist salute', they 'smiled rather self consciously' as the Spanish band played the

Irish national anthem.[68] When the recruits filed out onto the platform they looked to Tangye like the 'toughest-looking lot' he had ever seen, dressed in 'shabby suits and still shabbier overcoats'. Most were unshaven and without hats; some mere boys and others looked as though they could have served in the First World War. Those to whom Tangye spoke had 'no idea where they were going or what was to happen to them'. At the station they were issued with a plate and a spoon and marched off, 'arms once more outstretched in salute', to a nearby hall where they were served a meal (Tangye, pp. 55–6).

A member of the brigade, Peter Lawler, described their subsequent departure for Cáceres to Peter Kemp. After the men had drunk too much wine on empty stomachs at lunch, their officers had some difficulty loading them back on the train. As the band struck up the Spanish national anthem, the Spanish officers stood to attention and saluted beside the train. At the same time an Irish soldier, 'drunk as a coot', lent out the window and vomited down the neck of a general who remained ramrod straight and unmoving throughout.[69] Kemp took delight in this incident as he had little respect for O'Duffy and was scathing about his being accorded the rank of general when 'few generals can have had so little responsibility in proportion to their rank or so little sense of it' (*Ibid.*, p. 86). The Irishmen, however, Kemp considered were of a 'superb quality' and with better commanders could have made a fine battalion (*Ibid.*, p. 88).

The Irish were not well led. O'Duffy appointed his own associates to senior positions often only on the basis of their having a shared history in the Irish Right. The field commander was Major Patrick Dalton, a thin and wiry 40-year-old who had been in Sinn Fein with O'Duffy during the period of the Black and Tans. The second in command was Captain Sean Cunningham. Later, in the field, he and O'Duffy fell out and Cunningham so enraged the commander of the Foreign Legion that he ordered the Irishman's arrest. Tom Hyde, also a captain, had been a commander with O'Duffy in the Blueshirts movement. Captain Tom Gunning, the only Spanish speaker and O'Duffy's private secretary, was an ex-priest who had been a journalist on the London *Weekly Despatch*. An outspoken anti-Semite, Gunning, later in Berlin with Goebbels, joined John Amery and Jane Anderson, who also were denizens of franquista circles in Salamanca.[70] Two legionnaires, Lieutenants Michael Fitzpatrick and Gilbert Nangle, English Protestants whose real names, respectively, were Skeffington-Smyth and O'Brien, were transferred from the 5th Bandera of the Foreign Legion to the Irish Brigade. Neither was happy about the switch. Nangle, a Sandhurst graduate and ex-officer in the Indian Army, had previously served with the French Foreign Legion. Kemp notes that he suffered episodes of 'cafard'[71] or 'legionnaire blues', an ailment that was an occupational hazard among soldiers in the desert. When overcome with these episodes of mild insanity, they might shoot up their comrades or become stinking drunk.[72] Father Mulrean was the unit's chaplain, a bluff and cheerful Irishman, who trained in the diocesan seminary in Madrid and served in the parish of Gibraltar. He knew a great many people in the Spanish church hierarchy but McCullagh noted that his lack of discretion and interfering nature made him increasingly unpopular with the Irish men.[73]

From November 1936 until February 1937, the Irish Brigade remained in comfortable barracks in Cáceres honing their Spanish drills and practising ceremonial formations. The *bandera* was a regular feature on Sundays as they marched through the town to Mass at the Franciscan Fathers' church of Santo Domingo. Whatever the occasion, O'Duffy was pleased to show off his troops at ceremonial gatherings around Cáceres and the neighbouring region. General Franco inspected the unit as did the Foreign Legion's commander, Colonel Yagüe; O'Duffy relished such visits.

While they were in Cáceres there were various, predictable hiccoughs that arose from misunderstandings of language on both sides and the difficulties of having to work through interpreters and adjutants. The Irish considered that the Foreign Legion uniforms they were issued – serge outfits of German origin – were of poor quality and incomplete. They found the food cooked in too much oil for their taste and never acquired the sober Spanish habit of sitting for very long periods of time over a single drink. Instead, the Irish were prone to consume large amounts of cheap strong Spanish wine, to which they were unaccustomed. In consequence, when Irish soldiers were out on the town they were often drunk and rowdy. They were unimpressed with a bullfight that was put on for their entertainment. O'Duffy recalled that many Irishmen left early and most sympathized not with the matador but with the bull, the 'best sport on the field' (*Crusade in Spain*, p. 116). Nor did the Irish ever take to the regimen of the siesta.

Most painfully of all, the Irish suffered constantly from a lack of mail from home. O'Duffy eventually solved one of the problems by heading off to Lisbon and himself searching the warehouses on the docks until he found the undelivered crates of Irish mail. Overall, O'Duffy spent an enormous amount of time travelling about within Spain and back and forth to Ireland. The Badajoz headquarters of 'Felange', as he called it, gave him open access to their vehicle fleet and, with his bodyguards and coterie, he buzzed back and forth to his heart's content: Cáceres to Lisbon and off north to Burgos and Salamanca and back.[74]

During all this time, according to Seósamh O'Cuinneagáin who was one of them, ordinary soldiers pined for the front. At night 'the billets resounded to vociferous cries of "We want Madrid"'.[75] Finally orders came through that the Irish *bandera* was to move up to the Jarama front to the town of Ciempozuelos, north of Aranjuez about fifteen kilometres from Madrid. On 16 February 1937, the Irish marched through Cáceres to the station. The Dublin St Mary's Pipe Band played as they went with heads high, the Irish flag and the colours of the *bandera* – an orange Irish wolfhound on a ground of emerald green – fluttering proudly in front.

Almost immediately things began to go wrong. The train trip to Torrijos, from where they would march, took 26 hours instead of the expected five. The volunteers were told that it was because the driver was discovered to be a Republican spy with plans to blow up the train (O'Cuinneagáin, 'Jottings', p. 13). When they arrived at the disembarkation point there was no one to inform them which direction they should take to their next staging point at Valdemora. The accompanying Spaniards were unfamiliar with the area and it was not until a small boy had been found and agreed to show them the way that the unit moved off. With the delay, they arrived at Valdemora at midnight where no food awaited them. Equally uncomfortable was the discovery that they had been ordered to prepare to advance in the morning at 6 o'clock to occupy the first line of trenches at Ciempozuelos on the Jarama front.

O'Duffy was upset. First of all, he had understood that the Irish would be moved up to a second or third-line position while they became acclimatized to life at the front. It also seemed unreasonable to him that the men should be asked to turn out at dawn after they had passed such a strenuous day. In his inimitable fashion, O'Duffy jumped in the car and set off immediately for Navalcarnero to speak to General Orgaz, the overall field commander of the region. One can only imagine what Orgaz's response might have been but, when O'Duffy returned at 4 o'clock in the morning, the order was rescinded and an 11 o'clock departure planned for the next day. Exhausted, the men slept wherever they could with the sound of artillery thundering in the distance.

Meanwhile, O'Duffy hurried off in the car to Toledo to pay his respects to the military governor. By the time he came back the next day, the *bandera* had already moved off towards Ciempozuelos.[76]

The Irish left the main road for a side road that provided better cover. As they spread out in marching formation they saw troops advancing towards them. The Irish halted and, after a hurried conference among the officers, it was agreed that the oncoming troops were friendly and therefore Captain O'Sullivan, an interpreter and two Irish officers advanced to meet them. The Irish *bandera* remained about 400 yards behind. The other unit stopped, their rifles at the ready. Lieutenant Pedro Bove, the Spanish liaison officer, saluted and in Spanish identified his men as part of the Irish *bandera* of the *Tercio*. O'Sullivan advanced as well and began to speak in halting Spanish. Immediately, in O'Duffy's description which he gathered after the event, 'the opposing officer stepped back a pace, drew his revolver and fired point blank at Buve'. Even more extraordinarily, the shot missed. (O'Duffy, *Crusade*, p. 138). At this point, the other Irish officers drew their revolvers and fired, setting off a heavy fusillade from both sides. The exchange lasted for five minutes. Two officers and three men on the Irish side were killed, including Tom Hyde and, according to the Irish accounts, eleven, 40 or a half of the opposing soldiers lost their lives. It is an indication of their opponents' poor marksmanship that, in addition to the original failed shot at Buve, three of the other Irish group out in front, despite being in a close and direct line of fire, managed to scramble back to the safety of their own lines.

It was a mistake. The adversaries were Falangists from the Canary Islands and, like the Irish themselves, newly arrived at the battlefront. O'Duffy set off immediately to headquarters where he learnt that the first and second in command of the Canary Islanders had been killed and the remaining officers were on court martial. He was also gratified that Franco in person expressed his 'deep sympathy for the Irish losses' (O'Duffy, p. 140). Legionnaire O'Cuinneagáin, who was on the spot, was convinced that it was the 'thread-bare garments' on issue to the Irish which made them look different from the rest of the Nationalist forces and had caused their own side to 'mistake them for the Reds' (O'Cuinneagáin, p. 3). Whatever the reason, it was a disheartening start, as O'Cuinneagáin observed, to have 'splendid men' fatally wounded before they had even reached enemy lines (*ibid.*, p. 3).

O'Duffy took the Irish bodies back to Cáceres for burial and was glad to note that it was the largest funeral that had ever been held in that town.

In the highest compliment to them, O'Duffy described them as 'brave and popular with their comrades' (O'Duffy, p. 140). The bodies were interred in ceremonial sepulchres in the church of Santo Domingo.

Meanwhile, at Ciempozuelos the Irish had relieved a mixed platoon of Spaniards and Moors who had cleared out the town in ferocious fighting. When the Irish moved in, the Jarama front was quiet, though they faced the onerous duty of burying great mounds of bodies that lay scattered around the town. The Irish claimed that, because the Spaniards had not fought in the First World War, they knew little about digging trenches, which were too shallow and not constructed in zig-zag patterns for better protection. Their worst irritation, however, were the lice, which they attributed to the Moors, the last inhabitants. And it rained constantly until the dugouts and trenches were flooded. The men, perforce, were in wet clothes and as their boots were without waterproofing their feet constantly squelched in the mud and water that filled their boots. High on the meseta, Pozuelos at night was bitterly cold. Dozens of men came down with rheumatism, pleurisy and flu. The commander, Patrick Dalton, was struck with a severe attack of sciatica that could not be relieved with morphia and forced him to go to Lisbon for treatment and eventually home to Dublin. According to MacKee, the men began to 'growl about their grievances' and question why they had come to such a God-forsaken place (*Franco Soldier*, p. 25).

On 13 March they were ordered to move up closer to the line of fire, to take the village of Titulcia. Dalton had left by this time and O'Duffy was travelling somewhere away from the front. When the unit set off they faced a heavy barrage of fire from rifles, machine-guns and artillery. The forward line began to waver, then panic and fall back. Major Diarmuid O'Sullivan, who was now in command, ordered a retreat and the men 'ran like hares' (*ibid.*, p. 27). O'Duffy's memoirs claim that he was present when the retreat took place, but it is not clear what was the exact sequence. He also states, very dramatically, that, as they were being heavily shelled, the stretcher bearers were frantically bringing back the wounded. O'Duffy estimated that the unit would lose 'two to three hundred men'. But, in contradiction, when he had gone closer to look for himself, he had been 'delighted to find that there had been no fatal casualties' and only a few wounded (O'Duffy, p. 155). MacKee, who was also present, states that three men went down, mortally wounded, along with other casualties.

The unit was pulled back to Ciempozuelos. The next day, however, the order came down again that the Irish were to move up and man the same line. O'Duffy refused the directive. He gave orders that the men were to remain at the base while he set off to field headquarters, fifteen miles away. McCullagh, who was not present, claims he heard that Orgaz refused to give the order that the Irish Brigade could move to another place and offered only to send them back to Cáceres. In O'Duffy's version, a week later at Navalcarnero, Franco agreed with the Irish general that he had done the right thing to refuse to send his men back to Titulcia.

Whatever the reason, the Irish *bandera* was moved very soon to the La Marañosa sector. It was warmer though intermittently under fire. According to MacKee, discontent among the men increased. More and more of them appeared on sick parade. O'Duffy records at least 150 in one day, which he attributed to the after-effects of their spell in the wet trenches at Ciempozuelos. When McCullagh visited the Irish *bandera* he noted that there were now a number of Spanish officers appointed to the command and it had 'created an impossible situation that could not last' (McCullagh, *Franco's Spain*, p. 297).

McGarry and Stradling provide detail of the manoeuvres between Franco, Yagüe and the Free State's diplomatic envoy from de Valéra. All of them were anxious to be rid of O'Duffy. Yagüe visited the Irish camp, presumably in shock that a *bandera* had retreated in combat and dared to disobey an order to go forward. The commander of the Foreign Legion found the Irish unit in disarray, with soldiers drunk at their posts, and recommended the immediate dissolution of the *bandera* and the dispersal of Irish soldiers throughout the Legion. After an altercation with the Irish commander, O'Cunningham, who in the heat of the moment threatened to desert to the Republic, Yagüe placed him under arrest. While O'Duffy was away, Franco visited the Irish at the front and interviewed Irish and Spanish officers. On 14 April 1937, the Caudillo wrote a highly critical report to O'Duffy which listed, among other things, the *bandera's* 'lack of professional officers' and the general 'limitation of the military contribution' that the Irish had made overall.[77]

From MacKee's vantage point, the incident which brought to an end the Irish enthusiasm for Franco's Spain was quite different. The Irish ordinary volunteers had been greatly disturbed when Moorish troops executed prisoners from a captured Republican armoured train. MacKee notes that at the time the Irish were near a unit of British International Brigaders and often in the clear evening air the sounds of cockney voices wafted over the Irish lines. Presumably the fact that the executed could have been countrymen added poignancy to the deaths. In any event, as a consequence, Irish calls to return home became more insistent. Again, according to MacKee, it was at this time that O'Duffy produced the fiction of the six-month enlistment. It enabled him to withdraw the volunteers from Spain without losing face. He claimed that the Irish had fulfilled their contracts and were now free to elect to remain for another tour of duty in Spain, or return home.

The 15th Bandera returned to Cáceres and, almost unanimously, voted to return to Ireland. After some minor resistance by officers, who were anxious to retain their firearms, the Nationalists disarmed the Irish *bandera* and, provided with new civilian clothes, the Irish embarked by train to Lisbon on 17 June 1937 and then by ship to Dublin. In the 1938 Foreign Legion muster of foreign volunteers in Spain, there are five legionnaires identified as of Irish nationality.[78] At least three of them are from the original 15th Bandera.

More than six hundred Irish soldiers arrived home on the '*Mozambique*' on 21 June and, many wearing their Spanish Foreign Legion uniforms, marched through Dublin. Half of them split off to head in a separate parade. The French chargé d'affaires, François Brière, wrote to Delbos, the Foreign Minister in Paris, that a large Irish crowd turned out to see the men but greeted them in silence.[79] Brière explained the lack of enthusiasm as a function of 'Irish psychology'. They were a 'bellicose people' and were disappointed that O'Duffy and his men had not stayed in Spain and seen it out to the end. He also noted that, just beneath the surface of religiousness that O'Duffy affected, lay real personal ambition.

Conclusion

Franco's individual volunteers had a good deal in common. They were young, restless and avid for new experiences and their tendency to the Right meant that between 1936 and 1939 they headed to Franco's Spain. The two Protestants among them were perhaps less comfortable in an anti-Masonic, anti-Protestant franquista Spain than were their English-speaking Catholic comrades. The four, however, went to Spain because they favoured Franco over the Republic and because they were at a stage in their lives when they were free to quit home responsibilities and take off on what promised to be a great adventure.

It is hard to estimate their military contribution. War is a collective effort in which it is difficult to weigh up what difference an individual's participation alone may make. In the examples here, three of the four English-speakers were injured and spent a good deal of time in hospital, which perhaps suggests that they were in the thick of combat. Certainly it is possible to read their sojourn as having assisted Franco's victory. Patriarca, flying the planes that brought Franco's African forces to the mainland, certainly aided Franco in a significant manner as, perhaps in a less spectacular way, did Thomas, Bull and Kemp.

By contrast, it would be hard to argue that the Irish Brigade made a large practical contribution to Franco's military victory. As evidence of Catholic support outside Spain they were important, even though tight censorship may have muted the impact. At this time Franco was concerned about the workings of the Non-Intervention Committee and its ramifications on a Nationalist military victory. As we shall see with the *bandera* of the French Juana de Arco, the sequence of the committee's deliberations in London had a direct impact on the reception of foreigners in Nationalist Spain. In the Irish case, a strong impulse to publicize the support provided to *franquista* Spain by another Catholic country was counteracted by the equally powerful impulse to avoid giving any quarter to those who criticized Nationalist Spain about German and Italian involvement.

There is no doubt that Franco spent much more on maintaining the Irish Brigade in Spain than he ever received back, despite the collections taken up in parish churches throughout the country by the United Christian Crusade. These produced a few ambulances, a couple of nurses and the occasional visit from Patrick Belton and the movement's publicist, Aileen O'Brien.

Franco, with his customary wiliness, saw at first that O'Duffy could help Nationalist Spain and it was the anticipation of this outcome, presumably, that fostered the accommodating manner in which Franco originally treated O'Duffy. The Irish *bandera* were treated far more leniently and spent longer in preparation for combat than did other foreign volunteers in Nationalist Spain.

The leader of the Irish, Eoin O'Duffy, on the other hand, gained a considerable benefit from his involvement with Nationalist Spain. He was able to present himself as an important international figure on the edges of the European Right. With his continuous travel, O'Duffy was seen at all sorts of important gatherings: at the Grand Hotel in Salamanca or the Londres y Norte in Burgos and with people of importance in Paris,

London and Dublin. Without the Irish Brigade, O'Duffy would never have been able to pull this off because, by 1936, the Blueshirt movement was on the ebb and with it he faced an inevitable slide into obscurity.

Franco supported the Irish until it was apparent that they were not good soldiers: under fire they were unreliable and disobedient. When this happened, to Franco the soldier, the Irish and the long Catholic tradition they shared with Spaniards became irrelevant. They were simply soldiers to be disciplined and, if that failed, to be got rid of as fast as possible.

Notes

1 José E. Alvarez, *The Betrothed of Death: The Spanish Foreign Legion during the Rif Rebellion, 1920–1927*, (Westport, CT: Greenwood Press, 2001), p. 16.

2 Frank Thomas, *Brother against Brother: Experiences of a British Volunteer in the Spanish Civil War*, edited by Robert Stradling (Phoenix Mill: Sutton Publishing, 1998), p. 53; André Nicolas, on assignment for the French fascist paper, *Je Suis Partout*, divided the foreigners in the Spanish Foreign Legion he met into classic adventurer-types and those who had enlisted during the Spanish Civil War because of political beliefs. See 'La Guerre de Libération Espagnole', *Je Suis Partout*, No. 305, 26 September 1936. Franco himself referred to foreigners in the Legion as 'shipwrecked from life', quoted in Herbert L. Mathews, *Half of Spain Died: A Reappraisal of the Spanish Civil War* (New York: Charles Scribner's Sons, 1973), p. 83.

3 Edwin Rolfe, *The Lincoln Battalion* (New York: Random House, 1939), quoted in Michael Jackson, *Fallen Sparrows: The International Brigades in the Spanish Civil War* (Philadelphia: American Philosophical Society, 1994), [Memoirs Vol. 212], p. 53. Jackson's discussion of the explanations of the motivation of the International Brigaders is highly relevant to Franco's volunteers, pp. 36–59.

4 I am grateful to Daniele Patriarca in Naples for giving me access to some of his father's papers; to Enzo Pan, for facilitating the exchange; and for the assistance of the American consul in Naples, William A. Muller, and Anna Merola and John Carver Edwards.

5 *La 'Non intervention' dans les affaires d'Espagne. Documents publiés par le Gouvernement de la République Espagnole* [Valencia, 1936], pp. 22–3.

6 Vincent Patriarca, 'Two wars in one year', *American Cavalcade*, May 1937, p. 9. See also his 'Going to the bullfight', *American Cavalcade*, June 1937, pp. 105–11; and the Annexes to 'Déclaration faite par le sargent italien Vicenzo Patriarca, fait prisonnier le 13 septembre', *Documents publiés*, p. 22; National Archives, Washington, 852.00/3466, American Embassy Madrid, 21 September 1936, 'Transmitting documents from the Spanish Foreign Office regarding alleged military assistance of German, Italian and Portuguese Government to Spanish

Rebels'; and personal correspondence with Daniele Patriarca, Naples, 10 June 1998.

7 For the pre-war period, see Robert Wohl, *A Passion for Wings: Aviation and the Western Imagination 1908–1918* (New Haven: Yale University Press, 1994). For between the wars, see Evelyn Waugh's description in *Labels: A Mediterranean Journal* (Middlesex: Penguin Books, [1930] 1985), pp. 9–10. Alan Moorehead vividly describes the air aces he knew in North Africa in the Second World War who lived to fly and were 'restless and nervous when grounded for a day and therefore volunteered for every flight', *Mediterranean Front* (London: Hamish Hamilton, 1941), p. 68.

8 Bellville told Peter Kemp the story of his life when the two first met in Burgos in August 1936. See Kemp, *Mine Were of Trouble* (London: Cassell, 1957), pp. 15–16.

9 Virginia Cowles flew into Nationalist Spain with Bellville in his two-seater and was detained for 24 hours. See her *Looking for Trouble* (London: Hamish Hamilton, 1941), pp. 65–7; p. 76; pp. 99–100.

10 *New York Times*, 6 August 1936; 8 August 1936. Frances Davis was in the same convoy; see *My Shadow in the Sun* (New York: Carrick & Evans, 1940), pp. 147–9.

11 Alan Dick, *Inside Story* (London: George Allen & Unwin, 1943), pp. 150–2.

12 Dick, *Inside Story*, p. 138. See as well, John Carver Edwards, *Airmen Without Portfolio: US Mercenaries in Civil War Spain* (Westport, CT: Praeger, 1997), p. 111.

13 *New York Times*, 11 December 1936, p. 22.

14 *Foreign Relations of the United States Diplomatic Papers 1936 Volume II Europe* (Washington: Government Printing Office, 1954), Cordell Hull, 12 October 1936, p. 736.

15 National Archives Washington, 'Document File Note, Madrid, 15 October 1936 to The Secretary of State, Washington', United States Government, Spain, Internal Affairs, LM 74 852.00/3495; *Foreign Relations of the United States Diplomatic Papers 1936 Volume II Europe*, Hull, 12 October 1936, Patriarca, Vincent J/ 17:Telegram, p. 735–6; Wendelin, Patriarca J/ 18: Telegram, 13 October 1936, pp. 736–7; Wendelin, Patriarca Vincent J/ 30: Telegram, 6 November 1936, pp. 752–3.

16 H. Edward Knoblaugh, *Correspondent in Spain* (London: Sheed & Ward, 1937), pp. 114–15. See also Henry Buckley, *Life and Death of the Spanish Republic* (London: Hamish Hamilton, 1940), p. 249.

17 *New York Times*, 11 December 1936; *New York Herald Tribune*, 11 December 1936.

18 Vincent Patriarca, 'Going to the bullfight', *American Cavalcade*, June 1937, p. 111.

19 Frank Thomas, 'Spanish *Legionario*: a professional soldier in Spain', in *Brother against Brother: Experiences of a British Volunteer in the Spanish Civil War*, edited by Robert Stradling (Phoenix Mill: Sutton Publishing, 1998), pp. 35–153. The diary which Thomas kept in Spain was lost during the war; however, immediately on his

return home, he wrote his recollections of the Spanish Civil War with a view to their being published. See Robert Stradling's Introduction, pp. 16–20.

20 Francis Hywel, *Miners against Fascism: Wales and the Spanish Civil War* (London: Lawrence & Wishart, 1984).

21 See Robert Stradling's 'Introduction', *Brother against Brother*, p. 4.

22 *Western Mail and South Wales News*, 7 November 1936, quoted in 'Introduction', *Brother against Brother*, p. 5.

23 Michael Seidman has evoked the everyday way of life at the front in 'Frentes en calma de la guerra civil', *Historia Social*, No. 27 (1997), pp. 37–59.

24 See María Rosa de Madariaga, 'The intervention of the Moroccan troops in the Spanish Civil War: a reconsideration', *European History Quarterly*, 22 (1) (1992), pp. 67–97.

25 Verle B. Johnston, 'Battle of Jarama'. in James W. Cortada (ed.), *Historical Dictionary of the Spanish Civil War 1936–1939* (Westport, CT: Greenwood Press, 1982), pp. 276–7.

26 In the enlistment papers, the place of birth is 'Sidney in the United States of America'; on final discharge it is the 'province of USA, Australia' and a travel pass gives Bull permission to return to his 'residence in Barcelona'; the last word has been carefully crossed out and 'Australia' written over in the same hand. Servicio Histórico Militar, Comandancia General de Ceuta, Tercio Duque de Alba 2o de la Legión, Bull Family Papers; and Servicio Histórico Militar, Comandancia General de Ceuta, Tercio Duque de Alba 2o de La Legión, 530/SHMAB Número 1365 fecha 25. Nugent Bull 'Comisíon Liquidadora'.

27 I am indebted to family members Mrs Joan Harvey-Smith and Dr Anthony Bull, Mrs Mary Plant and Mr Clarrie Cullen QC and Father Barry for recollections and family papers. Mr Barry O'Neill kindly provided access to the family papers at W. N. Bull Pty. Ltd., Newtown, Sydney, and Brother Michael Naughton, the archivist at St Joseph's College, Hunter's Hill, to the school's archives.

28 Mr Clarrie Cullen QC, Interview, November 1983.

29 *Catholic Freeman's Journal*, the *Advocate* and the *Australian Catholic Truth Record* between 1931 and 1939 carried weekly news on Spain, via the Vatican. In 1931, and particularly in 1936, there were articles almost every week documenting the burning of Spanish churches, while on facing pages readers were urged to donate to school building projects. See, as well, *Australian Catholic Truth Society Record*, 30 Dec. 1936, No. 85, 'For God and Spain. The truth about the Spanish war'; 10 Dec. 1936, No. 83, 'The truth about Freemasonry all over the world and including Spain'; *Australian Catholic Truth Society*, 30 May 1938, No. 136, 'What to read. Books for discussion groups. The Spanish Civil War: Allison Peers; McNeil Moss and Knoblaugh'.

30 I am grateful to Bob Gould for this information.

31 The glamorous funeral cortège, with the attendants in dazzling white and the hearse and cars sprayed to match, appeared at a state funeral. Much to his

mother's horror, Bull's funeral innovations made front-page news. Joan Harvey-Smith, Interview, November 1983.

32 I am grateful to Mr Clarrie Cullen QC for sharing his recollections of Nugent Bull.

33 The marching song of the Spanish Legion begins 'Nosotros somos los novios de la muerte/ we are the bridegrooms of death'. See Judith Keene, 'An Antipodean bridegroom of death: an Australian with Franco's forces in the Spanish Civil War', *Royal Australian Historical Society Journal*, 70, Part 4 (April 1985), pp. 251–69.

34 N. Bull to Brother Gerard, Zaragoza, 16 March 1938, St Joseph's College Archive (SJCA).

35 SHM Documentación D. Joseph Bull Nugent, 530/SHMAB 5/Archivo 1310.

36 N. Bull to Brother Gerard, Baños de Montemayor, 1 May 1938, SJCA.

37 *Ibid.*

38 N. Bull to Brother Gerard, Tremp, Catalonia, 11 December 1938, SJCA.

39 *Ibid.*

40 N. Bull to Brother Gerard, Baños de Montemayor, Cáceres, 1 May 1938, SJCA.

41 N. Bull to Brother Gerard, Tremp, Catalonia, 11 December 1938, SJCA.

42 N. Bull to Greg Bull, London, 4 September 1939; 25 September 1939, Bull Papers, W. N. Bull Pty. Ltd., Newtown, Sydney.

43 N. Bull to Greg Bull, Mildenhall, 3 September 1940, Bull Papers.

44 Air Commodore in Charge of Records to W. G. Bull, Ruislip, Middlesex, 10 January 1941.

45 Peter Kemp, *Mine Were of Trouble* (London: Cassell, 1957). See also Imperial War Museum, Department of Sound Records, British Participation in the Spanish Civil War, 1936–1939, Acc. No. 009769/3. Colonel P. M. M. M. Kemp, DSO MA; and his *No Colours or Crest* (London: Cassell, 1958), for Spain, particularly pp. 1–12; and 'Peter Kemp', in Philip Toynbee (ed.), *The Distant Drum: Reflections on the Spanish Civil War* (London: Sidgwick & Jackson, 1976), pp. 67–74.

46 Kemp, *Mine Were of Trouble*, p. 8.

47 For Kemp's recollections of his initial enlistment with the Carlist, see Imperial War Museum, Dept. of Sound Records, Acc. No. 009769/3 Colonel P. M. Kemp, pp. 7–13; and *Mine Were of Trouble*, pp. 4–17; and 'Peter Kemp', in *The Distant Drum*, pp. 67–9.

48 Karl Robson describes this exotic figure in 'With Franco in Spain', in Wilfrid Hindle (ed.), *Foreign Correspondent: Personal Adventures Abroad in Search of the News by Twelve British Journalists* (London: George Harrap, 1939), pp. 265–6.

49 *New York Times*, 13 December 1936; see also *Mine Were of Trouble*, pp. 144–5, pp. 198–9.

50 See also Chapter 2, pp. 56–7.

51 Imperial War Museum, Acc. No. 009769/3, p. 27.

52 'Drawn by the sound of guns: survivors: a profile of Peter Kemp, veteran of many wars', *Spectator*, 17 August 1985, pp. 14–15.

53 See for example, J. Bowyer Bell, 'Ireland and the Spanish Civil War, 1936–1939',

Studia Hibernica, **9** (1969), pp. 137–63; Michael McInerney, *Peadar O'Donnell: Irish Social Rebel* (Dublin: The O'Brien Press, 1974), pp. 153–70; Maurice Manning, *The Blueshirts* (2nd edn., Dublin: Gill and MacMillan, 1987); and Mike Cronin, *The Blueshirts and Irish Politics* (Dublin: Four Courts Press, 1997).

54 Mike Cronin, 'The Blueshirt movement 1932–5: Ireland's fascists?', *Journal of Contemporary History*, **30** (1995), p. 315.

55 Sir Robert Hodgson, *Spain Resurgent* (London: Hutchinson, 1953), pp. 70–1.

56 Georges Oudard, *Chemises noires, brunes, vertes en Espagne* (Paris: Librairie Plon, 1938), p. 53.

57 Cronin, 'The Blueshirt movement', p. 320.

58 Fearghal McGarry, *Irish Politics and the Spanish Civil War* (Cork: Cork University Press, 1999); Robert Stradling, *The Irish and the Spanish Civil War 1936–39: Crusades in Conflict* (Manchester: Mandolin, 1999); and his 'Franco's Irish Volunteers', *History Today*, **45** (11 March 1995), pp. 40–7.

59 Stradling, 'Franco's Irish Volunteers', p. 40.

60 *Ibid.*, pp. 41–2.

61 See in particular his 'Epilogue', *Irish Politics and the Spanish Civil War*, pp. 234–43.

62 See, for example, Eoin O'Duffy, *Crusade in Spain* (Clonskeagh: Browne and Nolan, 1938), pp. 1–3, 10; and Seamus MacKee, *I Was a Franco Soldier* (London: United Editorial Ltd., 1938), p. 14.

63 Sir Percival Phillips of *The Daily Telegraph*, quoted in Captain Francis McCullagh, *In Franco's Spain: Being the Experiences of an Irish War-Correspondent During the Great Civil War Which Began in 1936* (London: Burns, Oates & Washbourne, 1937), p. 150.

64 See Michael Ledeen, *Universal Fascism: The Theory and Practice of the Fascist International, 1928–36* (New York: Howard Fertig, 1972), p. 113. See also the discussion in Chapter 4.

65 Stradling, *The Irish and the Spanish Civil War*, pp. 26–9.

66 MacKee, *I Was a Franco Soldier*, p. 6. MacKee was disillusioned with Spain and it is possible that the supporters of the Spanish Republic funded the publication of his story; however, the nuts and bolts of the information he provides about himself and his time in Spain are probably true, despite the antagonism that he displays latterly towards O'Duffy and Franco.

67 McCullagh, *In Franco's Spain*, p. 230.

68 Nigel Tangye, *Red, White and Spain* (London: Rich & Cowan, 1937), pp. 52–3.

69 Kemp, *Mine Were of Trouble*, p. 87.

70 Judith Keene, in preparation.

71 Kemp, *Mine Were of Trouble*, p. 109.

72 See John Whitaker, *Fear Came on Europe* (London: Hamish Hamilton, 1937), p. 45; and Kemp, *No Colours or Crest*, p. 75.

73 McCullagh, *In Franco's Spain*, p. 227.

74 See McCullagh, *In Franco's Spain*, Chs 20 to 25, for his contacts with the Irish Brigade.

75 Seósamh O'Cuinneagáin, 'The jottings of an Irish legionary in 1938', *The Echo* (Enniscorthy), Marx Memorial Library, Clerkenwell Green, Box A–1, File A/10, p. 10. See also Seósamh O Cuinneagáin, 'Saga of the Irish brigade in Spain (November 1936 to June 1937)' (Enniscorthy: Dunegin Print), Box A–1, File A/10, and Box A–1, File A/11.

76 MacKee, *I Was a Franco Soldier*, pp. 22–9, O'Cuinneagáin, 'The jottings of an Irish legionary', pp. 2–25; and O'Duffy, *Crusade in Spain*, pp. 133–64, all provide accounts of the exchange of fire on the road, O'Duffy's at second hand as it occurred just before he arrived, and of the subsequent days at Ciempozuelos and La Marañosa sector.

77 See Yagüe to Franco, 29 March 1937, quoted in Stradling, *The Irish and the Spanish Civil War*, p. 230, Note 37; and McGarry, *Irish Politics and the Spanish Civil War* (Cork UP, 1999), p. 268, note 167.

78 S H M Ávila, 2/168/30/5, Cuartel General del Generalísimo-Estado Mayor, Sección 1. 'Secreto. Despacho número 15.773 Relacionado con el número de extranjeros alistados a la Legión antes y después de iniciado el Glorioso Movimiento Nacional. Desp 13331. Relación nominal del personal extranjero filiado en la Legión a partir de la iniciación del Glorioso Movimiento Nacional, con indicación de la nacionalidad de cada uno, 21–8–1938'. They are 'Dailhe' V. Higgins, David O'Dea, 'Jhon' Madden, 'Andrés' O'Toole and 'Jhon' MacGuire.

79 See Ministère des Affaires Étrangères. Direction des Affaires Politiques et Commerciales. Espagne. Guerre Civile. Volontaires, 1937 juillet–novembre. 'Dublin le 3 juillet 1937, Chargé d'Affaires de France à Dublin.' The French Foreign Office kept close tabs on events in Ireland relating to Franco's volunteers as part of tracking non-intervention. The series above and 'Guerre Civile d'Espagne les Puissances, Irlande', contain a good number of letters and notes that relate to Franco's Irish volunteers.

CHAPTER 4

Spectators at their own drama: Franco's French volunteers

Introduction

In January 1937 the conservative French daily, *Echo de Paris*, raised a subscription to honour General Moscardó, the hero of the Alcázar, with a suitably inscribed ceremonial sword to mark the lifting of the siege.[1] There was money left over to strike a commemorative medal to present to the thousand or so people who had waited out the siege underground with him. A great ceremony was planned for Easter 1937 within the ruins of the Alcázar and several hundred French 'Catholics and patriots' prepared to make the pilgrimage to Toledo. They included the Catholic activist, Henry de Kérillis, and the *Echo*'s editor, Henry Bordeaux.

The leader of the delegation was General Edouard de Curières de Castelnau, the founder of the Fédération Nationale Catholique, which represented a broad strand of Franco's French supporters. A member of the nobility and father of twelve, Castelnau had fought in the Franco-Prussian War and the First World War, losing three sons in the latter. In addition, and to a remarkable degree, Castelnau was a chauvinist and xenophobe. Fiercely anti-German, he believed fervently as well that France was threatened by the insidious machinations of world Jewry and Freemasonry.[2] In his view, the Civil War in Spain pitted 'Western civilization against Muscovite barbarism'.[3]

In March, just as plans for the Toledo ceremony were well under way, the Socialist Minister of the Interior, Roger Salengro, refused to grant visas to the delegation and the expedition fell through. In Catholic and right-wing circles there was a great outcry. The minister's action, ostensibly to calm domestic agitation in France over the Spanish Civil War, was derided as further proof of the corruption of the 'Frente Crapular', to use Castelnau's scathing sobriquet.[4]

Politics under the Popular Front, according to Julian Jackson, had 'reached a level of passion unparalleled since the Dreyfus Affair'.[5] The Civil War across the border further exacerbated the febrile atmosphere of French public life. The similarities between Spain and France in 1936 were there for all to see. Both nations were governed by newly elected Popular Fronts which had been brought to office on the promise of large-scale social reform. On both sides of the Pyrenees, government and opposition had attracted almost equal electoral support. Similarly, in both places the Popular Front's enemies comprised religious Catholics, the majority of middle-class political parties and a good slice of the upper ranks of the military. The significant difference, of course, was that the Civil War that simmered below the surface in both countries had been brought to a head in Spain with the generals' *pronunciamento*. In France the opposition to the Popular Front watched the Spanish Civil War like 'spectators at their own drama'.[6]

This chapter examines the chequered history of the Joan of Arc company, a unit of French volunteers in Nationalist Spain during the Civil War. Because Franco was always at pains to downplay the contribution of foreigners to the Nationalist military effort, records of the French volunteers are scarce. There are, however, a few categories of sources that are useful. Spanish military records provide details of enlistments and trace the fluctuating progress of the Bandera Juana de Arco.[7] There are also French travel writings, which were produced to garner support for Franco's cause, much as we have seen with the English narratives in Chapter 2. As they shuttled about the front in delegations led by the Nationalist Press and Propaganda Department, foreign journalists and travellers were always delighted to catch sight of a countryman in Spanish uniform. In these pro-Franco narratives, the volunteers are depicted as soldierly males going about the admirable business of making war on the Spanish Republic. The volunteers, themselves, are usually clear in expressing their own ideological reasons for coming to Spain. Invariably, they are wholehearted supporters of Franco.

The individual recollections of Frenchmen, by contrast, often show daily life in Nationalist Spain in an ambiguous light. And an even less rosy depiction emerges from the French diplomatic correspondence which tracks the French ambassador's mostly unsuccessful efforts to repatriate his countrymen who were disillusioned with their enlistment in Nationalist Spain. These sources suggest that there was a high level of Francophobia within insurgent territory. Unlike the effusive Nationalist welcomes for leaders of the French Right, ordinary French civilians and regular soldiers were often treated very harshly.

For good or ill, Francoism and the Spanish Civil War was a significant marker in the political evolution of the French Right. In the recent spate of memoirs of Frenchmen who fought with Hitler on the Eastern Front, for example, many recall the Spanish Civil War as a critical event in their own political development. The collapse of the Soviet Union has spurred many recollections, suggesting as it does a vindication of anti-Soviet politics 60 years ago. As well, the passage of time has blurred the sharp postwar division between resisters and collaborators and the recent surge of the New Right may have prompted these old fascists to sniff the wind. Whatever the reason, it is notable that many were volunteers for Franco or saw Francoism and the Spanish Civil War as the central example in their own political evolution towards fascism.

The French volunteers in Spain were drawn from a range of extreme Right groups and their Spanish experiences are inextricably bound up with the fortunes of the French groups from which they came. In Spain, the volunteers' common objectives often masked the deep political differences between them. When soldiers in the Joan of Arc company identified their political affiliations, which happened not infrequently, they replicated the range of the extreme Right in France. In the same way, they were drawn by the fascist undertow that propelled many reactionary French rightwards in the 1930s.[8] Those who were disaffected with parliamentary politics and fearful of the Left looked to Franco and Nationalist Spain as an example of a strong leader successfully defeating the Left and replacing the 'decadence' of a parliamentary republic with an authoritarian and nationalistic state. The narrative of the Joan of Arc brigade and the social milieu which supported it, therefore, constitute a small but important fragment of the larger history of the French Right in the 1930s.

France and the international political context

Before 1936, the internal affairs of its southern neighbour carried no great importance in France. Once the Spanish Civil War began, however, France was the nation most closely affected. France had large commercial interests on the Iberian Peninsula. Geographically, Spain always had the potential to impinge on France's communication with its African colonial empire. As well, the war had immediate ramifications on France's internal politics and the country's position in international affairs.

Of all the major powers after the First World War, France had the largest investment in binding Germany to the conditions of the Versailles Treaty. In the 1920s, France had been the Great Power providing the linchpin that held together the network of alliances which constituted the Little Entente of Yugoslavia, Czechoslovakia and Romania. As well, France worked closely with Poland, a nation whose existence similarly depended upon the maintenance of the postwar settlement.

By the mid-1930s, a new wind had blown through European politics. Mussolini's ebullient fascism in Italy and the Nazi take-over in Germany skewed international affairs. Even before 1933 there had been a shift in the pattern of international trade in central and south-eastern Europe as the agrarian economies in these areas were increasingly linked into the orbit of German foreign trade.[9] As a consequence, Hungary, Romania and Yugoslavia began to gravitate away from France and towards Italy and Germany. In turn, from 1933 France attempted to juggle the contradictory foreign policy of trying 'to woo and resist' Germany at the same time.[10] Given the inherent problems, it is not surprising that the policy failed. France also attempted to shore up the crumbling eastern wall of the foreign policy edifice by paying more attention to the Soviet Union. France sponsored the Soviet Union's entry into the League of Nations and in 1935 the two nations signed the Franco-Soviet military pact.

All along, French diplomats worked hard to maintain a continuity of ties with France's key ally, Britain.[11] It was often more easily said than done, given British diffidence towards European involvement and what, until recently, has been seen as a notorious lack of interest in foreign affairs by Stanley Baldwin, the Prime Minister from 1935–37.[12] His successor, Neville Chamberlain, was equally reluctant to side with France, preferring at all costs to play the field in order to prevent European politics separating into two opposing blocs.

When Hitler remilitarized the Rhineland in March 1936, it appeared that France's worst foreign policy fears had been realized. The Versailles order, or the rejigged Locarno version of it, was dead. Britain had immediately poured cold water on any suggestion of military intervention. With Germany in occupation of the Rhineland, France's alliances in Eastern Europe were rendered outdated and remote.

The system of alliances was further strained in July 1986 when the Civil War began in the Spain. The Spanish Foreign Minister immediately appealed to France for planes and equipment.[13] Initially the cabinet agreed. By the end of July, however, faced with British opposition abroad and a huge public outcry on the Right at home when details were leaked to the press, French Socialist leaders backed away from outright support. Afterwards and somewhat uneasily, France fell into line with the arrangements for a Non-Intervention Committee to be chaired by Britain.

The primacy of Britain in French foreign policy meant that Blum could not afford to tack too far outside the wake of British foreign policy.[14] Nor could the Socialists become unhooked within the Popular Front from their Radical allies, a party entirely opposed to intervention in Spain. The stance caused some heartache, particularly to Léon Blum, Roger Salengro and Pierre Cot, the latter a Radical who shared the political instincts of the other two for supplying the Spanish Republic. As Blum explained at a rally of the Seine Federation of the Socialist Party, two days after the fall of Irún, he was appalled at the conflict in Spain but was doing his best to avoid triggering a situation that would embroil all of Europe in war.[15] From the start to the finish of the Spanish Civil War, French policy carefully attempted to remain in step with Britain while playing a balancing act at home.

It is a commonplace that the key to understanding foreign policy is often to be found in domestic politics. In France the strains within French domestic politics, what has been described as a near civil war between Left and Right in the 1930s, sowed an indecisiveness into French foreign policy. The conflict in Spain brought these tensions even further to the fore as the Iberian Peninsula offered the example to both Left and Right of what next awaited France.

French domestic politics

From the very beginning the French Right opposed any French involvement to assist the Spanish government, even though it was legal for the French to intervene, and the Spaniards had previously made a substantial order of French aircraft. The pro-Franco Spanish military attaché in Paris, General Antonio Barroso, leaked information to the newspapers, *Echo de Paris* and *L'Action française*, warning that the French cabinet was discussing ways to assist the Spanish Republic. In one of the first commentaries on the Spanish Civil War, the Catholic intellectual, François Mauriac, warned Blum that if he 'collaborated in the massacre of the Peninsula' it would mean that France was governed not by 'statesmen but by gang leaders acting under the order of the International of Hatred'.[16] The dire threats against intervention did not stop Frenchmen enlisting on both sides.

After 6 February 1934 and the great demonstrations provoked by the

Stavisky affair, the French Right had undergone a form of 'fascist impregnation',[17] manifested in escalating street violence and political disorder.[18] In a series of ugly incidents, one of the most disturbing was an attack on 13 February 1936 on Léon Blum as he was travelling home to lunch from the National Assembly. While his car was held up crossing the Boulevard Saint Michel by the tail of a funeral procession for a leading intellectual of the Action Française, the crowd recognized the passenger and began shouting 'Death to Blum' and 'String him up'. The Camelots du Roi, the bodyguards-cum-bully boys of the Action Française, broke the car windows, pulled Blum out and gave him a bloody beating. Later that afternoon, in response to the incident, the President of the Assembly banned Action Française and its associated student and paramilitary leagues, though the movement's daily newspaper, *L'Action française*, was not proscribed. Subsequently, Charles Maurras was convicted of incitement to murder and, after a series of appeals, imprisoned in the Santé. He remained behind bars, though free to read and write and entertain a constant stream of visitors, from October 1936 to July 1937.[19] On 18 June 1936, almost as soon as the Popular Front took office, the Minister for the Interior, Roger Salengro, dissolved all anti-parliamentary leagues and 'private militia and combat groups'.

The French Right, with the exception of a small splinter group including some notable French industrialists, was not pro-Hitler but intensely xenophobic and obsessed with the 'two great materialist leviathans' they perceived to be menacing Europe: Russian Communism and 'American hyper-capitalism'.[20] Added to the amalgam was a pervasive anxiety about being drawn into another war, a sentiment that was shared by many French citizens and, until very late in the decade, by Europeans in general. The virulent anti-Communism of the Right ratcheted up in response to the factory occupations by left-wing workers between May and mid-1936 and the Communist Party's gains in the voting urns and on the street. In June, when the Popular Front alliance of the Left, led by Léon Blum and the Socialist Party, took government, anti-Communist fears on the Right went into overdrive. The tensions over whether to support the Spanish Republic, or not, raised the tempo even further.

Action Française was the most important French influence on the circle that surrounded Franco at Military Headquarters in Nationalist Spain. The movement in France, founded in 1898 to rally anti-Dreyfusard intellectuals, was royalist, Catholic, anti-Republican and anti-Semitic. The total membership of Action Française fell away after the riots of

February 1934 as many activists abandoned the 'Inaction française'. Until the end of the Second World War, however, Charles Maurras and Action Française exerted a profound intellectual influence on French Catholic and right-wing thought. The movement also constituted a powerful and disintegrative force in French national life.[21] In Eugen Weber's assessment, whether they were revolutionary dissidents wanting to overthrow the Republic or returned soldiers embittered over postwar pensions, the French Right had been influenced in one way or another by Maurras and Action Française.[22] Furthermore, in his opinion, the existence of the movement in France, see-sawing on the edge of illegality, exuded a 'dirty stream of undifferentiated hate that distorted social realities'.[23]

In the movement's daily, *L'Action française*, Charles Maurras and the volatile polemicist Léon Daudet railed against the 'slut', their shorthand for the 'worthless Republic', which had permitted 'the national body of France' to become 'invaded' by the 'alien' influences of 'Protestants, Jews, Freemasons and foreigners'.[24] Maurras, himself an agnostic, advocated national Catholicism because it was the pillar of French civilization; and though no particular admirer of the French Pretender, Maurras was an outspoken royalist because the monarchy embodied French tradition, order and structure.[25] The 'integral nationalism', which Maurras offered in the place of 'shallow democratic republicanism' incorporated Catholic tradition, a revitalized hereditary monarchy and decentralized absolutism. These, Maurras claimed, were the manifestation of the essence of the French 'pays réel'.

When the Popular Front took government, Maurras and his supporters increased the vitriol of their attacks on Republican democracy. In *L'Action française*, like the main newspapers of the 'ultra Right'[26] – in descending order of circulation, *Gringoire, Candide* and *Je Suis Partout* – Blum's name was never used without a hyphen to 'the Jew' or to derogatory epithets like 'Shylock', 'human detritus' or the 'circumcized hermaphrodite'.[27] Readers were reminded daily that Blum and his 'Talmudic cabinet' were in the thrall of Moscow and were a front for Communist revolution, Freemasonry and world Jewish finance.[28] Perhaps most famous was Charle Maurras' sinister editorializing in *L'Action française* on 14 April 1935 that 'Blum is a man to shoot, but in the back'. Roger Salengro, the Socialist Minister of the Interior, who had dissolved the paramilitary leagues in June 1936, was driven to suicide in November by the unrelenting barrage of attacks from *Gringoire* and *L'Action française*.[29] As we will see below, Action Française leaders had close connections with Franco's headquarters; various close associates of Maurras and finally the old man himself made the pilgrimage to Nationalist Spain.

The Camelots du Roi were the 'storm troopers' of the Action Française.[30] They had begun as newspaper vendors selling the royalist press at church doors and, by the 1930s, carried out a 'holy war' against the Popular Front and the Left. Stand-over tactics, street brawls and violent bully-boy agitation constituted their mode of operation. When Frenchmen for Franco in Spain indicated their political allegiances, it was more often to the Camelots du Roi than to any other organization. Francoism provided a model of political existence that attracted many French Camelots du Roi. The organization's leader, Réal del Sarte, admired Franco greatly and visited him a number of times.

The returned soldiers' organization, the Croix de Feu, which was led by Colonel François de La Rocque, also had a strong following among French volunteers in Nationalist Spain. Begun as an organization of decorated returned soldiers, it opened the ranks to non-veterans in 1931. When the anti-parliamentary leagues were banned in 1936, La Rocque quickly transformed the Croix de Feu into a political party, the Parti Social Français. By 1937 it boasted between 700,000 and a million members and had become the largest formation on the French Right.[31] From the first days of the Spanish Civil War, a certain number of its supporters felt compelled to enlist with the anti-Republican forces.

There were also followers of Jacques Doriot's Parti Populaire Français among Franco's volunteers. It constituted the second largest group on the French Right in the mid-1930s. Doriot's sashay rightwards in 1935 had taken him out of the Communist Party to found his own openly fascist party. With strongholds in Paris, Marseilles and French Algeria, and in particular Oran, it supplied a recruiting centre of French volunteers for Franco.

The most sinister constellation on the Right in France was the Cagoule, the Secret Committee for Revolutionary Action, which had been founded on the eve of the Popular Front by Eugene Deloncle and Jean Filliol. Both men were ex-Camelots du Roi. The Cagoule functioned as a clandestine terrorist organization, carrying out political assassinations and sabotage against Communists, leading Jewish citizens or suspected Masons: all categorized in Cagoule circles as the 'enemies of France'.[32] Franco's Spain figured large on the Cagoule landscape. Cagoulards traded arms and smuggled weapons into Franco's Spain.[33] According to Philippe Bourdrel, a French journalist who has written extensively on the movement, the

Cagoule saw itself providing the 'link in a chain between Franco's Spain and Mussolini's Italy'.[34] With ties to individuals in the ranks of the second level at Mussolini's court and to Franco's brother Nicolás in Spain, the Cagoule's long-term objective was to draw France into the fascist orbit of Italy and away from Great Britain and 'Red Europe'.[35] Robert Soucy, similarly, emphasizes the importance of Franco Spain to the organization: Deloncle 'wanted for France what Franco had undertaken for Spain'.[36]

Whether as pious believers or practitioners from lifelong habit, most individuals on the Right sat under the wide umbrella of French Catholicism. French Catholics were conservatives because historically French Radicals and Republicans were anticlerical. The automatic association of the Republic with secularism had reified the opposite alliance; and by the early twentieth century, Throne and Altar were perceived as the natural configuration.[37]

When the Civil War began, French Catholics were easily convinced that the next round in an all-encompassing battle had begun in Spain. Having listened every Sunday for almost thirty years as the priest thundered against the twin evils of secularism and Bolshevism, it was not difficult to believe that Franco, the 'noble Moscardó' and the 'heroic cadets of the Toledo Alcázar' were leading the charge against the enemies of the Church worldwide.[38]

There were some dissenting voices. The liberal Dominican journal, *Sept*, argued that Franco's cause was not a Holy Crusade.[39] The fragility of the minority of Catholics that *Sept* represented, however, was revealed in February 1937, when there was such an outcry over the journal including an interview with Blum that it was forced to close down.[40]

The plight of Spanish Basques split some Catholics from the solid pro-Franco front. The Basque Countries, in the north-west of Spain, comprised some of the most Catholic regions in the land. At the same time, many Basques were loyal Republicans and valiantly defended the Spanish government. On 31 March 1937, the small Basque town of Durango was bombed by the German Condor Legion, killing two priests, thirteen nuns and a hundred parishioners in two churches as they were gathered for Mass. On 26 April, more than a thousand people died in Guernica when the Condor Legion carpet-bombed the town. Guernica is the capital of the Basque nation where, under the Tree of Euzkadi, the historic symbol of Basquedom, the Spanish kings had recognized the autonomy of the Basque region. It was market day when the bombing occurred, and locals and farmers from outlying districts were in town doing their business. Many of the dead perished in the fierce firestorm that the bombing unleashed.[41] At the end of June 1937, Bilbao, on the coast, fell to Franco's forces after a bloody and drawn-out siege.

Early in February, a group of Catholic intellectuals, including Jacques Maritain and Emmanuel Mounier, made a public appeal for the end of the Civil War. They blamed the Spanish generals for the conflict, called for a cessation to the bombing of Madrid and stated that it was time to tear away the 'mask of the holy war that covered a war of extermination'.[42] On 8 May, after Durango and Guernica had been destroyed, there was another call by French Catholic intellectuals to form a Committee for Civil and Religious Freedom in Spain. The manifesto included most of the signatories to the first document, as well as François Mauriac, the respected Catholic writer. Their statement began unequivocally: 'It is beyond doubt that Basques are a Catholic people whose devotion has never flagged'. They went on to decry the civilian deaths caused by bombing open towns.

Charles Maurras, from prison, replied to what he called 'this twice-odious fable' of Guernica. The town, he alleged, had been 'devoured by the fires set methodically by the Russians when they left'. The 'Reds' version of the story had gained credence, he claimed contemptuously, because 'the old guard had come in: one Jew, two Jews and then the Christian Democrats'.[43]

In July 1937, Maritain published a moving statement on the ethical response that Christians should adopt to the brutality taking place in Spain, whereby it was a 'sacrilege to profane the holy places and the Holy Sacraments' as it was to 'shoot men in Durango or Guernica'. Decent people should 'not fail to protest if a town in the White Zone is bombed by the Republican air force' or 'when the German air force destroyed Guernica'.[44]

The Catholic intellectual, George Bernanos, also expressed deep reservations about Franco's Christian crusade. A monarchist and outspoken anti-Semite, he had been a member of Camelots du Roi since 1908 and a senior Action Française figure. When the Civil War began Bernanos was living in Majorca in the home of a leading fascist family.[45] Bernanos's account, using a novelistic form, described the White terror in Majorca in the first months of the war. It appeared to an instant readership in 1938 under the title, *Les Grands Cimitières sous la lune*, and was quickly reprinted in a number of languages.[46] The figure of Bernanos, and what he stood for, increased the impact of the work a hundredfold.

The small group of Catholic intellectuals who were concerned about the treatment of Spanish Basques provided an important dissenting position. Individually and as a group, however, pro-Franco Catholics dismissed their anguished criticisms as Red propaganda from Jewish and Marxist stooges.[47]

L'Action Française was the French organization which exerted most influence on the group around Franco. Spanish monarchists had long been in the thrall of Maurras' ideas which since before the First World War had spread widely in Catholic and monarchist circles outside France.[48] The monarchist Madrid dailies *ABC* and *El Debate* frequently syndicated columns from *L'Action* in Paris and reported the doings of French royalists. When the monarchist newspaper *Acción Española* was founded in Madrid in 1931, it was influenced by *L'Action française* in more than just the name, promoting monarchism and fomenting anti-Republicanism among Spanish military officers.[49] Monarchist intellectuals in Spain, like Ramiro de Maetzu, espoused the instrumental monarchism that was Maurras' hallmark. As Hugh Thomas has pointed out, Acción Española monarchists were much more energetic in trying to overthrow the Republic than they had been in defending the king.[50] Renovación Española, the rejuvenated Spanish monarchist movement which began in 1933, was led by Calvo Sotelo, who had then returned from three years' exile in Paris where he had deeply imbibed Maurras' ideas.[51]

Several French, Swiss and Portuguese admirers of Charles Maurras travelled to Nationalist Spain in order to observe what they heralded as a Catholic corporatist revolution. Whether the visitors were important enough to meet Franco face to face, or not, they all left Spain with grist for the propaganda mill against the Republican government.[52]

In March 1937, Maxime Réal del Sarte, the French Catholic sculptor and relative of the composer Georges Bizet, brought Franco greetings from Charles Maurras, still incarcerated in the Santé. The narrative of Réal del Sarte's voyage was printed at the end of 1937 as *Au pays de Franco, notre frère Latin*.[53] In the frontispiece photographs Charles Maurras gazes quizzically from behind prison bars, while Franco, with wife and daughter, smiles plumply at the camera.

Despite having lost an arm in 1916, Maxime Réal del Sarte was the most distinguished religious and monumental sculptor in France between the wars. The French royal family's artist of choice, he produced heads, busts and likenesses for the various betrothal and wedding ceremonies of the Dukes of Guise and Orléans. In the great boom of commemorative monument building in the 1920s and 1930s, he designed more than fifty municipal and commemorative sites.[54] Indeed, a break in February 1937, while the armaments were mounted on the monument to commemorate General Joffre at Les Invalides, provided a window for travel in a busy schedule of commissions.[55] In Spain, Réal del Sarte took the opportunity to measure up the Caudillo for a bust for the exhibition of Anti-Communist Art in Paris later in the year.

While an aristocratic student at the École des Beaux Arts, Réal del Sarte had become a founder of the Camelots du Roi and, as a 20-year-old in 1908, had made a name for himself when he had been imprisoned for interrupting a case in the Supreme Court to accuse the judge of Dreyfusardism. Over the years, Réal del Sarte progressed from enthusiastic participant in street riots, to Camelot organizer and, by 1936, he was the leader of the Camelot movement as a whole.

Like many of his co-religionists, Réal del Sarte was a fervent devotee of the cult of Joan of Arc: the Maid provided the motif for many of his religious and municipal commissions. In 1930, he founded the Companions of Joan of Arc which promoted pilgrimages in her name and, within a few years, had spread throughout France to Spain and Portugal. Her devotees shared a belief that the saint was 'the symbol of the genius of the Latin race'.

In the mid-nineteenth century Joan of Arc represented French nationalists of Right and Left. The Dreyfus Affair, however, reformatted French nationalism against the myth of the Jew as the 'antipode of Frenchness'. Between the wars, according to Michel Winnock, Joan of Arc was transformed into the symbol of anti-Semitism and came to embody all the characteristics that were the opposite of Dreyfus and the Jew.[56] Her identity as an anti-Semite was hardened as increasingly she was associated with incidents that affirmed French anti-Semitism. With the Popular Front ascendant, the quintessential figure of the Jew transmogrified into the image of Léon Blum and the Maid's feast day, on 8 May, became the date for right-wing rallies. In Paris at the statue in the Place des Pyramides and at similar locales in provincial centres, strident cries of 'Death to Jews' and 'Death to Blum' were as common as 'Vive Jeanne d'Arc'.

At the start of the decade, Réal del Sarte had presented Mussolini with a statue of Joan; however, the spiralling diplomatic tensions between Italy and France consigned her to languish in the basement of the museum of the Italian Empire.[57] In 1937 in Spain, the sculptor made a similar offer to raise her statue in 'liberated Madrid' as soon as Franco's troops had entered the capital.[58]

Wherever Réal del Sarte went, he distributed engraved medallions of Joan's head. In Seville in 1937, he slyly left a medallion on Quiepo de Llano's desk, after having spent an hour being 'entranced' by the southern general's 'incantations' against the Republic's military leaders. It was to remind Quiepo that he spoke for 'Latinness' everywhere (ibid., pp. 26–7). In the same town, the sculptor presented the Portuguese ambassador with an ivory statue of the Maid to be taken to Lisbon as a present for the 'heroic dictator', Dr Salazar. A few days later, in a café in Salamanca, Réal del Sarte noted with satisfaction that several people were wearing the colours of Joan. Among them, at a neighbouring table, was General O'Duffy, the head of the battalion of Irish volunteers for Franco (ibid., p. 31). Presumably a stint in Nationalist Spain had elevated the Irishman to honorary membership of the Latin race. At a formal dinner later with Franco's staff, most of the guests wore the emblem of St Joan, and Réal del Sarte had the pleasure of pinning the insignia of the Companion of St Joan on the breast of General Franco's sister-in-law as she sat beside him at table (ibid., p 38).

The Frenchman's trip to Spain in February 1937 was arranged from Paris by José María Quiñones de León, a Spanish monarchist who had been the ex-king's ambassador in Paris. The visit began in Biarritz, at the villa of the Count of Los Andes, an active monarchist who was part of Franco's northern intelligence service.[59] Georges Massot, a Spanish-speaker, a Camelot du Roi and the head of Action Française in the south-west of France, accompanied Réal del Sarte (ibid., pp. 13–15). Massot had close ties to Nationalist headquarters and was in the habit of crossing the border frequently. For example, he was the go-between for the money raised in public appeals for Franco in French right-wing newspapers.[60] In 1937, once they were over the border, both men were glad to wear their Camelot colours and insignia, which were banned in France.

A French-speaking Catalan, who changed into Nationalist uniform as soon as they had crossed the International Bridge over the Bidassoa, escorted the party. The identity of their fourth companion, Henri Bonneville du Marsagny, was revealed at the very last minute. The French leader of the Jeanne d'Arc battalion, he headed directly to Salamanca once they had cleared the border (ibid., p. 15).

Réal del Sarte and Massot were treated to full military honours during the week they spent in Spain. General Franco sent a driver and a large car and it ate up the miles as they sped north to south touring the sights of Nationalist Spain. At Irún, the military governor, Major Julian Troncoso, welcomed them; the Falange militia trooped the colours. In Salamanca, they lunched with the head of Franco's diplomatic cabinet and, in Talavera de la Reina, interviewed a taciturn General Mola (*ibid.*, p. 15). The Frenchmen were entranced when military sentries snapped to attention as the car with 'Headquarters of the Generalissimo' swept into view. Réal del Sarte waxed lyrical over the 'discipline and the love' that even the sight of Franco's name could elicit and contrasted the smart Spanish response with the decadent 'sloppiness' of the French in the 'shallow democracy of the Popular Front' (*ibid.*, p. 19).

During two days in Seville, Réal del Sarte and Massot swapped recollections of the French and Iberian royal families with Spanish and Portuguese monarchists (*ibid.*, pp. 24–5). Shops in the southern city displayed portraits of Hitler and Mussolini along with Franco and shopkeepers, realizing their customers were not Spanish, inevitably greeted them with 'Heil Hitler'. An exchange with a young bootblack left Réal del Sarte crestfallen because the boy stated that 'French were bad and Communists, and the same as the Russians and the Chinese' (*ibid.*, p. 27).

In Andalusia they had their first view of Moorish troops. The presence of the Moors fighting in a Christian country was a sore point for many devout Christians. Betraying a very slight understanding of Nationalist military arrangements, and a determination to explain away difficult matters, Réal claimed that the Moors had come to Spain because their religion was equally 'menaced' by the 'frightful Jewish and Asiatic invasion' and therefore the Moors' presence was 'living proof of the glory of Franco's Crusade' (*ibid.*, p. 21).

Like many Franco admirers before him, the absolute highpoint of the trip was an audience with the Caudillo, the details of which Réal del Sarte recorded in an extravagantly reverential tone. Franco's eyes had 'filled with tears' when he heard that Réal's sister and her six children 'went down on their knees and prayed for General Franco' every night before going to bed (*ibid.*, p. 34). The Caudillo 'generously' accepted the volumes by Maurras and Pujol's history of the Camelots du Roi bound in leather in the French and Spanish colours. As well, the Caudillo allowed himself to be measured for a bust and had even brought photos of himself in profile, which the sculptor took as proof of Franco's 'superior understanding of the technicalities' of the Arts (*ibid.*, p. 38). Finally he 'graciously permitted' Réal del Sarte to unpin the silver badge of the Camelot du Roi from his own chest and repin it to the Caudillo's tunic (*ibid.*, p. 37).

During their conversation, Franco spoke 'good French in a soft voice' which contained a 'trace of hesitation' that Réal found 'added great charm' to the words (*ibid.*, p. 34). The Caudillo claimed that he was aware that 'France was like Spain' in that the 'real nation' was opposed to the 'barbarian hordes'. But Franco most firmly wished Réal del Sarte to make the French understand that the great sacrifice that Franco had undertaken was to protect the French from the 'same forces of evil' that threatened Spain. When he spoke about the Basques, the Caudillo's equanimity disappeared and, almost shouting, he pointed out that Spanish Basques were nothing without the support they were receiving from the 'Reds' over the border (*ibid.*, p. 35–6).

Subsequently, Réal del Sarte made several trips to Nationalist Spain and, as we shall see, attempted to use his access to monarchist officers in Burgos to repatriate Action Française volunteers. In November 1937, he went alone to present Franco with a bronze of Christ at Calvary.[61] At the start of May 1938, again with Georges Massot, and Pierre Héricourt, who was the parliamentary correspondent for *L'Action française*, Réal del Sarte accompanied Maurras on a four-day visit through Nationalist Spain. Maurras was treated like a visiting head of state, the crowning honour being his election to the Spanish Royal Academy.[62]

At the border, Franco's officials and a delegation of monarchists from Acción Española met Maurras and his party. In San Sebastian, French residents, all members of Action Française, and Spanish monarchists held a reception which ended with loud cheers for the 'King of France' and for Nationalist Spain.[63] In Burgos the next day, Maurras publicly expounded on the parallels between the monarchist in 'Real France' and what was taking place in Nationalist Spain. He also met Serrano Suñer, Franco's brother-in-law and the Minister of the Interior, who elaborated on the 'National Revolution' taking place under Franco (*ibid.*, p. 218). Réal del Sarte, enchanted as always by everything in Nationalist Spain, was transported by the 'youth of the leadership' in the New Spain which was in strong contrast with the 'gerontocracy' of Republican France (*ibid.*, p. 203). What the 70-year-old Maurras thought on this matter is unrecorded.

The second day culminated in a meeting with the Caudillo, who 'clasped Maurras's hand in both of his'; there were mutual thanks from 'Real Spain' to 'Real France' and vice versa. According to the mawkish newspaper report in *L'Action française*, as the Frenchmen withdrew, Franco made a 'moving and spontaneous gesture' in which he raised his arm and shouted 'Arriba Francia', to which his guests, in full voice, replied 'Vive l'Espagne'.[64]

In Saragossa they were welcomed by the military governor and the municipal council which named Maurras as 'honoured guest of the city' (*ibid.*, p. 221). After the requisite visit to the cathedral to kiss the statue of the Virgin of Pilar, the four Frenchmen set off briskly for the Aragon front. They paused to observe military operations on the Ebro and travelled to the furthest point of the Nationalists' advance. Maurras was 'transported' at the sight of the army in the field: young men in full physical form, as he said, 'danced' across the landscape, carrying their heavy weapons 'like bouquets of flowers'. His was the 'profound and melancholic curiosity of the civilian who vainly dreamed of another destiny' (*ibid.*, p. 154).

At Balaguer, General Moscardó turned on a full military salute with several hundred soldiers pulled from front-line duties (ibid., pp. 209–13) and, after an excellent lunch, Moscardó and Maurras sauntered through the town which had been newly captured from the 'Reds'. Maurras' own narrative records several 'unforgettable', and highly unlikely, 'examples of Franco-Spanish communion'. In one case, they allegedly came across a wounded Spanish peasant who recognized Maurras and insisted on 'kissing the hand that had written so much for the cause of Spain and Latin civilization' (*ibid.*, pp. 212; 224).

Back in Saragossa, on their last day, the mayor held a dinner at the Grand Hotel, after which each of the French visitors spoke over Radio Saragossa. By this time there was a regular broadcast in French being beamed from there.[65] Réal del Sarte used his slot to describe the demonstrations for Joan of Arc that would take place at Les Pyramides in Paris in a couple of days.[66]

Maurras' highly unrealistic observations of what he saw in the Spanish Civil War are probably a function of his age and his interests. He confessed to having little previous curiosity about Spain and, apart from Cervantes, knowing little of Spanish literature and having always found the 'brutality' of the bullfight unappealing. Like Réal del Sarte, he saw Nationalist Spain as the backdrop against which to play out his own ideological scenario which was based on his perception of politics in France. Maurras and his companion's world-view was grounded in the generation of the First World War. Franco's Spain provided Réal del Sarte

with the political model of the most desirable form of social organi
he retained a deep attachment to it for the rest of his life, even when his
admiration was no longer reciprocated in franquista Spain.

In October 1939, Réal del Sarte and Maurras prepared a second trip to
Spain in order to celebrate Franco's victory. They anticipated another
lavish welcome and Maurras looked forward to presenting an erudite
discourse on 'Integral Nationalism' before the Spanish Royal Academy.
General Pétain, appointed French ambassador to Spain at the end of the
Civil War in order to mollify Franco, counselled against the trip. By this
time anti-French sentiment in Spain was very high. It is very possible, as
well, that Maurras' endless trumpeting of the virtues of the monarchical
system was no longer to Franco's liking. In the months immediately after
the war, there were considerable strains between Franco's inner circle and
the Spanish monarchists, as the latter pushed for the restoration of the
king. In this environment, Maurras with his royalist connections was no
longer welcome.[67]

The depth of Réal del Sarte's continuing attachment to Franco Spain
was apparent in January 1940, when he was made a companion of the
Légion d'Honneur and insisted on the investiture taking place in the
French embassy in Madrid, even though the ceremony took place at a
small private gathering. By then, as he explained, he had no contact at all
with 'official Spain' because Spanish Francophobia had increased to a
remarkable degree. As a private tourist, he noted that Madrid was 'criss-
crossed with large cars flying the German flag and the cafés were full of
people with Nazi insignia in their buttonholes'.[68]

Even in the early days of the Civil War when Action Française's
influence was in its heyday, the red carpet was only ever rolled out for the
movement's leaders. Rank-and-file Action members in Nationalist Spain
often received a decidedly hostile welcome. There are a number of
examples of harsh treatment meted out to ordinary Frenchmen despite
them being supporters of the Right and having crossed into Spain
ostensibly to support Franco. The 28-year-old Julien Primat is one. In
February 1937, he obtained a safe conduct from his comrades in Action
Française in Hendaye to travel to Irún in order to obtain another pass
which would allow him to progress to Saragossa to visit his Spanish
fiancée.[69] Once in the Aragonese capital, Primat settled down in a hotel
and spent time with his girl and her family. At the end of a month a
Franco official told Primat that he should show some 'commitment' to the
Nationalist cause. As a result, Primat quickly joined the local Falangist

Auxiliary. After an aerial bombing of Saragossa by Republican planes, Primat was picked up at his hotel and thrown in prison. He was badly beaten by the prison guards and given no indication of why he was being held. After a week, he was transported to Irún and then to the border where, still in handcuffs, he was expelled. Primat attributed his bad treatment to the intense Francophobia in Nationalist Spain which, he claimed, was caused by the growing influence of Italy and, in particular, Germany in running the war.[70]

The *bandera* of the Juana de Arco

There is no agreement about the exact number of Frenchmen who crossed into Spain to join General Franco's forces. The French ambassador, who, as we shall see, spent a good deal of his time attempting to extricate disillusioned Frenchmen from Spain, provided the highest total of 500 of his countrymen who, he claimed, were with Franco's forces, including those with the Carlists Requetés and various Falangist militias.[71]

The Spanish Foreign Legion census compiled in August 1938 indicates 71 Foreign Legionnaires designated as having French nationality, plus 2 Swiss and a single Belgian.[72] These figures are most likely understated, as there were other French volunteers with the Requetés and the regular army. As well, it was not unusual for men to register under assumed names and false nationalities. The Spanish Foreign Legion list shows a French volunteer identified as 'Mauricio Chevalier' and several individuals who were definitely in the Spanish Foreign Legion at that time are not included. By then, as well, there had been a good number of French desertions.

A Swiss journalist, Georges Oudard, travelling in Spain in the first months of 1937, offers the figure of 250 men, including some 50 other French-speakers, predominantly Belgians and Swiss. Commissioned by several Swiss newspapers to examine the significance of foreign involvement in the military outcome of the Spanish Civil War, Oudard sought out foreign military personnel wherever possible and was careful to weigh up the evidence he presented.[73] Taking all the available head counts, probably somewhere between 250 and 500 French-speakers served with Franco's forces.

The impetus for the formation of a separate French company originated in the coincidence of the interests of Spanish Nationalist headquarters and the leaders of the National Front in France.[74] By mid-

1936, when the anti-parliamentary leagues and Action Française itself were banned, the possibility of operating openly across the border was very attractive. The French Right, whether Camelots du Roi, Croix de Feu, Parti Social Français or Doriot's men, could demonstrate their ideological agreement with Franco and display their military prowess on a real battlefield. The French backers of the Joan of Arc company saw Spain, too, as a training ground for the creation of the future leaders of an insurrection of the Right in France.[75]

For the military men at Franco's headquarters a designated unit made up of French volunteers served another purpose altogether. The pace of activity from mid-1937 to create a company of French foreign volunteers, and in August 1938 to carry out a census of foreign volunteers in the Spanish Foreign Legion, was probably tied to the rhythm of the negotiations which were taking place on the Non-Intervention Committee in London.

The 27 members of the committee had agreed in February 1937 to ban foreign volunteers from travelling to Spain, but serious talks about what was to be done with the volunteers already in Spain only began in earnest from July 1937.[76] In that month, the British government came up with a plan that linked the assignment of belligerent rights to both sides in Spain with an agreement to withdraw the volunteers already on the Iberian Peninsula.

It was an irresistible carrot to dangle before Franco. All along, he had agitated for belligerent rights, as it would accord legal equality to both combatants. This would boost Franco's international standing and, in practical terms, mean that it was legal for the Nationalists to stop and search shipping in Spanish waters and blockade Republican ports. With the clandestine support of Italian submarines and warships, the Nationalist navy was more powerful than the Republican fleet.[77] The possession of belligerent rights would increase the naval power which was already in Franco's camp. In order to bring the Nationalists and their allies on the Non-Intervention Committee, Italy, Germany and Portugal, to the negotiating table, the British Foreign Office tied together belligerent rights with the withdrawal of foreign volunteers. And indeed the strategy paid off. In November 1937, Franco sent word to the British ambassador at Hendaye that he would accept the British plan, though with a number of reservations that would have to be worked out later.

The Spanish government had little choice but to accept the trade-off, though it constituted a significant defeat. The Nationalist advantage on the ocean was increased. Far more serious was the fact that a stroke of a pen in London had transformed an illegal uprising against a legitimate government by insurgents into a conflict between two legal equals.

Much of the time that the Non-Intervention Committee spent in fits and starts of discussion and negotiation from July 1937 until October 1938 was taken up with three questions. The first was, how were the numbers of volunteers on each side to be estimated? And, what constituted a 'substantial' withdrawal? Finally, what would be the proportion of withdrawals on each side? The momentum of the cogs that turned the Non-Intervention Committee in London governed the sequence of events at headquarters in Nationalist Spain.

From Franco's point of view, if push came to shove from the London Committee, the Nationalists could agree to send home a designated battalion of foreign volunteers, for example, the *bandera* of the Juana de Arco, or even all the 'foreigners' who together made up only a small proportion of the Spanish Foreign Legion. The fact that these units were few and their loss would not compromise Franco's military capability was so much the better. The Nationalists could count as well the propaganda benefit in the visible difference between the size of Franco's 'White' French troops and the ten thousand or so 'Red' French in the International Brigades. The first group was a drop in the bucket in Franco's army while the French constituted the largest foreign nationality fighting for the Republic. Once Nationalist command had sent home the designated 'foreign volunteers' openly, Franco could stonewall all complaints about the large numbers of Italians, Germans and Portuguese that remained in Nationalist Spain. And, of course, it was these groups, particularly the Italians and the Germans, that were important for the military outcome of the war.

The French ambassador read the activity in Nationalist Spain to establish the Joan of Arc battalion as part of the process of rendering 'illusory' the withdrawal of foreign volunteers.[78] In July 1937, his source in Franco's Spain alerted him to an effort afoot to comb out all foreigners in the Requetés and the Falangist ranks and place them in a designated unit within the Foreign Legion. French soldiers who had reached officer grades were being skimmed off to lead a new French company; foreigners who were unwilling to transfer were summarily demobbed. The changes, which the French ambassador claimed were being pushed by the German representative in Spain, were an attempt to head off the demands of the Non-Intervention Committee and to create a unit of the Spanish Foreign

Legion which would be the equivalent of the Republican International Brigade.[79]

Almost as soon as the Civil War had begun, First World War veteran General Paul-Louis Alexandre Lavigne-Delville, a military correspondent for *L'Action française*, began encouraging Frenchmen to fight for Franco. Charles Trochu and his private secretary, Jacques Pecheron, ran a recruiting line which passed potential volunteers from Paris to Bordeaux where Captain Bonneville de Marsagny was forming up a battalion. A similar network operated to funnel volunteers to Nationalist Spain from North Africa, particularly from the Parti Social Français stronghold in Oran. Trochu was a member of the list of Parisian councillors of the extreme Right, associates of the Prefect of Police, Jean Chiappe, who had captured the Municipal Council in the early 1930s. It was their manifesto that had called out the demonstrators in February 1934 to march on the National Assembly. Trochu, as the President of the National Association of Returned Officers, had a network of contacts among French reservists and veterans. Several industrialists and businessmen, who shared the National Front's apocalyptic view that a Communist takeover was imminent in France, provided the financial backing to raise a French company to be sent to Franco's aid.[80] In Lisbon, at the same time, members of the French community raised a public subscription for a French-speaking battalion to fight the Spanish Republic.[81] The original backers predicted – quite incorrectly as it turned out – that there would be a great surge of comrades from France wishing to fight for Franco.[82]

By the end of May 1937, Nationalist Military Command began forming a designated French company within the Spanish Foreign Legion. Named after France's most famous Christian warrior, Joan of Arc, the unit would incorporate all French speakers in the militias and any future enlistments in the Spanish Foreign Legion, and would function under the command of French commissioned officers.[83] Initially, White Russians were included with the French because most came from Paris and were French-speakers of one sort or another. Their leaders, however, vehemently rejected being placed with the French, ironically perhaps, because they saw the French as pro-Soviet, and only a few White Russians ended up in the French unit.[84]

The *bandera* Juana de Arco marshalled at the Spanish Foreign Legion's headquarters in Talavera de la Reina. From the very start it was plagued by problems. Not the least of them was a shortage of volunteers. By mid-September 1937, recruitment and reorganization within the Spanish Legion had produced a captain, a sub-lieutenant and a dozen non-commissioned officers to lead 59 ordinary soldiers. They included regular Frenchmen as well as French-speaking Swiss, Belgians and a few Italians and Greeks resident in France.[85] At the end of 1937, the numbers had risen to no more than a hundred and included an Australian Catholic, whose schoolboy French landed him with the French speakers.

The calibre of the volunteers left much to be desired. As early as September 1937, General Juan Yagüe, the commander of the Spanish Foreign Legion, observed that it would better if most of the French recruits were sent back to civilian life because their pay was a drain on franquista revenues and they provided nothing in return.[86] The organization of the company was also inept and the unit's commanders unreliable, often much more interested in their own well-being than that of their men. Franco had been promised soldiers and money and, when both failed to materialize, franquista headquarters became hostile towards the French company.

The military backgrounds of the French commanders were unorthodox. Captain Henry Bournville de Marsagny had served in the First World War and led a Parisian section of the Croix de Feu. He had come to Nationalist Spain in the first place as a war correspondent for *L'Action française* and had shown bravery under fire: on one occasion, he had taken over command of the unit he was accompanying, when the Spanish officer had been killed. His move from civilian to military life, however, was less than happy. He was killed in October 1937, possibly in dubious circumstances, in the siege of Oviedo.[87]

A first-person account of George/Gaston Penaud as a French volunteer in Spain catalogues a series of bungles and mishaps, including his serving time in prison.[88] During his four months in Spain as a volunteer, he never lifted a rifle or made any gesture that could be considered to have assisted Franco's military effort. Penaud, 40 years of age and a member of the Military Reserves, had served as an artillery officer in the First World War. By April 1937, several business failures had brought him down on his luck and, unable to find work, he had sought the commander of the returned officers' association to which he belonged. Trochu had assured Penaud that he had come at exactly the right time, because Trochu was recruiting a French company to fight the Communists in Spain. He provided Penaud with the fare and sent him off to Bordeaux to present himself to Captain Bonneville de Marsagny, the commander of the company under formation. At first everything went swimmingly. Marsagny interviewed Penaud and, after examining his service record, offered Penaud a post in Spain as a lieutenant on 10 pesetas a day.[89] Back in Paris, Trochu was delighted with the outcome and told Penaud to prepare to leave for Spain within the week. When the day arrived, Penaud and another recruit, Albert Langer, set off by train to the Spanish border. Trochu's private secretary, Jacques Pecheron, accompanied them and arranged their accommodation in a hotel near St-Jean-de-Luz, where they were to wait for a signal to cross into Nationalist Spain. They cooled their heels for ten days until a guide arrived. He brought them fisherman's clothes and, carrying rods and reels, they climbed through the mountains and across the border at a remote part, disguised as men on a fishing holiday. Their guide left them at a forester's house just inside Spain, where a group of Spaniards in Falangist uniforms were waiting. After the Falangists checked the identification papers that the Frenchmen had been given in Bordeaux against a Falangist list, they took the two volunteers to the Military Command in Irún where they spent the night and, in the morning, were issued passes to travel to Saragossa to join the Joan of Arc company.

In Saragossa things began to go wrong. When they arrived there they could find no Spanish official who knew anything at all about a French *bandera*. The two Frenchmen were without money and knew nobody at all in Saragossa. After a few lean days, they sought out the French consul, M. Robarch, who arranged for them to travel back to Irún. At Falangist headquarters they were told that their commander Marsagny was expected at any moment and they should wait for him where they were, as he would know what to do with them. At first, the Falangists were very civil. They made no demands on the two Frenchmen, who kept their civilian clothes and hung around Falangist headquarters during the day, sleeping on the desks at night when everyone had gone home. Their rations consisted exclusively of chick peas. Without a peseta between them, the two could not supplement their food or even pass time in the bar. They waited three weeks. As the days went by, the attitude of the Spaniards at Falangist headquarters became more and more hostile and bullying. When Marsagny did arrive finally, he stayed only long enough to discover that Langer could drive a car and to gather him up to be the chauffeur on another trip off around Spain. Penaud remained behind, alone, camping at Falangist headquarters, without pay or kit, for another fifteen days. When Marsagny returned to Irún the next time he was in a great state of agitation because General Lavigne-Delville was on his way south from Paris to inspect the company of French volunteers. The very instant the general arrived in Irún, Marsagny ushered him into an automobile and took off with him on a whirlwind tour through Nationalist Spain. When they returned a day or so later, Penaud heard the two men arguing violently about the non-existence of the company of French volunteers and about the disappearance of the funds that had been raised outside Spain for the company.

At this stage Penaud realized that it was likely that he would never be paid or get to join the Joan of Arc company. He therefore asked Lavigne-Delville for funds to return to France, because his wife would be destitute as he had sent her no money because he had never been paid. Delville refused Penaud permission to leave Spain but promised to forward Mme Penaud money from Paris; and he duly did.[90]

By this time a second group of volunteers, despatched by Trochu, had arrived in Irún. Marsagny convinced them all that they should trust him to take care of their needs if they came with him to Talavera de la Reina. Between Irún and Salamanca, however, Marsagny suddenly left the group, saying that he had urgent business to deal with and he would meet up with them later. Still not having been paid, they made their way to Salamanca as best they could: they scrounged food and hitched whatever rides they could manage. One night they slept in a hotel and left very early in the morning without paying the bill. When they arrived in Salamanca, Marsagny was already there, staying in the home of a wealthy Frenchman who managed a nitrate mine in Chile. S. G. Guillemet was fanatically pro-Franco and had come from Chile to Nationalist Spain to drum up business. While the volunteers remained unpaid and on sparse rations, billeted with supporters, Marsagny cut a figure in Salamanca society. He was an habitué in the Hotel Grand and often seen in clubs and bars around the Plaza Mayor, always in the company of young and pretty women.

After two weeks, the group moved on to Talavera de la Reina where they found fifteen or so other French men waiting for them, among them a 17-year-old boy. All of the French volunteers had been recruited by Trochu in Paris. Another serious hitch emerged. It turned out that the Foreign Legion was only interested in recruiting men with experience in the infantry. This excluded many of the Frenchmen who were congregated, including Penaud, whose background was in the artillery. Disgruntled, the men who had been turned away pestered General Yagüe to change his mind and allow them to join up. While all of this was going on, Marsagny had left again, this time for three weeks in Saragossa where, he said, he would arrange new headquarters for the French volunteers. In Talavera, the penurious French volunteers scrounged food as best they could. In the mean time, another 25 recruits arrived, this time from Nancy. The Legion placed them in different barracks from the older French hands, in Penaud's words, because the new volunteers still had some 'illusions about joining up'. They, too, soon became discouraged and began demanding that Marsagny be telegraphed to return post haste from Saragossa and deal with the problems. Several of them approached the second in command of the French *bandera*, Captain Courcier, asking him to take over responsibility for the French. He haled from Oran and was a member of the Parti Social Français, but could do nothing as he too was on the very point of departure for Cadiz, where he hoped to meet 600 new French volunteers who had been recruited in Oran.

Penaud was determined to return to France in order to inform Trochu of the disorder and mismanagement of the French in Spain. He therefore asked at Foreign Legion headquarters for a safe conduct pass to travel north. He was told to wait. Four days later, the Military Police arrested him and took him off to the lock-up in Talavera, where he found himself in the company of several other Frenchmen.

After a few days, they were all transported to Ávila and passed several days in the cells, until they were moved again, this time back to Saragossa. There they were charged with espionage, currency fraud and having taken part in white slavery. Penaud claimed that Marsagny and associates from Bordeaux had illegally bought a considerable sum of pesetas in large denominations which they had squandered in franquista brothels. Whatever the rights or wrongs of the charge, the Frenchmen were terrified. They were kept in the provincial prison, which was built to hold two hundred prisoners and now was jammed with six times that number. They all faced a death penalty and every night, for many hours, could hear the staccato of clusters of single shots of the execution squad in action. After a month, Penaud managed to get word to the French consul and, like a miracle, M. Robarch appeared at the gaol, had the Frenchmen released and took them to a hotel. Within the hour, however, while the consul had gone to arrange their travel to France, the Nationalist Military Police appeared and rearrested the men and took them back to the packed provincial prison. And there they stayed.

Prisoners worked in road gangs during the day and slept at night in shifts, as there was not enough room for everyone to lie down at the same time. The guards and the trusty prisoners singled out political prisoners and foreigners for especially harsh treatment. Penaud was beaten and subjected to mock executions and nightly awaited his turn of the real thing.

The French consul attempted to contact Marsagny to request that he testify to the innocence of the incarcerated Frenchmen. By this time, however, Marsagny, following his peripatetic pattern, was travelling in France and refused to return. Trochu in Paris similarly washed his hands of the French volunteers. The persistence of the French ambassador and the consul eventually paid off and, on 14 July 1937, Penaud was taken from prison in Saragossa to the French border and expelled. Without a French passport, which the Spanish Military Police had refused to return, Penaud was considered to have left France illegally. He was therefore arrested in Hendaye and given eight days in prison by the court in Bayonne.

There is no reason to believe that the chaos which Penaud's experiences highlight changed in the *bandera* Juana de Arco. Towards the end of 1937 the unit moved to new quarters in Saragossa and a new commander, Major Victor Monnier, took over. When he was killed in a bombing raid at Getafe, his second in command, Captain Jean Courcier, became commander and led the company at the battle for Teruel and later at Calatayud.

The French unit continued to be troubled by scandal and mishap. Courcier was part of a sordid incident in February 1938 which produced a series of denunciations and prompted an official enquiry by the Judicial Section of Franco's Military Police. He was accused of embezzling money from the wealthy Frenchman, G. Guillemet, in Salamanca, who had lent funds to tide over the Joan of Arc company while it was set up. According to Guillemet's sworn statement, when he asked Courcier to return the money, the French commander had him arrested and imprisoned in Valladolid.[91] To add insult to injury, Courcier then ran away with Guillemet's Spanish mistress and set her up in Saragossa 'as a wife'.

Courcier's bad behaviour was further attested by his batman, Henri Renout. He accused the commander of stealing a valuable set of the *Diario de Alcázar* from another officer and blaming it on the previous French commander, the now deceased Major Monnier.[92] The *Diario* was the hand-printed newspaper produced by Moscardó in the Alcázar and since the siege had become sought after by collectors.

Henri Renout, perhaps, was not the most reliable witness. He had made his sworn testimony after he and another French volunteer had been arrested as deserters in Bilbao, when they had attempted to buy a sketch map of the terrain between San Sebastian and the French border with the routes that led to France. Renout testified that he was from Melilla, where he had enlisted for Franco. Without a word of Spanish, and never having crossed to the European mainland before, he had no idea where to find the French border.

Renout pleaded for leniency on the grounds that desertion had been caused by his mistreatment by Courcier and he would be happy to be reassigned to the regular army or the Carlist Requetés. Under no circumstances was he willing to return to the Juana de Arco which, in his opinion, was made up 'in major part' of men who were 'bandits' and who would 'take their revenge' on him if he were sent back. Another denunciation made to the Military Police claimed that the French were subject to ill treatment by their commanders in Spain and that it had led to levels of desertion as high as 90 per cent.[93]

Equally seriously, Courcier ran foul of senior Action Française leaders in Paris when he blocked efforts to extract several young volunteers who were from Action families.[94] Réal del Sarte intervened on behalf of a young Camelot du Roi, Maurice Barbarin, whose father, a colonel in the French army, had appealed to Maurras for assistance in getting his son out of Spain. Réal del Sarte went directly over Courcier's head to the monarchist, Major Barrosso, at Franco's headquarters. Barrroso had been the previous military attaché in Paris and, despite his providing a clearance, Courcier refused to release young Barbarin, who was killed in the battle for Teruel soon afterwards. Courcier also refused to release another son of an Action Française family, Jean de Morène, who had been held in prison in Talavera for several months on the charge of attempted desertion and spying against the Nationalist army. Even though Réal del Sarte, Marcel Guillon and Jean Conderc, all senior figures in Parisian Action circles, attested to the family's staunch pro-Franco background, the young man remained in prison. From Paris, Action Française people sent agitated letters to Franco, demanding a full military investigation into Courcier's command.

It may be that the disagreements among Franco's French followers arose from personality differences and conflicting perceptions of status and entitlements in Spain. It is not impossible, though, that the acrimony in Spain between Action Française and the French commander was fuelled by the political differences between these groups outside the country. Courcier belonged to the Croix de Feu/Parti Social Français and his treatment of Maurras' followers echoed the more general disdain of the new Right for the traditional royalists. These French groups had separate contacts among the monarchists, Falangists and Francoists at Nationalist headquarters. Correspondence in the file of denunciations against Courcier points to a disagreement between some sections within the Legion and the Nationalist Command. On 13 April 1938, the commander of the Spanish Legion ordered the dissolution of the Juana de Arco and the dismissal of Courcier. Two days later, a telegram to Franco headquarters attested to the fact that Courcier had shown 'excellent comportment, exceptional capacity, valour and military spirit and bravery in battle'.[95] According to the Legion's own internal history of the French battalion, Yagüe's order to dissolve the unit was countermanded eight days after it was given. For whatever reason, from this time on there were few references to the Juana de Arco as a separate company and increasingly the French volunteers who remained came under the supervision of the 17th Bandera.[96]

Whether the cause of dissension in the Courcier case or not, the full range of French right-wing groups was represented in Nationalist Spain. There were sightings of French royalist volunteers in the Carlist Requetés from the earliest days. A Frenchman killed with the Navarrese regiment in the Battle of Irún was buried with great pomp in Pamplona Cathedral in August 1936. At another funeral in San Sebastian in early October, the Count of Guilonière, a French royalist volunteer killed in a Carlist brigade, was also honoured. The French flag fluttered beside the yellow and gold of Nationalist Spain and a Spanish nobleman made a eulogy which concluded with a general cry of 'Viva Francia'.[97]

A Swiss Action Française supporter, Eddy Bauer, met French volunteers on his two voyages to Spain in August 1937 and May 1938.[98] While being shown over a hospital in Getafe, he came across a Frenchman, recuperating after being injured when he had been careless enough to light up a cigarette on an airfield and ignite a drum of petrol (Bauer, p. 25). A second man had 'thrown himself' at Bauer when he had heard a group of journalists speaking French, as they were being escorted around the battlefields by Pablo Merry del Val. This soldier had been a Camelot du Roi in Toulouse and had taught Greek and Latin in a secondary school. His reply to the perennial question about the soldier's welfare was that the 'food was good' and his comrades 'excellent, chivalrous and utterly devoted to the Nationalist cause' (ibid., p. 52). The Camelot from Toulouse was also optimistic that the military situation had picked up strongly and the 'Reds would soon be driven out'.[99]

In August 1936, a French deserter from the Spanish Foreign Legion had approached the consul in San Sebastian for help. He told the consul that he had been recruited in Oran by Franco supporters who had found him a space on a German plane to the mainland.[100] This man and the others from Oran were most likely to have been members of Doriot's Parti Populaire Français, which enjoyed great support in French Algeria.

Georges Oudard met another of the French volunteers from Oran on a warm evening in early 1937, as both strolled in the shade of the colonnades of the Plaza Mayor in Salamanca.[101] Oudard had noticed a 'well-built man with a shock of thick hair' wearing the khaki green open-necked shirt of the Foreign Legion. He sported a French tricolour ribbon on his shoulder flash, indicating that he was in the *bandera* of the Juana de Arco. The two men repaired to a nearby bar and passed an enjoyable evening together.

Oudard's companion told him that he had fought on the Oviedo front, evidently with some distinction, as he had earned a corporal's stripe. The Spanish officers he had encountered had treated him well and, since arriving in Spain, he had found a Spanish girlfriend, whose crumpled picture he proudly carried in his wallet. Before coming to Spain, the legionnaire had been a sleeping-car attendant in French Algeria and had joined up with Franco in order to 'fight Communists'. After a few convivial glasses of sherry, the Frenchman blurted out that he was an 'Anti-Semite' and that Oran was becoming 'overrun by a pack of Jews' who want to 'bludgeon us with the Popular Front'.[102] It was the same, he said, as in Spain, because 'all the Jews want is a future of communism'. Therefore he had come to Nationalist Spain 'to join up with the other side' (Oudard, pp. 55–7).

Later, in the bar, Oudard came across another volunteer wearing the tricolour ribbon on his tunic. A slight, tubercular, blond, French-speaking Swiss from Lausanne and not yet 20 years of age, this young man was full of complaints about Spaniards. They were backward, their women were prudish and their attachment to transportation by mules was positively antiquated. Another volunteer who hailed from the Paris suburbs and identified himself as 'Republican' (presumably not Action Française) had come south in order to 'stand up to the foreigners and the agents of Moscow' who were 'leading everyone by the nose' (Oudard, pp. 57–8). Overall, Oudard considered that the French men he met were not so much fighting for Franco and for Spain but were there to push their own barrows against Communism.

While travelling through Nationalist Spain with the fascist Mayor of Oran, François Roland, he also met a townsman in the uniform of a French volunteer.[103] He sported a Croix de Guerre and a row of medals on his chest from French colonial wars and saluted 'in the manner of Doriot'. The French volunteer claimed that he was fighting for the 'Latin Spirit and Western Civilization' which he perceived as presently under threat from barbarism. Behind his boastful bravado and patriotic talk, he expressed the fear that Spaniards at the front might not maintain a distinction between the 'Real French', like himself, and the tawdry French of the Popular Front. His worry was especially keen at a time when many Spaniards were being told that the French government was supplying the planes that were dropping bombs on Nationalist Spain.

Two French Croix de Feu members in the Carlist Requetés were interviewed in *El Pensiamiento Navarro* on 1 October 1936. Both were Parisians. The first, Edmond Lapegne, the son of a shoe salesman with eleven brothers and sisters, confidently expected to spend Christmas at home with them because, by then, Franco would have achieved decisive victory. In a convoluted manner, he explained that he and his companion had come south to aid 'real France' by fighting the French who were currently enlisted in the ranks of the 'Spanish Communists'. The 'most fervent hope' of both was that, by 'wearing the red beret' (that is of the Carlists), they would demonstrate to the Spanish that there were 'good Frenchmen' from 'Real France' who were part of the French Croix de Feu within the ranks of Franco's soldiers in Spain. The two, in unison, ended the interview with a rousing 'Vive la véritable France' and 'Vive La Rocque'.[104]

In April 1938, Robert Brasillach, the editor of the fascist newspaper *Je Suis Partout,* and two companions travelled extensively through Nationalist Spain.[105] Two years before, Brasillach's volume, written with his brother-in-law, Henri Massis, had lionized the 'noble energies' and the religious spirit of Moscardó and the cadets of the Alcázar. During the 1938 trip, Brasillach met a number of Frenchmen who were there to defeat the 'Red Marxists' of the Spanish government. Among them was the 'celebrated Frenchman of the Alcázar', a baker on the Zocodover Square in Toledo, who, having shared the siege for several weeks, had slipped out one night in order to collect flour to take back to feed the besieged. Caught by the Republicans, the baker was tried and would have been executed if the French consul in Madrid had not heard about his plight and raced to Toledo. On the day that the Frenchman's sentence was to be carried out, the consul obtained a stay of proceedings and, using the consular car, had carried him off 'in the best style of the American cinema' (Brasillach and Massis, p. 221).

Brasillach was greatly moved by the romantic story of a very young French boy whose father was a member of the Garde Mobile and had been killed in the Paris street riots in February 1934. As soon as the boy had heard about Franco's uprising, although only 16 and still at school, he had borrowed money from his sister and, 'with the school books still under his arm', had set off to Spain. Three days later he was in Irún and was accepted into the Spanish Foreign Legion so that he could 'fight the Communists who had killed his father'. Now two years older, he was a great favourite with the men. Despite his having been wounded five times, he was still a boy who 'did not drink or think about women' and, on his days off from the trenches near the University City in Madrid, he would go to Toledo and buy himself a kilo of sweets (*ibid.,* pp. 221–2).

An interesting sidelight on the French in Nationalist Spain is provided by an Australian, Nugent Bull, who enlisted with Franco in the Spanish Foreign Legion at Talavera de la Reina in October 1937. His story has been told in the previous chapter. Bull's lack of knowledge of the intricacies of European politics is a boon to the historian because, like a human *tabula rasa*, his correspondence records the attitudes and explanations of his French comrades concerning the Civil War in Spain and, in even more detail, their views on French politics and the Popular Front. With no competing voices, the sounds of the French volunteers in the Juana de Arco come through loud and clear. He shared the paranoia of his French comrades about Communist, Jews and Freemasons, and their anti-England attitudes resonated with Australian Catholic republicanism.

It is useful to attempt to establish the tenor of relations between French volunteers and their Spanish comrades. It was a question that interested Robert Brasillach as well. A French First World War veteran at the front insisted that Spaniards had nothing against French volunteers. As proof, he offered the evidence of his own unit, in which the commander had decreed that any Spanish soldier who spoke badly about the French would be placed immediately on the punishment squad (Brasillach and Massis, pp. 221–2). The example, however, might equally suggest the reverse of goodwill towards the French, whereby their unpopularity was so common that an official punishment was needed to dampen down the hostility.[106]

Francis McCullagh noted that Frenchmen were regarded with deep suspicion in Franco's Spain: a French accent was immediately suspect and French volunteers were warned to keep their mouths shut in public; any letter with a French postmark was always opened by the censor.[107] A degree of Francophobia is suggested, as well, by the exaggerated claims that Franco's headquarters made about the presence of the French on the Republican side. The statements, which the French government always officially denied, drove the French ambassador to distraction. For example, during the Teruel campaign, between December 1937 and February 1938, there were constant reports from Nationalist command about the great number of French soldiers fighting for the Republic. Nationalist press bulletins announced that Franco's headquarters had 'identified authoritatively' that French nationals were the majority among the 'hundreds and hundreds of bodies they had examined' that had been 'abandoned in the snow'. A patently ludicrous statement was broadcast over Radio Saragossa that 'authoritatively identified' the hundreds of bodies at Teruel as belonging to 'French Freemasons'.[108] Another news report claimed that 'a superior officer in the French Army' had led the Republican encirclement of Teruel.[109]

When the news was broadcast over the radio, there were anti-French demonstrations in Saragossa. The French ambassador in December 1937 warned French citizens in Nationalist Spain to exercise caution by not wearing French decorations or colours that might provoke hostility. At the same time, the French Foreign Minister, Yvon Delbos, published an official rejoinder in L'Agence Havas, denying that any French army officers were at Teruel. He noted the 'astonishment' of the French government to see 'blatant untruths' published in a press that was entirely under the control of Nationalist government censors.[110]

An even more unlikely story was circulating at the end of 1937 during the Republican push into Teruel, which was still in Nationalist hands. The governor of Irún, Major Julián Troncoso, claimed that Nationalist Border Police had picked up two Frenchmen who had injected themselves with 'dangerous viruses' which they intended to spread throughout Nationalist Spain.[111] Troncoso, relating the story to the Swiss journalist, Eddy Bauer, stated that he had seen the Frenchmen with his own eyes: their backs, bellies and arms were covered with 'thousands of needle marks from the bacillus for the plague, typhus, cholera or sleeping sickness'. Bauer, who in normal events was a stout supporter of General Franco, found the story doubtful.[112]

French volunteers, whom Oudard met, were troubled by a common attitude among Spaniards, expressed in a belief that all French people were Communists and that, after the Soviet Union, France was 'the great breeding ground' of world Bolshevism. Patriotic and anti-Bolshevik, French volunteers resented the slur on their nationality and felt duty-bound to disprove it by their own acts of valour in the field (Oudard, pp. 59–61).

There were also Frenchmen at the front who disparaged the military capacities of the Spaniards and their antiquated ideas of combat. One volunteer related an incident to Oudard in which an enemy machine-gun nest was dug in very near to them in the Nationalist lines. The Spanish commanding officer was reluctant to give permission to the Frenchman to lead a small group under the cover of darkness to take it out. When the mission was finally accomplished with no loss of life, the Spanish officer had remained displeased, because night raids were outside 'the rules' of the Spanish army. It similarly was not done, so the French volunteer reported, to carry out attacks at mealtimes. According to Oudard, it was only after the Battle of Brunete in mid-1937 that the Nationalist army had begun the practice of night raids.[113]

The French embassy and the volunteers in Spain

From the beginning of the Civil War, the French embassy operated from St-Jean-de-Luz, a short drive along the coast from the main crossing at the International Bridge at Hendaye. Like most of the foreign embassies, the French had been on summer holidays on the coast at San Sebastian in July 1936 and, instead of returning to Madrid, had set up temporary offices in France. The French ambassador, until he retired in October 1937, was Jean Herbette. His replacement moved to Valencia and a consul general operated across the border from the western zone.[114] Herbette had been appointed to Madrid in June 1931 and had been close to Azaña and the new government of the Second Republic, though it was always clear that his objective was to promote French commercial interests. He had spent the previous seven years in the French embassy in Moscow where his first-hand observations had made him strongly anti-Communist and fearful that revolutionary disorder would spill over and threaten the Western democracies. After the uprising, Herbette's enthusiasm for the Spanish Republic gave way in favour of the insurgents.

The biographer of Léon Blum, Jean Lacouture, described Herbette as 'spontaneously favourable' to Franco and more concerned to remain at a safe distance away from the war at St-Jean-de-Luz. This choice of location cast him in the role of an 'observer of the rebels' rather than an ambassador to the Republic.[115] In a similarly critical light, Claude Bowers describes Herbette as 'misrepresenting France, having gone over bag and baggage to Franco and the generals within three weeks'.[116]

Certainly Herbette assiduously cultivated Franco's military commander in Irún, Major Julián Troncoso, who was permitted to come and go across the French border. The Frenchman also maintained good contacts with Sangroniz at Nationalist headquarters in Burgos and with Franco's supporters and couriers, like the Count of Andes in Biarritz. It is possible that the ambassador chose this strategy in order to maintain the communication channels that would facilitate his diplomatic duties. Whatever the assessment of him by his contemporaries, Herbette's despatches, by contrast with those of Sir Henry Chilton and Sir Robert Hodgson, reveal profound mistrust of Nationalist headquarters. Similarly, Réal del Sarte in an interview with Franco cited M. Herbette as an example of the perfidious sort of Frenchman.[117] In any event, however, Leftist groups in south-west France and the Communist paper, *L'Humanité*, complained about Herbette's apparent pro-Francoism. Anti-Herbette feeling was brought to a head when a group of Franco's supporters attempted to highjack a Spanish destroyer in Brest harbour in mid-1937. Troncoso, the military governor, was one of the conspirators who was allowed to get away. Only later was he arrested, after there had been a great outcry from left-wing groups in France. Troncoso was picked up when he crossed into France on one of his frequent jaunts. Herbette, implicated by his relationship with Troncoso, was accused of being a 'traitor to France' and was recalled to Paris in October 1937 and very soon afterwards retired from diplomatic service.

A good deal of diplomatic time at the French embassy was spent in dealing with requests that French families had sent to the Foreign Minister in Paris, wanting assistance for their sons who had enlisted in Spain. The detail of these incidents sheds an interesting light on the recruits and their reception in Nationalist Spain. Behind the formal language of diplomatic minutes in the consular records, it is possible to catch a glimpse of the perplexity of the families at their sons' departure, especially if, as was common, they had left without warning.[118]

When a French citizen wrote to the government for help in locating a family member, whether a volunteer with Franco or a Republican prisoner in Nationalist Spain, the matter inevitably ended up on the desk of the French ambassador. While it may have been extremely irritating for embassy staff to have to deal with them, it seems that a conscientious effort was made in most cases to track the individual down and, if the Nationalists would agree, to begin the process of repatriation.

More common were the occasions when French embassy staff seethed at the uncooperative attitude of the Nationalists' high command and their reluctance to provide information about French citizens either in the Foreign Legion, or, equally, French International Brigaders who were prisoners in Nationalist Spain. Franco's headquarters were particularly unforthcoming about wounded French prisoners.[119] In a confidential note to consular staff, the Foreign Ministry pointed out that the Nationalists' attitude neither conformed to 'the elementary principles of humanity' nor to the international conventions of war that 'even Germans in the First World War had respected'.[120] In another communication, the ambassador offered a more dispiriting interpretation, and probably closer to the facts, that most prisoners of the Nationalists were executed on the spot. He added gloomily that French prisoners suffered particularly because of the 'widespread perception that has carefully been fomented in Nationalist Spain that France is pro-Communist and committed to the triumph of Communism and anarchism in Spain'.[121]

According to French law, all military recruits under the age of 20 were required to provide written consent from a parent or a guardian before they could enlist in the French army. The French ambassador used this legal precedent whenever he attempted to press the case for the repatriation of a minor who had enlisted on either side in the Spanish Civil War. In the case of minors whose parents or guardians had requested it, the French diplomatic service was instructed to assist in every possible way to find these young men and send them home.

The official position of the French Foreign Ministry was quite clear in relation to French nationals who wished to be repatriated. Long-standing international convention dictated that all foreign nationals were entitled to free access to their consular representatives. As well, any French volunteer who presented himself to a French consul and asked for repatriation was entitled to immediate diplomatic protection while the legal ramifications of his request were sorted out. On several occasions, the Foreign Minister reiterated that no obstacles were to be placed in the way of anyone who asked for repatriation. Quai d'Orsay added the rider that the repatriation negotiations should be carried out discreetly by consular officials, who, in all cases, should never behave as though France and Spain were in 'a state of war'.[122]

In practice, this common-sense policy did not always work. Because France had no official diplomatic relations with Nationalist Spain, the ambassador worked informally through his own contacts and via the French consuls in San Sebastian, La Coruña, Saragossa, Seville and so forth. Often a French soldier wishing to make contact with the consul would be denied leave to travel to wherever it was that the consul was located. In May 1937, for example, the French consul at San Sebastian sent a coded telegram to the ambassador about the cases of eight French volunteers who wished to return home. Among them were two men on the Madrid front with Carlist Requetés, one ill and the other wounded, who had been denied permission to travel by their commanding officer and were therefore unable to present themselves in person at the consulate.[123]

There were few successes in official repatriation from Franco's Spain. On 27 August 1936, Roger Dugenest, a 16-year-old Parisian, disappeared from his mother's flat in Rue d'Alma in the 16th Arrondissement.[124] His mother, Mme Cécile Boucher, was frantic. A month later, she received a letter with the return address 'La Légion, Bandera Juana de Arco, Talavera de la Reina, Provincia de Toledo', letting her know that her son had been accepted into the Spanish Foreign Legion to fight with General Franco. A second letter, this time postmarked Saragossa, arrived several weeks later. In it, her son indicated that he had made a terrible mistake and asked his mother to send his birth certificate as soon as possible. With it he hoped to prove that he was under age at enlistment, so that the Spaniards would let him return home.

Mme Boucher immediately contacted the Quai d'Orsay and requested the French government to retrieve her son. She explained that she was a widow from the First World War, which had left her with a dependent, disabled brother, and that she relied on her son for financial support. Subsequently, on several occasions she came to the Ministry of Foreign Affairs to ask about the progress of her son's repatriation.

The French ambassador pulled out all stops to extricate the boy. He activated his informal contacts with the Nationalist officials across the border, wrote formally to Franco's headquarters and directed the French consul in San Sebastian, who in the past had been successful in such matters, to go in person to Salamanca to try and negotiate the release of young Dugenest.

It was to no avail. On the last day of December, the Nationalist headquarters sent a crisp letter pointing out that, as Roger Dugenest had enlisted in the Spanish Foreign Legion 'voluntarily and of his own free will', there were no grounds for his contract to be rescinded. As a result, he was legally obliged to remain in the Foreign Legion until the contract had run its course.[125]

Another Parisian, M. Virgile Bressand, from the Rue des Petits-Hotels in the 10th Arrondissement, at the end of June 1937, asked the Foreign Minister's assistance in finding his 18-year-old son Jean-Marie, who had joined up with General Franco. The first and last word that his anxious father had heard had been in a letter written from Irún, telling him that his son had crossed into Spain and been accepted into the Spanish Foreign Legion. The consul, who took up the case because Bressand's son was a French minor, was unable to find any evidence of the boy, or even that he had crossed into Spain.

There were others. Mme Zamouth, a French citizen in Algeria, wrote for assistance on 18 June 1937 to the Quai d'Orsay. Her husband, Angel Zamouth, an electrical engineer, had left home in August 1936 with the intention, she thought, of enlisting with the Spanish insurgents. She had heard nothing from him until very recently when, in a 'private communication', she was told that her husband had been killed in battle in Spain on 10 December 1936. Having received no official word about his fate, she begged the French Foreign Office in Paris to help her establish whether her husband had died and if so, whereabouts.

Using his normal channels, Herbette was unable to find any information about Angel Zamouth. He received word, as well, from a contact that there was no record of Zamouth in the Foreign Legion. Eventually, the ambassador wrote to ask whether Mme Zamouth could provide any clue about the front on which her husband might have fought; however, in a postscript to Paris, Herbette added that it was very likely that the fellow had enlisted under another name or even a false nationality and, since they had tried all the regular channels, there was no way of tracking him down.[126]

The father of a 28-year-old commercial traveller in Toulon wrote to ask the French ambassador to get a letter to his son. The son had joined the Spanish insurgents and was known now to be in the Jeanne d'Arc battalion and his father wanted to know whether he was still in good health. The letter was sent on to the consul in San Sebastian to take up.[127] A mother in Tours, whose son had joined up with Franco, wrote that she was afraid that her son, not yet 21, did not know what he was getting into and she therefore asked for assistance in finding him.[128] It is not known whether the Consul ever managed to locate any of these individuals in Spain. Most likely they were not found.

Franco's French volunteers and French fascism

In the last couple of decades, the memoirs of French veterans who were on the Eastern Front with Hitler have begun to appear and now constitute almost a sub-genre of first-person writing about French fascism.[129] Many of them had been volunteers for Franco. Others, ideologues and adventurers, report that Francoism and the Spanish Civil War were major influences in their political development in the years leading up to the war.[130]

Eric Labat, a member of the French Légion contre le Bolchevisme in the Second World War, described a French comrade on the Eastern Front. Nicknamed 'Tito', his experiences in Nationalist Spain during the Civil War had created what Labat termed 'a certain international eclecticism' in his politics. It was this that, in 1942, predisposed 'Tito' to Germany and Nazism.[131]

The chequered career of Jean Fontenoy provides another good example. He was 'a storybook soldier of fortune' but with a shady past that probably included drug addiction.[132] A right-wing ideologue, he volunteered with the Joan of Arc company during the Spanish Civil War. Previously he claimed to have been a Havas correspondent in the Soviet Union and the Far East; however, in 1935, he was expelled from Havas and believed that it had been Blum's doing. Henceforth, he harboured a phobic hatred of Blum and the Popular Front, which he claimed was synonymous with Communism. In 1939, Fontenoy fought with the Finns against the Soviet Union and, more disreputably, in Occupied Paris, in 1941, Fontenoy was a founding journalist for the German Press Agency. Later, though without great success, he accompanied the French volunteers to the Eastern Front as a press officer cum political agent.[133]

Conclusion

The picture which has been pieced together in this chapter constitutes a fragment of the large and complex canvas of the extreme Right in France between the wars. It is probably true that the history of the *bandera* of the Juana de Arco makes a very small contribution to the historiographical debates about this decade. These have revolved around questions about whether French fascism grew from indigenous roots; was part of a counter-revolutionary tradition from 1789; or even existed at all. The experiences of Franco's French supporters in Spain reveal one part of the social reality within which, between 1936 and 1939, individuals on the Right made their choices for action.

The men of the Joan of Arc company, whether soldiers, organizers or backers, were motivated by a powerful combination of ideology and self-interest. Right-wing ideologues in France saw the Spanish Civil War as a critical event in a much larger struggle. They were convinced that on the other side of the Pyrenees they could lay down the glove to the Popular Front in Paris. In doing so, they cast their actions as the cutting edge of a 'White International' in which a blow struck against 'Reds' in Spain was a blow against 'Reds' everywhere, but particularly in France.

Frenchmen, like Charles Maurras and Réal del Sarte, who rejected the Republican tradition of 1789, imagined that what they observed in 'New Spain' was the dawn of the new order in which an authoritarian leader was forging a strong state: intransigently Catholic, intolerant of difference and implacably anti-democratic. But, of course, ideology provides only part of the story. Right-wing leaders who could be useful to the Nationalist cause were lavishly fêted in Spain with travel perks and honours. They were escorted on whirlwind tours through the western zone. Chauffeured in large cars provided by Nationalist headquarters, there were obedient flunkeys to wave them through every roadblock and provide comfortable accommodation at the end of the day. It is no wonder at all that these Frenchmen, like the equivalent English travellers, found Nationalist Spain irresistible. Nor is it surprising that the narratives of travel that they produced are peppered with details of flattering receptions and dinners held in their honour, while recording little that evokes a nation in wartime.

Despite the ideological patter they repeat in interviews, many ordinary French volunteer soldiers probably signed up for Franco because they were down on their luck and the prospect of reinsertion into military life was appealing. A whole swathe of veterans at the end of the First World War were ill-equipped to return to humdrum civilian life. Like Drieu la Rochelle's Gilles, they were nostalgic for the excitement of adventure and the male camaraderie that they recalled in the trenches.[134] Others were simply out of work and glad to find any billet that paid. The soldiers in the Juana de Arco company probably made no particular military contribution to Franco's success. General Yagüe's recommendation, that the unit be disbanded a few months after it had begun recruiting, is telling.

There is no reason to assume that they later lifted their game. Indeed, the evidence suggests that the French in command of the company continued to be of poor calibre and contributed to the high rate of desertions among French volunteers overall.

Franco's primary concern in forming the company was to make contact with backers and leaders of the Right in France who could be useful to his cause outside Spain. As well, there was the incentive that the Juana de Arco could provide a putative parallel to the International Brigades if the Non-Intervention Committee insisted on the withdrawal of all foreign volunteers in Spain. It is likely though, as well, that Franco expected from a French unit a more concrete contribution than he received in money, men and military prowess.

In the long run, it may be that the major impact of Francoism and the Civil War on the French Right was the example it left to Frenchmen in the chaos of the Second World War and the Occupation. Certainly, it influenced the younger generation. Christian de la Mazière was too young to fight in Spain but in 1942 threw in his lot with the Waffen SS and embraced National Socialism outright.[135] Mazière grew up in a military family that read L'Action française every day and believed that Jews were taking over the French nation. As a boy, Christian was riveted by the 'heroic cadets of Toledo' and wished fervently to share their adventure. In his words, within the 'interior mental theatre' on which people play out their dreams and plans, Francoism set the landscape and Moscardó defined the benchmarks of good and evil against which he rehearsed his future life.

In this sense, activists on the Right saw Franco's success as presaging a victory of the counter-republican tradition in France. As a consequence, many on the extreme Right in France confidently expected that the next Civil War would embrace Europe as a whole and in it, if they followed Franco's reactionary politics and his military example, they could achieve a similar outcome.

Notes

1 The details of the Moscardó presentation are included in PRO, London, FO 371/ 21285/ 47815, No. 106, Hendaye, 16 February 1937, p. 193; 8 March 1937, p. 70.

2 René Rémond, Les Catholiques dans la France des années 30 (Paris: Éditions Cana, 1979), p. 264; and James F. MacMillan, 'France', in Political Catholicism in Europe, 1918–1965, edited by Tom Buchanan and Martin Conway (Oxford: Clarendon, 1996), pp. 41–2.

3 *L'Echo de Paris*, 23 July 1936, quoted in J. R. Tournoux, *L'Histoire secrète* (Paris: Plon, 1962), p. 21. In *Gringoire*, 21 August 1936, Castelnau wrote that 'the civilized world trembles in disgust as the Bolshevik front in Spain machine guns, pillages, destroys and sets everything alight'.

4 Rémond, *Les Catholiques dans la France*, p. 264.

5 Julian Jackson, *The Popular Front in France: Defending Democracy, 1934–38* (Cambridge: Cambridge University Press, 1990), p. 252.

6 Rémond, *Les Catholiques dans la France*, p. 175.

7 Spanish documents at the time use both the French, Jeanne d'Arc, and the Spanish, Juana de Arco. The *bandera* is often translated as the English battalion, though in size a *bandera* more closely resembles an English company, which is the term often used in relation to the Joan of Arc unit and is used in this chapter. I am grateful to Grahame Harrison for his expert advice on this and a number of other Spanish military matters.

8 Robert Soucy, *French Fascism: The Second Wave 1933–39* (New Haven: Yale University Press, 1995). By contrast, René Rémond argues that radical Right movements maintained a continuity with French traditions, borrowing the 'ornaments and finery' of fascism rather than its spirit. See his *The Right Wing in France: From 1815 to de Gaulle* (2nd edn., Philadelphia: University of Pennsylvania, 1969), p. 281.

9 Hans Raupach, 'The impact of the Great Depression in Eastern Europe,' *Journal of Contemporary History*, IV (4) (1969), pp. 75–86.

10 Martin Gilbert, *The European Powers 1900–1945* (New York: New American Library, 1965), p. 165. See also Jean-Baptiste Duroselle, *La Décadence, 1932–1939, Politique étrangère de la France* (Paris: Imprimerie Nationale, 1979), which examines France's structural weaknesses and poor leadership after the First World War; and Enrique Moradiellos, 'The Allies and the Civil War,' in *Spain and the Great Powers in the Twentieth Century*, edited by Sebastian Balfour and Paul Preston (London: Routledge, 1999), pp. 96–126.

11 Though it does not alter substantially the broad pattern of relations between France, Britain and the Spanish Republic, which is the background to the discussion of Franco's Frenchmen in this chapter, it is worth noting that Nicole Jordan's study of French diplomacy during the Popular Front has shown that French foreign policy at the time was independently concerned with Eastern Europe and specifically Czechoslovakia, to isolate future war away from French territory. See her *The Popular Front and Central Europe: Dilemmas of French Impotence 1918–1940* (Cambridge: Cambridge University Press, 1992).

12 Sir Samuel Hoare, who was Foreign Secretary to Baldwin and Britain's ambassador in Madrid during the Second World War, noted that Baldwin 'never seemed to have any clear-cut idea of what foreign policy should be'; see Lord Templewood, *Nine Troubled Years* (London: Collins, 1954), pp. 290–1. It is worth noting that Philip Williamson, in *Stanley Baldwin: Conservative Leadership*

and National Values (Cambridge: Cambridge University Press, 1999), offers a major revision to the 'belittlement' of Baldwin's leadership. Although not substantially altering the position on Spain presented here, Williamson argues that Baldwin's leadership was positive and credible.

13 For a recent and detailed analysis which discusses the type and calibre of the planes and equipment, see Gerald Howson, *Arms for Spain: The Untold Story of the Spanish Civil War* (London: John Murray, 1998), pp. 21–7; 33–9.

14 There has been a long debate about whether Britain or France provided the impetus for non-intervention. For a clear analysis of the larger international picture and the Spanish Civil War, see Enrique Moradiellos, 'The Allies and the Spanish Civil War', in Balfour and Preston, *Spain and the Great Powers*. On French domestic politics, David Levy argues that Blum's policies favouring reconciliation were misapprised, in 'The French Popular Front 1936–1937', in *The Popular Front in Europe*, edited by Helen Graham and Paul Preston (London: Macmillan, 1987), pp. 58–83. See also, M. D. Gallagher, 'Léon Blum and the Spanish Civil War', *Journal of Contemporary History*, 6 (1971), pp. 56–64; J. Bowyer Bell, 'French reaction to the Spanish Civil War, 1936', in *Power, Public Opinion and Diplomacy: Essays in Honour of Eber Malcolm Carroll by His Former Students* (Durham, NC: Duke University Press, 1959), pp. 267–96; Dante A. Puzzo, *Spain and the Great Powers, 1936–1941* (New York: Columbia University Press, 1962); David Wingeate Pike, *Les Français et la guerre d'Espagne* (Paris: Presses Universitaires de France, 1975). See also note 28 in Chapter 1.

15 The crowd, which had been calling for arms for Spain, gave Blum a standing ovation. See the contemporary observations by the Manchester *Guardian*'s correspondent in Paris, Alexander Werth, 'Aeroplanes for Spain', in his *Destiny of France* (London: Hamish Hamilton, 1937), pp. 370–90.

16 *Le Figaro*, 25 July 1936.

17 Raoul Girardet, 'Notes sur l'esprit d'un fascisme français, 1934–1940', *Revue française de science politique* (July–September 1955).

18 See Joel Colton, 'The formation of the French Popular Front, 1934–6', in *The French and Spanish Popular Fronts: Comparative Perspectives* (Cambridge: Cambridge University Press, 1989), pp. 9–23; Samuel M. Osgood, 'The Front Populaire: views from the Right', *International Review of Social History*, 9 (2) (1964), pp. 189–201.

19 The police with a search warrant found Blum's blood-stained hat, collar and tie displayed by the Camelots du Roi as trophies of war at the Action Française's headquarters. An amateur's film of the incident enabled the police to prove what had happened. See Henri Noguères, *La Vie quotidienne en France au temps du Front Populaire 1935–1938* (Paris: Hachette, 1977), pp. 50–2; Philippe Bourdrel, *La Cagoule: histoire d'une société secrète du Front Populaire à la Ve République* (Paris: Albin Michel, 1992), pp. 37–8; and the Appendix to Decroix and Maurel, *Bandes armées* (Paris: Éditions du Comité National de Lutte

Contre la Guerre et le Fascisme, 1939). For the Action Française version, see Albert Marty, *L'Action Française racontée par elle-même* (Paris: Nouvelle Éditions Latines, 1968), pp. 326–34.

20 Pierre Milza, 'L'ultra-droite des années trente', in *Histoire de l'extrême droite en France*, edited by Michel Winock (Paris: Éditions du Seuil, 1994), p. 184. See as well Michel Winock's discussion of anti-Semitism and its links to historical and economic development on the Right and the Left, in his *Nationalisme, antisémitisme et fascisme en France* (Paris: Éditions du Seuil, 1990), pp. 218–23.

21 Ernst Nolte, *The Three Faces of Fascism: Action Française, Italian Fascism and National Socialism* (New York: New American Library, 1963); Eugen Weber, *L'Action Française* (Stanford: Stanford University Press, 1962); Samuel M. Osgood, *French Royalism since 1870* (The Hague: Martinus Nijhoff, 1970); Oscar L. Arnal, *Ambivalent Alliance: The Catholic Church and the Action Française 1899–1939* (Pittsburgh: University of Pittsburgh, 1982); and Michel Winock, 'L'Action Française', in his *Histoire de l'extrême droite en France* (Paris: Éditions du Seuil, 1993) pp. 125–56.

22 Weber, *L'Action Française*, p. 398.

23 Weber, *L'Action Française*, p. 402.

24 'Quatre états confédérés: Juifs, protestants, franc-maçons, métèques, in Charles Maurras, *Mes idées politiques* (Paris: Fayard, 1937), quoted in Winock, 'L'Action française', in his *Histoire de l'extrême droite en France*, p. 129.

25 Pius XI saw Action Française as a 'dangerous cuckoo in the Catholic nest' and in 1926 the Vatican placed Maurras' books on the index and forbade *L'Action française* to French Catholics on pain of being denied the sacraments. See John Cornwell, *Hitler's Pope: The Secret History of Pius XII* (London: Viking, 1999), p. 172.

26 Occupants of the territory at the extreme of the far Right. See Milza, 'L'ultra-droite des années trente', pp. 157–89.

27 Among a great many examples see the description of Blum in *Je Suis Partout*, as part of 'the sordidness of this squalid race of usurers, shady bankers and rag dealers', No. 312, 14 Nov. 1936; or the pastiche made from Blum's published speeches and writings that suggest that he was an embezzler and seducer of underage girls, *Je Suis Partout*, No. 342, 12 June 1937; and *Candide*, No. 699, 5 August 1937. See also Michel Winock, *Nationalisme, antisémitisme et fascisme en France*, p. 257; and Jackson, *Popular Front*, p. 250.

28 See Dominique Borne and Henri Dubief, *La Crise des années 30, 1929–1938* (Paris: Éditions du Seuil, 1989), which provides a lively view of the politics, society and culture of the decade; Jackson, *The Popular Front*; and Eugen Weber, *The Hollow Years: France in the 1930s* (New York: Norton, 1994).

29 With no basis in fact, both papers claimed that Salengro had been court-martialled as a coward in the First World War. For *Candide*'s response to the affair see 'Le suicide de M. Salengro et la guerre d'Espagne', No. 663, 26 Nov. 1936; and

Alexander Werth's commentary in the Manchester *Guardian*, reprinted in *The Destiny of France*, pp. 391–8.

30 Nolte, *Three Faces of Fascism*, p. 128. The Camelots' song, chanted as they marched shoulder to shoulder through the Latin Quarter pledged to 'wipe out insolent Jews'.

31 See Robert Soucy, who argues that it was a fascist organization, in his *French Fascism: The Second Wave 1933–1939*, pp. 104–203. By contrast, Rémond's view is that its activities consisted of 'political boy-scouting for adults', in *The Right Wing in France*, p. 290, while, for Michel Winock, the fact that the movement was careful to exist within the bounds of legality precludes its being fascist; see *Nationalisme, antisémitisme et fascisme en France*, p. 264.

32 Philippe Bourdrel claims that Cagoulards had close connections to Franco's brother Nicolás and General Mola, *La Cagoule: histoire d'une société secrète du Front Populaire à la Ve République* (Paris: Albin Michel, 1992), pp. 165–79.

33 According to Louis Ducloux, ex-Director of Criminal Investigations of the French National Security Service, Deloncle negotiated the purchase of Mauser weapons and ammunition manufactured in Toledo in *From Blackmail to Treason: Political Crime and Corruption in France 1920–1940*, translated by Ronald Mathews (London: André Deutsch, 1958), pp. 169–70. When the Cagoule's Parisian armoury was uncovered by French Security in November 1936, two Cagoule agents, Juif [*sic*] and Jean-Baptiste, were assassinated in southern France. Jean-Baptiste's death was covered up by official reports in the Nationalist Spanish press that he had died a hero fighting the Communists with General Franco in Nationalist Spain; see Bourdrel, *La Cagoule: histoire d'une société secrète*, pp. 162–74.

34 Philippe Bourdrel, *La Cagoule: 30 ans de complots* (Paris: Marabout, 1970), p. 136.

35 Bourdrel, *La Cagoule: 30 ans de complots*, pp. 148–50.

36 Soucy, *French Fascism: The Second Wave*, p. 47. The Cagoule had links to the Italian Secret Service. Their most notorious achievement was the contract murder of the Rosselli brothers in June 1937. Carlo Rosselli, an anti-fascist Italian exile in France and editor of the anti-fascist paper, *Justice and Liberty*, had fought in the Matteotti Column of the International Brigades and published identity papers taken from Italian soldiers with Franco which documented Mussolini's involvement. See Philippe Bourdrel, *La Cagoule: 30 ans de complots*, pp. 153–69, and Louis Ducloux, *From Blackmail to Treason*, pp. 178–82.

37 MacMillan, 'France', in Buchanan and Conway (eds), *Political Catholicism in Europe*, pp. 34–68.

38 See the comments by Jean-Louis La Roy, who fought on the Eastern Front with Hitler, that every Sunday in his Breton church the congregation prayed for the defeat of Bolshevism and the return of Russia to the 'bosom of the Catholic community', in *Histoire d'un marin breton alcoolique engagé volontaire dans la L.V.F.* (Paris: Tema Éditions, 1977), p. 44.

39 See MacMillan, 'France'; and Paul Christophe, *1936: les Catholiques et le Front Populaire* (Paris: Desclée, 1979), pp. 119–34.

40 The journal had suggested that as Blum was the Prime Minister Catholics could support him. See René Rémond, *Les Catholiques dans la France des années 30* (Paris: Éditions Cana, 1979), pp. 216–24.

41 Herbert Southworth's exhaustive study has traced the evidence of the incident, the official cover-up by Franco's supporters and the continuing polemic, in *Guernica! Guernica!: A Study of Journalism, Diplomacy, Propaganda and History* (Berkeley: University of California Press, 1977). Most famously, the horror of the deaths of civilians in the bombing of Guernica was captured in Picasso's *Guernica Guernica* (1937).

42 *Euzko-Deya*, Paris, 7 Feb. 1937, quoted in Southworth, *Guernica! Guernica!*, p. 150.

43 *L'Action française*, 6 May 1937, Maurras writing as 'Pellisson'. See also the scathing attack on Catholics and Basques who are 'allied to Marxists' in H. Joubert, *L'Espagne de Franco* (Paris: Sorlot, 1938), pp. 27–36.

44 *Nouvelle Revue Française*, 1 July 1937, and as an introduction to Alfredo Mendizábal, *Aux origines d'une tragédie* (Paris: Desclé de Brouwer, 1937). See also Southworth, *Guernica! Guernica!*, pp. 136–79. Writing years later, François Mauriac stated that it had been difficult to change his position to opposition to the Nationalists when he knew that the legal Spanish government was supported by Marxists and anarchists. He had shifted his allegiances because of the presence of Moors fighting Christians, the 'atrocious methods of total war', the suffering of the Basques and, most of all, the horror that the 'pretension' of the Spanish generals had produced in him when they claimed that they were leading a holy crusade as 'soldiers of Christ the King', in *Figaro littéraire*, 4 May 1963.

45 This did not prevent Robert Brasillach from pouring contempt on Bernanos, 'a coarse hairy man who like an intoxicated lion shakes his head and endlessly repeats the same fuliginous phrases', and whose book left Brasillach 'flabbergasted' and convinced that the author is 'mad'. See Brasillach, *Une génération dans l'orage* (Paris: Plon, 1950), p. 215.

46 Nolte, *The Three Faces of Fascism*, pp. 592–3; and Michel Winock, 'Le cas Bernanos', in his *Nationalisme, antisémitisme et fascisme en France* (Paris: Éditions du Seuil, 1990), pp. 397–415.

47 At the ceremony to celebrate the anniversary of the fall of Bilbao on 19 June 1938, Franco's brother-in-law, Ramón Serrano Suñer, described Maritain as a 'converted Jew who speaks in an accent that recalls the Sages of Israel and the fake manner of Jew-democrats', and whose 'work had received high homage in the synagogues and the lodges of Freemasonry'; quoted in Herbert Southworth, *Le Mythe de la croisade de Franco* (Paris: Ruedo Ibérico, 1964), p. 141.

48 Oscar L. Arnal, *Ambivalent Alliance: The Catholic Church and the Action Française 1899–1939* (Pittsburgh: University of Pittsburgh, 1982).

49 Weber points out that French royalists marked Alfonso XIII's abdication as a day of mourning; *L'Action française*, p. 379. For Spanish monarchists, see Paul Preston, 'Alfonsist monarchists and the coming of the Spanish Civil War', *Journal of Contemporary History*, 7 (3 and 4) (July–October 1972); and Martin Blinkhorn, 'Conservativism, traditionalism and fascism in Spain 1898–1937', in his *Fascists and Conservatives: The Radical Right and the Establishment in Twentieth Century Europe* (London: Unwin Hyman, 1990).

50 Hugh Thomas, *The Spanish Civil War* (New York: Torchstone Books, 1986), p. 59.

51 Thomas, *Spanish Civil War*, p. 151.

52 See for example, Bernard Fäy, *Les Forces de l'Espagne: voyage à Salamanque* (Paris: SGIE, 1937); Eddy Bauer, *Rouge et or: chroniques de la 'Reconquête' Espagnole, 1937–1938* (Paris: Éditions Victor Attinger, [1938]); H. Carlier, *En Espagne Nationaliste: impressions de voyage* (Geneva: Courrier de Genève, [1938]); Jérôme and Jean Tharaud, *Cruelle Espagne* (Paris: Librairie Plon, 1937); Robert Brasillach, *Une génération dans l'orage, mémoires: notre avant-guerre. Journal d'un homme occupé* (Paris: Plon, 1950); and with Henri Massis, *The Cadets of the Alcázar* (New York: The Paulist Press, 1937); and with Maurice Bardèche, *Histoire de la guerre de l'Espagne* (Paris: Plon, 1939); H. Joubert, *L'Espagne de Franco: synthèse de trois conférences données du 17 janvier au 10 février 1938* (Paris: Sorlot, 1938); and Generals Duval and Jouart and Admiral Joubert in *La Tragédie Espagnole: conférence donnée au Théâtre des Ambassadeurs, 27 avril 1938* (Paris: 1938), reprinted in *The View from the Right: Support for the Nationalists Vol. II* (Nendeln: Kraus Reprint, 1975).

53 The alternative title is À *travers l'Espagne Nouvelle sous la signe de Jeanne d'Arc* (Paris: Collection la Caravelle, 1937).

54 Anne André Glandy, *Maxime Réal del Sarte, sa vie–son oeuvre*, preface by Henry Bordeaux (Paris: Librairie Plon, 1955); and Jay Winter, *Sites of Memory, Sites of Mourning: The Great War in European Cultural History* (Cambridge: Cambridge University Press, 1996), pp. 88–9; 95. The figure of the sculptor Mercador in Bertrand Tavernier's *La Vie et rien d'autre* (1989) evokes Réal del Sarte.

55 Réal del Sarte, *Au pays de Franco*, p. 11.

56 Michel Winock, 'Jeanne d'Arc et les Juifs', in his *Nationalisme, antisémitisme et fascisme en France*, pp. 145–56.

57 Pius XII oversaw St Joan's placement in a public place in 1954; Glandy, *Maxime Réal del Sarte*, pp. 166–7.

58 Réal de Sarte, *Au pays de Franco*, p. 16.

59 José Bertrán y Musitu, *Experiencias de los Servicios de información del Nordeste de España (SIFNE) durante la guerra* (Madrid, 1940), quoted in Thomas, *Spanish Civil War*, p. 505. In 1935, Réal del Sarte had bought a house at St-Jean-de-Luz and, during the Civil War, the Nationalist border commander, Colonel Ortega, was a regular visitor. Major Julián Troncoso, the military governor of Irún, also shared a warm acquaintance with the French sculptor. Troncoso at the end of

1936 was implicated in a Cagoulist terrorist attack on Republican ships in the Bordeaux harbour and spent several months in a French prison.

60 Réal del Sarte, *Au pays de Franco*, p. 13. The first appeal appeared in *Candide*, No. 648, 13 August 1936.

61 In November 1937, the French refused Henri Massot, the Camelots du Roi organizer from Hendaye, permission to leave Spain and Réal del Sarte travelled alone. See Glandy, *Maxime Réal del Sarte*, p. 198; Charles Maurras, *Vers l'Espagne de Franco* (Paris: Éditions du Livre Moderne, 1943), p. 205.

62 The description of his and Maurras' voyage is contained in Maurras, *Vers l'Espagne de Franco*, including the Appendix by Réal del Sarte, 'En Espagne avec Charles Maurras', pp. 202–28; and the 'Extraits de Press', pp. 214–28.

63 Maurras, *Vers l'Espagne de Franco*, p. 216.

64 In the Appendix, 'Extraits de Press', in Maurras, *Vers l'Espagne de Franco*, pp. 214–28.

65 One of the main broadcasters was Jean-Hérold Paquis, who had moved rightwards from Action Française into Doriot's Parti Populaire Français. Paquis had been wounded and transferred to the radio service in Saragossa, where his call sign 'Extranjeros: étrangers' was a regular feature. During Vichy, Paquis was a principal broadcaster in the collaborationist Radio Journal de Paris. See his *Des illusions ... désillusions!* (Paris: Bourgoin Éditeur, 1948), p. 161; and Cl. Lévy, 'L'organisation de la propagande', *Revue d'Histoire de la Deuxième Guerre Mondiale* (October 1966), p. 14.

66 Maurras, *Vers l'Espagne de Franco*, pp. 244–5.

67 See, for example Maurras' discussion on Spanish royalism and the need for a strong monarchy that avoids the modern pitfall of 'reigning but not governing' in the future of Spain, in *Vers l'Espagne de Franco*, pp. 188–91. The Duke of Alba, who resigned as Spanish ambassador to Britain, fell out with Franco because Franco failed to restore the monarchy at the end of the war; see Rafael Rodríguez-Moñino Soriano, *La misión diplomática de Don Jacobo Stuart Fitz James y Falcó, XVII Duque de Alba, en la embajada de España en Londres (1937–1945)* (Valencia: Editorial Castalia, 1971), p. 129.

68 Glandy, *Maxime Réal del Sarte*, pp. 198–201. Michel Catala discusses the delicate relations between France and Spain and that the Spaniards in 1940 rejected Maurras as 'too Germanophobe'; see *Les Relations franco-espagnoles pendant la Deuxième Guerre Mondiale* (Paris: Harmattan, 1997), p. 97.

69 MAE, Nantes, Direction des Affaires Politiques et Commerciales Espagne Guerre Civile Volontaires, Vol. 237, July–November 1937, Commissariat Spécial d'Hendaye, pp. 17–18.

70 His view on the predominant role of Germany is echoed in the observations of the British pro-Franco journalist, K. S. Robson, 'The third winter of the Spanish War', *Nineteenth Century and After*, **CXXIV** (742) (December 1938).

71 MAE, Nantes, Direction des Affaires Politiques and Commerciales, Espagne.

Guerre Civile, Volontaires, Vol. 237, July–November 1937, 19 July 1937, 'Secret, volontaires français dans l'Armée du Général Franco', p. 21.

72 Servicio Histórico Militar, Ávila, 2/168/30/5, Cuartel General del Generalísimo, Estado Mayor, Sección 1. 'Secreto. Despacho número 15.773 Relacionado con el número de extranjeros alistados a la Legión antes y después de iniciado el Glorioso Movimiento Nacional. Proyecto de Organizacion de dos banderas del Tercio'. 'El número de extranjeros alistados en la Legión con anteriordad a la fecha de iniciación del Movimiento Nacional', 29–8–38. 2/168/31/27 Cuartel General del Generalísimo, Estado Mayor, Sección 1.29 Div, 10. 'Relativo a que remita con urgencia relacionados por bandera los legionarios extranjeros que existen en ese Cuerpo haciendo constar la nacionalidad. Desp. 13331. Relación nominal del personal extranjero filiado en la Legión a partir de la iniciación del Glorioso Movimiento Nacional, con indicación de la nacionalidad de cada uno y unidades en que se encuentran encuadrados', 21–8–1938.

73 George Oudard, *Chemises noires, brunes, vertes en Espagne* (Paris: Librairie Plon, 1938), p. 59. Though favouring a victory for Franco, Oudard was a careful observer and indicates the evidence for his conclusions. He accepted the total provided by a Frenchman who had been in Nationalist Spain since the war began.

74 It constituted a coalition of extreme Right leagues; Weber, *The Hollow Years*, p. 140.

75 The contracts that some of the volunteers signed in France before departing for Spain included a clause that, in the event of a revolution in France, the volunteer undertook to return immediately to France, *Le Populaire*, 28 August 1937, 'La Bandera fantôme'.

76 The Non-Intervention Committee used the term 'foreign volunteer' to cover all those fighting in Spain who did not hold Spanish nationality. As the Spanish Republicans constantly pointed out, this was a misuse of the term 'volunteer', because it placed International Brigaders, who had come to Spain in small groups or singly and without their governments' support, in the same category as Italian, German and Portuguese troops, whose trips were organized, paid for and, in many cases, commanded by regular army officers. The best analysis of the workings of non-intervention is Gabriel Jackson's *The Spanish Republic and the Civil War* (Princeton: Princeton University Press, 1965), which sets the dense detail of the workings of the policy against the large picture. See also P. A. M. van der Esch, *Prelude to War: The International Repercussions of the Spanish Civil War (1936–1939)* (The Hague: Martinus Nijhoff, 1951), pp. 118–38; Enrique Moradiellos sets the Civil War within the broad configuration of international politics; 'The Allies and the Civil War', in Balfour and Preston, *Spain and the Great Powers*, pp. 96–126; and on non-intervention and the armaments involved, see Howson, *Arms for Spain: The Untold Story of the Spanish Civil War*, pp. 33–9.

77 See Howson, *Arms for Spain*, p. 30.

78 MAE, Nantes, Direction des Affaires Politiques et Commerciales, Espagne, Guerre

Civile, Volontaires, Vol. 236, July–November 1937, Saint-Jean-de-Luz, 19 July 1937, 'Secret, Volontaires français dans l'Armée du Général Franco', p. 24.

79 *Ibid.*, pp. 21–4.

80 Emile Decroix, *Complot contre la France. Sous la Cagoule qui ???* (Paris: Collection Paix et Liberté, 1938), p. 21.

81 SHM, Ávila, 1/46/100/44 Año de 37, 38 y 39, 'Copia que se cita', pp. 12–13.

82 'Síntesis histórico de la XVII Bandera' from 'Publicación del año 1983 para el uso didáctico de la Academia de Formación de Mandos Legionarios'. I am grateful to Colonel José Espartero Nievas, Comandancia General de Ceuta, Tercio Duque de Alba 2 de la Legión, for providing me with this material.

83 'Síntesis histórico de la XVII Bandera'.

84 See the discussion in Chapter 5.

85 'Síntesis histórica de la XVII Bandera'.

86 SHM, Ávila, 1/46/100/44, 17–9–1937; General Yagüe's letter is included in the file 'Denuncia sobre irregularidades de Captain Courcier'.

87 AGM, Ávila, 1/8/93/7, Año de 1937, Cuartel General del Generalísimo, Estado Mayor, 'Mr Henry Bourneville Marsaingy'. He was awarded a posthumous *Medalla Militar* with the proviso that it not be acknowledged in the *Boletín Oficial del Estado*. Marsagny's wife was given permission to visit the grave. George Penaud, who is discussed further below, suggested that Marsagny may have been killed by disgruntled franquistas, in 'La Bandera fantôme', in *Le Populaire*, 2 Sept. 1937.

88 *Le Populaire*, the daily newspaper of the French Socialist Party, serialized the account over eight days under the heading of 'La Bandera fantôme' (28 August to 3 September 1937). Setting aside the exultant commentary that framed the narratives, the detail rings true and can be verified against the French diplomatic correspondence of the ambassador and the consul in Saragossa who dealt with the same individual. *Le Populaire*'s subject is called Gaston Penaud while the ambassador refers to Georges Penaud; however, the dates and the events are the same. Penaud avoided telling the French ambassador that he was a volunteer in the Joan of Arc company, presumably because he was breaking the Non-Intervention Pact. Instead, Penaud described himself to the ambassador as a bankrupt businessman, who crossed into Nationalist Spain looking for work. See MAE, Nantes, Direction des Affaires Politiques et Commerciales Espagne Guerre Civile, Volontaires, Vol. 237, July–November 1937, Commissariat Spécial d'Hendaye, p. 16.

89 This was a rate of pay three times higher than that of foreigners in the regular Spanish Foreign Legion; see Michael Seidman, 'Frentes en calma de la guerra civil', *Historia Social*, **27** (1997), p. 38.

90 In fact, Penaud notes that Lavigne tried unsuccessfully to recruit Mme Penaud as a nurse for the Joan of Arc unit, when he heard that she had studied some medicine.

91 AGM, Ávila, 1/46/100/44, Cuartel General del Generalísimo, Estado Mayor,

'Denuncias sobre irregularidades del Captain Courcier'. The file contains a number of detailed sworn statements collected in 1938 by the judicial unit of the Nationalist army against the Juana de Arco commander as well as a biography and profile of his activities.

92 *Ibid.*

93 AGM, Ávila, 1/46/100/44, Cuartel General del Generalísimo, Estado Mayor, 'Denuncias sobre irregularidades del Captain Courcier'. SIPM, Burgos, 22 Feb. 1938; the claim is contained in the summaries of the letters of denunciation made against Courcier by Jean Conderc from Paris.

94 *Ibid.*

95 AGM, Ávila, 1/46/100/44, 'Denuncias sobre irregularidades del Captain Courcier', Legión Mando Telegrama Postal a Mano, 15 April 1938.

96 'Síntesis histórico de la XVII Bandera'.

97 *Diario de Navarra* 2 October 1936; MAE, Nantes, Série B, Vol. 563, 2 October 1936; Télégramme au départ, 19 Avril 1937, p. 545.

98 Eddy Bauer, *Rouge et or: chroniques de la 'Reconquête espagnole' 1937–1938* (Paris: Éditions Victor Attinger, 1938).

99 From mid-1937, Nationalist forces increased the pressure on Republicans who were cooped up in the Asturias, cut off from Republican Spain, and, after the fall of Irún, from the French border. By October 1937, Oviedo had fallen to the Nationalists.

100 MAE, Nantes, Série B, Vol. 564, Madrid Ambassade, Télégramme par fil San Sebastian, 28 August 1936.

101 Oudard, *Chemises noires, brunes, vertes en Espagne*, pp. 55–7.

102 He was presumably referring to Blum and the Minister of the Colonies, Maurice Viollette's proposed reform to extend French citizenship to a select group of educated army officers and public servants in Algeria, Morocco and Tunisia. The reform, which Dominique Borne and Henri Dubief describe as 'timid', aroused extreme opposition among the European French in the colonies and was finally dropped. See their *La Crise des années 30: 1929–1938. Nouvelle histoire de la France contemporaine, 13* (Paris: Éditions du Seuil, 1989), pp. 169–71.

103 François Roland, *Avec l'Abbé Lambert à travers l'Espagne nationaliste* (Oran: Plaza, 1938), pp. 15–17.

104 See MAE, Nantes, Série B, Vol. 563, 2 October 1936, 1034.

105 Brasillach, *Une génération dans l'Orage: notre avant-guerre*, p. 221. On this trip Brasillach was preparing notes for the history of the Spanish Civil War by Brasillach and Bardèche, *Histoire de la guerre d'Espagne* (1939). Brasillach's earlier volume with Henri Massis, *Les Cadets de l'Alcázar*, on the siege of Toledo, had been read widely in France and translated into English and American editions.

106 Jérôme and Jean Tharaud met a French soldier who confessed that he was 'fed up' with the Foreign Legion because French soldiers were always sent to the most dangerous positions. The proof of his statement, perhaps, is that he was killed

very soon afterwards. See their 'Choses vues, le siège de Madrid', *Candide* **664**, 3 December 1936.

107 Francis McCullagh, *In Franco's Spain: Being the Experiences of an Irish War-Correspondent during the Great Civil War Which Began in 1936* (London: Burns, Oates & Washbourne, 1937), pp. 49, 64, 205.

108 MAE, Nantes, Direction des Affaires Politiques, Espagne, Guerre Civile, Volontaires, Vol. 239, 28 July 1938, p. 32.

109 MAE, Nantes, Direction des Affaires Politiques, Espagne, Guerre Civile, Volontaires, Vol. 238, St-Jean-de-Luz, 10 Jan. 1938, pp. 49–51.

110 MAE, Nantes, Direction des Affaires Politiques, Espagne, Guerre Civile, Volontaires, Vol. 238, Paris, 13 Jan. 1938, pp. 54–5.

111 Troncoso had close links to the Cagoule network in the south-west of France. After a terrorist commando attack on French shipping in Brest harbour, Troncoso, with several French and Spaniards, was arrested in France and imprisoned.

112 Bauer, *Rouge et or*, pp. 78–9.

113 Oudard, *Chemises vertes*, pp. 130–31. See also Jérôme and Jean Tharaud's comment that 'it is always the same thing. As soon as Spaniard meets a Frenchman the first question is, "so when will the revolution break out in France", in 'Choses vues, le siège de Madrid', *Candide*, **664** (3 December 1936).

114 José María Borras Llop, 'Relaciones francoespañolas al comienzo de la guerra: la embajada de Jean Herbette (1936–1937)', in Octavio Ruiz-Manjón Cabeza and Miguel Gómez Oliver, *Los nuevos historiadores ante la Guerra Civil española* (Granada: Diputación Provincial de Granada, 1990), pp. 107–24.

115 Jean Lacouture, *Léon Blum*, translated by George Holoch (New York: Holmes Meier, 1982), pp. 318–22.

116 Claude G. Bowers, *My Mission to Spain: Watching the Rehearsal for World War II* (New York: Simon & Schuster, 1954), p. 291.

117 Glandy, *Maxime Réal del Sarte*, p. 198.

118 Most are to be found in the series of the Ministère des Affaires Étrangères, Nantes, Direction Politique et Commerciale, Espagne, Guerre Civile, Volontaires.

119 On a number of occasions, the ambassador noted that it was very nearly impossible to offer assistance to French prisoners in Nationalist Spain because Franco had given 'categorical instructions not to negotiate with any prisoners they had captured' and, though a great many may have been detained, they were usually executed on the spot, as were most of the wounded. He noted as well that the survival, or not, of prisoners depended upon the officer in charge and the 'state of excitation' of the insurgent soldiers who had captured the opposing soldier; MAE, Nantes, Direction Politiques, Vol. 235 122, 24 Feb. 1937, p. 122. This accords with the general observations of foreign contemporaries who were volunteers with Franco. See Kemp, *Mine Were of Trouble* (London: Cassell, 1957), Ch. 2; and Thomas, *Brother against Brother* (Phoenix Mill: Sutton, 1998), pp. 60, 64. As well, the French ambassador to

Spain received requests for information about Italians in Franco's army who had disappeared. There were also enquiries for Italian flyers for Franco who had been shot down in Republican Spain. These requests came via the French ambassador to the Vatican from family requests made through parish priests and Church representatives in Italy, presumably because the Italian government was reluctant to admit the presence of Italian nationals in Spain. See, for example, the requests concerning an Italian soldier who his family feared had been killed at Guadalajara, in MAE, Nantes, Vol. 236, April–June 1937, p. 213. Before the Civil War, the situation had been different. In 1934, for example, the mother of a Frenchman, who had joined the Spanish Foreign Legion in 1929, had contacted the Quai d'Orsay because, having had no word from her son for two years, she was very worried about him. With the full assistance of the Spanish army, the French ambassador had been able to find the man, give him a letter from his mother and report back to her that he was in good health and had been promoted within the Foreign Legion. See MAE, Nantes, Madrid, Série C, Ambassade, la Légion Étrangère, 4 October 1934, pp. 59–65.

120 MAE, Nantes, Série B, Madrid Ambassade, Paris, 27 Feb. 1937, No. 237, Box 563. According to Dr Marcel Junod, the agent of the International Red Cross, members of the Nationalist Red Cross placed obstructions in the way of prisoner exchange because they were reluctant to 'swap caballeros for Reds'. See Junod, *La troisième combattant: de l'esprit en Abyssine (1939) à la bombe atomique d'Hiroshima (1945)* (Paris: Payot, 1947), pp. 83-7. See also Caroline Moorehead, *Dunant's Dream: War, Switzerland and the History of the Red Cross* (London: HarperCollins, 1999), pp. 316–28.

121 MAE, Nantes, Direction Politique, Vol. 235 122, 24 Feb. 1937, p. 122.

122 MAE, Nantes, Série B, Madrid, Ambassade, Vol. 563, 1 March 1937, No. 225, No. 4; 8 May 1937, 'pour le Consul Général St Sebastian'.

123 MAE, Nantes, Série B, Madrid, Ambassade, Vol. 563, 15 May 1937, No. 4. The others were two under-age youths and four regular volunteers wishing to return home.

124 MAE, Nantes, Direction Politique et Commerciale (1930–1940), Guerre Civile, Volontaires (1930–1940), Vol. 238, April–June 1937, pp. 218–9; 221; 227–8.

125 MAE, Nantes, Direction Politique et Commerciale, Vol. 237, Espagne, Guerre Civile, Volontaires, Vol. 237, July–Nov. 1937, p. 106; pp. 263–4; Vol. 238, Nov. 1937–June 1938, pp. 29–30; p. 43.

126 MAE, Nantes, Direction Politique et Commerciale (1930–1940), Guerre Espagne, Volontaires, Vol. 238, April–June 1937, pp. 202; 220; Nov. 1937–June 1938, p. 16.

127 MAE, Vol. 237, 22 July 1937, p. 26.

128 MAE, Nantes, Série B, 12 Feb. 1937, p. 563.

129 The term is Pierre Milza's, in his 'L'ultra-droite des années trente', *Histoire de extrême droite en France*, edited by Michel Winock (Paris: Éditions du Seuil, 1994), pp. 157–87.

130 In Lyons in 1941, for example, French ex-veterans for Franco ran the shopfront which served as a recruiting centre for the Légion contre le Bolchevisme, the unit that consisted of French volunteers who fought with Hitler on the Eastern Front. MAE, Nantes, Série C, Vol. 326, 51–1, URSS Madrid, Fond C, La Légion des Volontaires français contre le Bolchevisme.

131 Eric Labat, *Les Places étaient chères* (Paris: Table Ronde, 1969), p. 35. Labat himself had spent time in Franco's Spain during the Civil War and used the country as an escape route in 1940 and again at the end of the war, when his pro-German sympathies made him a wanted man.

132 Owen Anthony Davey, 'The origins of the Légion des Volontaires Français contre le Bolchevisme', *Journal of Contemporary History*, 6 (4) (1971), p. 43.

133 Davey, 'The origins of the Légion des Volontaires Français contre le Bolchevisme', Journal of Contemporary History, 6 (4) (1971), p. 43; Victor Barthélemy, *Du Communisme au fascisme: l'histoire d'un engagement politique* (Paris: Albin Michel, 1978), p. 176; Lévy, 'L'organisation de la propagande', p. 12; Paquis, *Des Illusions*, p. 25. Some of his associates attributed his drug addiction to his years in the East; others, including Otto Abetz, the German ambassador to Paris during the Occupation, claimed he was unsteady because he had suffered severe frostbite on the Finnish front and his body was unable to withstand even small amounts of stimulants. See, as well, Fontenoy's series of articles on European politics in *Je Suis Partout*, No. 342, 12 June 1937; No. 348, 23 July 1937; No. 349, 1 July 1937. He was killed in 1944 in a freak accident when German soldiers shot him during the chaos of the Paris collaborationists' flight to Germany.

134 For example, André Sernin, one such individual himself, described these men as either 'in love with a fight or with the mess tin' in *Le Réprouvé ou le rouge et le brun: un communiste à L.V.F.* (Paris: Éditions Hors Commerce, 1975), p. 43.

135 Christian de la Mazière, *Le Rêveur casqué* (Paris: Éditions Robert Laffont, 1972); and Marcel Ophuls' interviews in *The Sorrow and the Pity* (1969) and *The Sorrow and the Pity: A Film by Marcel Ophuls* (New York: Outerbridge, 1972), pp. 53–5; 83–4; 145–53.

CHAPTER 5

Snow boots in sunny Spain: White Russians in Nationalist Spain

Introduction

It is impossible to know exactly how many White Russians served in Spain. Probably there were between eighty and a hundred who crossed the frontier to join General Franco. There were ten Russians who enlisted in the Spanish Foreign Legion in 1938 and at least two larger groups serving with Carlist regiments, as well as another smaller number scattered through the ranks of the regular Nationalist army.[1] One of the most senior White Russian officers, General Anton Nikolai Shinkarenko, notes in his memoirs that he had met some 50 White volunteers in Nationalist Spain between February 1937 and the end of the war.[2] The ex-Tsarist Captain Anton Prokof'evich Yaremchuk, also a volunteer with Franco, gave the higher figure of 80 Russians. And he produced a larger figure again from a Soviet newspaper in October 1937 which listed the names of 128 White Russians in Nationalist Spain. At least 180 men from the Kornilov battalion in exile were ready to enlist in the last months of 1936, though it is not clear whether they all reached Spain.[3] In addition, an alleged Georgian prince brought six of his countrymen on a quest to re-establish links between 'Ancient Iberia and Georgia'.[4]

It was not a large number, even if an additional dozen or so are added for high Russian casualties. Yaremchuk and Shinkarenko, separately, bemoaned the shortage of volunteers. According to Yaremchuk, many of his ex-Tsarist military colleagues 'had sunk so far into despair in migrant life that they had come to believe that there was nothing they could do to make a change'.[5] Similarly, Shinkarenko railed against the 'softness' of White Russian emigré youth. Despite their having been provided with 'scout troops, cadet units and sports organizations', which in Imperial times would produce men of military calibre, young White Russians had turned their backs on their traditions and 'foregone a golden opportunity in Spain to achieve military experience that could aid Tsarist Russia'.[6] Equally important in keeping down the numbers was the fact that the Nationalist command placed tight restrictions on the entry of White Russians into Franco's Spain.

White Russians endorsed Franco's belief in the Civil War as a 'Crusade against Communism'. There were distinct differences, however, between Spaniards and Russians over what consequences should flow from their shared enterprise. For the White Russians, the Spanish Civil War appeared to provide an opportunity to set in motion a grand, if wildly romantic, plan to regroup the White Volunteer Army scattered in exile. With officers and men back in military harness, White military morale would improve and regenerate the entire exile community. After delivering a decisive blow to the Bolsheviks on the Iberian Peninsula a regalvanized Imperial Russian army would be ready to return and recapture the Russian Motherland. The flaw in this sweeping scenario was General Franco and the Nationalist military command. They had little interest in White Russian military veterans or their organizations and no sympathy at all for phantasmagorical plans to use Spain as a marshalling ground for the White army in exile.

This chapter examines the background to the Russian emigré volunteers in Spain and the exile community from which they came. The career of General Shinkarenko, who became the senior White Russian in Spain, highlights the difficulties which many Tsarist Russians experienced during the Civil War. Shinkarenko was forced to face the fact that what the leaders of the White Russian army in exile had assumed would happen in Spain was contrary to the expectations of the Spaniards with whom they served.

The White Russian community

Almost all Franco's Russian volunteers came from the emigré community in Paris.[7] There were some men from Brussels but few from Berlin.[8] The largest community of Russian emigrés that had left after the Bolshevik Revolution gathered in Paris. According to the official statistics, collected in 1930 and in 1936 the total Russian emigré population consisted of between 355,000 and 503,000 members and, of them, between 100,000 and 200,000 lived in France, predominantly in Paris.[9] From the mid-1920s, Paris was the centre for emigré organizations and the wellspring of a distinct Russian emigré culture.[10] The pre-revolutionary Russian intellectual elites had been based in St Petersburg and Moscow and it was natural that in exile they would gravitate to large European cities.

In the French capital there were Orthodox churches that served the separate Muscovite and St Petersburg emigré populations with a great many Russians settling in the 17th Arrondissement near Rue Daru and the St Alexander Nevsky Cathedral. There were Russian neighbourhoods as well around Rue de Vaugirard in the 15th Arrondissement, and in Boulogne-Billancourt and Vincennes, on the eastern and western outskirts, respectively, of the city. In these neighbourhoods bookstores, tea rooms and meeting places catered to Russian needs. A thriving exile literature had sprung up in journals, newspapers and books that came out of specialized emigré publishing houses. This literature nourished the web of contacts between exiles in Europe and elsewhere.[11]

The interwar emigré communities suffered continual and often vicious internal divisions, as well as what Olga Andreyev Carlisle calls a 'metaphysical longing for Old Russia' and an overriding fear of 'denationalisation'.[12] All of the communities shared a characteristic unwillingness, either from choice or inability, to integrate into the host societies. In Marc Raeff's words, the Russian exiles had 'never unpacked their trunks' but rather preferred to 'sit on them' and wait it out until the Bolsheviks were overthrown and the exiles could return home to take up their previous lives.[13] Vladimir Nabokov has described the troubled years of his deracinated youth within the 'compact communities' of White Russians in Europe. Between 1919 and 1940 he led 'the odd life' of the exile 'among spectral Germans and Frenchmen in whose more or less illusory cities we emigrés happened to dwell'. It was an intensely lonely time. Among the 'sprinkling' of Germans and Frenchmen whom Nabokov met, he made no more than two good friends.[14] Nina Berberova, too, emphasizes the emigrés' isolation. The French people she knew were restricted to 'landlords who rented rooms, proprietors who rented apartments', and 'coal-dealers, bakers, butchers, and the concierges who followed us with sharp eyes'.[15]

One of the more unsavoury sides of the alienation of the exiles was that they were open to political conspiracy. Michael B. Miller has characterized White Russians as the 'ubiquitous intriguers' between the wars.[16] They were perceived as the archetypal figures of interwar espionage. The fraught relationship between the White Russian community and the Soviet Union heightened the problem. The connections between the two were so labyrinthine yet symbiotic that it was often hard to tell where the affairs of one stopped and the other began. In Miller's words, with 'preposterous ambitions, bizarre enterprises and plans that were invariably inept in execution', the Russian emigration was filled with seedy characters. Intriguers and 'ex-czarist officers on-the-make' seemed always to be available for any hare-brained scheme (Miller, p. 143).

Among the displaced emigrés, the ex-officers from the Tsar's army were perhaps the least able to manage the disorientation of civilian life. Trained in the Imperial military academies to serve as a military caste, these men were poorly qualified for life outside. The military organization for White veterans in exile continued to provide the nucleus and the structure of the ex-soldier's life. In 1924, General Wrangel had created the Russian Armed Services Union, *Russkie Obschche-Voinsky Soyuz* (ROVS), which held together the remnants of the White army. It maintained military control and cohesion in exile, and kept alive the struggle against Bolshevism. With the headquarters in Paris, it provided welfare for destitute White military families and, in particular, helped to find employment for the veterans.

From the mid-1920s, ex-White officers were employed as miners in northern France and at the Renault works in Paris. The suburb of Billancourt, where Renault was located, became a distinctly Russian neighbourhood, with tea rooms, Russian grocery stores and rooming houses. Nina Berberova recalled Billancourt as it was in the 1930s: when the knock-off whistle sounded, every fourth man pouring out of Renault's iron gates was a 'high-ranking officer of the White Army'. They formed a close-knit community. All were members of the military veterans' organizations and at home kept their 'regimental distinctions, epaulettes and Saint George Crosses and medals' carefully stored in their trunks.[17] In interwar Paris, the White Russian officer at the wheel of a taxi or waiting on restaurant tables was a stock figure, as was the uniformed Cossack, the doorman in countless hotels.[18]

The trajectory of General Mikael Peshnia's life is typical. He was a strong advocate of enlistment with General Franco and a commander of a White military union. A veteran of the First World War and the Russian and Bulgarian Civil Wars, Peshnia had come to France in 1926. For the first six months he was a coal-miner. He then moved to Paris, where he worked on the floor in a resin factory. After three years, he began driving a taxi, an occupation in which he continued until his death in early 1938. At his funeral, the coffin, and the 100 mourners that accompanied it, were transported to the cemetery by a fleet of taxis flying the Russian Imperial colours, driven by the veterans of his own Markov regiment and the Kornilovs.[19]

Peter Ustinov's play, *House of Regrets*,[20] has captured the paranoia and disarray of life among the White Russians abroad. On the eve of the Second World War, in a West Kensington house stuffed with the bric-à-brac of a bygone life, three generations of White Russians celebrate Easter. Deeply traumatized by the rupture of revolution and exile, older members of the family's circle pine for Imperial times. Like many White Russian exiles who were 'consumed by the pursuit of a lost way of life',[21] they existed within an enclosed emigré society. The main topics of conversation concern the details of how their Russian acquaintances are eking out a living. From day to day they await some signal from friends or family abroad which will bring money or an introduction to take them out of their hand-to-mouth existence.

The three old Russian military men who live in Madame Baranova's house, in Ustinov's play, spend their days poring over the map of Europe, laying out the battle strategies to retake St Petersburg. The 78-year-old grandfather, General Andrei Cherevenko, and his aged military batman are contemptuous of the Red army, made up as it is of ignorant peasants and factory workers. The old soldiers plan to overwhelm the Bolsheviks with a single White cavalry charge. A friend from St Petersburg days, Admiral Konstantin Papanin, gave his best on the bridge of a Russian imperial navy destroyer. Now with failing eyesight and in exile, he writes long articles on naval strategy for a White Russian newspaper.

At the start of 1939, the two old infantry men confidently expect that the White armies will re-enter Kiev with the help of Germans and conduct a 'victorious campaign against Lenin, Stalin and his anti-Christs' (Ustinov, *House of Regrets*, p. 22). On the morning of 3 September 1939, in anticipation of Britain declaring war on Germany, the old general dons his military uniform and prepares to apply to the British War Office to lead a Russian army to Kiev via Salonika, Bulgaria, Roumania and Poland. Or, if needs be, the old general contemplates disembarking his troops in Karachi in order to advance on Kiev through Afghanistan.

These characters, profoundly out of kilter with the times, are drawn from Ustinov's own childhood. They resonate strongly with other first-person accounts of White Russians between the wars, including those military men who volunteered with Franco. Michael Ignatieff evokes the 'crazy Russian circus' of emigrés who gathered at his grandmother's dairy farm in Sussex in the 1920s. While demonstrating total ineptitude at farm tasks, the old military men endlessly reworked the past 'disastrous battles'.[22] A similar figure is the worn-down and threadbare Bologovsky in Nina Berkenova's novella, 'The Slut and the Waiter'. An ex-lieutenant in the Tsarist army, Bologovsky waits on restaurant tables in Paris and drinks himself into oblivion on his days off, lonely for the companionship and order of the old military life.[23]

At the other end of the social scale, two aristocratic White officers weathered very similar experiences. Prince A. Lobanov-Rostovsky, an ex-Royal Guardsman from St Petersburg, was engulfed by the 'overwhelming despondency of exile' at the end of the Civil War. In Paris, he took a job in an insurance office where 'every day from eight o'clock in the morning until six in the evening he added columns of figures and multiplied them by a given number'. No one ever explained what it was for. Ahead of him 'stretched drab, humdrum meaningless days'.[24] In a similar frame of mind, Grand Duke Alexander, part of the family of the Pretender Grand Duke Cyril, fled to the United States in order to escape the 'senseless regrets and continuous sighs' that prevailed in Paris.[25] As well, the community was riven by factional arguments that revolved around political and personality differences, or often simply arose from the 'snarling resentments which proceeded from material discomfort'.[26]

International events and Russian emigrés

By the mid-1930s, international politics had begun to bear down directly on the White emigré communities. The ebullience of the Nazi state and its sabre-rattling anti-Communism created a split over the correct stance of White Russians towards Nazism. The 'defeatists' (*Porazhentsy*), who included most of the right-wing groups, adopted an accidentalist position towards Germany. In judging the main objective to be the defeat of Stalin, they were willing to ally themselves with Hitler if that would help bring down the Bolshevik regime. In contrast, the 'defensists' (*Oborontsy*) argued that patriotic Russians must support their own country when it was under threat from another nation. Their number included most left-leaning emigrés and the Socialist Revolutionary groups but also General Deniken and some of his supporters.[27]

In relation to the Spanish Civil War, an event with international ramifications, the emigré community was also split. Most Socialist Revolutionary and Menshevik journals editorialized against Franco. His victory would boost fascist Italy and Nazi Germany and in France strengthen the Fascist Leagues which were violently anti-immigrant and anti-White Russian. This reading of the political situation was correct. Léon Blum's Popular Front administration, the object of continuous and virulent attack by French fascists, had done more than had any other French government to regularize the legal situation of Russian emigrés resident in France.[28]

The majority of Orthodox Russian exiles rejected the French Popular Front and supported Franco, as shown in an incident in October 1936. In a liberal Orthodox journal, a teacher at the St Serge Theological Institution criticized the 'hypocrisy' of Franco in carrying out a 'crusade in the name of Christianity while resorting to brutal oppression'. His comments created a storm among Orthodox Russians in Paris who publicly demanded the teacher's dismissal. He was admonished by the Orthodox Metropolitan in Paris, though he eventually managed to keep his job.[29]

General Deniken was strongly pro-Franco but categorically opposed to Russian volunteers intervening in Nationalist Spain. In this position, Deniken was out of step with the ROVS organization, whose leaders were urging their members to enlist with Franco. In any event, by this time, Deniken had withdrawn from ROVS and army politics in order to lead a quiet life in which to pursue his writing.[30]

For the ex-officers of the Imperial army and the veterans' organization ROVS that represented them, the Spanish Civil War came more and more into focus. From mid-1936, there were reports in the French press about the left-wing international volunteers who were arriving in Paris on their way to Spain to join the International Brigades. From this time, as well, ROVS began to promote the parallels between Nationalist Spain and Imperial Russia. The organization regularly ran courses on military and political history for its members. In July 1936, Valery Levitski, the ex-head of Wrangel's Crimean Political Department, taught a course on international relations that covered the murder of the Spanish monarchist Calvo Sotelo, the event in Madrid that triggered the Civil War. The lecture emphasized the parallel between the ROVS' own desire to defeat the Bolsheviks and restore Imperial Russia and Franco's cause in Catholic Spain. The Russian Orthodox Church in Paris and elsewhere was sympathetic to the overtures of the Catholic Pro Deo movement, which was committed to defending the Roman Catholic Church against Communism. In the Pro Deist view, the laicizing policies of the Mexican Revolution, the Russian Revolution and the Spanish Republic were part of an international atheist conspiracy to promote secularism and Satanism.[31]

There appeared to be a coincidence of interests between White Russians and Franco's Nationalists. ROVS and its men welcomed the possibility of joining up with Franco. At the end of 1936, General Miller sent General Chatiloff, part of the old Kornilov Shock Regiment, to Spain to make contact with Nationalist headquarters about the possibility of gathering a large troop of the White army in exile on the Iberian Peninsula. His efforts came to nothing. He needed large amounts of money, which were supposed to be funnelled through a complex series of negotiations in Italy, to transport White soldiers from all over Europe. The Italian government at some stage provided uniforms for the White Russians and some entered Italian Mixed Brigades, but the larger enterprise failed.[32] Franco's terse and consistently negative responses to any efforts to set up a separate White Russian battalion outside the Foreign Legion knocked the schemes on the head. Franco had no desire for Nationalist Spain to become a marshalling area for the reconstitution of the White armies in exile.

Chatiloff returned to Paris with the information that the Nationalists would only permit small groups of Russian volunteers to cross the frontier. As a consequence, the 58 members of the Kornilovs, who were keen to depart immediately for Spain, were broken into small contingents and ordered to be ready to move under the command of Captain Maximovich.[33]

Relations between the exile community of Russians and their French hosts were always strained. In May 1932 a deranged Russian exile, Paul Gorgouloff, had assassinated the President of the French Republic, Paul Doumer, when he had attended a ROVS memorial ceremony for Imperial Russian soldiers who had served in the First World War. The event and Gorgouloff's subsequent execution caused an enormous public outcry against Russians and calls for the wholesale expulsion of the exile community.[34] A year into the Spanish Civil War, Russian exiles were placed in the national spotlight again by another sensational event. On 24 September 1937, General E. K. Miller, the commander of ROVS, was kidnapped by three men in broad daylight from the street outside his apartment. Seven years before, Miller's predecessor at ROVS, General Kutepov, had disappeared in a similar fashion. The subsequent police enquiry established that General Nikolai Skoblin, Miller's second in command at ROVS, had also disappeared on the same day. Skoblin was implicated along with a Soviet NNKVD agent, it was claimed. Newspaper reports suggested that he had returned to the Soviet Union, or been smuggled into Republican Spain by the NKVD and got rid of. Whatever the case, Skoblin was never heard of again.[35] His wife, the famous Russian folk singer and darling of the emigré community, Nadezhda Plevitskaya, was arrested. She eventually stood trial and was sentenced to fifteen years in a French prison.[36]

The press was full of sensational reporting of the affair. On the Left and the Right there were declamations about the undesirability of having large foreign communities in France. The Socialist Party newspaper, *Le Populaire*, claimed that rightists in the Russian community had been antagonistic to Miller because he had not been outspoken in advising men to enlist with General Franco.[37] As well, *L'Humanité*, the organ of the French Communist Party, hammered home the complicity of the military organization, ROVS, in the affair. Both papers raised the unpleasant spectre that France was harbouring within its borders a reactionary Russian army in exile which would constitute a threat to national security if there was ever a break-down in law and order in France. For their part, White Russians felt that the French government allowed Bolshevik agents to roam with impunity in France, while blaming every unsavoury happening on White exiles.[38]

For ROVS and the displaced ex-Tsarist officers that the organization represented, the Spanish Civil War across the border could hardly have been more opportune. Faced with a climate of growing political unrest within France and the increasing mistrust towards all foreigners, particularly Russians, they could put it aside and join Franco in their true vocation as military men. The enthusiasm of the White veterans for the military adventure in Spain was equalled by their relief at abandoning civilian life.

Shinkarenko, at 48 years of age, was delighted to leave behind what he described as 'eleven unhappy and friendless years' in Paris, living with an aged mother. Yaremchuk, 47 in 1937, paid up his rent, gave away his few personal belongings and set off with a small suitcase containing a change of underwear and his identity documents. When the French clerk at the government office in Paris, where he was required to apply for a permit to travel, asked whether he would be prepared to serve in the French army, Yaremchuk vehemently refused. The French government, he claimed, was 'full of Jews' and hostile to White Russians so that he was overwhelmed with relief to leave 'Godless France for God-fearing Spain'.[39]

White Russians in Spain

The Russians went to Nationalist Spain in the hope that the way back to St Petersburg would be through Madrid. This sentiment echoed a similar though contrary idea of many exiles who were members of the International Brigades.[40] In the long term, the Russians' mission was to defeat the 'Godless no-gooders' of Bolshevism in Spain and from there carry on to 'the Motherland' for a second round with the Bolsheviks in which, this time, the Whites would be victorious.[41] The biographies of 38 of the volunteers reveal men who were middle-aged and all had been career officers in the Imperial army and veterans of the First World War and the Russian Civil War. Almost all of them, as well, had been part of General Wrangel's Crimean expedition.[42]

Baroness Wrangel, the late general's wife who lived in Belgium, established a committee to help the families of the soldiers who enlisted in Nationalist Spain. During the war, her group in Brussels raised funds to send an Orthodox priest, Father Alexander Shabashev, to Spain to minister to the spiritual needs of the Russian volunteers. In the First World War, Shabashev had been decorated for bravery while serving the Tsar as a military padre and in the Crimea, during the Civil War, he had accompanied Wrangel's troops in battle. Shabashev spent ten days in Spain travelling around the Aragon front, holding Orthodox services and giving Communion.[43] There were three other orthodox priests fighting in Spain. They included Prince John Shakhovsky, who later ministered to the Orthodox community in Berlin during the Second World War, and eventually became the Orthodox Archbishop of San Francisco.[44]

The journal *Chasovoi* (*The Sentinel*), part of the ROVS organization, was outspokenly pro-Franco, and its editor, V.V. Orekov, took an active part in setting up the first contingent of recruits to go to Nationalist Spain. While the men were away, ROVS raised money to send clothing, cigarettes and chocolates to the front, while *Chasovoi* dispensed aid to their families from a list drawn up by the ROVS leadership.

Throughout the Civil War, *Chasovoi* ran admiring articles about Franco and Nationalist Spain and the horrors of life under the 'Reds'. Shinkarenko went so far as to claim that General Franco sent funds to Orekov. Whether this is the case or not is hard to say. Certainly, Franco's speeches were reprinted regularly in the paper and Franco himself wrote several times to acknowledge its support. For example, on 13 October 1936, he thanked the editor for warm congratulations on the Nationalist leadership and on 'the great victories of the heroic armies against the "red Huns" '. The Caudillo also described *Chasovoi* as a 'remarkable journal' which was contributing to 'our common good'.[45] A substantial part of each issue during the Civil War dealt with Spain and it carried a regular section, 'Letters from Spain', in which Russian volunteers reported on life at the Spanish front.

Despite the shared opposition to Communism and the belief that Republican Spain was entirely 'Red', the integration of the White volunteers into Franco's armies was not straightforward. The tenor of relations between Franco's Spaniards and the White Russians reflected an increasing lack of trust on both sides.

The first hurdle for the Russians was how to get across the Spanish frontier in order to enlist. The Whites travelled south in small groups. Rather like the international volunteers crossing the Pyrenees on foot from France into eastern Spain, the Russians at Hendaye paid smugglers to lead them at night across the mountains. The first party to cross like this managed the trip in October 1936.

On 12 February 1937, the two senior generals, Fok and Shinkarenko, accompanied by Captains Kiwvocheya and Poloukhin, reached San Sebastian. The local gentry greeted them with great courtesy and put them up in a comfortable hotel. The next day, the Russians travelled to Burgos to enlist. Here they struck their first problem. The authorities at Franco's military headquarters were unwilling to take in General Fok, even though he was the most senior officer among the Russians and had seen military service in both the First World War and the Russian Civil War. The Spanish recruiters ruled that, at 57, he was too old to fight and told him to return to France. Fok was dismayed. He unsuccessfully urged them to ignore his military seniority and allow him to enlist as a simple soldier. They refused. Ever resourceful, Fok said that they should judge his age for themselves and before their astonished eyes, he seized the rifle of a guard on duty nearby and, holding it aloft, promptly performed a series of Russian acrobatic exercises and strenuous army drills. Before such a display of fitness and zeal, the Spaniards relented and signed him up.

The second hurdle the Russians faced was where in the Nationalist armies they would serve. Nationalist High Command initially intended to place the White Russians in the Bandera de Juana de Arco. None of them spoke Spanish and as most of them came from Paris, it was assumed that they would be French-speakers. It offered a sensible solution. The ROVS leadership, Shinkarenko and Fok, however, refused to be placed in a

French *bandera* as they had 'little sympathy with the Godless French'. Instead they wished to join the Carlists, where they felt at home. The Carlist slogan of 'God, Fatherland and King' was close to their own 'Faith, Tsar and Motherland'. As well, the Carlists allowed the Russians to fly the Tsarist flag on parade and sew on their sleeves the white, blue and red colour patches of Imperial Russia.[46]

Shinkarenko, Fok and their companions were eventually assigned to the regiment led by the Carlist General Zumalacárregui and provided with army kit and green camouflage uniform topped off, 'like poppies in a field', with bright red Carlist berets (Pt. 4, Ch. 1). Another group of seven White Russians left Paris on 16 March 1937 and arrived at Irún via St-Jean-de-Luz, to be followed several days later by two other separate contingents. At least two other units of the Whites were placed in Carlist regiments. The largest group of White Russians enlisted in the Tercio de Marco de Bello. They fought courageously with the unit in the fierce battles at Belchite between August and November 1937.[47] As well, there were Russians involved in radio broadcasts made from the Nationalist side into Republican lines. The project presumably reflected the franquista assumption that all foreigners with the Republic were Russians in one form or another, though in reality there were very few Russian soldiers among the International Brigades.

Spanish authorities did not recognize Russian ranks and therefore all Russian officers began again as ordinary soldiers. This was galling to military men, especially as many of them considered their Imperial training and experience in at least two major wars to be superior to that of the Spaniards, though the truth was that the Russians had lost the two main wars that they had been involved in most recently. Like the other foreign volunteers in Nationalist Spain, the Russians had to learn Spanish commands and become habituated to different routines and military codes. The initial training that Fok and Shinkarenko received mostly involved marching in formation, which the generals rather contemptuously referred to as 'no better than a joke'.[48] Needless to say, these attitudes did not endear the Russians or the Spaniards to each other.

A problem which the Russians found particularly dispiriting was that most of the Spaniards they met were unaware that there were Russians of any colour other than red. Spaniards were also ignorant of the fact that Russia was a country with a religious and imperial tradition as long and as glorious as Spain's own. In Nationalist Spain, the terms 'Russian', 'Red', 'Komintern' and 'Communist' were used interchangeably. As a consequence, it was often hard for Spaniards to believe that Russians could be 'white', monarchist and anti-Communist.[49]

Typical were the complaints made by a White volunteer, who reported in *Chasovoi* that it was profoundly annoying in Spain to be told that 'Trotsky had murdered Lenin' and even worse, that 'King Stalin had overthrown the previous Tsar'.[50] Another *Chasovoi* correspondent pointed out that he had been tremendously heartened when a fellow Spanish soldier revealed that, since he had met the Whites in Spain, he now knew better than to assume that all Russians were Communists. Previously, he had been faced with widespread incomprehension about their situation and over and over had been obliged to prove that 'Russia and the USSR were not the same thing'.

Spanish ignorance of Russian history, and of the fact that since 1917 the Russian communities had been split into Bolsheviks and anti-Bolsheviks, meant that Russian volunteers in Spain often felt isolated within their battalions and under pressure to prove their military and political worthiness. An ex-officer who was placed with a Carlist battalion was relieved when he arrived to find several other Russians on his section of the Aragon front.[51] Although the men had been recruited as 'simple soldiers', they had soon demonstrated their military capacities and 'in practice' held officer responsibilities. He was also reassured that this meant that the Russians were treated in a 'very brotherly manner'. In a long piece to *Chasovoi*, the same volunteer emphasized how important it was to sustain 'the good reputation of the Imperial Russian soldier'. Grateful to wear the Tsar's colours and his Russian medals, the soldier opined that the 'place to fight the Bolsheviks was at the front in real military acts, not in the dining rooms and meeting halls in Paris'. He urged his readers to recognize that a Russian officer must prove by his actions that Russian emigrés are not 'only empty talkers and gentlemen who can only be effective after a few vodkas'. But instead they are 'military people who crave to translate their hatred of Bolsheviks into real action'.

The Spaniards' lack of knowledge about Russian exiles and their history was reciprocated in the blinkered Russian perception of the Spain around them. According to an 'aristocratic Baltic officer' who had been in Spain, Russian officers were 'hostile to Communism as a matter of caste'.[52] The Whites' Iberian experiences were refracted through the prism of the Russian Civil War and the givens of that conflict were simply transferred to Spain. It was in that cataclysmic event that the Whites' world-view and patterns of understanding had been forged. As a consequence, in most Russian descriptions of the Spanish Civil War, the specifics of Spain are obscure.[53] The Spanish landscape serves simply as the locale of the familiar tableau of the predetermined battle between Russian Whites and Russian Bolsheviks: like the puppet show, the wicked Red Punch tricks the heroic White Judy against a series of backdrops, one of which is Spain between 1936 and 1939.

The language that the Russian volunteers use to describe their Iberian experiences is predictable and formatted. Typical is the narrative by a Russian emigré who had enlisted for Franco in Spanish Morocco. He was placed in the regular army and his first military engagement took place in Andalusia, but it is Russian Bolsheviks, not Republican Spaniards who are his adversaries. He pointed out: 'here the Bolsheviks have carried out the same terrible atrocities, just as they did in Russia'. Everywhere there are 'burnt churches and the bodies of priests' and in a small town the 'Whites captured portraits of Stalin and Lenin' and 'disgusting anti-religious placards and atheistic brochures'. All of these, he tells us, were produced under the specific orders of Stalin sent through his agents in Madrid. The Red army behaved in Spain exactly as it did in the Soviet Union. The Spanish Civil War was controlled entirely by Stalin: Stalin gave personal orders that generals and soldiers were to be shot every time the Red army lost. The 'White Army in Spain', just as it had in Russia, will defend 'our Church, our faith and the culture of Europe'. His final comment was that he was grateful to be back under military orders and able to fight and fulfil his duty as a 'former Russian officer'.[54]

Another *Chasovoi* correspondent emphasized the links that Spain provides in the worldwide 'Judeo-Bolshevik plot', whereby there is an 'inevitableness' that Republican leaders, Stalin's officers and the members of the Non-Intervention Committee all have Jewish names. In the same vein, a victory for Franco will be a 'cruel blow to World Communism where Red Power in Spain is a further step towards the Bolshevization of Europe'.[55] A *Chasovoi* editorial suggested, in a rerun perhaps of General Wrangel in the Crimea, that the fate of the Spanish Civil War would depend upon the sea. In a strategy analysis that had little to do with Spanish geography or the actualities of the war, the editor opined that 'if the Soviet Union sends arms and troops through Catalonia it could overrun Nationalist Spain and drive it into the sea and, like the Civil War in 1920, produce nothing but death'.[56]

All of the *Chasovoi* reports on Spain made the tie connecting Spain and Imperial Russia. A ROVS correspondent wrote from Spain that, the more he thought about the two events, the less he could understand how it was that the Whites had lost in Russia in the first place. If they were the 'white counterrevolutionary Hydra' as the Bolsheviks claimed, and everyone seemed to agree that they would win in Spain against the Bolsheviks, why in three years of Civil War had they been vanquished in Russia?[57]

There were other more mundane but pressing matters that bore upon the daily life of the Russian volunteer. These concerned pay and rank. In Spain, only volunteers in the Foreign Legion were paid. This left Russians with the Carlists and the regular army in considerable hardship. Most were without financial backing; many had left behind destitute families. The ROVS organization did what it could to assist families but it was not well-off.

Shinkarenko raised the fraught matter several times with Franco and General Staff headquarters. He pointed out that the Russians were unlike ordinary Spanish soldiers who could call on their families from time to time for financial assistance. Because of the 'unfortunate accident of history', White Russians had 'no country' or anyone at all to fall back on.[58] Shinkarenko, without success, asked Franco to provide a small allowance to Russian soldiers. Nothing was forthcoming, either, from his own private plea for some personal funds from Franco to tide him over as he was unable to make ends meet. Even the appeal framed in terms of a request from one military man – 'veteran of three wars and five times wounded' – to another military man drew a stony response.

All the Russians were enlisted as 'ordinary soldiers' in the Nationalist army. None was able to retain his rank from his previous Imperial career. The lack of recognition of their previous military experience greatly irked them. A number of Russians complained as well that even when they were recommended for promotion in the field it was never processed at headquarters, and therefore they were prevented from being promoted to officer rank, in which case they would receive pay. Promotion in the field and the payment it brought was the conventional military mode of reward.[59]

There is an intriguing reference by Yaremchuk to an incident in which a White Russian volunteer had shown particular bravery in the field and was promoted within the Tsarist army, presumably by his senior White officer in Spain, though not within the Nationalist army. This suggests a highly anomalous situation whereby the Russsians were operating as an army within the Nationalist army.[60] Any hint that Russian volunteers had competing allegiances or were answerable to an alternative authority structure would have been anathema to Franco's High Command, as it would in any conventional army.

At the end of the war, in the celebrations for Franco's victory and the distribution of honours among the victors, all White Russians were promoted to the level of lieutenant. The distinction was appreciated, and presumably, to a certain extent, made up for the lack of recognition while the war was on. Some years later, during the Second World War, Shinkarenko was astonished and delighted to find that his promotion entitled him to a small war service pension from the Spanish state.

As already noted, Shinkarenko had begun with a Carlist Tercio de Zumalacárregui. Fok and the other two with whom he came to Spain fairly soon transferred to the Tercio Doña María de Molina where there were already a number of White Russian volunteers. Shinkarenko refused to go with them because he felt it would jeopardize the possibility of forming a separate Russian unit if most of the Russians were already gathered together under a Spanish command. He also described the Russian volunteers in the Doña María de Molina as a 'repulsive bunch' and rife with 'backstabbing and squabbles' (Pt. 4, Ch. 4) When Fok committed suicide at the Belchite front in October 1937, rather than retreat before Republican troops who had overrun his position, Shinkarenko became the most senior White general in Spain.[61] Four months after his enlistment, Shinkarenko received a serious head wound and spent a month in a military hospital in Saragossa. Once recuperated, he transferred into the Spanish Foreign Legion where he hoped his military experience would count for more. Within the Legion he manoeuvred his assignment several times, unsuccessfully as it turned out in each case, to obtain a more senior position.

Fok, Shinkarenko and the other Russian officers were military men of the old regime. The importance of class had been drummed into them from birth and the way in which its minute gradations finessed the behaviour of a gentleman.[62] Shinkarenko believed that 'people from the same social class are the same everywhere'. There were certain ineffable if arcane characteristics that constituted their common culture: they all 'held a knife and fork in the proper way'; they had 'all read Robinson Crusoe' and usually all of them were 'perfectly acquainted with the life of Julius Caesar' (Pt. 4, Ch. 4). With an almost visceral belief in social hierarchy, Shinkarenko was humiliated when he was treated like any ordinary soldier, especially by those whom he considered his social and military equals.

In early 1938 while with the 9th *bandera* in Toledo, Shinkarenko shrugged off the commendation of his immediate commander because he did not consider a 'Spanish major's praise meant much for a Russian general'. Indeed, in his diary, Shinkarenko notes that his own opinion of his commander – that 'he knew the rules of the book and not much else' – carried more weight than ever could a Spaniard's opinion of a Russian who had come up through the imperial military school (Pt. 4, Ch. 6).

As a senior Russian officer in Spain, Shinkarenko was particularly cut by the snubs he received from Spanish officers. When he transferred to the Spanish Foreign Legion, Shinkarenko assumed that he would meet General Yagüe in person and, to that end, waited for hours, fuming, outside Legion headquarters. Shinkarenko 'could not believe that the Commander of the Spanish Foreign Legion was unaware that a Russian Brigadier General awaited his attendance'. He was perplexed by Yagüe's behaviour which he read as disdain. In Shinkarenko's view, the Spaniard must realize that 'it wasn't every day that a Russian general paid a visit'. When the two finally came face to face some months later, when Yagüe was inspecting the troops which included Shinkarenko, the Russian stood to attention as straight as a flag pole, but the Legion commander simply passed on down the line, not indicating even by the flicker of an eyelid that he had seen the ramrod figure, wearing the narrow ribbon of the Russian tricolor. Again, later in 1938, when Shinkarenko, grown weary in the 'fruitless siege of Madrid', had managed to have himself transferred south to the headquarters of the Moroccan Regulars, Yagüe again cut him dead (Pt. 4, Ch. 4). Shinkarenko had hardly settled into his billet, when an order from Yagüe arrived that the Russian was to return immediately to the unit from which he had come and await further orders. Five days later, word came through that Shinkarenko was to go north to join a *bandera* in Saragossa, even though Franco's office had agreed to Shinkarenko's transfer to the Moroccans and he had the paper to prove it. The only explanation Shinkarenko could think of for Yagüe's 'mysterious' behaviour was that he was 'jealous' of the Russian's rank and experience.

Transferred to Saragossa, Shinkarenko 'sat about playing chess' until he could wangle himself an appointment at General Varela's headquarters in Teruel (Pt. 4, Ch. 4). Here, too, in his last assignment of the war, Shinkarenko felt unjustly overlooked. He joined Varela's administrative staff in February 1939, first at Teruel and then during the mopping up operations in Catalonia. After having enjoyed the pleasure of dining with the corps commander and the Chief of Staff on the first night that he had arrived, Shinkarenko was mortified the next day to be told that, owing to 'an acute shortage of cutlery', he should eat henceforth with the junior officers. He attributed this insult to General Varela's 'ignorance of social niceties', which in turn was caused by his 'humble origins' in Cadiz. While admitting that 'one couldn't smell the plebeian' about Varela, in Shinkarenko's estimation the Spaniard as a commander was 'not too bright and certainly very vain' (Pt. 4, Ch. 4).

From the Spaniards' point of view, Shinkarenko was not an ideal subordinate. He had an exaggerated idea of his own importance and was a prolific and persistent petition writer. Similarly, his tendency to take matters into his own hands and set off to headquarters in person to negotiate a more desirable billet would not endear him in any military operation. Most likely, as well, the Spanish generals' attitude towards Shinkarenko and the other Russian officers reflected General Franco's own assessment. The Caudillo was extremely cold towards Russian grand plans for the exiled White armies. In holding the Russian generals at arm's length he kept their schemes in check.

What the ROVS wanted was to resuscitate the Imperial army, disbanded and dispersed across half the globe. Central to the project was the need for a distinct Russian unit on Spanish soil. It was important for Russian discipline and experience that it be led by Russian officers. Chatiloff, Fok and Shikarenko saw this arrangement providing the skeleton of the future military grouping. In a long petition to Franco in July 1937, prefaced by the reminder that he was writing about 'White Russians' – and in case there should be any misunderstanding he placed the word in block letters and underlined 'White' – Shinkarenko laid out the plan.[63] If Franco would give him the independence to set up a separate Russian unit, there would be many Russian soldiers all over the world who would answer the call. Shinkarenko envisaged an infantry unit with machine-gunners and artillery. The latter, as he explained to Franco, was a Russian 'speciality' for which Russian armies throughout history had been famous. Already, he said, he was receiving piles of letters from ex-Tsarist officers asking how they could get to Spain in order to enlist. Even if a separate unit might appear ludicrous at present, when there were so few Russians in Spain, if Franco would go along with the plan, the numbers would surely swell.

In particular, Shinkarenko wanted Franco to give the Russian recruiters the right to decide who could cross the border in order to enlist. At present, the restrictions were so narrow that good soldiers with real war experience who would make excellent recruits were being turned away. Shinkarenko cited the case in point of a colleague from Marseilles. He had served in the Crimea at Shinkarenko's own headquarters and on his recommendation had come to enlist, but at St-Jean-de-Luz he had been turned back and sent home. Having very little money, this summary treatment had caused 'this excellent recruit' considerable hardship and produced ill will towards Nationalist Spain (p. 9). In conclusion, the petition reminded Franco that White Russia and Nationalist Spain shared 'the noble cause of defending European Christian culture' and that Russians had been fighting 'our mortal enemies', the Reds, since 1917 (p. 11). Five days later, Franco sent a single sentence reply. He thanked Shinkarenko for 'the interest he showed in National Spain' but denied his request.[64]

Ever since coming to Spain, Shinkarenko had been extremely keen to meet Franco in person. He placed great store in face-to-face communications, 'one military man to another', as he always put it. He was sure that, if he could speak to the Caudillo himself, his plans would receive a better hearing. In the July 1937 petition, he had asked to be allowed to 'greet' the Spanish leader in person so that he could 'communicate to him what an old soldier of Imperial Russia feels' (p. 12). Shinkarenko had been wounded in July 1937, spent a month recuperating in Saragossa and made use of his time in hospital to draft the long petition setting out the plans of the White army. While in Saragossa, a monarchist acquaintance introduced him to General Alfredo Kindelán, the strongly monarchist head of the Nationalist air force. He in turn introduced Shinkarenko to José Antonio Sangroniz y Castro, Head of Foreign Affairs in Franco's cabinet, who eventually arranged an appointment with Franco.

Shinkarenko's meeting with Franco took place on 5 August 1937, by which time Franco had received and rejected the Russian petition. Shinkarenko found Franco dressed in camouflage fatigues and 'thinner than the photographic likeness' but 'still chubby' (Pt. 4, Ch. 4). The Caudillo, 'like many Spaniards', was 'prone to baldness' but had a 'beautiful, virile Nordic face'. They spoke to each other in Spanish. This probably put the Russian at a disadvantage because even in the 1950s, after having lived for many years in Spain, and having 'taken a great many lessons', Shinkarenko spoke Spanish with great difficulty. Although Franco smiled and asked after his injury, Shinkarenko felt a 'certain coldness' with the question. Shinkarenko requested that he be promoted as he was, after all, a Russian general. Franco replied that, certainly it was an aspiration to work for, and agreed with alacrity to transfer Shinkarenko into a 'more distiguished regiment'. On the spot Franco called the Chief of Staff and ordered that the Russian be transferred forthwith into the Foreign Legion.

Though he longed to raise the matter of the separate Russian unit, Shinkarenko sensed that Franco did not wish to speak about it. After having waited so long for a personal interview with the Caudillo, Shinkarenko was disappointed. Although Franco had been polite, it was with a 'particular nuance of distance in his manner'. With chagrin, Shinkarenko noted in his diary that if their roles were reversed and had Shinkarenko 'faced a distinguished foreign general like himself', he would have 'pulled a medal from his own breast and decorated the officer on the spot, not for merit but out of respect for the other's extraordinary life'.[65]

While recuperating in hospital from his head wound, Shinkarenko also met Carmen Polo Franco when she came through his ward and spoke briefly to several patients including himself. He was touched by her 'modesty and dignity,' though the exchange was all too fleeting. Much more satisfying was the attention he received from the far-flung White community. News in the exile press of a White general who had been injured while fighting in Spain for General Franco produced a flurry of letters with get-well wishes from women emigrés as far away as Harbin and the Congo.[66] In Spain, Shinkarenko was probably most at home among the aristocratic women whom he had first met on arrival in San Sebastian early in 1937 and whose acquaintance he renewed on his periodic excursions to Franco's headquarters as he tried to arrange a more elevated posting for himself. An Old World ladies' man, he passed enjoyable afternoons in their charming company, speaking French and playing bridge. After the war, he retired to San Sebastian to live in genteel poverty on his small Spanish government pension.

Conclusion

It is not easy to determine what the military contribution of the White Russians was to Franco's victory. They considered themselves fine soldiers with a dynasty of military traditions behind them. Not surprisingly, in their recollections of Spain they describe in glowing terms their own valorous exploits. Between the lines, the picture was less cheerful. They were men who were living in a world in which the dream of a possible rerun of 1918–21 leading to a victorious outcome was the only compensation for the psychological alienation and physical displacement of exile. Their casualty rates in Spain were high. Indeed, Shinkarenko was careful to emphasize this fact in attempting to convince Franco to accept his petition to allow more Russians into Spain. At least 34 Russians were killed out of the putative figure of 100 who had enlisted in Spain. It is hard to know, however, whether high mortality rates and many casualties indicate military prowess or the reverse. Shinkarenko and Fok considered it a point of honour always to walk with ramrod backs and, even in the trenches, they refused to bend down, which meant that they were literally standing targets to the enemy. As a consequence, Shinkarenko was seriously wounded in the head by a sniper as he walked tall along the trench to his position. This may indicate courage and military-mindedness but strikes the laywoman as foolhardiness. It suggests, too, an old-fashioned view of combat more fitting the era of Imperial hussars and the cavalry strung out across the steppes than the battle strategies on the eve of the Second World War.[67] Among the Russian casualties Yaremchuk lists, Nikolae Zotoff was wounded five times, and left with one leg shorter than the other. Konstantin Kontstaniff, wounded three times, lost the sight of an eye, and General Fok, himself, chose suicide at Belchite, rather than fall into the hands of the 'Reds'.[68]

A good number of the White Russians who remained in Spain went on to serve in the Blue Division on the Eastern Front or in the Italian army in the Second World War.[69] This continuity of military service probably reflects the paucity of other occupational options as much as military commitment, though conventionally volunteers are considered better fighters than draftees. And these White Russians were volunteers several times over.

Shinkarenko and his Russian comrades were contemptuous of the 'passivity' and the 'lack of initiative' of Nationalist soldiers.[70] In battle, Shinkarenko claimed that many Spanish soldiers wanted only to 'avoid the bullets', not defeat the enemy. Russians claimed also to find that, even when Spanish soldiers were brave, 'their commanders were uneducated in the art of warfare' (Pt. 4, Ch. 2). It is hard to determine the truth of this assessment. It may result from a combination of Russian sour grapes that they were so often passed over in preferment and a compensatory sense of superiority. They were fond of pointing out that they had participated in more European wars than had the Spaniards, though they never added the fact that they were defeated in the last two wars in which the Imperial army was engaged. Instead, Shinkarenko offered various examples where Spaniards on both sides were cautious under fire. At Mondragón, for example, the two sides faced off for several weeks and, though there was not much distance between them, no one had been killed even in the artillery barrage.

Whatever the reason, Shinkarenko was adamant that battles he saw in Spain were less modern than the European wars he had known between 1914 and 1921 and were characterized by passivity and slowness (Part 4, Ch. 2). For example, between spring and winter 1938, Shinkarenko and his comrades had been in only one engagement and in this soldiers were more anxious to avoid the 'whizzing bullets' than to 'stamp on the enemy'. It was not through lack of bravery, according to Shinkarenko, but that the officers were bereft of initiative. The exception to this damming assessment were some of the Basques, who in his view were 'level-headed, practical and good soldiers', though their officers, too, were a disappointment, knowing 'only military warfare by the rules of the book' (Pt. 4, Ch. 1).

Setting all of this aside, what did Franco gain from his White Russian volunteers? All things considered, the answer must be that it was very little. There were very few of them and the effort of enlistment and training that they required was barely worth the trouble. Certainly the notation on the files in relation to Shinkarenko's grandiose requests indicates official irritation with him at Nationalist High Command.

In Franco's victory parade in Madrid, the White Russians marched proudly as a distinct unit under the Imperial Russian flag.[71] With the war over, they faced penury. Their exile organization had few funds to help with demobilization, leaving many Russians in Spain to scrounge for a living. The more enterprising few formed themselves into performing groups and travelled around Spain giving displays of traditional Russian music and dance. Those who returned to Paris were interned as stateless people when the Second World War began and, along with the other refugees in France, were treated very harshly.[72] In 1942, a number of White Russians enlisted in the Légion Contre le Bolchevisme, which was recruited in Paris by Jacques Doriot to fight with Hitler on the Eastern Front. This was hardly a way out. Once the Legion had entered Russian territory, the Russians among them were confronted with the same dilemma that they had faced in exile in 1930. Some deserted to Soviet units rather than fight their countrymen on the soil of the Motherland, while others, believing that in fighting with the Nazis they were helping to defeat Bolshevism, were put to the work of flushing out partisan units in the borderlands of the former Poland and the Ukrainian Soviet Socialist Republic.

When the Second World War broke out, Shinkarenko returned to France and attempted to enlist in the French army. He was refused because of his age and his anomalous legal situation as a stateless person. At the time, he took it as one more outrageous slur on his Imperial background but, when France capitulated in mid-1940, he was 'relieved' to have escaped being part of such a 'cowardly military outfit'. Shinkarenko died at the age of 78 in San Sebastian in 1968.

Notes

1 Archivo Histórico Militar, Ávila. Cuartel General del Generalísimo-Estado Mayor, año de 1938. 2/168/30/5 and the list in the series año de 1937. 1/168/18/12, 'Copia, Legionari Russi del Tercio' which provides names of twelve White Russians transferred into the Italian regiments. The historian of the White Russians in exile, the late Professor Viktor Bortnevski of the Hoover Institution, was enormously helpful with manuscript sources as was Hoover archivist, Carole Leadenham. Sheila Fitzpatrick suggested useful White exile memoirs and Yavor Siderov and Kira Raif assisted with translations.

2 Anton Nikolai Shinkarenko I Vsevolovich, [Typescript Memoirs], [TSM] 7 pamphlet boxes, Hoover Archives IDCSUZ68020-A, Stanford University, Part 4, Chapter 4. The voluminous diaries range over a huge number of issues and events. The sections which relate to Spain are Part 4, Chapters 1 to 11, and are arranged partly by chronology and partly by topic.

3 Anton Prokof'evich Yaremchuk, *Russkie dobrovol'tsy v Ispanii 1936–1939* [*Russian Volunteers in Spain 1936–1939*] (San Francisco: Globus Publishers, 1983), p. 51.

4 Shinkarenko, TSM, Part 4, Ch. 2.

5 *Russkie dobrovol'tsy v Ispanii 1936–1939*, pp. 8, 365.

6 Shinkarenko, TSM, Part 4, Ch. 1; and letter in *Chasovoi* [*The Sentinel*], No. 174, 1937.

7 According to Yaremchuk, 53 Russian volunteers came from Paris, though only 35 of the group managed to cross the border into Spain. See *Russkie dobrovol'tsy v Ispanii 1936–1939*, pp. 2–3. An appendix provides their biographies, pp. 365–73. For the Russian Expeditionary Forces in France during the First World War and afterwards, see Jamie H. Cockfield, *With Snow on Their Boots: The Tragic Odyssey of the Russian Expeditionary Force in France during World War I* (London: Macmillan, 1998).

8 Shinkarenko, TSM, Part 4, Ch. 1. In Berlin, Boris Toedtl, a Russian of Swiss-German origin and a member of the Swiss National Front, established links with

the right wing of Russian emigrés in Berlin to raise a unit of volunteers for Franco. In October 1934, his star had risen briefly in Nazi circles in Berlin when he organized the defence of the Swiss publishers of the Protocols of the Elders of Zion against a prosecution by Swiss Jews. Robert C. Williams, the historian of Russian emigrés in Berlin, states that Toedtl's writings were fantasy and his plans amounted to nothing. See *Culture in Exile: Russian Emigrés in Germany, 1881–1941* (Ithaca: Cornell University Press, 1972) p. 342.

9 Marc Raeff, *Russia Abroad: A Cultural History of the Russian Emigration, 1919–1939* (New York: Oxford University Press, 1990), pp. 202–3. Ryszard Wraga gives a higher figure of 400,000 White Russians in France, in his 'Russian emigration after thirty years of exile', in George Fischer (ed.), *Russian Emigré Politics* (New York: Free Russia Fund, 1951), p. 42.

10 Temira Pachmuss argues that the emigré intellectual community in Paris created a 'positive conspiracy' to sustain and develop non-Soviet culture in exile. See her 'Introduction' in *A Russian Cultural Revival: A Critical Anthology of Emigré Literature before 1939* (Knoxville: University of Tennessee Press, 1981), pp. 3–10.

11 Catherine Andreyev quotes statistics from the Russian Historical Archive Abroad that, in 1936, outside the borders of the USSR, there were 108 newspapers and 162 journals produced for a readership of more than 2 million, in *Vlasov and the Russian Liberation Movement: Soviet Reality and Emigré Theories* (Cambridge: Cambridge University Press, 1987), p. 12.

12 Olga Andreyev Carlisle, 'A Parisian childhood', in her *Voices in the Snow: Encounters with Russian Writers* (London: Weidenfeld & Nicolson, 1962), pp. 13–25.

13 Raeff argues that the situation continued until the Second World War which integrated many refugees into the societies in which they had settled. After the war, exile communities were diluted by Displaced Persons from the Soviet Union. As well, by then many of the generation of 1917 refugees had died. See Raeff, *Russia Abroad*; and George Fischer's *Russian Emigré Politics* for an overview of White exiles.

14 Vladimir Nabokov, *Speak, Memory: An Autobiography Revisited* (London: Weidenfeld & Nicolson, 1967), pp. 276–7.

15 Nina Berberova, *The Italics Are Mine*, translated from the Russian by Philippe Radley (New York: Alfred A. Knopf, 1992), p. 281.

16 Michael B. Miller, *Shanghai on the Metro: Spies, Intrigue and the French between the Wars* (Berkeley: University of California Press, 1994), p. 130; p. 139.

17 Nina Berberova, *The Italics Are Mine*. See also Richard D. Sylvester's introduction to *Valentina Khodesevich and Olga Margolina-Khodasevich, Unpublished Letters to Nina Berberova* (Berkeley: Modern Russian Literature and Culture Studies and Texts, Vol. 3, 1979).

18 Milchail Bulgakov's *Exiles* (1928) also evokes the unreality of White exiles and their disorientation in civilian life.

19 Viktor Bortnevski, personal communication, August 1985; and the obituary in *Chasovoi*, No. 204, 10 January 1938. Peter Ustinov described his uncle Nicholas, a regular officer in the ex-Russian army, as 'following the great tradition of emigré officers': driving a Paris taxi. Peter Ustinov, *Dear Me* (London: Heinemann, 1977), p. 37.

20 *House of Regrets; A Tragi-Comedy in Three Acts* (London: Jonathan Cape, 1943).

21 The expression is Serge Schmemann's, in *Echoes of a Native Land: Two Centuries of a Russian Village* (New York: Alfred A. Knopf, 1997), p. 16.

22 Michael Ignatieff, *Russian Album* (London: Vintage, 1997), pp. 151–4.

23 Nina Berberova's collection of stories about White Russians in Paris is contained in *Three Novels*, translated from the Russian by Marian Schwartz (London: Chatto and Windus, 1990). See also the historical novel of the life of Russian exiles living in a *pension* in the 16th Arrondissement in J. Kessel, *Nuits de Princes* (Paris: Calmann-Lévy, 1948).

24 Prince A. Lobanov-Rostovsky, *The Grinding Mill: Reminiscences of War and Revolution in Russia 1913–1920* (New York: Macmillan, 1935), pp. 380–1.

25 Grand Duke Alexander of Russia, *Once a Grand Duke* (London: Cassell, 1932), p. 374.

26 Nabokov, *Speak, Memory*, p. 261.

27 See Andreyev's discussion in *Vlasov and the Russian Liberation Movement*, pp. 12–13; and Dimitry V. Lehovich, *White against Red: The Life of General Anton Deniken* (New York: Norton, 1974), pp. 450–2.

28 Raeff, *Russia Abroad*, pp. 150–5.

29 The journal *Novyi grad* [*New City*] was published by three exiles in Paris. See Raeff, *Russia Abroad*, p. 151, and footnote 26, p. 216.

30 Lehovich, *White against Red*, p. 454.

31 Typical is the 1937 pamphlet, *Nos frères catholiques sous la Croix en Espagne. Conférence faite à l'église orthodoxe Russe de Genève, par le docteur Lodygensky, membre de conseil de paroisse et du bureau de la Commission Internationale 'Pro Deo'* (Zaragoza: Talleres Gráficos de 'el Noticeo', 1937). As in this case, Pius XI's 1937 encyclical *Divini Redemptoris*, which argued that Communism and Christianity were incompatible, was widely quoted, though less so was the bracketed encyclical, *Mit brennender Sorge*, warning against Nazism. The former argument was often made in *Chasovoi*. See, for example, No. 172, August 1936.

32 AGM, Ávila, Cuartel General del Generalísimo-Estado Mayor, 2/168/18/2, Delegazione Italiana, No. 349, DIS Salamanca, 29–5–39, pp. 3–5.

33 Yaremchuk, *Russkie dobrovol'tsy v Ispanii 1936–1939*, p. 2.

34 On the assassination and the execution see Mary Knight, 'Girl reporter in Paris', in Eugen Lyons (ed.), *We Cover the World by Sixteen Correspondents* (London: George G. Harrap, 1937), p. 283.

35 See Lehovich, *White against Red*, p. 448.

36 See Anatoli Rybakov's historical novel based on the incident, *The Fear*, translated

by Antonia W. Bouis (Boston: Little, Brown and Co., 1992). For the trial see Berberova, *The Italics Are Mine*, pp. 331–4; and Lehovich, *White Against Red*, pp. 437–8.

37 *Le Populaire*, 24 September 1937; 29 September 1937; *L'Humanité*, 21 September 1937; 24 September 1937; 25 September 1937; 28 September 1937. See also A. Beucler, 'Russes de France', *Revue de Paris*, **44** (2) (1937), pp. 866–96.

38 Robert H. Johnston, *New Mecca, New Babylon: Paris and the Russian Exiles, 1920–1945* (Montreal: McGill-Queen's University Press, 1988), pp. 100–2.

39 Yaremchuk, *Russkie dobrovol'tsy v Ispanii*, pp. 5–7.

40 At least one ex-Kornilov officer acted on his longing to return to Russia by joining the International Brigades. His older brother, profoundly shamed, blamed the defection on the dissolute life of exile in Paris in which his younger brother had 'met up with all sorts of scum'; Yaremchuk, p. 368. John Cornford met a similar group of homesick White Russians in Barcelona, who had enlisted in the International Brigade in the hope that it would facilitate their return to Mother Russia. In a curious time warp, they referred to Stalin as the 'little Father' and when drunk became maudlin and sang old Russian folk songs. See Keith Scott Watson, *Single to Spain* (London: Arthur Barker, 1937), pp. 104–7.

41 *Chasovoi*, No. 173, 1 September 1936, p. 4.

42 Yaremchuk, *Russkie dobrovol'tsy v Ispanii 1936–1939*, pp. 365–73.

43 *Chasovoi*, No. 226, 15 December 1938, p. 13; No. 226, January 1939, pp. 32–3.

44 See Shinkarenko, TSM, Part 4, Ch. 4, and *The Berlin Diaries 1940–1945 of Marie 'Missie' Vassiltchikov* (London: Methuen Paperback, 1985), pp. 203–4.

45 Reprinted in *Chasovoi*, No. 178, 15 November 1936.

46 *Chasovoi*, No. 173, September 1936, p. 4; Yaremchuk, *Russkie dobrovol'tsy v Ispanii*, p. 12.

47 Luis Fabián Blázquez, *Riesgo y ventura de los Tercios de Requetés* (Madrid: ACTAS, 1995), p. 102–3.

48 See Shinkarenko, Part 4, Ch. 1. There are innumerable references to Russian military superiority in Shinkarenko's diaries.

49 See the comments from the Russian volunteers recruited in Spanish Morocco, in *Chasovoi*, No. 173, 1 September 1936.

50 *Chasovoi*, 'Letters from Spain', No. 209, March 1938, p. 16.

51 *Chasovoi*, No. 172, August 1936.

52 The character, who the author claims is true, came from the region between Prussia and Latvia, which fell to Germany at Brest Litovsk. After the Russian Civil War he fought with Franco in Spain and Mussolini in the Second World War. See Marguerite Yourcenar, *Coup de Grace* (London: Secker & Warburg, 1957).

53 See also General Krasnov's comment on the 'irrelevance' of whether victory against Bolshevism is celebrated in Spain or Russia, though he speaks about Russia, in *Chasovoi*, No. 205, February 1938.

54 *Chasovoi*, No. 172, August 1936, pp. 5–6.

55 *Chasovoi*, No. 176, October 1936, pp. 1–2.

56 *Chasovoi*, No. 169, July 1936, pp. 1–29.

57 *Chasovoi*, No. 186, March 1937.

58 AGM, Ávila, 2/168/18/2, Cuartel General del Generalísimo-Estado Mayor, N. Schinkarenko, Hospital Militar Seminario, 7 July 1937, p. 10.

59 Frank Thomas mentions that the White Russian he knew was an ex-officer in the Imperial navy and a veteran of Wrangel's army but was never promoted despite his bravery in the field; *Brother against Brother: Experiences of a British Volunteer in the Spanish Civil War* (Phoenix Mill: Sutton Publishing, 1998), p. 95.

60 See Yaremchuck, *Russkie dobrovol'tsy v Ispanii*, p. 48.

61 In his memoirs, Shinkarenko suggests that Fok had become disheartened in Spain and came to doubt that there would ever be a Tsarist restoration and therefore withdrew from Shinkarenko's grand plan-cum-fantasies for the future.

62 See a similar life story in Vladimir S. Littauer, *Russian Hussar: A Story of the Imperial Cavalry 1911–1920* (London: White Mane Publishing Co., 1993).

63 AGM, Ávila, 2/168/18/12, Cuartel General del Generalísimo-Estado Mayor, Sección 1a, Organización unidades Rusas. Petición del ex-general ruso Nicolas Schinkarenko para que se forme una unidad a base de oficiales y soldados rusos que hoy sirven a nuestro lado como voluntarios, pp. 8–12.

64 AGM, Ávila, 2/168/18/12, Cuartel General del Generalísimo Salamanca, 16 July 1937, a General Nicolas Schinkarenko, p. 6. In the same file there is a similarly curt refusal, dated 7 June 1937, to another letter of request (p. 1).

65 Shinkarenko, TSM, Part 4, Chapter 4.

66 There is a dramatic, unsigned letter in *Chasovoi* that is probably by Shinkarenko as it contains his trademark description of himself, though now having been in 'four wars and suffered six injuries'. See No. 173, 1937.

67 See the pre-First World War values and ethos evoked in Littauer, *Russian Hussar*.

68 See note 7.

69 As indicated in Yaremchuk's biographies of the 38 recorded biographies of the survivors in Spain, in note 7.

70 If this is the case, it accords perhaps with Michael Seidman's conclusions that as the war dragged on Spanish conscripts became increasingly reluctant to engage in combat that would endanger their lives. See his 'Frentes en calma de la guerra civil', *Historia Social*, **27** (1997), pp. 52–8.

71 Fabián Blázquez, *Riesgo y ventura de los Tercios de Requetés*, pp. 102–3.

72 See Arthur Koestler, *Scum of the Earth* (London: Jonathan Cape, 1941) which described the travails of stateless internees in France at the start of the war.

CHAPTER 6

Slaying Satan, saving Franco: The Romanian Iron Guard in Nationalist Spain

Introduction

In the light of ideology and practice, the eight members of the Romanian Iron Guard who became volunteers for Franco embody in a striking form a particular set of the features of Franco's foreign volunteers. The Romanians believed that with Franco they were on a worldwide crusade to defend Christ and the Cross against, in their graphic parlance, 'Satan and his Judeo-Masonic henchmen'. Their identification with Nationalist Spain was such that, in many cases, they conflated Romania and Spain into a single entity. Their contribution to Franco's war, however, was symbolic rather than practical or military. The Iron Guard contingent joined up at short notice and were in battle very briefly. The real impact of their enlistment with Franco was felt only after the volunteers had returned home to Bucharest.

The legionaries of the Romanian Iron Guard came to Spain because they saw the Nationalists and themselves on a 'historic mission in defence of the Cross, of culture and Christian civilization'.[1] It is easy to see why they identified with Francoism. The political objectives, the cultural aspirations and the Manichean language employed in both movements were almost interchangeable.[2] The core elements of franquista ideology extolled Family, God and Patria, which resonated strongly with the sensibilities of Romanian nationalists. Similarly, the figure of the Virgin of the Pillar, who served a powerful symbolic function for the Nationalist army, was very much like the Archangel Michael, who provided inspiration to the Romanian Legion.[3] The Virgin of the Pillar, named the military Captain General of Saragossa, was carried out of the cathedral on ceremonial occasions to lead her troops. In much the same way, images of the avenging St Michael, with wings outstretched and sword aloft, led the Iron Guard ever onwards.

Familiar within a Romanian context was Franco's castigation of 'los rojos' ('the Reds'). This hold-all category in both Romania and Nationalist Spain embraced Communists, Masons, Jews, atheists, liberals and all of those who led cosmopolitan and secular lives. That the existence of these 'Reds' was inimical to traditional Spain – Catholic, rural, patriotic and united – confirmed the Romanian nationalists' own beliefs. In their view, Old Kingdom Romania was a sort of Castile of the Balkans. Just as Spanish nationalists feared that the essential 'Hispanidad' of Castile was threatened by states on the Spanish periphery, Romanian nationalists saw the values of the Old Kingdom under siege from the minorities in the new territories that after the Versailles Peace Settlement encircled the Old Kingdom to form Greater Romania. Rather as traditional Spaniards rejected the language and separatist aspirations of Catalans and Basques, Romanian nationalists feared the dissolvent elements of Jews, Hungarians, Ruthenians, Russians and Bessarabians who, from 1919, were equal citizens within the expanded territory of Romania.

It is not surprising that the figure of General Moscardó was revered by right-wing Romanians, just as he was admired by a whole segment of the interwar Right, many of whom were ambivalent about postwar society in which the certainties of religion and tradition had been swept away. In Romania, too, the expansion of territory that was won in the First World War was counterbalanced by the influx of non-Romanians into the national body politic. Moscardó steadfastly leading the besieged in the Alcázar symbolized a bygone and better era: part of the pre-1914 world of heroism and old-fashioned military valour. In Romania, the narrative of the siege was told and retold in a series of editions.[4] Franco's supporters everywhere greeted with jubilation the news that the Nationalists had relieved the siege at Toledo. In Romania, when word came through that the Nationalists had routed the Republicans, members of the Iron Guard decided to travel to Spain to meet Moscardó and mark the historic event in some memorable way.

Historical background

Although it existed before the First World War, Romania faced some of the same strains and structural dislocation that confronted the new states formed in Eastern Europe after the war. The paramount issue was how to form a modern democracy that could incorporate newly enfranchised groups and meet the letter and the spirit of the Versailles settlement.

Countries in Central and Southern Europe, which were reliant on agriculture, had to operate against a backdrop of economic instability.[5] Increasing competition from cheap agricultural exports from the New World forced rural prices down, tipping the negative balance of payments even further and sending many agricultural communities into decline.

While sharing their economic problems, Romania's political situation was unlike that of its neighbours. Hungary, Austria and Russia suffered the loss of territory and, as a consequence, were left with an oversupply of unemployed state functionaries embittered at lost livelihoods and diminished status. Romania, by contrast, had gained a great deal at the end of the war. The Treaty of Saint Germain in 1919 doubled national territory and population.[6] As well, the nation's industrial base was greatly strengthened with the inclusion of industrial regions such as the Banat.

In the pre-war Old Kingdom, less than 8 per cent of the population had been members of minorities, the largest of which were the Jews. In Greater Romania after 1919, the non-Romanian population was close to 30 per cent, consisting of Hungarians, Germans, Ukrainians, Russians and a large group of Jews, the latter predominantly in the urban areas of the old and new territories. Despite the new influx of other ethnic groups and the fear that they generated among Romanian nationalists, in fact, among the hotchpotch of minorities and races that constituted the new state, ethnic Romanians were still in the majority and occupied the box seat.[7]

In the new territories (Banat, Transylvania, North Bukovina, Bessarabia and Dobroudja) rural Romanians were, at the stroke of a pen, transformed from 'savage beasts',[8] at the bottom of the social hierarchy, into the core national group. Governments in power in Bucharest between the wars were all Nationalists and, whatever their party, were committed to Romanizing the newly acquired regions in order to ensure Romanian political and cultural hegemony. Central to the enterprise was the creation of a self-conscious Romanian elite and the promotion of Romanian culture. A core element was the production of a national history that privileged the Romanian past in the heterogeneous history of the region.

There were serious structural disjunctures in Greater Romania: for example, many more educated young people graduated than there were jobs to employ them. In the normal course of things, however, and in the longer run, it would be young men – ethnic Romanians like those who went off to Spain – who would constitute the new national elite. The Iron Guard movement, despite its archaic rhetoric, was part of a modernizing process that threw up a generation that was upwardly mobile. The youth organization, the Brotherhood of the Cross, led by Ion Motza, later one of Franco's volunteers, is a good example. It was created with the express purpose of establishing between the Old Kingdom and the new regions a new Romanian 'intellectual and moral youth bloc'.[9] The eight comrades who travelled to Spain represented the new order. Except for the two aristocratic Cantecuzinos, they were from poor and unprepossessing provincial backgrounds. The young men had risen as leaders in student politics, through a Romanized national education system, and become players in the national arena. The presence of the Cantecuzinos in the group, similarly, underlines the fact that a profound shift had taken place in Romania after the war. These young men, scions of the old aristocracy, saw the future with the New Right and were happy to work towards it as equals with comrades in the Iron Guard.

The Iron Guard movement exemplified reactionary modernism. Despite their medieval rhetoric and Old Regime garb, they were firmly plugged into the twentieth century. With an excellent nationwide organization they used the national railway system to move their supporters quickly to wherever they could have maximum effect. Codreanu's own wedding ceremony in mid-1925 provides an example of the archaic secured to a solid twentieth-century technological foundation. It was a peasant wedding with all the traditional trappings. Bride and groom wore national dress as did the guests. He, with ribbons and flowers in his hat, embroidered white linen blouse and sash, narrow white trousers and laced-up leather sandals, rode on a white horse. She, in flowing peasant skirt and ribbons laced into a bodice, travelled to the church in a flower-bedecked wagon drawn by six white oxen. Afterwards, there was a peasant fiesta in the forest with folk music and dancing and feasting in the open air. The archaic nature of the proceedings was belied by the thousands of spectators who turned up and the fact that the entire event was filmed and screened later to what were reported as enthusiastic audiences in Bucharest. The response was so great that the government became fearful and banned the film.[10]

Despite all of their real advances in political power, Romanian nationalists were uneasy at the changed ethnic composition of Greater Romania and afraid that they would be overrun by minorities. They saw these groups – Jews and Hungarians in particular – as threatening Romanian power, even though the entire new state after 1918 was Romanized and the government in Bucharest was committed to ensuring and retaining Romanian hegemony. This fear of denationalization was translated into a series of political and cultural responses to keep minorities in a subordinate place and Romanians in the saddle. This was the context in which the Iron Guard flourished.

The Legion of the Archangel Michael, after 1930 the Iron Guard, was formed by Corneliu Zelea Codreanu in 1927 from a split within several Romanian nationalist and anti-Semitic groups. The nucleus of the movement consisted of five comrades who became blood brothers while jailed with Codreanu in Vacaresti prison near Bucharest at the end of 1923. Their attachment to the Archangel Michael dates from this time. An icon in his image was in the prison chapel and the military demeanour of the warring saint greatly appealed to the future legionaries. St Michael became their protector and talisman. The French interwar travel writers, Jérôme and Jean Tharaud, in Bucharest in 1938, interviewed Codreanu at the Legion's headquarters where statuettes and images of Archangel Michael covered every available space. On the wall behind Codreanu's desk hung a large statue of the saint with wings raised in the characteristic pose. Whether by chance or design, the leader's chair was so placed that his body was in front of the angel's trunk so that the outstretched wings appeared to rise out of Codreanu's shoulders.[11]

The members of the Iron Guard were Christian revolutionaries on the extreme right of Romanian politics. According to Eugen Weber, the movement combined a 'mystic nationalism' with 'fervent anti-Semitism' and a high tolerance for violence that could promote their cause.[12] The absence of an organized working-class movement on the Romanian Left, or a moderate middle-class opposition on the Right, enabled the Iron Guard to operate in a political climate which encouraged untrammelled revolutionary nationalism and anti-Semitism. The Legion's mission was 'to reclaim Romania from Hungarians, Jews and Bolsheviks for the Christian faith of the original Dacio-Roman descendants of the Danube Basin'. In their literature the Iron Guard were greatly exercised over the effect of Romania's 'internal enemies' personified by 'the Jew' who 'daily robbed' virtuous Romanians of 'their wealth, the right to their own race, and their own home'. In this omnibus of wickedness, Jews and Bolsheviks were synonymous and were often referred to interchangeably with 'Freemasons and foreigners'.[13]

The movement's leaders, in their writings and from the dock in several famous court cases, railed against that other postwar political innovation which was also the bane of the extreme Right in many parts of Europe.

This was the 'pernicious doctrine' of citizenship as a political right. According to Codreanu, a strong people is not 'led by itself through elections' but by an elite: men with 'special aptitudes and qualifications'. This elite cannot be elected by the people: elections only cause 'all the scum of the people to rise to the surface'.[14] For the Iron Guard, citizenship and nation were synonymous and could only ever be based on race and birth and, in the case of Romanians, must be tied to a clear 'Dacio-Roman pedigree'. The latter was a reading back into the past to produce an invented history of Romanianness. The 'real Romania', as the Guardists saw it, was to be found among the peasantry and those who lived in small towns away from the cities which were the source of Jewish/Bolshevik contagion. In a parallel circumstance in Spain, Franco, too, always claimed to draw his strength from the 'Real Spain' of peasants and rural areas against the 'Reds' who controlled the urban areas.

The Iron Guard's programme was not so much political as moral and cultural. It aimed at 'regenerating the spirit of the Romanian nation'. Rather than promulgating a programme, the Legion promoted a state of being.[15] With rituals, initiations and a cult of death they hoped to invoke the cleansing powers and the sacrifices that would produce a new Romanian. The followers of the Iron Guard were exhorted with such slogans as 'Who knows how to die will never be a slave'; or, 'you are in God's hands and you can only die once'; and 'he who knows death will never be enslaved'.[16] The similarities between Iron Guard necromanticism and the Spanish Foreign Legion are noteworthy. In both organizations the recruit, on enlistment, became a new man with a fresh identity and new allegiances.

Codreanu's organization was based on a central structure: the 'nest' of three to thirteen members who had sworn brotherhood and loyalty to each other. A cluster of nests made a locality and a larger group again became a region until finally the whole nation would be incorporated. The legionaries' uniform consisted of a green shirt and, embroidered over the heart, the broken cross of the swastika, a symbol used by Romanian nationalists long before it gained favour with the Nazis. As well, many legionaries, even in urban occupations, made a point of wearing national dress.

The Iron Guard movement believed in practical action and collective work. From the mid-1930s they set up work camps in which legionaries voluntarily provided the labour for public works in rural areas to construct schools, roads and bridges, as well as community centres where the committed legionaries could spread the word among rural communities. Codreanu claimed that it was in the egalitarian spirit of camaraderie and collective work that the personality of the new Romanian man would be forged.[17] In certain areas the Legion also set up shops in order to cut out Jewish middlemen.[18]

In late 1929 and early 1930, the Legion carried out a series of pilgrimages throughout the new territories.[19] Contemporaries have left graphic descriptions of the drive. The leaders on horseback and in Romanian national dress, with turkey feathers in their caps, carried the banner of St Michael. Their mode was to arrive in the village square and begin to sing traditional folk songs. When curious peasants began to gather, a legionnaire would announce that the hour of resurrection had arrived and Jews, who were the anti-Christ, must be driven out to make way for a new era in the Fatherland. In this imminent new epoch, virtuous Christians would enjoy their rightful place. Peasants, who by definition were blessed with the power of faith and the righteousness of their souls, would inherit the earth. When the cavalcade moved on to the next hamlet, often a great tail of villagers would accompany them. At night there were lantern-lit processions and, as the word spread, the peasant audiences grew larger and larger. It was not uncommon for whole villages to come out on the road to meet the caravan and leave with them when the legionaries moved on.

The extraordinary procession traversed Transylvania and Moldavia and, by the time it crossed the River Pruth into Bessarabia, it had grown into seven columns of thousands of pilgrims. In Bessarabia the proportion of Jews was the highest in the population of Greater Romania and many Bessarabian Jews were Leftists and pro-Soviet Union. The cavalcade of columns provided an impressive sight. By this time the legionaries at the head carried great wooden crosses and their horses, like the mounts of medieval crusaders, were draped in white stoles with large crosses embroidered on the chest. At each stop speakers proclaimed the need to drive out Jews and corrupt politicians in the name of Christ and the Cross. Increasingly, as the cavalcade grew, other anti-Semitic groups joined. After several weeks the local police, acting on the agitated orders of the government in Bucharest, closed down the rallies and dispersed the columns.

After the enormous success in Bessarabia, Codreanu reformed the Legion of the Archangel Michael into the Iron Guard. It became like Mussolini's militia or the SS in Germany, a military organization with grades and emblems, rituals of passage, and an oath of allegiance sworn to Codreanu – 'the Captain' – as he was always called. From the mid-1920s, Codreanu and his associates were involved in a series of highly publicized assassinations which brought great publicity to the movement. In the trials of all of them the Guardists were acquitted, which drew even more members to the movement.

The Spanish Civil War in Romania

News of the insurgents' uprising against the Spanish government galvanized the Right in Romania. Henceforth the red and yellow flag of Nationalist Spain shared pride of place beside the banners of Italy and Germany on the rostrums of the Right.[20] According to the French consul, the 'lessons of Spain' were propounded at every nationalist forum.[21] The Spanish ambassador, Pedro de Prat y Soutzo, Marqués de Prat de Nantouillet, immediately declared for Franco and became the spokesman for Nationalist Spain.[22]

The Romanian government, at Britain's instigation, attended the Nyon conference and was a signatory to the Paris Naval Agreement in October 1936 which laid out the conventions of non-intervention. In Bucharest the government issued instructions to all the police authorities to prevent Romanian citizens from going abroad if they intended to take part in the Spanish Civil War. Despite an apparent official toeing of the line of non-intervention, the British consul in Bucharest opined that 'it would be no exaggeration to say that the vast majority of Romanians [of his own class and politics] prefer the Nationalists or the military elements in Spain'.[23] As well, he commented that 'there was plenty of evidence' that the efforts of Prat to further the interests of the Nationalist government in Spain 'were undertaken with the connivance of the highest Romanian authorities'. King Carol stepped in swiftly to prevent the Spanish Republic importing oil in tankers from Romania and, when the Spanish government attempted to transport arms, bought in Poland through the Romanian Black Sea port of Constantsa, the Romanian government, alerted by Señor Prat, impounded the ship that was carrying them.[24]

In early 1937, the Spanish government sent a new consul general, M. Manuel Lopez Rey, to replace the ambassador who had defected to the rebels. The Romanian government accepted the appointment, but with clear reluctance, and indicated unequivocally that the new Republican emissary should not attempt to reoccupy the Spanish embassy building which since July 1936 had been transformed into premises for Franco's government. Prat y Soutzo enjoyed strong contacts with journalists and editors of the right-wing press in Bucharest and used his influence to blacken the reputation of the new Republican consul general. The most outlandish stories were circulated about him and his dastardly doings in Madrid.[25]

Prat y Soutzo recalls in his memoirs that the funds to maintain the legation, once he had severed contact with the Spanish government, were paid by the 'Sephardic Jew' Max Ausnit with some extra help from the National Bank of Romania.[26] The British ambassador described Ausnit as 'standing high on the Iron Guard's black list' because he had converted to Christianity in 1934 in order to marry a beautiful and much younger Romanian Christian. His donations to Franco's ambassador may have been part of an attempt to ingratiate himself with the Iron Guard and the Romanian Right.[27] Prat claims also that, from the start, the embassy was 'inundated with hundreds of potential volunteers for Nationalist Spain' but the legation had no funds with which to send them.[28] Henri Prost, a French resident in Bucharest for more than thirty years, tells a slightly different story. Professor Octavian Goga, the Transylvanian nationalist poet and leading anti-Semitic theorist, had told the Spanish ex-ambassador that, if he gave the word, Goga could produce 100,000 volunteers. Not for Spain, he added, but to march past under the balcony of the Spanish legation and salute the victory of General Franco.[29]

The first Romanian to enlist with Franco was Prince Michael Sturdza, descendant of a very ancient aristocratic family of Moldavian princes. He greatly admired Codreanu, becoming later in the 1930s one of the captain's closest advisers. In 1940, after King Carol's abdication and the installation of a pro-Guardist government, Sturdza became Foreign Minister, a position which he also held in the postwar Romanian government-in-exile.

Sturdza had been a member of the Romanian diplomatic service since before the First World War. An admirer of Mussolini and, in particular, Hitler, Sturdza worked actively against the Little Entente and its government supporters because he saw it drawing Romania through the network of alliances with France into the orbit of the Soviet Union. In contrast, he argued that Romania's historic enemy was to the East, that is the Soviet Union, while the Little Entente ensured that 'Romania was precluded from alliances with her real racial and geopolitical ally which was Germany in the west'.[30]

From the Foreign Ministry, Sturdza had watched with increasing concern what he described as the 'anarchy' of the Spanish Republic and its secularizing 'Masonic' government, which he perceived was bent upon 'degrading churches' and 'turning them into brothels'. While the Republican government looked away, 'priests were shot like flies' and nuns subject to 'Satanic and necromaniac orgies, as disinterred they were lined along the graveyard walls with the pipes of the profaners stuck between their teeth' (Sturdza, p. 96).

In early July 1936, Sturdza travelled to Paris for an operation on a stomach ulcer. There, he was 'horrified' by the 'judeo-masonic' machinations of the French Popular Front under Léon Blum. When he heard that a group of generals had staged an uprising against the Popular Front in Spain he determined to offer his services to help in 'a victory that could prevent the establishment of the Franco-Spanish-communist-dominated empire that had been predicted by Lenin' (p. 96).

Sturdza crossed the frontier at Hendaye at the end of July and obtained permission to enlist from General Fidel Dávila in Franco's headquarters at Burgos. Before he could be sent to the front, however, Sturdza collapsed with a stomach haemorrhage and was immediately rushed to hospital. As luck would have it, as he tells us in his memoirs, while he was in Paris, his kinswoman, Queen Nathalie of Serbia, had given him a box of sweets to take to Spain for her nieces, his cousins, Chiquita and Margarita de Pedroso y Sturdza. Ill in Burgos, he enlisted their help to obtain a private room in the overcrowded military hospital. Their ministrations, and those of his wife, who on hearing of his illness had 'come running from Bucharest', managed to 'soothe considerably the bitterness of the misadventure'. After two months 'completely immobile' in Burgos, he left Spain and travelled home via Rome, where he took the opportunity to exchange views with an old acquaintance, Mussolini's Foreign Minister, Count Galeazzo Ciano (Sturdza, p. 97).

The siege of the Alcázar had been followed closely in Bucharest by right-wing Romanians, including the Iron Guard. In honour of the relief of General Moscardó's siege in October 1936, General 'Zizi' Gheorgio Cantacuzino Granicerul, the deputy leader of the Iron Guard's political party, 'All for the Fatherland', obtained permission from Franco's ambassador to lead a delegation to Toledo. The plan was that they would present General Moscardó with a special ceremonial sword recast from the one that had been given to Cantacuzino for heroism in the First World War. The original had been cast in Toledo and it would be remade to replicate the sword that the Spanish King Philip III was reputed to have presented to the Romanian Prince Michael the Wise early in the seventeenth century.

Eight members of the Iron Guard left Bucharest for Toledo to make the presentation. The most senior of them was General Cantacuzino. A white-haired 70-year-old with a monocle, he was from a very ancient aristocratic Romanian family and a famous First World War hero. A contemporary described him as, despite his age, 'infatuated' with Codreanu and an enthusiastic member of the Iron Guard movement.[31]

The youngest legionnaire for Spain was Banica Dobre, a 20-year-old Transylvanian school inspector from the Department of Education in Cluj. Dobre, who always wore national dress, was a charismatic speaker and a dedicated nationalist.[32] As well, there was Nicolae Totu, 32-years old, a lawyer and good-humoured agronomist, whose practical skills had been honed while working in the Legion's brick kilns and orchards in north Moldavia and Bukovina.[33] With them went the 47-year-old engineer, Gheorge Clime,[34] and Prince Alexandru Cantacuzino. At 30 years of age, Alexandru was a lawyer in the diplomatic service and hailed from a branch of the same distinguished aristocratic family as did the General Cantacuzino. Alexandru's mother, Princess Alexandrine Canta-cuzino, was a leading proponent of women's rights in Romania.[35] An Orthodox priest, Dimitrescu Borsa, in full clerical regalia with a large silver cross, travelled with the contingent to take care of their spiritual needs.

The remaining two legionaries, Ion Motza and Vasile Marin, were close friends, activists and the leaders of the group in Spain.[36] Marin, 32 years of age, led the Iron Guard in the Bucharest region, where he had been born and raised.[37] His widowed mother was a pious but impoverished laundress who had struggled hard to educate her children. From an early age, Marin showed intellectual brilliance. An outstanding student with a wide interest in literature, language, architecture and music, he had majored in law and political science at Bucharest University. In a familiar pattern for young men like himself in the early 1920s, he was active in student politics, first in the Law School and then rising to become the president of the Bucharest Student Movement. While at university he caught the attention of Ion Lugojeanu, a leader of the National Peasant Party and the Romanian Minister to Rome, who hired the bright young man in 1927 as his secretary. A year later, when the National Peasant Party took over government, Lugojeanu became Under-

Secretary to the President of the Council and Marin his chief secretary to the cabinet. Subsequently, with great distinction, Marin headed the Secretariat of the Ministry of Industry and Commerce. During these years he took the opportunity to travel abroad, to France and to Italy. There he was fascinated to observe what he perceived to be the great success of Mussolini's corporate state. Marin became more and more involved in full-time activism with Codreanu's Legion until, at the end of 1932, he swore allegiance to the captain and abandoned his government job to work full time as an organizer for the Iron Guard.

In that year he had enrolled for a doctorate of Law in Bucharest. His thesis laid out the philosophical, institutional and historical bases of fascism and argued that the movement had a close relationship with Catholicism. His study was published later as a book and was the main vehicle for spreading the knowledge of Italian fascism among members of the movement.

Marin was active in anti-Semitic organizations and, while in the Law School, had set up conferences and symposia in which the 'scientific' bases of anti-Semitism were elaborated. In 1932, however, he met and married Ana Maria Ropala, a Jewish medical student from Moldavia, who was studying pediatrics at Bucharest University. Her presence is intriguing. She has claimed that Marin and all his friends knew that she was a Jew but did not care. Sturdza recalls that Codreanu gave Marin 'permission to marry a Jewish girl' (Sturdza, p. 55). Whatever the arrangements, the situation is striking, as is the fact that she was a medical student. High Jewish enrolments in Romanian medical schools was perhaps the most raw of all the issues that abraded Romanian and Jewish student relations between the wars.[38]

Ana Maria has left a tender description of her meeting with Vasile while she was on a walking holiday to the monasteries of Moldavia near her grandmother's house.[39] Her first impression of her future husband was of a 'blonde boy', very tall and thin, with intense blue eyes and wearing a threadbare but newly laundered cotton jersey. She was struck by his clear voice and the eloquence and intensity of his talk about Romanian poetry and literature. They met at a party and she assumed that what he saw was 'a young girl in a flowered skirt' who was good to dance with. He continued to seek her out, however, and when they returned to Bucharest, despite her parents' objections, they spent more and more time together. Without telling either of their parents, they married on 9 February 1933. She insisted on the condition that, if in a month either was not happy with marriage, they were free to go their own way. By this time Marin was writing his doctorate, which he dedicated to Ana Maria, and working full time for the movement.

Marin's wife notes that Vasile would be gone for long periods engaged on his 'mysterious projects' and that she realized that, though he loved her dearly, she was not the centre of his universe. When the Liberal Prime Minister Ion Duca was assassinated by Iron Guards on the railway station at Sinaia on New Year's Eve in 1933, Marin was arrested. Several months later, he was released, after a military tribunal found him not guilty. Deeply committed to the role he had to play in a 'battle for good against evil', Marin believed very strongly that they were at 'a cross roads' in history and that he must seize the moment and promote the movement. According to Ana Maria, his dedication to Codreanu and the Legion was total.[40] While he was at home, ill with pleurisy, in mid-November 1936, he heard that Motza was raising a group to travel to Toledo. Marin insisted that he be included. To Codreanu's objection that there were no funds, Marin sold some books and raised the money himself. His wife accepted his decision with resignation but, as the departure grew closer, she was filled with a feeling of cold foreboding (Marin, pp. 101–15).

Ion Motza, the final legionnaire was the leader of the Romanians' expedition to Toledo and a senior organizer in the movement. Born in 1902 in Orastie, Transylvania, which until 1919 was part of Hungarian territory, Motza came from a long line of Orthodox priests and Romanian Nationalists. His father, Ion senior, an Orthodox clergyman, had dedicated his life to the defence of 'oppressed Romanians' in Transylvania. Arrested several times by the Hungarian authorities, Motza senior crossed the Carpathians as soon as Romania entered the First World War and enlisted in the Romanian army. In 1919, when the postwar settlement of the Balkan frontiers was being worked out, Motza and a delegation of Romanian nationalists travelled to the United States of America to drum up support for the creation of a Greater Romania at the Versailles Settlement. After the war, he returned to settle in Transylvania, now part of the Romanian State. In the 1930s, from Cluj, he began to publish a journal, *Libertatea*, dedicated to defeating the two enemies of Romanian nationalism, which he identified as Hungarians and Jews.

As a small boy before the First World War, Ion had begun school in a Hungarian lycée. While his father was at the war, his mother managed to take the family into Romania proper, settling eventually in a village near Iassy in Moldavia. There Motza was able to begin Romanian schooling.

During the German invasion of Moldavia, he joined other Iassy high-school students to serve as a runner for the Romanian soldiers. At the end of the war, Motza took his baccalaureate at the Liceo Santa Sava in Bucharest and, in 1920, went on scholarship for a year to the Sorbonne to study law and political science. When the scholarship money dried up, he returned to complete his studies in Cluj, where his family had settled.

The first years of the 1920s were a period of great turbulence in the universities throughout Europe. In Romania, students protested against overcrowded lecture theatres and poor conditions. The creation of a national Romanized education system after 1919 brought minorities, Hungarians, Germans, Ruthenians, Russians and Jews – often better educated than Romanian students – to compete within the education system. In her study of students in the 1920s, Irina Livezeanu has pointed out that Romanian nationalists reduced the complex problems facing the universities in this decade into a single complaint against the presence in tertiary education of 'minority students', a code word which most often stood for Jews.[41] Anti-Semitic student groups flourished and national student organizations increasingly called for the application of *numerus clausus* laws in education and employment.

Motza was a leading student activist, first in the Law faculty at Cluj and, from 1923, as the president of the Student Council. In an article at the end of 1922, in the student journal, *Dacia Noua*, Motza argued that the *numerus clausus* laws were part of Christ's will and essential to 'preserve the health and the future of the Romanian people'.[42] In the opening week of the autumn session of the 1922–23 academic year at Cluj, Romanian students rioted because more Jews than Romanians had been admitted into first-year medicine. The protesters occupied the medical school, driving Jewish students out of the dissecting rooms and proclaiming that Jews must use Jewish bodies for dissection rather than have access to the cadavers of gentiles.

Confronted with student unrest right across the country, the government in Bucharest closed the universities for the academic year of 1922–23. At the same time, a number of student leaders, including Motza, were precluded from future enrolment in any Romanian institution. It was during this period of heightened political tensions and student activism that Motza met Codreanu, who was to become the leader of the Iron Guard movement. The two men became inseparable companions, growing even closer in 1927 when Motza married Codreanu's sister, who enjoyed the redolent name of Iridenta.

In March 1923, Motza, Codreanu and Professor Cuza, the doyen of the political movement of anti-Semitism in twentieth-century Romania, founded a new political party, 'The League for National Christian Defence'. The core platform for the blue-shirted National Christians was to prevent the 'Jewish leprosy which was spreading like eczema over the whole country'.[43] The party opposed the minority protection provisions in the Treaty of St Germain, proposing instead the retention of Article 7 of the Old Constitution, thereby abolishing Jewish emancipation. The party also called for the expulsion of Jews who had arrived after 1914, and the application of *numerus clausus* in education, industry and government service. These anti-Semitic demands were totally unrealistic because Jews in Banat, Transylvania, North Bukovina and Bessarabia, unlike Jews in the Old Kingdom, already enjoyed full citizenship. In the new states of the post-Versailles order, no new national constitution would be acceptable that stripped a segment of the population of the rights of citizenship which they already enjoyed.[44]

By the end of 1923, it was clear that the national campaign to introduce *numerus clausus* had failed. Motza next masterminded a plan to assassinate prominent Jews and the politicians who supported them. On the tip-off of a fellow student, the police arrested all of those involved. Motza, Codreanu and three associates were placed in the freezing cells of Vacaresti prison. On the day of the trial, Motza, who had obtained a revolver, shot in full view the man who had been identified as the police informer. Despite the clear evidence against them, and after a public trial, Codreanu and another three were released in March 1924 and six months later Motza was also acquitted.[45]

As they had both been suspended from university in Romania, Motza and Codreanu determined to complete their studies in Grenoble. With Codreanu's wife, they travelled in September 1925 to France through Berlin and Strasbourg. They were horrified on the way by what they viewed as the predominance of Jewish businesses. Codreanu recollected that Strasbourg was a city 'infested with Jews', where they had had to search long and hard to find a Christian restaurant in which to eat. The Jews he saw were exactly as those he knew in Romania: 'same satanic eyes in which one can divine behind the obsequious facade the ruthless envy of the robber'.[46] Even in Grenoble, only five of the eighteen Romanians registered as foreign students were 'real Romanians'; as he noted, the others were all Jews.

In Grenoble, the three Romanians lived in penury, surviving on the monthly pittance sent by Motza's family and what Elena Codreanu could bring in with her embroidery. Motza completed his licentiate in law despite the fact that, as his biographer described it, the university was 'hostile' to Motza's work because 'the majority of the professors were infected by the judeo-masonic virus'. The thesis, which examined the shortcomings of the legal powers of the League of Nations, was later published under the imprint of the Romanian Studies Centre Library in Bucharest, with the title of *The League of Nations as a Vicious and Dangerous Ideal*.[47] Motza passed his exams in autumn 1926 and returned to Romania.

Motza was a Christian fanatic with the corollary of an unswerving commitment to the broad cause of European anti-Semitism. Eugen Weber has made the perspicacious observation that there was a 'violent wistfulness' in Motza's anti-Semitism, that almost constituted an 'inverted wish fulfilment'. Motza's Jews seemed to have in abundance all the qualities that Romanians lacked: they were industrious and 'united, powerful, dangerous to cross and devious'.[48]

In 1923, on his return from Paris, Motza translated from French the *Protocols of the Elders of Zion*, which was published in Orastie under the imprint of his father's journal, *Libertatea*.[49] The first Romanian edition of the tract, it is dedicated to the student movement of 1922–23 and to 'all Romanians in order to alert them to the source of national debilitation, improvidence and veniality and to awake in them the sacred flame of the struggle against the invasive Jew'.[50] In 1925, Motza, with Professor Cuza, attended the World Anti-Semitic Congress in Budapest, where he was elected to edit the Statutes of the Section of the World Youth Anti-Semitic Congress.

At the end of 1934, he regenerated his international contacts in the cause of anti-Semitism, when he travelled to Montreux in Switzerland to attend the Congress of the Fascist International. The historian, Michael Ledeen, has argued that Motza's intransigence towards the Jewish question at the congress was out of step with the positions of the other thirteen national fascist parties present, but incidentally not with the Irish, Eoin O'Duffy, who supported Motza's anti-Semitic recommendation. Motza's insistence that the final resolution of the congress include a shared international objective to exclude the Jews was unavailing. Motza spoke fervently in favour of a combined stand because he claimed that the presence of Jews was incompatible with a fascist state. In Romania, he explained, Jews had infiltrated every area of national existence with the intention of subverting the national culture and daily life.[51] In January 1936, Motza offered to send food parcels from the Iron Guard in Romania to Italian soldiers in Ethiopia, suggesting to Mussolini that the Ethiopian invasion could be linked to an international crusade against the Jews. The offer was refused.[52]

Before his departure to Spain, Motza consoled his father with the example of General Moscardó and his son, and urged his wife, the eponymous Iridenta, to keep up her spirits in his absence. Most emphatically he told her, as well, to follow his instructions and meet the publication schedule of *Libertatea*.[53] The journal was a way for him to exercise some control over the movement from abroad and would provide an income for his wife and two children.

Romanians in Spain

The eight Iron Guards left Bucharest on 22 November 1936 by train for Poland and then on to Hamburg. There they embarked on the 'Santa Olivia' bound for Lisbon.[54] On 7 December at Soria near Toledo, there was an impressive ceremony where the sword was handed over to Moscardó and General Cantacuzino spoke with great emotion about the patriotic and religious ties between Nationalist Spain and the 'old Christian lands of Romania'. Later, the Romanians were entertained at a reception at the local Falange headquarters. In both ceremonies they were received with full Spanish military honours.[55]

On the way to Spain, Motza had brought up the suggestion that they should enlist with Franco. Alexandru Cantacuzino recalled that, initially, the group was not enthusiastic. Individuals worried that they did not have Codreanu's permission and the younger Cantacuzino raised the possibility that Franco might not want foreigners in his army.[56] Motza read the cards, which were favourable to the venture, and promised to write to Codreanu for permission as soon as they had landed.[57] General Cantacuzino, whose days of rough bivouacking and combat were long past, returned to Bucharest alone.

The explanations that the legionaries offered for their own enlistment emphasize that Franco was doing 'battle with the Red Beast of the Apocalypse'. His crusade, which would defend the Church in Spain and in Russia, would strike a blow as well for Romanian Christians. They reiterated many times that 'the destiny of Christian nationalists in Romania was directly tied to the victory of the Spanish Nationalists' on the Iberian Peninsula.[58] Writing afterwards, Alexandru Cantacuzino stated that detractors were 'stupid' who claimed that the legionaries should have stayed in their own country. When a 'act of sacrilege' takes place it matters not where it occurred but only that it occurred and must be avenged everywhere. He also argued that when 'far away nations honoured the Iron Guard, as was the case in Spain, it then rebounded to their merit in their own country of Romania.'[59]

Despite their distance from Bucharest, the Iron Guard in Spain remained entirely absorbed in Romanian affairs. It was while he was at the Spanish Front that Motza received the news that he had been promoted to second in command of the Romanian Iron Guard. As well, in Lisbon, Motza edited the December and January editions of *Libertatea*. Indeed Motza wrote a staggering number of letters in the short period he was away; it was claimed that there were some two hundred or so. In their recollections his comrades note that Motza spent much of his spare time writing letters home. These appeared in his journal under the heading of 'Letters of the Romanian Legion from the Spanish front' and provided a commentary on the Guards' travels as well as a stream of advice on Romanian affairs and their relation to events in Spain. After his death, there were enough of Motza's letters to sustain a separate section in *Libertatea* for several years.

Perhaps as a consequence of the fundamentalism of their beliefs, the Guardsmen were attuned to potential signals from their divine mentors. Motza recorded as a positive portent that he had come across a statue of St Michael in Hamburg and was reassured to glimpse St Anthony in tiles on a wall near his lodgings in Lisbon. He and his colleagues were equally heartened to note that the embroidered pattern on the tablecloth in the Portuguese hotel included a part of the Iron Guard's cross-hatched insignia. The volunteers read these signs as runes that the Virgin and St Michael were pleased with the progress so far.[60] In their writings home, both Motza and Marin exude a certainty of their own invincibility. Because they were crusaders 'defending the Cross and battling the Antichrist' they were sure that God and his divine powers would protect them just as he would ensure the righteous victory of Franco and the Nationalists.

The Romanians reached Talavera de la Reina from Toledo just before Christmas 1936 and were placed 'as ordinary soldiers' in the 21st Company of the 6th Bandera of the Foreign Legion. They spent Christmas billeted in a monastery between Toledo and Talavera with a group of

Germans who were also newly arrived in Spain. The Welshman, Frank Thomas, met them there on his 'Bank Holiday', as he called it, and looked over the damaged church in the town with them. He and they were appalled at the destruction; the crucifixes had been 'torn down' and the altar and interior 'befouled'.[61]

In an exuberant letter from this time, Motza described the transcendence they had experienced in a Christian Christmas with fellow crusaders against Satan. Presumably, the enterprise they saw themselves sharing with Franco papered over the differences that had historically plagued relations between the Orthodox and the Roman Church. Motza reported, as well, that they were eager to begin the New Year with 'gun or grenade or machine-gun in hand in the arduous struggle against those who have tried to blind the Saviour and defile the mother of God and her Holy Child'.[62] A few days later, on 4 January 1937, they went up behind the front on the Madrid sector located on the road near Majadahonda.

According to Alexandru Cantacuzino, their life at this time was not easy.[63] They spoke no Spanish and had only the most cursory initial training. As well they had no proper pack or kit because they had not planned to remain in Spain. They were expected to scavenge most of these things at the front as they went along. Without tents, they slept in the open, lying on the ground in freezing temperatures. As Cantacuzino points out, too, except for the schoolmaster Dobre, the Romanians were older than many of the ordinary ranks of Spaniards around them. Again, with the possible exception of Totu the agronomist, they had all come from sedentary occupations and found army life very rugged, especially in the trenches. However, as Cantacuzino recalls, they were undaunted by these hardships, even revelling in them because they saw them as part of the physical sacrifice they were making for Christ the King.

On 13 January, at about 10 in the morning, the word came through that they were all to move up and occupy positions lining the Majadahonda road at Las Rosas. The Spanish sergeant ordered everyone to dig in behind parapets. Motza was the only one of the Romanians with a small shovel which he had found abandoned in a Republican trench as they moved into position. Cantacuzino, with no shovel, dug with his mess tin and some of the others used their hands. Motza was absolutely determined that the Romanians as soldiers must excel in front of the Spaniards and therefore he executed all orders completely, almost obsessively, and with tremendous speed. He and Marin dug energetically until they had made not just a parapet, but a small fortress, the walls of which they strengthened with stones and bricks that they collected from round about. At 2 o'clock, the order came down that they were to move out and leave their positions to the Moroccans. The Nationalist army, the Romanians with them, withdrew back towards Majadahonda, occupying trenches that had already been prepared and evacuated. In the new position, Cantacuzino was in the centre with Motza and Marin on his left and Clime and Father Borza on his other side. Except for Motza, they were all in high spirits, delighted that they had finished for the day. While they opened a tin of sardines and some conserves and shared out the sausage, everyone was laughing at the jokes Marin made about their predicament. Motza, however, was soulful and began feverishly to write to the captain describing what had happened to them in combat so far.

Half an hour later, and quite suddenly, shells began to pound the ground around them and on the hill in front, three Republican tanks rolled into view, heading towards their trenches. Nationalist anti-tank guns sputtered into action and the reports of their fire echoed with a staccato crack as they hit the lumbering tanks. The firing became more intense and great plumes of dirt spurted into the air as the shots from either side ricocheted around. The order came through to stay down in the trenches and Motza, above the din, shouted dramatically that if they were surrounded nobody was to surrender so that they could all die together.

Cantacuzino stood up briefly to see what was happening. When he looked he saw Motza and Marin together, the latter with a 'Moroccan face'. Marin had grown a beard at the front and his skin was stained brown with dirt. The Republican lines were about 500 metres in front and the soldiers from there had begun to advance towards them. Over his shoulder Cantacuzino could see Nationalist soldiers bent over, running back through the trenches. Behind them again were streams of wounded heading back to the rear, some with shattered arms and legs, one man crawling and crying out, his face the colour of the soil, darkened with pain and with very white lips. Cantacuzino, however, was relieved because none of his comrades was wounded. He picked up a small machine-gun abandoned nearby and began to fire out straight ahead over the wall of the trench towards the advancing enemy. The sharp report of the gun's shot made him close his eyes for an instant and when he opened them he saw a metre and a half away, along to his left, Motza lying face down in the bottom of the trench. At another metre's distance was Marin splayed backwards, with his back propped against the wall of the trench. Cantacuzino raced towards them, trying to shout to the others over the roar and the chaos that Motza and Marin were dead. When they had all managed to gather around, they noticed that Motza's watch, dangling on a chain, had been smashed and the time had stopped at 4.30 p.m. As they bent over him, they saw through his torn shirt that he had wrapped the Romanian flag around his body under his clothes so that he could produce it for them to march under if there were to be parades when the Nationalists were victorious. They removed Motza's tunic, unwrapped the flag and spread it over the bodies. According to Cantacuzino, at that moment they all felt 'the attraction of death' drawing them ineffably closer.

Suddenly a burly Spanish lieutenant appeared above them and ordered them back to their places. He shouted, 'Bad luck, that's war.' Cantacuzino picked up the gun and moved back along the trench. In the same engagement, Bonika Dobre and Nicholas Totu were wounded and withdrawn behind the lines. When the fighting subsided, one of the Romanians scavenged a stretcher and placed the two bodies on it. Cantacuzino then begged a Spanish sub lieutenant to allow the priest, Borsa, to accompany the bodies and carry out the proper religious ceremonies over them. When the priest departed with the stretcher, Marin and Motza's places were taken by fresh Spanish troops, who spoke no Romanian and were unaware of the ordeal that their trench mates had gone through earlier in the day.

Clime and Cantacuzino remained together on duty until midnight. They embraced each other tightly and, as the frost whitened their coats, comforted each other, talking in low voices about their comrades' deeds. They mourned their loss but also recalled the sacrifices that the parents had made for the dead men and the steadfast example that Codreanu had always upheld in their years together in Romania. Cantacuzino at this time felt utter devastation and an emotion towards Motza and Marin that 'almost bordered on envy' because they had made their sacrifices, and heroically, and therefore completed their earthly trials (Cantacuzino, p. 21).

There is a fable-like quality to the narrative of the legionnaires' last hour, from the detail of the time piece which had stopped at the moment of death to the tattered flag wrapped around the body. Much like the legionnaires in the Spanish Foreign Legion, the Romanians heroicized death in battle, which was a central element of the collective myths that sustained each group. The descriptions of the battle scene itself, however, resonate strongly with those from other eyewitnesses on these fronts around Madrid, as does the sudden and unexpected mortal event.

The Romanians were fearful that Motza and Marin would be buried in a common grave along with all the other dead from Majadahonda and their bodies would be lost. Cantacuzino sought permission to report to the commander of the *bandera* to request that the Romanians be given permission to escort the dead men to Toledo. The captain to whom he applied was 'a dirty, burly soldier with a bottle of cognac in front of him' (*ibid.*, p. 22). He dealt very roughly with Cantacuzino's request. The Romanian was appalled that the Spaniard offered no word of condolence and behaved as though such a request in wartime was impossible and quite absurd.

Somehow news of the deaths had reached Toledo, perhaps via the priest Borsa, and from there was telegrammed to General Cantacuzino in Bucharest. He immediately contacted Franco. The younger Cantacuzino obtained an authorization and managed to find the bodies of Marin and Motza lying with others in a shed in Majadahonda. At 5 o'clock the next evening, the five Romanians were allowed to leave the front for Toledo, riding in the back of an old truck with their own dead and the bodies of 20 others. It was a nightmare trip. The temperature was well below freezing and the living and the dead bumped about together, knocking arms and legs and covered with blood and dirt.

General Cantacuzino arrived from Bucharest on the last day of January 1937. He had sent a cable to Franco, in French, requesting permission to collect the bodies and bring them back to Romania. He had claimed that a 'symbolic gesture was sufficient' and, as he did not wish the other senior members of the Iron Guard to be lost in Spain, he wanted Franco's permission to let him bring the whole group back to Romania. Surprisingly, Franco agreed. In the normal course of events, it was extremely difficult to leave the Foreign Legion once a soldier had enlisted of his own volition.

The Iron Guard's return to Romania was a rerun in reverse of their arrival. When the bodies reached Toldeo, they were embalmed and placed in two magnificent coffins covered with the Spanish and Romanian colours. Representatives of the military, the Falangist Party and civilian dignitaries from the city of Toledo formally bid them farewell, as the surviving Romanians in uniform stood to attention behind the coffins on the square outside the Hospital de Sangre del Colegio de Doncellas. A fife band played the Romanian anthem and a column of Spanish infantry slow-marched past and saluted. The Civil Governor of Toledo evoked 'the heroism of their Romanian brothers' and the generosity of their contribution to the Spanish Legion and the franquista cause. Cantacuzino, in French, thanked the Spaniards and said that all Romanians were proud soldiers willing to struggle and die for the Cross and for civilization in Spain where the Nationalist fight was for the highest Christian ideals. As the cavalcade passed through Salamanca, the Foreign Minister, José Antonio Sangróniz y Castro, presented each of them with an official citation of gratitude for their bravery and awarded them the medal of the Red Cross of Bravery for the wounded.[64] It was, he said, 'a sign that Spain and Romania were both Latin nations, and part of Christian Rome eternal'. Old Cantacuzino again spoke for the whole group to say that his men were glad to have been able to make a symbolic gesture that tied together Catholic Spain and the Romanian Orthodox Christian nation. And after that they 'all prayed that General Franco would have a complete victory which will not only save Spain but the entire civilization'. [65] The cortège of hearses and followers then drove in slow convoy to Irún and across the International Bridge to be loaded onto a French train to Paris and on to Berlin.

Despite the hyperbole of the farewell speeches, the military contribution of the Iron Guard in Spain was negligible. Their ceremonial presentation of a sword to Moscardó brought some publicity for the Nationalist cause but the real impact of their Spanish expedition was felt only back in Romania. The coffins, received with 'special honours' in Berlin, travelled overland through Poland.[66] At the Romanian border the widows, 'like two shadows',[67] joined the train, which made a long looping voyage through Bukovina and Transylvania to Bucharest. As it passed through stations on the way, kneeling Iron Guard supporters with arms raised in the fascist salute solemnly greeted the coffins. At the same time, special trains brought legionaries to Bucharest from all over the nation.

On 13 February 1937 the funeral for Motza and Marin closed down the capital. Even the National Assembly was unable to raise a quorum as deputies joined the procession, or carefully stayed indoors at home. In the British consul's words, 'the police were conspicuous by their entire absence', as traffic and the crowds were controlled by two thousand green-shirted Iron Guards.[68] Thousands more lined the streets and another several thousand marched behind. Leading the procession was the Patriarch, the head of the national Church of Romania, with four hundred clergy and bishops following. Then came the coffins on two gun carriages drawn by six glossy black horses. Beside them marched the pall-bearers, wearing white cloaks on which were embroidered the great black crosses of the order of St Michael the Brave. Helmeted soldiers, protecting the coffin and the pall-bearers, surrounded them on all sides. Then came the high functionaries, officers in the uniform of the Royal Guard, and then the foreign ambassadors: the German ambassador, Herr Fabricius, the Italian ambassador, Ugo Sola, and the Portuguese chargé d'affaires, Freire de Andrade. Beside them strode Pedro de Prat y Soutso, Franco's representative in Romania. The presence of the consular representatives provoked a minor diplomatic incident later, as the parliamentary opposition claimed they had violated diplomatic conventions by participating in internal political affairs.[69] The diplomats were followed by a great crowd of Romanian and Polish students in national dress, carrying icons and banners. Then, with a small break, came the columns of the Iron Guard. At the head marched Codreanu, dressed like the others in green shirt and military uniform but wearing a long military greatcoat. Around him, in their first public demonstration, was gathered the Legion of Death, the special armed militias raised to protect the whole movement. Behind marched row upon row of green-shirted Iron Guards from every region in the country. The people lining the streets stood in silence, most with their arms raised in the fascist salute. The only sound was the squeak and thud as the legionaries' boots hit the pavement in perfect unison. A friendly bystander commented later that it was as though 'all of Romania was taking Holy Communion with the Iron Guard.'[70]

It was the Romanian equivalent of the March on Rome and few official observers could mistake its significance. Sir Reginald Hoare informed Whitehall that the Spanish veterans' funeral showed that the Greenshirts had become 'a serious menace' and were 'the beginning of a Nazi movement whose fanatical spirit would gather irresistible impetus'. He also predicted that it presaged a serious future threat to King Carol's monarchy.[71]

It was an accurate prediction. From 1937 to 1941 the Iron Guard were the central players on the national political scene. The main political changes that took place were in response to their growing power in combination with the increasing penetration of Germany into Romanian economic and political affairs.

In Hugh Seton Watson's assessment, King Carol gave the leaders of the Iron Guard 'material assistance and police protection' and used them to terrorize the Romanian Left. Once it appeared that 'the movement was no longer willing to be a tool of others' and had begun to 'capture the imagination of the masses' the king had them massacred.[72] King Carol established a royal dictatorship from March 1938 to 1940. He first banned the Iron Guard and, when that was unworkable, he had Codreanu arrested and, at the end of November 1938, shot with twelve of his companions in prison. In March 1939, one of the gunmen of Horia Sima, Codreanu's successor, assassinated the new Prime Minister, Calinescu. King Carol ordered a massive retaliation against the Iron Guard and across the country hundreds were executed and their bodies displayed as a warning; others were rounded up and interned. In 1940, in the rightist surge that went with Nazi expansion, members of the Iron Guard joined Carol's government. The monarchy collapsed when the Soviet Union occupied Bessarabia and Germany backed Hungary's annexation of Transylvania, the territories that Romania had acquired in 1919. There was, briefly, an Iron Guard government which from September 1940 to January 1941 oversaw a reign of terror. Once war in Eastern Europe had decisively begun, however, Germany abandoned the Iron Guard. The Nazis were interested, not in labyrinthine local rightist politics, but in efficaciously extracting Romanian resources.

Conclusion

The Iron Guard volunteered to fight for Franco because they believed that Franco's crusade in Spain was synonymous with their own in Romania. On a symbolic level, among others, the two movements had much in common: both employed a rhetoric about supporting traditional forces against the 'sinister powers of Communism, Freemasonry and world Jewry'. The Iron Guard, however, were reactionary modernists. Their polemic was about wishing to turn back the clock to some imagined halcyon epoch before liberal democracy, when race and ethnicity were supreme and the region of the Danube was free of the new-fangled notions of citizenship and equal political rights. The paradox was that it was in the so-called new democratic era after the First World War that Romania gained territory and Romanian nationalists were able to strengthen their cultural and political hegemony.

In Spain, at first, it was as though the volunteers had never left Romania. Reality bit deep and painfully when they encountered full-scale warfare. After their brief engagement in front-line combat, which resulted in Motza and Marin's death and two others wounded, the whole delegation abandoned Spain in order to accompany the bodies back to Romania.

The real impact of their enlistment was felt at Motza and Marin's giant funeral in Bucharest, which provided an opportunity for the first time to display the real muscle and the numbers that the Iron Guard could marshal across the nation and it was here that lay the real significance of the Spanish episode of the Romanian volunteers for Franco.

Notes

1　The words are from Zelea Corneliu Codreanu's *Manifesto* in 1937 and in similar form appear over and over in Iron Guard writings. See Codreanu, *La Garde de Fer: pour les Légionnaires* (Paris: Éditions Prométhée, 1938), p. 237. See also the manifesto and a commentary on it in PRO FO 371/21188/47815, 2 December 1937, p. 226; and FO 371/20429/47029, 20 November 1936, R. H. Hoare to A. Eden, pp. 167–83.

　　In preparing this chapter I have benefited from the generosity of Vlad Protopopescu, who shared with me his knowledge of the movement and of interwar Romanian history and made available volumes from his library. Although he may not agree with my reading of the Romanians in the Spanish Civil War, I greatly appreciate his assistance.

2　Horia Sima, the leader of the Iron Guard after Codreanu's death, has argued that Codreanu and José Antonio Primo de Rivera, the founder of the Spanish Falange, had independently developed the same ideas, in *Dos movimientos nacionales: José Antonio Primo de Rivera y Corneliu Zelea Codreanu* (Madrid: Ediciones Europa, 1960). For the attraction that Romanians felt for Spanish Latin culture, see Francisco Veiga, *La mística del ultranacionalismo: historia de la Guardia de Hierro Rumania 1919–1941* (Bellaterra: Publicaciones de la Universitat Autónoma de Barcelona, 1989), pp. 14–17.

3　The patron saint of Spain, the *Virgen del Pilar* was supposed to have appeared in a vision to the Christian soldiers fighting the Moors during the Reconquest.

4　See, for example, Dr Rudolf Timmerman, *Alcázar*, traducere din limba Germana de Roland Radler (Bucharest: Editura Ofar, Nov. 1936 [1943]).

5　Hans Raupach, 'The impact of the Great Depression on Eastern Europe', *Journal of Contemporary History*, **IV** (1969), pp. 75–86.

6　The population increased from a pre-war 7.7 million to 14.6 million in 1919 and the area of Romania increased from 137,903 to 295,049 square kilometres; Institul central de statistica, *Anuarul statistic al Romaniei 1937 si 1938*, pp. 58–61; table quoted in Irina Livezeanu, *Cultural Politics in Greater Romania: Regionalism, Nation Building and Ethnic Struggle 1918–1930* (Ithaca: Cornell University Press, 1995), p. 284.

7　*Institul central de statistica, 1937*, pp. 58–61.

8　The term is from Gregor von Rezzori describing rural Romanians. His family were Austrian aristocrats serving the Austro-Hungarian Empire in North Bukovina. See

The Snows of Yesteryear: Portraits for an Autobiography (New York: Vintage International, 1989), pp. 5–13. Walter Starkie emphasizes the primitive character of Romanians but as a virtue for the ethnographer and folklorist. See *Raggle-Taggle: Adventures with a Fiddle in Hungary and Roumania* (London: John Murray, 1933), pp. 171–81.

 9 Codreanu, *La Garde de Fer*, p. 237.

10 Jérôme and Jean Tharaud, *L'Envoyé de l'Archange* (Paris: Plon, 1939), pp. 54–5.

11 Tharaud, *L'Envoyé de l'Archange*, pp. 2–3.

12 Eugen Weber, 'Men of the Archangel', *Journal of Contemporary History*, 1 (April 1966), pp. 101–26; and his essay on Romanian history in 'Romania', in *The European Right: A Historical Profile*, edited by Hans Rogger and Eugen Weber (Berkeley: University of California Press, 1965), pp. 501–74. See also Nicholas M. Nagy-Talavera, *The Green Shirts and Others: A History of Fascism in Hungary and Roumania* (Stanford: Hoover Institution Press, 1970); and Zev Barbu, 'Romania', in *Fascism in Europe*, edited by S. J. Woolf (New York: Methuen, 1981); and the brief but apposite introductory discussion of interwar nationalism and the Romanian intellectuals, in Katherine Verdery, *National Ideology under Socialism: Identity and Cultural Politics in Ceaucescu's Romania* (Berkeley: University of California Press, 1991).

13 Among many examples in his collected writings, see Codreanu's statement 'quand je parle des communistes, j'entends les juifs' (p. 353) in the discussion, 'La Garde de Fer. Un organisme de combat contre le communisme juif', in his *La Garde de Fer*, pp. 352–3.

14 PRO FO 371/2188/47815, 'Roumanian Iron Guard Movement', 26 March 1937, p. 51.

15 Horia Sima states: 'The essence of a nation is not the institutions, the language, the territory or the historical past but a species of obscure and uncontrollable social will' (p. 27); or 'the keystone of the Legion is the man not the political programme. The new man will have all the virtues of our human soul and the qualities of our race' (p. 94), *Dos movimientos nacionales* (Madrid: Ediciones Europa, 1960). See as well the discussion of the common Romanian usage of 'Jew' as synonymous with 'Communist', in PRO FO 371/211901/47217 Annual Report, 1936, Roumania, para. 152, p. 29.

16 See Tharaud, *L'Envoyé de l'Archange*, p. 66. Like the Foreign Legion's anthem, the Romanian Legion's song refers to 'death as a gladsome wedding'; quoted in Weber, 'Romania', p. 523.

17 See Codreanu, *Garde de Fer*, p. 446.

18 Pierre Predesco, 'Lettre de Roumania. La politique intérieure. La Garde de Fer', *Mercure de France*, Tome CCLXXXV, 1 July–1 August 1938, p. 264.

19 See Codreanu's description in *Garde de Fer*, pp. 339–57; and PRO FO 371/21188/47815, 'Roumanian Iron Guard Movement', 26 March 1937, p. 49.

20 Prost described the National Christian Party Congress in Bucharest in November 1936 where hymns were sung 'to the Glory of Christ, Cuza, Goga, Hitler,

Mussolini and Franco' and Jews everywhere reviled. See *Destin de la Roumanie* (Paris: Berger-Levrault, 1954) p. 85.

21 MAE, Nantes, Série Europe, 1918–1940, Vol. 173, Bucharest, 18 Oct. 1936, pp. 19–25. PRO FO 371/21283/47217, 30 January 1937, pp. 323–4.

22 PRO FO 371/21190/47217, Roumania, Annual Report, para. 98 p. 47.

23 PRO FO R 5252/282/37, Sir R. Hoare to A. Eden, Bucharest, 27 August 1936, p. 186. Unfortunately the Public Record Office at Kew has culled these documents from the series. The letter is reprinted in Bela Vago, *The Shadow of the Swastika: The Rise of Fascism and Anti-Semitism in the Danube Basin, 1936–1939* (London: Institute of Jewish Affairs, 1975), p. 186.

24 Gerald Howson, *Arms for Spain: The Untold Story* (London: John Murray, 1998), pp. 73, 108; and for armaments, pp. 213–14. See also PRO FO 371/22466/47217, Confidential, Archives, Roumania, Annual Report, 1937, p. 18.

25 For example, he was supposed to have 'hands dyed with the blood of the 20,000 victims' he personally had executed when he was the Police Chief in Madrid and his diplomatic posting was in order to save him from certain death when the Nationalists entered Madrid. See PRO FO 371/21189/47029, Report on foreign Heads of Missions at Bucharest, 1937; FO 371/21393/47217. Sir R. H. Hoare to Anthony Eden, p. 2. FO 371/22466/47217, Confidential, Archives, Roumania. Annual Report, 1937, pp. 17–18. FO 371/20429/47029, Sir R. H. Hoare, p. 80.

26 Pedro de Prat y Soutzo, 'Effectul revolutiei nationale Spaniole in Romania', in *Ion Mota y Vasile Marin 25 ani dela moarte* (Madrid: Editura Carpatii, 1963), p. 19.

27 See PRO FO 371/21189/47029, 'Records of leading personalities in Romania', 21 January 1937, No. 7, p. 5. The figure of the Jewish banker Druker in Olivia Manning's *Balkan Trilogy* (Harmondsworth: Penguin, 1960) is probably based on Ausnit.

28 Prat y Soutzo, *Mota y Marin*, p. 19.

29 Prost, *Destin de la Roumanie*, p. 85. On Goga and his politics see PRO FO 371/21189/47029, 'Records of Leading Personalities in Roumania', 21 January 1937, No. 34, pp. 11–12.

30 Sturdza, *The Suicide of Europe: Memoirs of Prince Michel Sturdza, Foreign Minister of Romania* (Boston: Western Islands Publication, 1968), pp. 96–7.

31 A. L. Easterman, *King Carol, Hitler and Lupescu* (London: Victor Gollancz, 1942), pp. 144–6; Prost, *Destin de la Roumanie*, p. 69.

32 Gheorge Costea, 'Echipa legionara din Spania. Crâmpee din viata lor', 'Banica Dobre', in *Ion Mota y Vasile Marin*, p. 228.

33 *Ibid.*, 'Nicolae Totu', pp. 227–8.

34 *Ibid.*, 'Gheorge Clime', pp. 229–31.

35 PRO FO 371/21189/47029, 'Records of leading personalities in Roumania', 21 January 1937, No. 20, p. 8. The British consul general, Sir Reginald Hoare, described her as 'indefatigable in espousing all questions to do with Romanian women's rights'.

36 The biographical detail is taken from *Los legionarios rumanos Ion Motza y Vasile*

Marin: Caídos por Dios y por España. Prologue by Juan Aparicio (Madrid: Editorial 'Cuibul Legionario', 1941), (Biblioteca Legionaria Rumana, No. 1), p. 67. See also Costea, 'Echipa legionara din Spania', pp. 227–31.

37 See the biography 'Vasile Marin', in *Los legionarios rumanos*, pp. 36–48; and his wife's recollections, Ana Maria Marin, *Poveste de Dincolo ... (Amintiri din tara cutropita)* [Stories from the Other Side: Memories from the Occupied Country] (Madrid: Editura Autorului, 1979); and Costea, 'Echipa legionara din Spania', 'Vasile Marin', p. 231.

38 Sturdza, *Suicide of Europe*, p. 55. Ana Maria Marin relates a story that provides insight into her own perception of her Jewishness. She came across an old Jewish man she knew while visiting her Moldavian grandmother. He asked her whether the malaise of anti-Semitism was still widespread in Bucharest. She replied tartly that, if he wasn't happy in Romania, he should go back to wherever it was that he came from, and noted with satisfaction that the old man hastily assured her that Romania was a wonderful country because it allowed a Jew like him to make money and enjoy freedom. See Ana Maria Marin, *Poveste de Dincolo*, p. 102.

39 Ana Maria Marin, *Poveste de Dincolo*, p. 102.

40 Ana Maria Marin, *Poveste de Dincolo*, pp. 101–15.

41 Livezeanu, *Cultural Politics in Greater Romania*, pp. 245–7.

42 *Dacia Noua*, 23 December 1922, quoted in *Los legionarios rumanos*, pp. 15–16.

43 PRO FO 371/20429/ 47029, Sir R. Hoare to A. Eden, No. 342, Bucharest, 9 November 1936, p. 37.

44 The Cuza-Goga government in power for 44 days between December 1937 and February 1938 implemented restrictive legislation against Jews. However, it produced a political and economic crisis in which investment drained out of the country and the economy began to fail. The king stepped in and dismissed the government.

45 For Codreanu's recollections of this time, see *Garde de Fer*, pp. 157–79.

46 Codreanu, *Garde de Fer*, p. 248.

47 *Los legionarios rumanos*, p. 29.

48 Weber, 'Romania', in Rogger and Weber, *The European Right*, p. 521.

49 *The Protocols of the Elders of Zion* was a fraudulent document, originally produced in Russia in 1903 by the Tsar's secret service. It reported a discussion that was supposedly heard among Jewish elders in a cemetery outlining plans to subvert Christian civilization and create a world Zionist state. See Norman Cohn, *Warrant for Genocide: The Myth of the Jewish World-Conspiracy and the Protocols of the Elders of Zion* (Chico, CA: Scholars Press, 1981).

50 Quoted in *Los legionarios rumanos*, p. 17.

51 Michael Ledeen, *Universal Fascism: The Theory and Practice of the Fascist International, 1928–1936* (New York: Howard Fertig, 1972), pp. 118–21.

52 In ACS Minculpop, Busta, 181, f. 7. Quoted in Ledeen, *Universal Fascism*, p. 126.

53 Motza, letter to his parents, Bucharest, 22 November 1936, reprinted in *Los legionarios rumanos*, pp. 49–51.

54 *New York Times*, 23 November 1936, p. 13.

55 *ABC*, December 1936. *El Alcázar; Diario Tradicionalista*, 15 January 1937; *Heraldo de Aragon*, 15 January 1937; *Arriba*, 13 January 1957, J. L. Gomez Tello, *Motza y Marin veinte años después*.

56 Alexandru Cantacuzino, *Opere Complete, Colectia 'Omul Nou'* (Munich: Traian Golea, 1969), pp. 1–30.

57 Cantacuzino, *Opere Complete*, p. 10.

58 See Marin's letter to his wife, 26 November 1936, in *Los legionarios rumanos*, p. 47; and Motza's 'En la Natividad del Señor' from *Libertatea*, Nos. 37 and 38, Christmas 1936, *Los legionarios*, p. 56.

59 Cantacuzino, *Opere Complete*, p. 28.

60 Motza, 'Lisboa (Portugal), a 3 de diciembre de 1936', *Los legionarios rumanos*, pp. 66–7.

61 Frank Thomas, *Brother against Brother: Experiences of a British Volunteer in the Spanish Civil War*, edited by Robert Stradling (Phoenix Mill: Sutton Publishing, 1998), p. 82.

62 Motza, *Libertatea*, No. 1, 3 January 1937; *Los legionarios rumanos*, p. 58.

63 Cantacuzino, *Opere Complete*, pp. 10–11.

64 Marin's and Motza's widows were awarded their husbands' posthumous medals.

65 *El Alcázar; Diario Tradicionalista*, 30 January 1937; 31 January 1937; 1 February 1937; Madrid, 16 January 1956; *Arriba*, 13 January 1957.

66 Sir Reginald Hoare stated that the Germans had funded the return journey. See the letter to Anthony Eden, No. 92 (12/20/37. R 1484/162/37), Bucharest, 24 February 1937, pp. 5–9. For another contemporary description of the funeral see Prost, *Destin de la Roumanie*, p. 86; Tharaud, *L'Envoyé de l'Archange*, p. 147. On the day of the funeral Princess Alexandre Cantacuzino had a serious altercation with her son Alexandru who tried to stop the concert she had arranged to bid farewell to the Duchess of Atholl, Eleanor Rathbone and Lady Layton, who were in Romania as members of the League of Nations. See PRO FO 371/21190/47217, 23 February 1937, pp. 112–15.

67 Ana Maria Marin, *Poveste de Dincolo*, p. 129.

68 PRO FO 371/22466/47217, Annual Report, Roumania, 1937, 24 March 1938, para. 129, p. 28.

69 See *The Times*, 17 February 1937; 25 February 1937; *The Daily Telegraph*, 18 February 1937; PRO FO 371/21188/47815, 24 February 1937, Sir R. Hoare to R. H. Anthony Eden, p. 71.

70 Tharaud, *L'Envoyé de l'Archange*, p. 148.

71 PRO FO 371/21187/47534, Decipher, Sir R. Hoare, 22 February 1937, p. 34; FO 371/21188/47815, 24 February 1937, p. 9; FO 371/21189/47029, Sir R. Hoare to Viscount Halifax, Bucharest, 11 March 1938, pp. 9–11.

72 Hugh Seton-Watson, *Eastern Europe Between the Wars 1918–1941* (Cambridge: Cambridge University Press, 1946), pp. 209–10.

CHAPTER 7

With Flit and phonograph: Franco's foreign female supporters

Introduction

During the Spanish Civil War, a dozen or so women travelled to Nationalist Spain for short and longer periods to support Franco. The largest group were the writers and publicists who, having looked around briefly, went home to turn out laudatory commentaries about New Spain from a woman's point of view. A smaller number worked in wartime medical service. These two groups experienced quite different Spanish Civil Wars.

Rather like those of the male travellers in Nationalist Spain, the women's narratives often reflect nothing so much as their own class and political perceptions. These were simply carried over into Spain from England, France or from wherever it was that they had come, and in light of some other defining political experience they had lived through elsewhere. The medical volunteers remained in Spain longer and the nature of their work meant that they engaged in a practical manner with Spaniards caught up in everyday life at the front during war. As a consequence, their observations of Nationalist Spain and the Civil War are more realistic; and the contribution they made to Franco's victory is more straightforward.

In most wars, the presence of women at the front has been accepted only grudgingly, if at all.[1] On the Nationalist side, the figure of the woman in combat evoked nothing but hostility. The *miliciana* symbolized for Franco's supporters the disorder and 'unSpanishness' which they had rejected in the Spanish Republic.[2] Despite an overt commitment to the Nationalist side, Franco's foreign women embodied a way of being that resembled much more the New Woman of the Spanish Republic than the much vaunted Angel of the Hearth in Nationalist Spain.

Franco's foreign female supporters were upper class, independent and travelled about unchaperoned as they pursued the projects that had brought them to the Iberian Peninsula. Since their business was with the war, they were highly visible in public spaces that were male and militarized: whether staying in hotels, coming and going into military headquarters to obtain safe conduct papers or driving on roads crowded with military convoys of trucks carrying soldiers from one place to another.

Before tracing the experiences of the publicists and then the medical workers, it is useful to sketch out broadly the social context of women in Nationalist Spain as it provides the backdrop against which Franco's foreigner women functioned.

Spanish women in Nationalist Spain

Nationalist Spanish ideology was an amalgam of traditional Catholic values grafted onto an amorphous fascist corporatism. The whole was leavened with an unflinching discipline from Franco's own military model of how society should run. At the head of the state, with overriding authority, was the Caudillo. Below him were generals and administrators and, at the bottom, like obedient soldiers, were the citizens. In the parallel realm of family and private life, the pyramid of authority was replicated with fathers at the head of families exerting an unchallenged authority over women and children.

Between the wars, most right-wing movements shared the belief that strong nations required a social order in which men were the soldiers and fathers and women the nurturing and fecund mothers. Whether framed in terms of Nazi patriarchy that privileged male power or in fascist complementarity of the sexes, there was no argument that what was required was a clearly delineated gender division. Timothy Mitchell has argued, even further, that in Franco's Spain a 'monolithic unanimity' about the proper place of women prevailed because the Catholic Church, the Falangist Movement and the Nationalist Army shared a coincidence of ideas about family and gender.[3] The case in Spain was in contrast with Mussolini's Italy where, as Victoria de Grazia has shown, the Italian fascist movement gave out 'mixed messages' to Italian women which simultaneously 'exploited the desire to be modern and at the same time attempted to curb it'.[4]

Women in Franco's Spain were marginalized in the conceptualization of the new Nationalist state. According to the cultural anthropologist,

Giuliana di Febo, women in Nationalist Spain were offered the 'model of the beehive'.[5] Like busy bees they were expected to carry out constant and essential labour for the community, but quietly and out of sight. Sequestered at home, females, young and old, attempted to realize their only true destiny as virtuous and religious mothers.[6] Di Febo argues that the Nationalists' myth of the Franco crusade grafted the franquista soldier onto the heroic figures of the conquistadors and the great warrior priests that figured in an idealized version of Spain's past. In the process, maleness and military values were sacralized and in turn came to represent what was seen to be 'authentically Spanish'. In addition, a simplification took place between the 'true Spain' of the Nationalists and the 'un-Spanishness' of the Second Republic. While the symbolic order of Franco's New Spain configured men as heroes in the military tradition of the great crusades, women were relegated to the 'reconquest of the hearth'.

This was the ideology, but what of the practice? As often happens in wartime, during the Spanish Civil War, women took over many male tasks. Similarly the exigencies of war were a solvent of the rigid conventions that governed relations between the Spanish sexes. While the transformation was most marked in the Republican zone, in the Nationalist areas, as well, the conflict drew women into war work.[7] For example, the Falangist women's organization, the *Sección Femenina de la Falange Española* recruited young women for public service. From October 1937, single women between the ages of 17 and 35 were expected to volunteer for six months' social work. The largest welfare organization, the *Auxilio Social*, was modelled on the Nazi's Winter Aid. Its members, wearing the distinctive blue uniform and white apron, fed children, made and distributed clothes, and provided crèches and care for the orphaned and the displaced. In their own descriptions, however, women in these Falangist sections emphasized that their aim was always to empower the family within a patriarchal state and encourage the submission of women within the patriarchal family.[8] Similarly, the Margaritas, comprising women in the traditionalist Carlist organization, were energetic in carrying out works of public charity but always within a narrow religious mission to recreate an earthly version of the Holy Family in every Spanish home whereby fathers oversaw pious mothers and obedient children.[9]

Frances Lannon has also highlighted the paradox of female leaders of the *Secciones* leading busy public lives as they preached the need for women to stay at home.[10] There were also tensions between young women Falangists and their homebound sisters. Although at the end of the war some young Falangist women were reluctant to give up their posts, they were cajoled into returning home by inspiring past examples of traditional women who carried out their partiotic duties away from the limelight.[11] In general, though, whatever the variations in particular experience, Nationalist values in the New Spain shunted women firmly out of the public sphere and into the obscurity of family life.[12]

In Republican Spain, by contrast, the New Republican Woman represented the new and the progressive. Between 1931 and 1936 women were enfranchised and made steady gains in politics and the professions. For many traditional Spaniards, such female advances were a palpable reminder that the Second Republic was a degenerate and 'unSpanish' institution. Conservatives declaimed that women's liberation overrode patriarchal authority and the secular individualism of females had shattered the Catholic family and destroyed Spanish religiosity. Indeed, it was exactly from this sort of 'degenerate progress' that the insurgents in July 1936 had promised to 'save Spain'.

During the Civil War, Nationalist literature and priests in the pulpit railed against the 'shameless egoism' of the Republican woman, holding up instead the *'mujer castiza'* – the modest and pure – woman of traditional Spain. The Republican *miliciana*, the woman in combat, was castigated throughout Nationalist Spain as epitomizing the debauchery of Spanish womanhood in the Republican zone.[13] In Falangist novels the 'decent women' of Catholic Spain – maternal, asexual and sacrificing – were offered as a foil to the depraved, obscene and violent 'hyena-women' of 'Red Spain'.[14] A similarly undesirable stereotype of Republican womanhood in Falangist literature was the aristocratic woman who had become a leftist for no other reason than to indulge her own debauched sexual perversions.[15]

Single, foreign women in Nationalist Spain, even though they were there to promote Franco's victory, transgressed franquista notions of the correct demeanour of respectable women. These foreign women were away from their families, living alone and travelled about unchaperoned as they pursued various projects.

In the light of all this, it was perhaps not surprising that these foreign women often made patriotic Nationalists uneasy. And they were right who claimed that that these independent foreign visitors were part of the cohort of the New Woman in Europe between the wars. Indeed the contrast in the 1930s between them and the typical Spanish woman could hardly have been greater: a third of Spanish women were illiterate and most of those who worked were unsalaried and laboured within the family.[16] In contrast, Franco's foreign women supporters were aristocratic, or at least upper middle class, educated and well travelled. They exuded a self-confidence and independence that was contrary to the franquista social order. In several cases there was a tension between the perception of the good work that Franco's female volunteers were doing for the Nationalist victory and the anomalous way in which they were seen to be going about it.

Franco's female publicists: the writers

Not so well-known as their male counterparts, there were women travellers on the Iberian Peninsula who gathered information that they later used to promote Franco's cause. In most cases, the political analyses that underpinned their commentaries were pitifully shallow. Without speaking Spanish and following restricted itineraries within narrow circles, their observations of what was taking place around them in Spain reflected political understandings that had been formed elsewhere. The narratives they produced when they returned home, however, were quoted as irrefutable proof of what was happening in Spain because they constituted eyewitness accounts and were used to buttress already established pro-Franco sympathies.

Helen Nicholson in Granada

Helen Nicholson, the Baroness de Zglinitzki, an American long resident in England, was visiting her married daughter in Granada in July 1936. Her son-in-law enjoyed the status due to a successful lawyer with a position at the University of Granada. As was fitting, his family lived in an elegant house which shared a boundary with the Alhambra; a cascade from the Generalife flowed through their large, flower-filled garden.[17] Mrs Nicholson learned about the 'black cloud' of Republican Spain (Nicholson, p. 14) from her son-in-law and his upper-class associates and their wives and the groom who accompanied her daughter, Asta, when she went riding every morning. Alfonso, the son-in-law, had become 'violently depressed' during the Republic as he felt that 'all dignity and beauty has gone from the law' as, in his view, it became harder and harder to defend 'right-wing clients' (*ibid.*, p. 15). The groom, Joaquin, a 'manly man', was deeply shocked by the evidence of sexual decadence that was 'almost prevalent in Spain before the outbreak of the war' and in which 'effeminate men were everywhere and on the increase'. He and Mrs Nicholson 'sighed for the good old days when women were women and pansies were flowers' (*ibid.*, p. 71).

Mrs Nicholson, herself, heard the first shots of the war as her personal maid, a doughty tea-drinking woman, was putting down the morning tea tray on the bedside table. The women in the family drank cups of tea while listening to Quiepo de Llano's 'bed time stories' and as they waited expectantly for the news that Madrid had fallen to the insurgents. When Granada was bombed by Republican planes, Nicholson's maid similarly fortified everyone with more cups of strong English tea.

According to Mrs Nicholson, she had long known that 'Spaniards were capable of the unthinking brutality and cruelty of children' and therefore she was not surprised by the stories her English expatriate friends told her such as that in Seville 'the Red mob' had cut off the head of a foreigner and used it as a football (*ibid.*, pp. 16–19). Similarly, while taking afternoon tea, mother, daughter and maid stoically contemplated having 'their nose and ears sliced off by the Red Army' who at that moment were reported to be walking 'gaily' towards Granada with their pockets full of 'strange objects' which turned out to be 'girls' eyes which they had already gouged out' (*ibid.*, pp. 35–6).

When the Foreign Legion arrived in Granada, on 'August Bank Holiday', as Mrs Nicholson notes, she, with a lump in her throat, and the family had cheered until they were hoarse. First came the 'tough and bronzed' legionnaires with a 'peculiar swinging gait', wearing their 'unconventional costumes of flannel shirt, baggy breeches, sandals and jaunty little cap'; followed by the khaki-clad troops of the regular army and then behind, in lorry-loads, the young fascists in blue overalls shouting 'Arriba España' (*ibid.*, pp. 37–8). Later the cafés 'swarmed' with soldiers: 'laughing Legionaries, serious-looking Fascists and Spanish Patriots', the latter in blue overalls and sporting 'really lovely enamel badges' (*ibid.*, p. 100). As well, there were Requetés with picturesque red bonnets and Civil guards in patent leather hats' (*ibid.*, p. 68). As she watched it was as though 'a miracle was taking place: the miracle of the rebirth of the Spanish soul'. It seemed that what the fascists had predicted was coming true: 'Spain should at last be united, free and great' (*ibid.*, p. 41).

Nicholson presents unquestioningly the Red atrocity stories that she heard, even those that were so outrageously unlikely that they could hardly have been true. In Malága, the 'Russian system of terrorization' had been implemented in a 'most fiendish fashion' (*ibid.*, p. 73), whereby the good men were impaled on stakes and as they endured a slow death they were forced to watch their wives and daughters first raped and then burnt alive (*ibid.*, p. 73). In Antequera, so she was told, 'nuns were exposed naked in shop windows' and priests ravaged and mutilated (*ibid.*, p. 73). In the small town of Loja, nearby, the advancing Rebel army had discovered a great stash of Russian money, including a pile of 50,000 rouble notes. As Nicholson noted, 'it was no news to us that the Communists were being financed from Russia'; she and the family were only 'startled' to find 'proof' that the Russians were getting so near to the house (*ibid.*, p. 74). All of these extravagant, and unlikely, details in Nicholson's telling were simply repeated in a matter-of-fact tone.

The nightly executions in the cemetery above their house also worried the Granada family very little because the victims were 'Communists and Reds'. Even when among the executed was a former friend, they simply accepted the old adage that where there was smoke there must be fire. And indeed, since everyone in their circle said that these people had been found guilty, it simply followed that they must be shot (*ibid.*, p. 34).[18]

There are only a few places in the narration where Mrs Nicholson's equanimity wavers, and then it is only momentarily. In each case it occurred when she was confronted with a reality that was close to home and therefore harder to dismiss. A neighbour, a widow, from all accounts perfectly innocent, had fallen under official suspicion. An ugly incident ensued. Forty Fascists turned up at her door, pistols drawn, and turned her house upside down. They ripped open mattresses, cushions and upholstered chairs and emptied out all the drawers onto the floor, ostensibly in the search for weapons. Several days later, the same Falangists picked up the Nicholson family's handyman, who was the fiancé of their cook, on the grounds that he could tell them where the caches of arms were hidden. Uniformed men took him up the hill towards the cemetery, which served as the execution ground (*ibid.*, p. 80). Luckily, Alfonso was at home and was acquainted with some of the young Falangists and vouchsafed the handyman's politics. It was a close shave. The next morning, 60 men were executed against the cemetery wall in connection with the same search for hidden weapons.

The caretaker at the cemetery, who lived with his large family in a small cottage at the gates, begged Alfonso to help him find other lodgings, because the nightly shootings and the 'cries and screams of the dying' had made their lives a 'nightmare' (*ibid.*, p. 82). As well, the nearby neighbour's kindly gardener, who lived in a cave on their property and did part-time gardening for Mrs Nicholson's family, had provided a bed for his brother-in-law, who came from an outlying village. Men in the Falangist militia came across the stranger and claimed he was a Communist on the run. They beat the gardener and his brother 'in order to make them confess' and, when Mrs Nicholson saw them later, they were in the back of a truck, hands bound, covered in blood, and the gardener was deathly pale and fainting. When the little boy of the house sobbed as the prisoners were driven off, a Falangist militiaman berated the child and told him to 'be a man and behave like a patriot' (*ibid.*, p. 88). The adults went quickly inside and closed the doors and windows.

On 30 August, Helen Nicholson with her maid, a mountain of baggage and hampers of food, left Granada on the train. Like the intrepid English woman she perceived herself to be, she was undaunted by the prospect of travelling alone by rail through the war zone. In Seville, they spent the night with a comfortable room and bath in the Hotel Majestic, where she noted a marked decrease in the number of women in the dining room; and that 'everyone in ear-shot spoke Italian' (*ibid.*, p. 131). The next morning the two women travelled by bus to Algeciras and then to the safety of Gibraltar and home to London to write the book.

Eleonora Tennant in southern Spain

At the end of 1936, Eleonora Tennant published an account of a ten-day trip she made through the southern part of Nationalist Spain.[19] She was the daughter of a prominent Catholic Italo-Australian family and had met her husband, a wealthy English industrialist, while he was on a business trip to Australia in 1911. They had married in Italy the following year.[20] Ernest had considerable financial interests in Germany and, as a founder of the Anglo-German Fellowship, was a strong Germanophile. In London, the Tennants as a couple socialized with the von Ribbentrops. The Nazi ambassador had sponsored several of their visits to Berlin where on a number of occasions Ernest had met Hitler.[21]

Eleonora was an independent woman in her own right. In 1933, much to Ernest's dismay, the redoubtable Lady Lucy Houston, the eccentric owner of the *Saturday Review*, had sponsored Eleonora as the unsuccessful Tory candidate to a London dockland seat.[22] In October

1936, Eleonora motored 'alone and unmolested' (though sitting behind a chauffeur wearing the uniform of the Falangist Party) from the Portuguese border to Huelva, Seville, Talavera de la Reina and finally to Toledo. Like any sensible lady traveller, she came armed with her own 'Flit' which she used every night when faced with a foreign bed to 'calm [her] suspicions by a plentiful spraying with this excellent chemical' (Tennant, *Spanish Journey*, p. 35).

Tennant possessed an unswerving self-confidence in her own perspicacity which was probably grounded in the xenophobic certainties of a world in which Great Britain and the Empire were at the centre. Empowered by her Englishness, she interrogated the soldiers and citizens she met in the hotels and restaurants she patronized on the road. And after having been in Spain 'for several days', she was glad to note that she had 'accumulated sufficient first-hand information to understand the main reasons for the outbreak of the war' (*Spanish Journey*, p. 24).

Everywhere she went she found 'business as usual'. Bread, potatoes and first-class hotels were cheaper than in Britain and, except for most of the population in uniform, she would scarcely have known there was a war. The German who set her hair in Seville was enthusiastic that the bourgeois hair-do was back in style. The British manager of a factory near Huelva told her that his workers previously 'used to scowl at him', but since the Glorious Uprising they were 'more happy and content than they had been for years' (*Spanish Journey*, pp. 23–9). Among the 'Spanish Tommies', even in Talavera de la Reina at the headquarters of the Spanish Foreign Legion, she 'never saw one single action that any Britisher could take exception to' (*ibid.*, p. 36).

Though Mrs Tennant's right-wing political instincts were unswerving, her grasp of political taxonomy was unsteady. At pains to point out that Franco was not a fascist and had not overthrown an elected government she claimed instead that he was 'Republican' but of a sort that had nothing to do with the 'Reds' on the Republican side (*ibid.*, p. 103). Everyone she met praised General Franco: he was 'universally beloved' and 'a military genius'. Although 'short in stature' he was blessed with 'a remarkable personality'. A 'man of few words', in southern Spain it was said that 'when he does speak it is like receiving a telegram' (*ibid.*, p. 107).

In almost equal amounts to the enthusiasm for Franco, she heard the 'most frightful stories' about the behaviour of the Communists with the Republic. All of the events that were retold, perhaps fortuitously, took place in parts of Spain other than those in which Mrs Tennant found herself. Many of the stories are highly salacious, with a sharp scatological edge and a leaven of sexual transgression which serves to underline the abnormality of the whole situation.[23] Probably this mix is the result of the genre of Spanish anticlericalism embellished with the charges of sexual aggression and degeneracy against the enemy which are common in wartime.

A 'refined English woman' told the fastidious Mrs Tennant about 50 men and women, 'prisoners of the Reds' who had been 'cooped up' in a single room 'without conveniences' and 'no opportunity of changing clothing of any kind'. The centre of the room became a latrine and the 'atmosphere so horrible that some died and others continually lost consciousness' (ibid., p. 28). Near Málaga, it was said, a respectable family had been terrorized by a notorious 'Red' woman, a courtesan and the head of the Popular Tribunal. A 'column of Reds' led by women had arrived and begun 'to loot the village' (ibid., pp. 65–9).

In Seville, Mrs Tennant heard a particularly grotesque story about an aristocratic woman in another province who had a fine house by the seashore. She had been terrorized by sexually depraved, cross-dressing 'Reds'. When the houses of the woman's neighbours were 'ransacked', the Reds decked themselves out in women's dresses they had stolen. All the looted furniture was stacked up and the lot was set on fire and the woman watched a 'terrible spectacle' as 'the furniture blazed and the Reds dressed as women danced around yelling madly' (ibid., pp. 71–3). In the Málaga harbour, 'Red sailors' carried off several hundred innocent young virgins. Those that returned to their houses were 'found to be all diseased' (ibid., p. 83). Even more grotesque things had happened in Madrid where there were 'compulsory marriages' between priests and nuns. The 'unfortunate bride and groom were stripped naked and forced to consummate their marriage in the street surrounded by Reds' and, after participating in their own sexual violation, the couple were killed (ibid., p. 83).

Perhaps her own colonial background fostered Mrs Tennant's intense interest in the relations between Spaniards and their colonial peoples, the Moors. She wished to dispel the 'most dastardly' misinformation that 'Franco was using black non-Christian troops against Spanish white Christians'. Citing 'scientific' evidence, Mrs Tennant explained that the 'Moors of Africa are not a black race and have no racial connection whatever with the Abyssinians or the Negroes'. Indeed, the 'very name' Moor is a corruption of 'the real name' which means 'Occidental Arabs'. In Spain, Mrs Tennant pointed out, people do not 'look down on the

Moors'. Quite the reverse, 'many well-known Spanish families are proud of their Moorish blood' and many more have 'migrated to Morocco and become Mohammedans'. It is nothing but a 'calumny of the Reds' to depict the Moors as indulging in atrocities against their victims. Certainly, the Nationalist officers Mrs Tennant asked were 'loud in their praise of the exemplary behaviour of the Moors'. According to those who know them well, 'the Moors' treatment of women is ordered by their religion' and 'lays it down as a crime to maltreat women since the Arab regards the female as the weaker sex'. It was even said by a Nationalist officer that he knew Moors who 'objected to firing on the battalions of Red women' fighting for the Madrid government (*ibid.*, p. 118).

The most frequent complaints among the English expatriates around Huelva were that the British policy of non-intervention was wrong and the BBC and *The Times* of London were pro 'the Reds'. In judging correct behaviour Mrs Tennant's touchstone was the fair-playing Britisher. She stated that, although 'every Englishman knows that the British would never ill treat women and children' even the steady Britisher might lose his equanimity before the 'Red' provocation that Spaniards had faced. What is more, if there were a civil war in England, English Communists could not be relied upon as Englishmen because they take orders from Moscow. Mrs Tennant herself allegedly had heard an English Communist 'openly boast' that when they came to power they would 'strap all members of the boss class to the cannon's mouth and blow them to pieces' (*ibid.*, pp. 60–4).

Just as the 'open and welcoming outstretched right arm in the fascist salute' was a different greeting from 'the menacing gesture of a clenched fist of the Communists', in equal contrast were the possible outcomes in Spain. Communism would 'never bring happiness to the world' but when he had defeated it, General Franco would make Spain 'a great nation' (*ibid.*, p. 5).

The Duchess de la Rouchefoucauld

The Duchesse de la Rouchefoucauld, a Parisian aristocrat, travelled in Nationalist Spain in early 1938. An enthusiastic advocate of Mussolini's fascism and a close friend of the Italian ambassador's wife in Paris, the Duchess believed quite incorrectly that only fascism could 'regenerate the privileges of the aristocracy'.[24] In her narrative she discounted all those who claimed that Franco was not a monarchist because, in Spain, her monarchist contacts had assured her equally incorrectly that Franco would re-establish the monarchy as soon as possible.[25] The wives of generals and of the ex-Spanish ambassador to France met her at the border and, with a young woman from the Falangist *Sección* as chauffeur, drove her about.

As soon as she had left Hendaye, she was 'rendered practically speechless' by the recollection of the First World War: the ruined houses of Irún, the wounded soldiers, the sense of the place occupied by men in uniform (Rouchefoucauld, p. 3). Everything she saw 'plunged' her into a 'depressing sensation' of reliving the war atmosphere of 20 years before.

She visited *Auxilio Social* dining rooms and watched 'with hands clasped' as 'the tiny guests and the grown ups stood with arms outstretched in Roman salute towards a large picture of Franco'. Greatly applauding the revival of that Old Regime charitable institution, 'the portion of the poor', she saw the custom as a part of Christian charity that had sensibly been adopted by totalitarian countries (*ibid.*, p. 14). The courses foregone during one-course-meal days went to fund the Auxilio dining rooms.

La Rouchefoucauld was at pains to emphasize that all the women's work for the war effort in Nationalist Spain was done by volunteers. Not to be found here were feminists or professional women expanding their own horizons but rather women in self-abnegation, sacrificing themselves for others. Everywhere she found Pilar Primo de Rivera's proclaimed fit between the 'egoism of the male and the self-abnegation of the woman'.

Florence Farmborough

In April 1937, the Nationalists established a radio station, Radio Nacional Salamanca, which broadcast propaganda in various languages,[26] Florence Farmborough offered her services and began broadcasting in English regularly on Sunday nights. Her talks ranged over the virtues of the Franco state versus the 'horrors of Red Spain'.[27] Farmborough had come to Valencia in 1926 to teach English. A staunch monarchist, she had enthusiastically welcomed the insurgents' uprising and very soon moved to Rebel territory.

Twenty years before, Farmborough had been a nurse in Tsarist Russia, and it was here that her political understanding was forged. In her Spanish radio broadcasts there is constant slippage from observations about the Civil War in Spain to her previous first-hand experiences in Russia during the Bolshevik Revolution. This skew gives a particular power to her opinions but an edge that is strongly anachronistic as well.

Florence had led an adventurous life. Born in 1887, the fourth of six children of 'stout Buckinghamshire stock', she was raised an Anglican in a tolerant household.[28] From childhood, Florence 'longed to travel' and when, in her teens, she expressed an intention to go abroad, her father encouraged her to do so. At the age of 21, she became a governess to two daughters of a distinguished Moscow surgeon and for the next decade, with breaks in England, Florence was an English teacher and family-companion in Russia. During this time she came to speak good Russian and German.

In August 1914, when the First World War started, she and two of her charges became volunteers in a Moscow military hospital. Florence passed her entrance exams and joined a Voluntary Aid Detachment posted to a front-line mobile nursing team. Leaving Moscow in December 1914, it took the nurses a month by rail to find their unit on the Galician Front. Almost immediately they were caught in the Russian army's retreat eastwards back into Russian territory. The nurses, and Florence, endured great hardship as they moved one step ahead of the German invaders in the chaos and mismanagement of the Russian Imperial army. The women were the objects of soldiers' bawdy jokes and had to fend off frequent and hostile attention.

Florence, a 'firm Royalist' and an admirer of the 'August Tsar' – whom she described as the 'Heaven-chosen representative of Church and country' – was horrified at the ascendancy of the Bolsheviks and the speed with which the Russian soldiers 'were infected with the disease of Bolshevism' (Farmborough, p. 20; p. 357). By early 1917, 'the comrades', as Florence noted they called themselves, defied their officers openly, refusing categorically to take orders and, as she noted, 'Theft and Pillage had become the order of the day'.

In December 1917, in the Ukraine, the nurses were told to make their own way home as best they could. It was a terrifying time. The women, afraid of 'unruly men, as drunk with freedom as they were with alcohol', were forced to hide at night to avoid bands of marauding soldiers. Florence was separated from the other nurses in a great stream of soldiers and refugees hurrying on foot before the advancing Germans. Eventually she made her way to Moscow, partly on foot and then, in a frightening ten-day trip, alone, on a troop train. A young unchaperoned woman wearing the Tsarist nurses' uniform, she was the object of constant hostile male attention.

Back in Moscow Florence found that the 'Red Guards' had turned the city on its head. Her observations in Moscow are reminiscent of those she made 20 years later in Spain. In some cases, the detail is the same: respectable bourgeois people hide their wealth under shabby clothes; their possessions are looted by their servants; the Bolshevik state in Russia in 1918 and in Spain in 1936 introduced 'Free Love' and the offspring of the grotesque couplings became the property of the state, and so on.

In the description of Republican Spain, the sound of Farmborough's terrifying 1914–1918 years in Russia comes through loud and clear. Republican Spain, like Bolshevik Russia, is chaotic, irreligious and 'in the grip of the iconoclasts'. The 'Brotherhood of the Open Hand' of the Falange is in contrast with 'the clenched fist of Red Hatred'. Franco's opponents are 'Bolshevik Spaniards' aided by the 'Red Hordes from Russia': the International Brigades are under the 'subjection and control of Soviet Russia'.[29] The war is not about two Spains but about 'true Spain defending the church' against 'Russian Spain which Lenin wants to form into the brightest diadem in the Soviet Republic'. Under the 'yoke of Azaña the Atheist, Red Vandalism spills blood and sews rapine, ravage and ruin'. Those who oppose 'Franco's noble stand' are of 'Jewish nationality with lucrative business interests in the Mediterranean' (ibid., p. 60).

In her broadcast of a classic 'Red atrocity' story, it is Russia that pulls the strings. Farmborough described the 12-year-old son of a man tortured to death because he refused to give 'three cheers for Red Russia', itself a curiously English salutation in either country. As a consequence, and in detail that would make the blood of a VAD nurse run cold, 'the infuriated inquisitors cut out his tongue before sending him forth on his homeless, orphaned way' (ibid., p. 28).

Many of Farmborough's broadcasts draw on the most common English stereotypes of Spain. Under Franco, the old order of *mañana* has given way to a new religious and industrial era. Franco's generals, in her descriptions, are Anglicized rather than Old Regime Russified, perhaps because there were few Tsarist military heroes to dredge up in 1930. Franco and his generals in Farmborough's broadcasts would have been instantly recognizable and acceptable to an English audience with similar politics. General Mola, touched by the inexorable 'Finger of Fate', was 'very English in type and style'. Although he was a 'hard man of inflexible honour and virtue', Farmborough also made the somewhat incongruous claim that it was Mola who wanted 'Love, love, love to be the motto of today's Spaniards' (ibid., pp. 97–112). Millán Astray, the founder of the

Spanish Foreign Legion, remained un-Anglicized, probably because Farmborough found it impossible to produce an English equivalent. He remained, in Farmborough's words, the 'great Mutilated Gentleman of Spain': without an arm and an eye he was a living symbol of the 'life of a soldier filled with thrilling events'. Although he had many decorations and medals, 'his physical disfigurements' were the 'most superb war decorations of all' (*ibid.*, p. 73).

Not surprisingly, all Nationalist heroes in the Farmborough pantheon give way before the Great Liberator himself. In appearance General Franco was 'a classic Latin type of medium height, robustly built, oval face and dark hair', in which in the last months have appeared a 'few threads of silver'. Even as a small boy he 'showed the sign of extraordinary capacity of analytic and critical studies of military movements'. In battle, frequently mounted on a white horse and always out in front of his troops, at home the real Franco is 'most content within the domestic circle, within the charm of the tree-shaded garden' and within earshot of the 'melodious chatter of his little daughter and her tiny cousins' (*ibid.*, p. 17).

The English also would 'not find wanting' the Spanish woman in Nationalist Spain. Even though 'her place is in her home miles away from the front line, her heart is in the trenches' (*ibid.*, p. 30). Because 'every soldier is a mother's son, men must work and women must weep'. The Spanish woman's heart is filled with pride 'born of self-sacrifice and self-abnegation'. Social Aid women by their tenderness are winning over 'Red children' who hitherto have had the 'seeds of class hatred sown by their parents'. They come to the dining rooms with hearts filled with 'hereditary malice' and, as 'wild woodland creatures', they leave as human being transformed by the 'white-aproned women of Spain' (*ibid.*, p. 41).

According to Farmborough, women's main practical contribution was in knitting garments. A self-confessed 'non-knitter', Farmborough had never seen such energy expended with the needles: women at every gathering sat singly or in groups with great baskets of wool at their sides. In Navarre between September 1936 and February 1937, women of the province produced 42,018 garments and, at the same time in Galicia, 8200 women knitted 2 million garments. Indeed there were enough socks, gloves, vests, helmets, mufflers and belts to deck out an army. In Franco's Spain, in Farmborough's broadcasts, war is 'won in the vanguard with shot and shell' and in the rearguard with 'work and wool' (*ibid.*, pp. 34–6).

Jane Anderson Cienfuegos

Jane Anderson was a publicist for Franco on the American lecture circuit from 1937 to 1939, when she spoke at large Catholic gatherings about the horrors of her experiences as a prisoner in Republican Spain. She also briefly ran a travel agency in the United States that promoted wartime tourism, running tours around battle sites in Nationalist Spain. All these activities were eclipsed, however, by her subsequent identity as 'Lady Haw Haw', the broadcaster from Berlin who, from 1942, touted Hitler as the 'Saviour of European Christianity'.[30]

Jane Anderson turned heads wherever she went. A 'round-faced, voluptuous, blue-eyed blond, baby doll', she had brains as well as beauty.[31] A series of men helped her in a life trajectory that took her from Atlanta, Georgia, to Berlin via New York, London, Paris and Madrid. Born in Atlanta in 1893, she was raised a Presbyterian, the only child of a 'Southern belle and a gentleman-adventurer'. Her father Robert 'Red' Anderson was a larger-than-life American. Reputedly a friend of Buffalo Bill and later the Sheriff of Yuma, he wore a ten-gallon hat, packed a revolver with 29 notches to mark the criminals he had killed and was reputed to have 'a bottle of whisky and 2 pounds of steak' each day for breakfast.[32] After her mother's death, Jane began junior college in Texas, until an affair with a Mexican boy caused her father to take her out of school. She headed to New York for the start of a life that was 'destined to wreck more hearts, break up more homes and raise more international hell than a wagonful of Scarlett O'Haras'.[33]

By the age of 18 she had married a New York music critic who was many years her senior. Always with a yen to write, she begged friends to help her raise the fare to London when the First World War began in order to break into newspaper reporting. An introduction to Lord Northcliffe landed her a job on the *Daily Mail* and she eventually became a great favourite of the press baron. During the First World War she reported from the Western Front and, from all reports, was very brave under fire. In 1918, when she returned to New York to divorce her first husband, her friends noted that her southern twang had been overlaid by a strong upper-class British accent. And, by then, she 'could speak French like a native'.[34]

Anderson made her mark in journalism by writing about herself as an intrepid young woman engaged in adrenalin-producing adventures. In 1916, for example, she was nearby to cover the downing of a Zeppelin over London; she was also the first woman to travel in a submarine; and later in a biplane belonging to the British Air Ministry, she 'looped the loop at 7,000 feet over London'.[35]

During the 1920s in London, both Joseph Conrad and H. G. Wells became her mentors and she had a series of torrid affairs with middling-famous men.[36] In 1934, in the great cathedral in Seville, she married Eduardo Alvarez de Cienfuegos, whom she had met in Paris at a reception in the American embassy. He was variously reported to be a marqués with a high position at the Spanish court; and to have some interests or other in Cuba, either as a large landowner, or the manager of a casino or even as an employee in a large hotel.[37] Whatever the situation of her husband might have been, henceforth Jane Anderson was the Marquesa of Cienfuegos.

When the Spanish Civil War began, she claimed to have been living near Alicante and to have become an accredited correspondent with the *Daily Mail*.[38] Though the paper contains nothing under her byline or anything that sounds remotely as though she might have written it, subsequently she wrote gripping pieces about this period that suggested that she had accompanied the heroic Nationalist army as it moved up the Iberian Peninsula. She also claimed to have seen the horrifying Red atrocities that she described. What is certain is that, towards the end of September 1936, Anderson was arrested by the Spanish government on a charge of espionage and held for two weeks in the Madrid Women's Prison. The United States consul, Eric C. Wendelin, who at this time was also busy negotiating the release of Vincent Patriarca, managed to obtain Anderson-Cienfuegos's release on the condition that she left Spain for good. Freed on 13 October 1936, she travelled to the United States and from there to join her husband in Cuba.[39]

The exact details of her imprisonment are not clear. In later writings and lectures, Jane Anderson was prone to extend the length of time of her prison ordeal and exaggerate the details of 'the torture by the Reds'. Similarly, the sequence of events of her time in Spain that she has offered does not stand up to close scrutiny. In a piece written several months afterwards, she described her arrest on 22 July 1936 as having been by a 'dark-skinned man with Mongolian cheekbones and slanting black eyes', who turned out to be a 'feverish flat-fingered Russsian'.[40] He made her sign a blank sheet of paper and informed her that the 'next world war' had begun: after they had 'finished with' Spain these sinister men planned to 'move on to Portugal and France'. Eventually he let her go when she explained that she and her husband had done everything they could for 'their people': they 'let the poor in the countryside take water free from the mountains' and she herself learnt Spanish to teach the children in the local school.

In this narrative, she says she made her way to Madrid via Valencia where, in a highly exaggerated style, she described a series of incidents whose horror comes from the sexual deviance implied, much like Eleonora Tennant's descriptions. In the main Valencia market Anderson heard a 'little flower seller' say that 'it cannot be a crime to believe in God'. No sooner were the words out of her mouth than a hideous harridan selling bread took out a huge bread knife and 'drove it down into the girl's white throat' producing a 'thin stream of blood'. Astonishingly, this dreadful act does not seem to have killed the girl. Instead a group of hideous men, 'brandishing the Marxist salute', carried the flower seller off in a limousine with her head propped up on a rifle butt. Later in the day, Jane Anderson saw the girl again, this time she was on the beach 'tied to a stake, naked under the scorching sun' her 'head lolling on her chest'. And, as she slowly bled to death soldiers stood about 'mouthing obscenities and exulting in her agony'.

On the same trip, but on the other side of the country, indeed near Talavera de la Reina at exactly the time that Mrs Tennant was motoring about to 'business as usual', Jane Anderson saw a 'lad crucified in a church'. His tormenters had 'girded his loins with the red banner of communism' and 'driven nails into his hands and feet from which heavy drops of blood glinted as they fell on his lacerated feet'. In Segovia, Anderson saw anarchists rape and pillage a brace of Catholic nuns, while a 'hideous virago' at their head urged on the others.

In 1937, Jane Anderson undertook the first of a series of speaking engagements in the United States, eventually making over one hundred appearances around the country, all of them to Catholic audiences.[41] At a meeting of the National Council of Catholic Women in September 1937, Anderson described her prison experiences. In the Biltmore Hotel in February 1938 she addressed 900 women at the annual Catholic women's Communion breakfast, describing her '43 days in four Spanish prisons'. Arrested at 5, she was tried by midnight and taken to the execution grounds before sunrise. They let her go only because of her American citizenship.[42] She warned that Communism could 'happen any where' and therefore people 'should be vigilant and arm themselves'.[43] She also pointed out that Russia was using Spain as a 'stepping stone', concluding that there was scarcely time before they would see 'Catholic dead in the streets of Washington', because there was 'no social strata in the United States that was not contaminated with Communist propaganda'.

Several members of the audience at these events reported to the FBI investigator later that they were sceptical about Jane Anderson, because she changed the detail of her experiences with different tellings. Some informants found her presentation 'overly dramatic' and her stories exaggerated and unbelievable.[44] As well as its evident truth, this assessment probably reflects American common sense and the diffidence of American Catholics confronted with the details of sexual depravity and violence so much a part of the genre of Spanish anticlerical writings.

In early 1938, Jane Anderson returned to Spain, probably in the wake of Merwin K. Hart, the radical right-wing free trader, whose State Economic Council was devoted to blocking Roosevelt's social legislation. He founded the American Union for Nationalist Spain and, when he visited the insurgent zone in early 1938, Franco's men in the Press and Propaganda department gave him the red carpet treatment.[45]

In the middle of that year, Jane Anderson began to use her speaking contacts to set up a travel bureau in the United States that would take tours of American Catholics to visit the battle sites of Nationalist Spain. Her outfit was called the Spanish State Tourist Service and was run out of an office in Philadelphia; it was linked to Luis Bolín's tourism in Nationalist Spain. At least one full tour to Nationalist Spain took place in the second half of 1938. It was a success, though there were the sorts of complaints that are probably typical from package tourists. Though they had received what they had contracted for, some travellers were disappointed because they had not met any of the 'famous Spaniards' that Anderson had promised in the publicity material in America. One traveller remarked sourly to the FBI investigator that the Marquesa of Cienfuegos was not as famous as she had led people in the United States to believe, because none of the Spaniards they met in Spain had ever heard of her.[46]

In 1939, Jane Anderson and her husband returned to live in Spain. Franco awarded her a Military Medal for bravery during her ordeal with 'the Reds';[47] by the end of 1940, however, she was in Berlin and part of Goebbels' media unit. Her broadcasts from the Nazi capital, praising Hitler as the Saviour of world Christianity, earned her the sobriquet of 'Lady Haw-Haw'. Rather curiously, as she had never been a nurse in Spain, it was reported that she often wore a Nationalist Spanish nurse's uniform for her German broadcasts, in which in lurid detail she raked over her time in Spain during the Civil War. At the end of the war, she and her husband were captured in Austria and, despite a Grand Jury indictment for treason, she was released and slipped across the border into Franco's Spain.[48]

Franco's medical volunteers: Gabriel Herbert and Pip Scott-Ellis

Two young English women served as volunteers in the Nationalist medical service during the Spanish Civil War. Gabriel Herbert was the moving spirit behind the Anglo-Spanish Mobile Medical Service and Pip Scott-Ellis was a nursing assistant with the Spanish *Sanidad*. They represented the main strands of support for Franco in the United Kingdom.

Gabriel Herbert was the administrator for the Anglo-Spanish Medical Service and was in Spain from late 1936 until almost the end of the war. Twenty-five in 1936 and well travelled, Gabriel frequently spent summers at the grand Italian house her family owned near Portofino.[49] Her father, Aubrey Herbert, the second son of the fourth Earl of Carnavon, was a Conservative MP, a distinguished Orientalist and, it was claimed, had twice been offered the throne of Albania. Before his death in 1923, he had been drawn increasingly to Catholicism, and very soon afterwards his wife and children embraced the Roman Church.[50] The family was part of the cohort of converts that constituted the Catholic Renaissance in England between the wars.[51] As well, there was a family connection with Spain through Gabriel's uncle, Lord Howard of Penrith, also a Catholic convert and the British ambassador to Madrid between 1919 and 1924.[52]

In the First World War, Gabriel's mother, Lady Mary Herbert, had run a military hospital in Egypt with Lady Margot Howard de Walden, the mother of Pip Scott-Ellis. The commitment to the national war effort of these two women perhaps gives some insight into the independent characters of their daughters. In Spain, the daughters' paths occasionally crossed.[53]

When the Civil War began, Gabriel's uncle, Lord Howard, and a group of prominent English people, mostly Catholic and many with family and business interests in Spain, formed a committee to support General Franco.[54] The Bishops' Fund for the Relief of Spanish Distress raised considerable amounts of money to purchase and ship medical supplies to Nationalist Spain. The total was £14,500, some of which came from large single donations.[55] Eventually the Fund supported a network of mobile surgical units and dressing stations behind the lines in northern Spain.[56]

When members of the Bishops' Fund made their first contact, Nationalist agents told them that money was what Franco most needed. The committee declined when it discovered that cash could be used to buy arms and therefore would violate the stipulations of Non-Intervention. The only gifts that were legal under the Non-Intervention Agreement were medical supplies which had been purchased outside Spain.

Early in September 1936, the committee sent Gabriel Herbert to Spain to establish exactly what medical supplies would be most useful. She crossed the Bidassoa into Nationalist territory the day after Irún fell. The Anglophile Duke of Lequerica[57] escorted her to Saragossa and, acting as her translator, introduced her to a couple of Nationalist doctors who explained the dire state of Franco's medical services. In Burgos she met General Mola and General Cabanellas. On the London committee's suggestion, she also took advice from Father Henson, the rector of the English St Alban's College in Valladolid. On returning to Biarritz, there being no direct phone link from Burgos to London, she reported to members of the Bishops' Fund, who instructed her to tell Mola that the programme would go ahead.

A week later, Gabriel was back in London with a long list of urgent requests. They included anaesthetics, painkillers, antiseptic lotions, sterile dressings and all the instruments and supplies needed to fit out a mobile surgical hospital.

The Bishops' Committee began fund-raising immediately. In a few short weeks, duly blessed by Cardinal Hinsley, two Austin ambulances were despatched to Spain. Each was equipped with stretchers and a mobile theatre, consisting of a portable operating table and a full kit of surgical instruments, and was packed to the roof with bandages, cotton wool and surgical dressings.[58] Herbert headed back to Hendaye to await their arrival at the border. In her recollections, she noted that the French railways had been 'impossible' in dealing with the committee's gifts: surgical gear was stolen on the way; French Customs impounded one of the ambulances; and boxes of cotton wool were seized at the border as illegal materials of war. Eventually the second ambulance was despatched by sea to Lisbon where Herbert and a chauffeur drove it overland to Salamanca.[59]

The Bishops' Committee was generous in supporting the Anglo-Spanish *equipos*. The committee raised money through events and talks and by regular appeals in the Catholic weeklies. They supplied the medical service with whatever was requested and sent the best quality materials that money could buy. Eventually, the medical service in Spain had at its disposal eight ambulances with portable operating tables and instrument sets, four large lorries packed with 200 dismountable beds and bedding, and a smaller lorry in which to carry staff.

The importance of independent transport for medical services in wartime cannot be overestimated. When the army was on the move transport allocation was always scarce and chaotic. There would be long delays as the medical services waited for trucks to be assigned to them. Similarly, Herbert's unit had the beds and gear to equip a full field hospital so that they could re-establish themselves quickly once they were in a new location. In the normal sequence of setting up a hospital in the field, the medical staff had themselves to set about requisitioning all the beds they could find in the local area. When there was a push at the front, there would never be enough beds to accommodate the wounded.

The Anglo-Spanish team also had its own mobile X-ray unit. It speeded up the treatment of head injuries and broken bones which could be diagnosed on the spot. Herbert recalled her 'delight' that the committee had produced the X-ray machine. She had requested it, 'half thinking that it would be out of the range of the possible'. She noted her constant 'astonishment' at the committee's generosity in managing to send 'an unending stream of goods of excellent quality'. So well endowed were the English team that very soon the committee established a depot in a secure barn south of Saragossa to store their supplies. From there Gabriel Herbert fetched by lorry whatever was needed and transported it to wherever it was required. Eventually their own mobile units stretched across the extended Aragon front. By the committee's policy, the Anglo-Spanish service was generous in sharing supplies with local Spanish medical services.

All of these provisions made a great deal of difference to the level of medical care in the north. Before the war, the hospitals and medical expertise available in Spain were concentrated in the large cities of Madrid and Barcelona. As Herbert had been told, at the start of the Civil War there was a single, poorly supplied, mobile unit serving the whole of northern Spain. As a consequence, wounded soldiers were transported enormous distances to medical attention, often travelling slung in a blanket between two swaying mules.

The administrative arrangements which Herbert oversaw increased the efficiency of the service as well. The staff was Spanish, with Gabriel Herbert acting as *enlace*, the go-between, for the London committee and the Spanish service. She was in charge of orders and supplies and the day-to-day relations between London and the workers in Spain and, although there were a few hiccoughs caused by the languages, for example, an order was sent for '10,000 baby eels of different sizes' (*anguilas*) instead of needles (*agujas*), most things went smoothly. The committee in London had chosen the chief medical officer, Ignacio Urbina, who in turn had selected the four doctors and nurses who made up the initial team. By the time the service was at full strength it consisted of six doctors, seven nurses, a Spanish administrator, two permanent ambulance drivers, a head mechanic, a radiologist and a dentist. The appointment of the latter was enlightened. A dentist in the surgical team made a difference when there were soldiers with serious jaw and cranio-facial injuries. As well, the group included the inevitable priest to say Mass daily and provide sacraments for the dying.

The Nationalist army command automatically accorded military rank to the Anglo-Spanish doctors and paid them equivalent military salaries. Franco's headquarters also provided enlisted men to serve as stretcher-bearers and guards. The rest of the medical team was maintained by the Bishops' Committee. The whole Anglo-Spanish medical enterprise was administered independently and was fortunate to exist outside the ramshackle bureaucracy of the Nationalist *Sanidad* and *Frentes y Hospitales*. In both the latter, orders to medical units at the fronts passed through labyrinthine bureaucratic channels. Often hospital teams were ordered to pack and move and move again according to plans that were incomprehensible to those at the end of the chain of command.

In the course of the war, Anglo-Spanish staff were never transferred to other hospitals or surgical teams, but stayed with their own original formation. In Pip Scott-Ellis's experiences, as we shall see, medical teams were often broken up and individuals were shuttled about, so that many hospital staff wasted time seeking assignments and transfers. This made for unsettled working conditions and less than satisfactory co-ordination, all of which was reflected in the team's performance. In contrast, the stability of the Anglo-Spanish teams in their original formation promoted efficiency and solidarity. In Herbert's words, they 'worked together, played together and became friends'[60] and, as a consequence, their medical interventions were effective.

In October 1936, when the Anglo-Spanish Medical Service was first formed, it occupied a single floor in a large three-storey building in Samaniego near Vitoria. Two other separate medical services worked on the other floors, but drew on Anglo-Spanish supplies. In this location Herbert's group dealt with the wounded from the northern fronts, predominantly Carlist Requetés, and the overflow sent from the fronts around Madrid. Once they were set up with their gear and personnel in shape, the service began to send out mobile first aid units to the front. Their aim was to stay as close as possible to the battle lines; the faster the wounded were handled and given preliminary care the better the survival rates.

By October 1937 the service had moved their main base of operations eastwards to Huesca province. The city of Huesca became their main staging point after that city was taken by the Nationalists. Until the end of the war, the Anglo-Spanish service ran a network of mobile units strung across a far-flung line from the sierras in the north to the Ebro in the south. As Franco's army moved through Aragon, across Catalonia, to open the way to Vinaroz and the Mediterranean before heading north to Barcelona, Herbert's medical teams followed close behind.

Throughout, it was probably Herbert's administrative skills and, even more so, the abundance of material sent from London that enabled the Anglo-Spanish Medical Service to maintain harmonious relations with the Nationalist army command. The London committee at various times sent extra volunteers. For example, Tom Burns drove an ambulance for Herbert in the summer of 1938.[61] Other observers travelled with Gabriel Herbert as she drove the laden lorry from the border to the Saragossa depot and then to the medical people in the field. A number of the first-hand accounts of 'Red atrocities' and conversations with franquista personnel that appeared in London, for example by Arnold Lunn and Hilaire Belloc, can be tagged back to journeys with Gabriel Herbert in Northern Spain.[62] When the war ended, Gabriel Herbert was awarded the *Medalla Militar* with merit for her work in the medical service for Nationalist Spain.

Pip Scott-Ellis

Pip Scott-Ellis, a young woman of 20 in 1937, was the middle daughter of the six children of the eighth Lord Howard de Walden and Seaford. Her father, who served in the British forces in the Boer War and the First World War, was a distinguished medievalist and author of several well-received volumes on English heraldry and an exponent of Gallic culture. He was interested in the contemporary stage and cinema, being among the early backers of the fledgling art of film-making. He produced plays and operas, including several of his own compositions. A keen sportsman, an Olympic fencer and a turf enthusiast, he also loved sailing and was an early advocate of the new sport of motor boat racing.[63]

His wife, Lady Margot Howard, as her First World War nursing attests, was a woman of great independence. She was one of the select group of 'upper-crust English ladies' who took up flying. These adventurous women, with husbands wealthy enough to indulge their passions, enjoyed being daring young women in their flying machines.[64] Lady Margot had a pilot's licence and flew her own Gypsy Moth. Pip, too, when she turned 18, obtained a flying licence. In Madrid at the end of the Civil War, while she was working in a canteen for the Spanish flyers at Barajas Aerodrome, Pip spent several exhilarating mornings with her 'hand on the joystick' in a two-seater soaring above Madrid. Between the wars, flight was 'the metaphor for a bright and shining future'; and pilots the very symbol of modernism and the new postwar age.[65] Even more for women, flying embodied the mastery and liberation of the New Woman.

Pip, raised an Anglican, spent her childhood between a large house in Belgrave Square and her father's seat at Chirk Castle in north Wales. In the country, the children enjoyed healthy and unrestricted days, left to their own devices to roam on their ponies as they wished. As a young girl, she accompanied her father to the United States and to Kenya. Educated by governesses and at day schools, Pip boarded in the last couple of years with her younger sister at Benenden. In the familiar pattern of young women of her class, she was finished in Paris and then spent some months with German family friends in Munich. Her sister, Gaenor, recollected that, though from childhood they all spoke a sort of 'franglais' acquired from French governesses, Pip's years abroad before 1936 had had 'no discernible effect' on her language skills. She was blessed, however, with a 'musical ear', which allowed her later, when it was needed, to become fluent in Spanish, French and Polish and acquire passable Portuguese, Italian and Russian.[66]

Pip Scott-Ellis has left a lively record of her 20 months in Nationalist Spain. Her diary entries are unsentimental, displaying a flair for the pungent observation. For example, the first time she saw General Franco in the flesh, she noted that he was a 'weeny little man, the size and shape of a tennis ball' (13 May 1939; Scott-Ellis, p. 231). In Spain, Pip divided her time between sporadic bursts of strenuous work as a nursing assistant and a highly diverting social life with the family of the Infante de Orléans, the first cousin of the Spanish king.

Lady Margot's family were close friends of the Spanish Infante, Alfonso de Orléans Bourbon, grandson of the Duke of Montpensier and first cousin of the Spanish king, Alfonso XIII. The Infanta, Princess Beatrice of Coburg, was the niece of the Spanish Queen Ena and a granddaughter of Queen Victoria. There were three sons, Alonso, Alvaro and Ataulfo, the youngest, and Pip's particular friend. In 1931, when King Alfonso XIII withdrew from Spain, the Infante and his family went too, spending the years in exile shuttling between Switzerland, the United States and England.[67] As soon as the war began, the sons returned to Spain and joined the Nationalist air force. The eldest brother, Alonso, was shot down very early. The youngest, Ataulfo, was attached to the German Condor Legion. Later, when Franco permitted it, the Infante himself returned to Spain to fly for Franco.[68]

Pip came out in London in 1934. By mid-1936 she was bored by the social round of the London season and determined to join her friends in Spain by volunteering as a nurse. Her mother insisted that she undertake a nursing aide's course and learn some Spanish. In October 1937 when Princess Bee – as Pip called her – left to work for Franco's *Hospitales y Frentes*, a charity providing food and medical care in captured areas, Pip went with her.

A photo of Pip Scot-Ellis at this time shows a dreamy girl with a soft, light complexion and curly fair hair. Her future husband, José Luis Vilallonga, with some embellishments from the hindsight provided by later events in their life together, recalled the first day he saw Pip standing beside an ambulance at Teruel. Tall and fair, she stood aloof from the chaos around her. With a long blue nurse's cape down to her feet over what he describes as an (unlikely) immaculate white nurse's uniform and (even more unlikely) a Hermés silk scarf around her neck, which brought out the bright blueness of her eyes, she might have been out of an English *Harper's Bazaar* or lunching in the Grill at Claridges. He was struck by her 'Englishness': the coolness and the 'horsey' elegance of the English upper classes. She offered him a cigarette from a silver case and a swig of gin from a silver hip flask and then invited him to lunch which, he claimed, consisted of fine food and wine from Fortnum and Mason which was stacked in an immaculate English Daimler with English registration plates that had been converted into her own private ambulance. The vehicle was fitted out inside with comfortable beds, one of which, according to Vilallonga, they shared at Pip's instigation after the meal.

Vilallonga's image is cinematic and probably an embellished composite of Gabriel Herbert in her English ambulance and Pip, the front-line nurse with her own car. It is likely that these two figures fed the powerful portrait of the aristocratic English woman he presents in *Fiesta*, the autobiographical novel about himself as a young man in the Spanish Civil War. As Vilallonga tells us, the young woman is based on Pip.[69] She has come to Spain because she is sympathetic to Francoism but, once in Nationalist territory, is horrified by the violence of Francoism. She seduces the young hero in a gesture of tenderness to compensate for the violence into which his father has foisted him.[70]

Pip's own diary reveals her high spirits and enjoyment of life. Her Spanish medical supervisors often found her headstrong and even wild. By the yardstick of what was conventional behaviour for a young Spanish woman of good family, she probably was. Her writing reveals little political underlay, except a perfunctory scorn for the 'Reds', and an abiding irritation with the English news: 'bright red and lies all through' (Scott-Ellis, p. 23). Overall, she exuded a cheerful and unexamined disdain for the lower orders which was typical of her class.

When she arrived in Spain, Pip and Consuelo, the daughter of the Marqués de Montemar, undertook some nursing training in a hospital near the Infante's country estate at Sanlúcar de Barrameda. They learnt to give injections, take blood from a vein and identify and clean the instruments used in the operating theatre. For the first time they observed an operation and were shown how to dress a wound. Nursing assistants also made beds, washed patients, emptied pans, rolled bandages and sterilized compresses and dressings.

In the hospital at Sanlúcar, many of the patients with whom Pip dealt were 'filthy smelly Moors', and all of them were 'very low class and just shout and snatch things and swear, or even worse become cheeky and make lewd remarks in Arabic'. But, as she noted in her diary, it was 'all madly interesting' and she 'loved the work': even when she 'disliked the people intensely', she still 'liked their wounds' (14 November 1937, p. 11).

Pip's free time was spent with the family at Sanlúcar and, later, when the flying base for the Condor Legion was relocated to Saragossa and the Infante moved to a rented country house 40 miles outside the city at Epila, Pip travelled there from hospitals in Aragon. With the Infante's family she enjoyed leisurely lunches and lively dinners with handsome young men.

The flyers from the Condor Legion and their friends came frequently to the house. Many mornings at Sanlúcar Pip fell into bed at 5.30 a.m. after 'getting plastered' and having danced for hours to the phonograph. The extended family and their intimate circle were 'great fun' and 'as mad as hatters'.

When it came to physical work, Pip was no shrinking violet. Faced with the demands of a front-line medical service, she pitched in with energy and common sense. When, for example, no local women were available, she spent the day on her knees at the river bank, washing hospital linen until her 'hands were raw'. She also learnt to deal with the many 'unattractive things' that nurses must face in their everyday routines, such as pumping out stomachs and dealing with the most intimate parts of a patient's body. For example, one day while washing 'an over-sexed head wound', he had suddenly thrown off the cover and 'with a wild shout produced his penis', which 'left to its own devices proceeded to spray fountains in all directions'. Pip, to no avail, 'rushed for the pot' and 'chased after the fountain'. Finally, she simply had had 'to grab the damn thing and hang on'. She noted ruefully that she could not imagine how nurses could look at a man after all the things they had to do with them as patients (23 March 1938, p. 61).

From October 1937 until May 1939 – with five weeks' rest in England in the middle of 1938 to recuperate from paratyphoid – and becoming more run down and suffering chronic abscesses on her arms and legs, Pip showed that she could keep her head through very trying times to become a hard-working nurse with a real vocation for the job.

The organization of the Spanish nursing service was ramshackle and the assignment and supervision of nursing staff haphazard. Pip and Consuelo spent several weeks at the start of their careers trying to find a hospital that needed them. After shuttling about from location to location, they were sent to a posting at Cella, a town 'crammed with soldiers and mules and ambulances come and go in a continual stream' (30 January 1938, pp. 30–1). The hospital commander, however, knew nothing of their appointments and, short of food and accommodation, wanted no more nurses. Eventually, they bumped into a medico who needed staff. He took them into his unit to become part of a team of four. Pip noted that the other two were 'very common' and the senior surgeon Captain Ramón Roldán, himself, was 'very common', too. Pip reported that 'watching him eat nearly killed' Consuelo and Pip 'with suppressed laughter'. Perhaps not surprisingly, he was 'abrupt and rude' with the two new nurses. A Falangist and therefore anti-monarchist, Roldán was probably less than enthusiastic about having two bright young aristocratic things sailing onto his ward. For whatever reason, Pip felt he resented her aristocratic friends and went out of his way to assign her the least interesting tasks (2 February 1938, pp. 32–3).

The relocations of the medical services behind the front were always carried out in a 'state of chaos', with the maximum of 'muddle and bothers'. Frequently, the soldiers assigned to load the trucks left behind swags of hospital gear: in one incident in freezing weather, the blankets and sheets were forgotten so that patients had only their greatcoats to huddle under on their beds. Another time, a patient was found abandoned in the empty ward after the lorries had driven off (20 May 1938, p. 95; 29 November 1938, p. 157; 30 November 1938, p. 158).

The medicine practised also left much to be desired. Pip was 'horrified' at the 'dirtiness of some of the doctors' and that often their 'ideas of antisepsis were very shaky'. It 'gave [her] the creeps' to see the 'casual way that medical people picked up sterilised compresses with dirty fingers' (3 February 1938, p. 33). As well, the chief doctor was often bad-tempered, shouting at the patients and the staff and leaving Pip 'all of a flop' (3 February 1938, p. 33).

The rhythm of work see-sawed. After periods with little to do or much locating and relocating to no discernible purpose, the hospital would be inundated with wounded and the staff would 'work like blacks'. In the first week of February 1938, the push into Teruel sent a wave of injured to the hospital, some six miles away. In a single stretch of twelve hours on 5 February 1938, and in temperatures which fell below –12°F, Pip's team performed nine major operations. There was 'one elbow shrapnel wound, three amputations, two arms and one leg; two stomach wounds, one head and one man who had shrapnel wounds in both legs, groin, stomach, arm and head'. The stomach operations were 'foul'. One patient had to be 'cut right down the middle and his stomach came out like a balloon and most of his intestines'. The other had a perforated intestine with 'all his guts out'. The amputations included a soldier's hand, and another above the elbow of an old man who had been hit in an air raid on his village. The amputated leg was taken off above the thigh. Pip was on her feet all day in a theatre filled with chloroform fumes, washing rubber gloves and sterilizing an 'endless quantity of instruments' (5 February 1938, p. 35).

She also observed an operation by another surgical team in which a man with shrapnel wounds had lain on the ground for two days and was full of gangrene. The surgeon stripped all the flesh from the man's back and side so that his spine was exposed and one side of his ribs and shoulder blade. Needless to say, he died an hour later (5 February 1938, p. 35).

In the same surge of wounded, she assisted at the removal of a spleen damaged by shrapnel and was unnerved to see it sitting on the table 'like a piece of liver in a butcher's shop'. There was also a man with his jaw a 'mass of teeth and bone splinters' and 'his mouth hanging loose by a single strand'. He looked 'so frightful when he was patched up' that the staff averted their eyes (9 February 1937, p. 37). Another soldier came with a pulverized femur bone so that, when Pip held it to bandage, it was 'limp like a sausage and sagged everywhere' (9 February 1937, p. 37).

Perhaps the most startling development took place a week later. While on night duty at three in the morning, Pip acted as the anaesthetist for an amputation. Never having done anything like it in her life, she 'was scared to death'. The ether knocked the patient out for an hour and a half but, in between times, he kept 'coming to life and trying to swallow his tongue' (16 February 1938, p. 39).

Three days later, in a single bloc, their team did ten major operations. An exhausted Pip was greatly disturbed by a young man with massive lung wounds, who had lain 'unconscious and pale as a sheet' on a stretcher. When he died, she found in his pocket a crumpled letter from his fiancée telling him that, at last, her parents had given their blessing for the marriage. In the chaos of the wounded arriving, this man in death throes had been sent prematurely to the morgue. Pip was saddened to think of him, still alive, being taken away with the others 'piled anyhow, half naked in a lorry' (19 February 1938, p. 41).

On another day in the same wave of wounded the team carried out eleven operations, on a table which consisted of two wooden trestles with a sheet thrown over. They 'just followed on one another without a pause'. As a soldier was carried to the table 'the next was on the stretcher being prepared', while the nurses 'hectically sterilized the instruments for the next one and washed up the one before'. Among them was a soldier with a head wound that turned out to be inoperable because he had 'a big lump of brains the size of a fist sticking out the top of his head', which made Pip and Consuelo 'feel rather ill' (21 February 1938, p. 42). Of the patients they dealt with during these days, Pip noted the depressing fact that nine out of ten would be dead before the next morning.

On her days off from this harrowing schedule, Pip took her car and drove up to the Teruel front line. On a hilltop they came across an anti-aircraft encampment staffed by 'friendly and informative' Germans. The nurses stayed several hours, 'too enthralled to leave', watching as 'the sky was full of aeroplanes shooting up and down the Red trenches'. The 'whole landscape all around was covered by pillars of smoke'. Pip noted that 'the noise was incredible, a continual roar like thunder with intermittent different-toned bangs'. Then bombers began to arrive, 'a continual stream for hour after hour till the Red lines were black with the smoke of the bombs' and 'occasionally a Red shell would wallop down about a hundred metres away aimed at our battery'. They could hear it 'whizz through the air with a high-pitched scream' and then crash, followed by 'a huge cloud of smoke below' (17 February 1938, p. 40).

The next morning Pip and friends returned to the same anti-aircraft battery, she noting 'the extraordinary thing, that no-one minded us being there'. The Germans, photographing them 'from every angle', asked only that they sit down so as not to obstruct the view. In the early afternoon a Spanish general 'turned up and politely said to scram' (18 February 1938, p. 41).

When Teruel was taken by the Nationalists, on 22 February Pip's entire medical team went to see what had happened in the city. Pip drove her car with the four nurses and the men followed in another car. Four kilometres outside they were stopped and told that they must turn back because women were not allowed in the area. With perhaps unintended irony, Captain Roldán said that the four were 'not women but nurses'. Leaving the cars, they proceeded on foot across a landscape scarred with shell holes, trenches and barbed wire rolls. A pall of smoke from the burning houses hung over everything and made it impossible to go into the streets (22 February 1938, p. 42).

Four days later, on a 'gorgeous day full of spirit and interest', the medical team was able to get into the city. It had been 'utterly destroyed', with 'not a single whole house', and the others all 'covered in bullet holes and shot by bits of cannon with great gaping holes from air bombardment'. The place was a shambles, and everywhere 'soldiers were busy looting all they could, which was very little'. Pip and her friends 'wandered in and out of shops', she collecting a 'bracelet and some much-needed field glasses'. In a bar that had been destroyed she played jazz tunes on a grand piano which by some miracle had been left untouched. She noted that 'everyone was crazy with joy' and the soldiers danced in the streets wearing 'queer straw hats they had looted' (22 February 1938,

p. 44). Until Captain Roldán absolutely forbade it, Pip made several trips to the flattened Teruel.

To the Spaniards who met Pip, what probably was most striking were her high spirits and independence. In Spain, Pip always drove her own car. A month after her arrival her father had shipped out to Gibraltar a new small car. 'Fiona', as she called it, was her pride and joy: 'black with green leather inside and a dream of beauty' (2 November 1937, p. 10). After it was stolen and wrecked in August 1938, her father sent another: 'very large and impressive, black with brown leather inside' (24 August 1938, p. 106).

Without a qualm and at great speed, she covered long distances to spend the days off with the Orléans family. Having her own transport was very useful, as she could drive herself and Consuelo from hospital appointment to hospital appointment. Commonly, on her nights off she would drive a carload of friends into the nearest town for an evening at the bar, getting 'squiffy' and 'tight as ticks'.

A young woman spinning along behind the wheel of a shining new car invariably drew comment in Spain. Driving alone near Cáceres in 1937, and low on petrol, she freewheeled to the aerodrome to beg some from the soldiers, 'much to their amusement'. Later, when her oil tank sprang a leak near Béjar, she stopped at a garage and, to the astonishment of the locals, filled up the tank and replenished the oil and water. She was aware that 'everyone was quite enthralled to see a young girl travelling alone and busying herself in the engine of a car. Girls here don't' (22 December 1937, p. 18). When she and Consuelo were driving back from Saragossa, a carload of soldiers drew alongside, 'made funny remarks', and then passed, splashing Pip's car with mud. She immediately speeded up and at 'the next patch of muddy water returned the compliment'. The two cars chased each other, overtaking until the bad road slowed them down (8 May 1938, p. 89). Again, while she was stopped with Consuelo in the car, they were surrounded by a crowd of boys convinced that, because they were smoking cigarettes and driving the car, the two women were really men in disguise (9 May 1938, p. 89).

An encounter with a Guardia Civil at Burgo de Osma near the Condor Legion's base was typical. It was early in the morning and Pip had just dropped Ataulfo at the aerodrome when the Guardia Civil flagged her down and asked for her pass. When she explained that she had none, he 'became vastly suspicious as a young girl driving alone in the early hours of the morning is unheard of in Spain'. He assumed that she was German and with the German aviators. When she said she was English, the Guardia became suspicious about why she was on the road so early. On learning that she had just driven an aviator back to the base, the Guardia was 'distinctly horrified' and asked if she were married. When she said she was not, he assumed she was 'leading a life of sin' and 'was so horrified he nearly burst'. He only let her go when Pip pointed out very firmly that she was a friend of the local military commander (15 January 1938).

Pip's mother kept her supplied with comforts: books, magazines, fur-lined gloves, brandy, thousands of cigarettes, a radio and the most treasured possession of all, a wind-up portable phonograph and a trunk of dance records. In every sort of rough accommodation, she set herself up with the phonograph and the records. On occasion, when billeted with poor families in the countryside, Pip brought out the radio to 'give the peasants a shock' (4 February 1938, p. 34). Off duty, when times were slack and, indeed, at any opportunity, Pip and the staff who shared her passion would dance to the phonograph. In Calaceite at the end of a gruelling day, Pip set it on the verandah in the moonlight and danced the rumba by herself, oblivious to the amazement of the patients and staff who were watching from the windows upstairs (2 October 1938, p. 129).

The Inspector General of the Nationalist nursing service, Mercedes Milá, strongly disapproved of Pip and of Consuelo. Pip's own family and her close ties with the Infantes placed her within the monarchist circles of the Kindeláns, the Bourbons, the Medinacelis and the Montemars. Although these aristocratic connections could be a handicap among Spanish Falangists on the wards, they provided her a measure of protection. It was not enough, though, to prevent Milá, after a tearing row with the Infanta, removing Consuelo from front-line hospitals. In her early forties and educated at an English convent, Milá saw her primary responsibility to protect the good name of the Spanish nursing service. In her eyes, Pip, a freewheeling young woman on her own in a foreign country, spelt trouble. At first, Milá tried to stop Pip going to the front, saying that she was too young and irresponsible to be assigned to a battle front service. And it must have seemed to Milá a number of times that her worst fears had come true. On several occasions, she reprimanded Pip and Consuelo for smoking cigarettes and wearing make-up (24 March 1938, p. 61). The Duchess of Vitoria, the head of the Spanish Red Cross, also 'ticked them off' in the Grand Hotel in Saragossa, when she saw them smoking in uniform, and threatened to 'make a great row' about it in Burgos (3 May 1938, p. 84). There were official complaints that Pip had been seen drinking in bars in her nurse's uniform. Princess Bee sent Ataulfo to say that she had heard 'bad rumours about Pip's behaviour' and Pip should leave the front immediately. At a family lunch in Saragossa, she shocked the wife of General Kindelán by 'making jokes about dead corpses' (10 April 1938, p. 70).

Exactly like the medical staff on the Republican side, and in wartime everywhere,[71] Pip and her comrades let off steam by consuming large amounts of alcohol and becoming rowdy and 'hysterical with mirth' over silly things. There were food fights and, with very little encouragement, Pip would give yodelling displays. There were also high jinks and practical jokes on the ward and, whenever there was an opportunity, the young staff would dance to the phonograph or to dance music on the radio. Towards the end of October, Pip and two other nurses at the hospital were invited to lunch by a group of officers and their chauffeurs. There were about 20 young men in the party and a riotous time was had by all. People became 'squiffy' and threw plates of food and 'played balls with the glasses up and down the table'. They all stayed until 5.30 p.m., 'behaving like lunatics, singing at the top of their voices and dancing around the table holding hands'. When the nurses returned to the hospital, there was a 'terrible row', because no one had taken the temperatures upstairs and the doctors were rude to the nurses and they in turn were rude back to the doctors (2 October 1938, p. 129).

An older trained nurse, Isabel, who had served in the First World War and was a friend of the Infanta's, was assigned to be the matron at Pip's hospital in Calaceite. She was greatly perturbed at Pip's apparent disregard for modesty and she gave her a stern lecture about 'being correct' with the doctors, standing up when they came into the room and always addressing them with the formal 'usted' rather than the informal 'tú'. The older woman was shocked that Pip drank brandy and was not mollified when Pip explained that it was 'quite usual for girls in England' (16 November 1938, p. 150). The matron was beside herself at a rumour that Pip, on night duty, had gone into the bedroom of the doctor on duty and berated Pip and Consuelo when she discovered that one of the wardsmen had visited their room when one of the women was ill in bed. The matron fumed that 'a girl should never be seen in bed by a man' (3 January 1939, p. 172).

Over the year, Pip had become very friendly with Margellon, a surgeon with whom she worked. In the diary she noted that she admired his skill and conscientiousness as a doctor, enjoyed his company and had learnt a great deal from him about professional nursing. When she went out to the village one evening with him unchaperoned to visit the family where he was billeted, even Consuelo became agitated (16 November 1938, p. 150). The matron sent Pip to Coventry and Princess Bee became more and more worried.

From a functional perspective, these concerns about propriety that overrode everything else seem hypocritical and antiquated, especially considering that the nurses were living in the harsh conditions of wartime and dealing with life and death in the raw. Certainly, Pip found extremely aggravating the constant remonstrances from 'old trout' who were 'old fashioned'. She mused that she herself 'could not help it that she had been brought up to a lot of liberty' and that 'it drove [her] mad to be spied on and followed about and treated like a bloody child or a tart who must be reformed' (16 November 1938, p. 150). In any event, the criticisms of her behaviour seem to have been to little effect. The effort to control these young women is more comprehensible, however, in light of the Nationalists' ideological stance, in which self-effacing women were the centrepiece of the Catholic family, which in turn was the linchpin of Nationalist Spain. In a similar vein, the hostile response that Pip sometimes evoked provides an interesting insight, via the refracted reflection, of the ideology and practice towards single foreign woman.

There were only a few times when Pip recorded that she was fearful of the men around her. In general, she appears to have dealt with drunks and patients with bossy aplomb. When a legionnaire escaped from her ward with 'nothing on except his bandage and an overcoat' and 'got sozzled and went about lifting his coat for the edification of all the girls', she 'ordered him to bed with great gusto' and took away all his clothes (20 November 1938).

There were other times, though, that Pip had a strong sense of being a vulnerable female in male space. A less important incident was when she and four other nurses on their night off from the hospital in Aragon drove to the cinema in Monzon. They were the only women in a cinema full of Italian soldiers who 'pinched one of the women all through the film' (11 December 1938, pp. 162–3). In a less cheerful incident, she was at the Intendencia in Calaceite, where she had gone to try and round up women to clean and wash for the hospital, and was crammed in with soldiers who 'made silly remarks and shoved [her] about' (29 November 1938, p. 157). With the hospital on the move to Tremp, Consuelo and Pip were stranded in town when the wardsmen they had come with went to drink in a bar.

Reluctant to be seen in their uniforms inside the bar, having been strongly warned about such behaviour, the two women finally decided to go inside with their friends. It was 'the lesser of the two evils', because standing outside unchaperoned they had immediately been 'surrounded by an unpleasant crowd of rude soldiers' (9 December 1938, p. 161).

On the move from Cella, Pip was confronted with a town full of soldiers who were 'foul drunks' and was 'scared pink' every time she went out, 'especially at night'. Ataulfo had given her a pistol which, in her pocket, 'cheered' her up somewhat. In the same town, the most frightening incident occurred in which she almost suffered 'a fate worse than death'. A group of soldiers forced their way into Pip and Consuelo's room one afternoon, when Consuelo was ill in bed. As the men became increasingly aggressive and refused to leave, Pip 'suddenly realised that things were not as they should be'. One soldier tried to 'paw Consuelo about on the bed' and another 'poked and prodded' Pip. Eventually, the men left but later returned and even more aggressively insisted that they had come to sleep the night. Pip was 'definitely disconcerted, not to say frankly frightened'. At the same time, she realized that the soldiers billeted in the house were away and, even if she had been able to call them, 'they might well have taken sides against the women'. Finally, Pip convinced the intruders to leave. The two women slept with the window shutters locked and their 'bayonets' at their sides (4 March 1938, pp. 49–50).

These were remarkable experiences for a young woman just out in the London season, who only a few months before had seen her first operation and had never before seen a battlefield or its consequences. During the strain of getting through the siege of Teruel, Pip noted in her diary that she was sleeping shallowly and dreaming constantly about the war, often waking with a start. She had also begun to worry about another war. Reflecting the attitudes of those around her, she was bitingly anti-French, noting that, in a war against Germany, she would certainly not be willing to fight with France. Not surprisingly, when news came through of Chamberlain's return from Munich, she was filled with relief.

When the war ended in April 1939, Pip rejoined the Infante's family in Madrid, where Prince Alvaro was overseeing the restructure of the Spanish air force. At the Barajas aerodrome the Infanta, with Pip assisting, ran a canteen for the pilots. As well, the two women were volunteers in an organization providing charity to the 'deserving poor' in the capital and surroundings.[72] They were part of the process whereby franquista Spain retook Madrid. The old pre-Republican elite that had supported the insurgents joined with Franco's men in putting into place the institutions of the dictatorship. Spanish aristocrats returned from exile and reopened their houses and Franco's supporters, who had spent the war sequestered in the foreign embassies and their apartments in Goya and Salamanca, came out of hiding.

Feeling rather lost, Pip returned to England at the end of May 1939. For her valiant contribution to the Nationalist victory she was awarded the *Medalla Militar*. Five months later, when the Second World War began, she crossed the Channel to join a mobile ambulance unit, managing to escape through Bordeaux just before the fall of France. Later, she ran a hospital for Polish refugees in Scotland and, towards the end of the Second World War, married José Luis Vilallonga, a Spanish nobleman, with whom she lived in Argentina and France. Pip Scott-Ellis died in Los Angeles in 1983.

Conclusion

The foreign women who volunteered to assist the Franco movement shared many characteristics. In all cases, before they went to Spain they were militantly anti-Communist and advocates of right-wing causes, whether conservative monarchism, outright fascism or some variant of the two. They were also adventurous and able to leave their home surroundings to transpose themselves to the unfamiliar setting of Franco's Spain. Once across the Nationalist border, however, they presented the Nationalists with something of a paradox. Even though dedicated to promoting Franco's victory, their presence transgressed franquista ideology concerning the place and proper demeanour of respectable women. Single and in most cases travelling alone, they moved about in public places that were male and military, occupied as they were by soldiers fighting a war.

The society of wartime Nationalist Spain occupied a place that was structurally distinct from other right-wing states between the wars. In the classical examples of Italy and Germany, the change to an authoritarian regime had been undertaken in peacetime – by back-room electoral deals, political pressure and disorder in the streets – but the transition that took place incorporated the whole of society. As well, the authoritarian governments in Italy and Germany had physical control of the national territory in its entirety. Even though all inhabitants were not necessarily supporters of these right-wing states, government initiatives applied to everyone who lived within the territory. Paradoxically, this meant that government policies in Italy and Germany were less totalitarian, in the sense of all-encompassing, than they were in Nationalist Spain, where Franco occupied only a part of Spanish territory. In Italy and Germany it was a given that the government had to deal with blocs of the population who were not avid supporters either because they were outright opponents, were passively opposed or simply uninterested. In this case, expulsion and extirpation were options, but the less complicated position was to ignore pockets of opposition as long as minimum compulsory requirements for participation were observed.

In Nationalist Spain the situation was quite different. Nationalist territory consisted of the part of the country that opposed the Spanish Republic. In this area Franco was creating a 'New Spain' in opposition to the ideology and policies of those existing in Republican Spain. The Constitution of the Second Republic was modelled on the 'professorial constitutions' of the post-Versailles new states which, in theory at least, enshrined individual rights regardless of gender, religious freedom or region. Franco's Spain was based on an explicit rejection of these principles. As an aside, the existence of the Two Spains, the progressive and its antithesis, explains the extraordinary ferocity with which Franco dealt with his opponents once he had won the war. Having taken their territory in battle, there was no need for restraint in dealing with the inhabitants that lived there.

Women were a distinguishing hallmark in the two conceptions of society. In Franco's Spain, a woman's place was first and foremost as the Angel of the Hearth within the traditional Catholic family. Throughout Nationalist territory, franquista values prevailed to a remarkable extent. Those who did not accept were in the Republican zone. The geographical configuration of Republican and Nationalist Spain entrenched even further the differences between the places of women. In the Nationalist zone there were no large cosmopolitan centres, like Barcelona or Madrid, where women, single or married, could go about their business without raising any eyebrows.

The female populations of Salamanca and Burgos were the wives of military men, or cowed widows of Republican supporters, waiting out the war. In addition, the Nationalist zone was never drawn into a 'total war' where the front line and the home front were blurred and gender lines dissolved. As well, in the western zone there were few food shortages to fray social structures. It was common for travellers in Nationalist Spain to remark upon the the peace and order away from the war zone. The difference was between female/family space and male/militarized space. The ethos of the first was Catholic, and the second military. Brothels for the soldiers were part of a militarized and therefore male public space as were medical services. This is probably the reason that the director of the Nationalist Nursing Service expended so much energy trying to maintain the reputation of Spanish front-line nurses whose position by definition was in male space and therefore transgressive. The head of Spanish nurses was as concerned about maintaining a tight control over the nurses' behaviour as she was about the level of care they were providing the wounded.

Franco's foreign female volunteers, Catholic or not, came from particularly tolerant families that had placed no obstacles in the adventurous ways of their daughters. Even the oldest among them, Florence Farmborough, had been encouraged to travel as a 20-year-old, 30 years before. They were self-confident, well travelled and able to look after themselves. The aristocrats among them were in a long tradition of upper-class women who did not see the rules that applied to ordinary women hampering themselves.

Franco's publicists, engaged in what today would be seen as public relations work, spread the word about Franco's cause, and equally importantly provided chapter and verse on the 'horrors' of 'Red Spain'. What they actually saw, however, is another question. Rather like Franco's other foreign travellers, and indeed many of the volunteers, these women filtered Spanish events through their own political views and frameworks of meaning which had been formed elsewhere. In Britain, France and the United States, where they took back the good word on Franco's Spain, support or opposition to the Nationalists was well established into fixed configurations that changed very little over the course of the war. In the light of this, their efforts probably made little difference in converting people, but they provided details and anecdotes to be trotted out by those who already supported Franco.

The women involved with the front-line medical service were engaged in a different war. Their contribution to Franco's military victory is less ambiguous as well. Gabriel Herbert's Anglo-Spanish medical units made a significant improvement to the level of care that the wounded received in northern Spain. Without doubt, the equipment that was sent from London, the effectiveness of their transport arrangements and the speed with which they were able to deal with the wounded, probably reduced wartime deaths among the soldiers in their care. In a less well-run outfit, Pip Scott-Ellis, an energetic, hardworking and committed nurse in Nationalist front-line hospitals, probably also helped wherever she was stationed. Her descriptions of the medical practices of which she was a part do not suggest great medical success; however, her own presence was undoubtedly valuable.

In their various ways, these women assisted in Franco's victory. The irony of it is that, in the Franco dictatorship which followed the Civil War, there was no place for independent women like themselves. Women on the Republican side who were known to have been independent, active in politics or to have eschewed conventional family life were arrested and served long and arduous prison sentences.

Notes

1   See, for example, Margaret H. Darrow, 'French volunteer nursing and the myth of war experience in World War One', *American Historical Review*, **101** (1) (February 1996), pp. 80–106.

2   Margaret R. Higgonet has pointed out that in civil wars, 'dissidents are aligned with unnatural women', in 'Civil wars and sexual territories', in *Arms and the Woman: War, Gender and Literary Representation*, edited by Helen M. Cooper, Adrienne Auslander Munich and Susan Merrill Squier (Chapel Hill: University of North Carolina Press, 1989), p. 81. According to Joan Scott, in wartime gender often provides the language with which to speak about the disruption caused by war and in which peace implies a return to 'traditional gender relationships' and war represents 'sexual disorder', in 'Rewriting history' in *Behind the Lines: Gender and the Two World Wars*, edited by Margaret R. Higgonet, Jane Jenson, Sonya Michel and Margaret Collins Weitz (New Haven: Yale University Press, 1987), p. 27.

3   Timothy Mitchell, *Betrayal of the Innocents: Desire, Power and the Catholic Church in Spain* (Philadelphia: University of Pennsylvania Press, 1998), pp. 120–1.

4   Victoria de Grazia shows that the Italian Catholic Church, the state and the Fascist Party were never in step over the proper place of women in Italian society. See *How Fascism Ruled Women: Italy 1922–1945* (Berkeley: University of California Press, 1992), p. 147.

5   Giuliana di Febo, 'El *Monje Guerrero*: identidad de género en los modelos Franquistas durante la Guerra Civil', in *Las Mujeres y la Guerra Civil Española, III, Jornadas de estudio monográficos*. Salamanca, October 1989 (Madrid: Ministerio de Cultura, 1991), pp. 202–10.

6   Mitchell points out that in Franco's Spain a 'woman's identity was defined by her relationship with the sacrament of marriage' and in postwar Spain, where women

outnumbered men, the possibility of becoming an old maid (*solterona*) 'inspired genuine terror', *Betrayal of the Innocents*, p. 116.

7 For the Republican zone, see Mary Nash, *Defying Male Civilization: Women in the Spanish Civil War* (Denver: Arden Press, 1995).

8 Marie Aline Barrachina points out that the Falangist Women's Section was always conscious of the need to ensure that, at the end of the war, women would return to their traditional place within the family, 'Ideal de la Mujer Falangista. Ideal Falangista de la mujer', in *Las Mujeres y la Guerra Civil Española*, pp. 211–17. See also María Teresa Gallego Méndez, *Mujer, Falange y franquismo* (Madrid: Taurus, 1983), pp. 175–201. Victoria Enders, drawing on her own interviews, offers an interesting methodological intervention on the relationship between the historians of the movement and the Falangist women as historical subjects. The *Sección* leaders that Enders interviewed rejected a feminist assessment of their work as repressive to women. Instead they shared a gendered franquista conception of the world but disagreed about the meaning that feminist historians have assigned to it. See 'Problematic portraits: the ambiguous historical role of the *Sección Femenina* of the Falange', in *Constructing Spanish Womanhood: Female Identity in Modern Spain*, edited by Victoria Lorée Enders and Pamela Beth Radcliff (Albany: State University of New York Press, 1999), pp. 375–97.

9 See Florencia Carrionera Salimero, A. Fuentes Labrador, M. A. Sampedro Talabán and M. J. Velasco Marcos, 'La mujer tradicionalista: las Margaritas', in *Las Mujeres y la Guerra Civil Española, III, Jornadas de estudio monográficos*, Salamanca, October 1989 (Madrid: Ministerio de Cultura, 1991), pp. 188–201. In April 1937, the Falangist Sección Femenina was joined with the Carlist Margaritas to become *La Sección Femenina Tradicionalista*.

10 Frances Lannon provides the example of Pilar Primo de Rivera, the head of the Falangist Women's Section, railing at large public rallies against the 'detestable type of female orator' who was not content to stay at home. See 'Women and images of women in the Spanish Civil War', *Transactions of the Royal Historical Society*, Sixth Series, 1 (1991), p. 225. See also Paul Preston, 'Fascism and flower arranging: Pilar Primo de Rivera', which presents the psychological and famial background to Pilar Primo de Rivera's self-abnegation, in his *Comrades! Portraits from the Spanish Civil War* (London: HarperCollins, 1999), pp. 111–39.

11 Marie-Aline Barrachina, 'La reécriture de l'histoire: le mythe des grandes figures de Castille. 1938–1945', *Entre émancipation et nationalisme: la presse féminine d'Europe 1914–1945*, under the direction of Rita Thaelman (Paris: Deuxtemps Tierce, 1990), pp. 183–203.

12 Assumpta Roura argues that women were the main focus of the restrictive morality of the franquista state because they were to provide a 'bulwark for the new moral order', in her *Mujeres para después de una guerra: informes sobre moralidad y prostitución en la posguerra española* (Barcelona: Flor del Viento Ediciones, 1998), p. 43.

13 In Nationalist descriptions militiawomen are violent and filthy; see Shirley
    Mangini, *Memories of Resistance: Women's Voices from the Spanish Civil War*
    (New Haven: Yale University Press, 1995), p. 93; or Constantino Bayle, 'La Cárcel
    de mujeres en Madrid', *Razon y Fe*, No. 113 (April 1938), pp. 435–50. For example,
    Dolores Ibárruri, 'La Pasionaria', in franquista literature was supposed to have
    torn open the jugular of a priest with her teeth; quoted in Paul Preston, 'Pasionaria
    of steel: Dolores Ibárruri', in *Comrades! Portraits from the Spanish Civil War*
    (London: HarperCollins, 1999), p. 277.

14 Albert Machthild, '*La Bestia y el Angel*. Imágenes de las mujeres en la novela
    falangista de la Guerra Civil', in *Las mujeres y la Guerra Civil Española, III,
    Jornadas de estudio monográficos*. Salamanca, October 1989 (Madrid: Ministerio
    de Cultura, 1991), pp. 371–7. The psychiatrist, Dr Vallejo-Nágera, after the war
    produced several studies that were supposed to prove the psychopathology of
    Republican women prisoners, quoted in Timothy Mitchell, *Betrayal of the
    Innocents: Desire, Power and the Catholic Church in Spain*, pp. 99–100.

15 Julio Rodríguez Puértolas, *Literatura fascista española* (Madrid: Akal, 1987), 2
    vols, quoted in Mitchell, *Betrayal of the Innocents*, p. 97.

16 Amparo Moreno Sardá, 'La réplica de las mujeres al franquismo', in *El feminismo
    en España: dos siglos de historia* ed. by Pilar Folgera *et al.* (Madrid: Editorial Pablo
    Iglesias, 1988), pp. 86–91; Adrian Shubert, *A Social History of Modern Spain*
    (London: Unwin Hyman, 1990), pp. 23–56.

17 Helen Nicholson, *Death in the Morning* (London: Lovat Dickson, 1937).

18 Ian Gibson provides the figure of 572 executions in Granada in August 1936,
    among whom was one of Spain's most distinguished writers, Federico García
    Lorca, executed in mid-August. See *The Death of Lorca* (London: W. H. Allen,
    1973), p. 77 and pp. 167–9.

19 Eleonora Tennant, *Spanish Journey: Personal Experiences of the Civil War*
    (London: Eyre & Spottiswoode, 1936).

20 Ernest W. D. Tennant, *True Account* (London: Max Parrish, 1957), pp. 54–5.

21 Richard Griffiths, *Fellow Travellers of the Right: British Enthusiasts for Nazi
    Germany, 1933–9* (London: Constable, 1980), pp. 182–7.

22 Tennant, *True Account*, pp. 117–18; Griffiths, *Fellow Travellers of the Right*, pp.
    233–7.

23 Eleonora Tennant's atrocity stories, classic Lévi-Straussian bricolage, exemplify in
    their content Joan Scott's notion of war as sexual disorder and Margaret
    Higgonet's suggestion that, in civil wars, dissidents are seen as sexually unnatural.
    See Note 2.

24 Geneviève Tabouis, *Ils l'ont appeleé Cassandre* (Paris: Éditions de la Maison
    Française, 1943), p. 385.

25 Edmée de la Rouchefoucauld, *Spanish Women* (New York: Peninsular News
    Service, 1938), p. 16.

26 SHM, Ávila, 2/169/2/4, Año de 1937, 16 April 1937, *Orden al Regimiento de*

Transmiones: la inmediata creación de una companía con personal e especializado en radio para atender la propaganda en los frentes. The Germans set up a transmitter at Salamanca which broadcast programmes under the signal of Radio Nacional Salamanca. When Franco moved his headquarters to Burgos, the transmitter was moved there. During the Second World War it operated from La Coruña to track Allied ships and submarines; see Ortwin Buchbender and Reinhard Hauschild, *Radio Humanité: les émetteurs allemands clandestins*, translated from Germany by Wanda Vulliez (Paris: Éditions France-Empire, 1984), pp. 28–9. The Rector of St Alban's College in Valladolid also made broadcasts in English towards the end of the war; see Michael E. Williams, *St Alban's College, Valladolid: Four Centuries of English Catholic Presence in Spain* (New York: St Martin's Press, 1986), p. 216.

27 Florence Farmborough, *Life and People in National Spain* (London: Sheed & Ward, 1938). The fourteen chapters each constitute a broadcast on contemporary topics. The extra chronological chapters presented as two parts presumably constituted two separate broadcasts.

28 Florence Farmborough, *Nurse at the Russian Front: A Diary 1914–18* (London: Constable, 1974), Preface.

29 Farmborough, *Life and People in National Spain*, p. 23, p. 43.

30 Jane Anderson has a voluminous FBI file, No. 65–36240, comprising more than 1000 pages. It was compiled in 1943 for the Grand Jury prosecution for treason based on her Berlin broadcasts which were 'designed to aid an enemy with whom the United States was at war'. This section draws heavily on the FBI material. The source has great strengths and weaknesses. The FBI's dragnet spread far and wide to encompass a whole generation of Anderson's acquaintances and to dredge up a wealth of detail. The source's shortcoming is that unsubstantiated statements are written into FBI file summaries and become part of the record. See, as well, John Carver Edwards, *Berlin Calling: American Broadcasters in Service to the Third Reich* (New York: Praeger, 1991), pp. 41–56.

31 Chas. Neville, 'The Georgia peach who became Lady Haw Haw', *New York Journal American*, 5 May 1943. The FBI description of Jane Anderson is '5.6", blonde hair, blue eyes small nose and mouth, round chin, oval face with fair complexion', FBI File 61–68, Summary, 'Baltimore', 'Jane Anderson with aliases', Los Angeles, 4/1/43, p. 39.

32 The latter details are from a description by Jane's lover, Joseph Retinger. See *Joseph Retinger: Memoirs of an Eminence Grise*, edited by John Pomian (Sussex: The University Press, 1972), pp. 37–9. See also FBI File No. 100–5791, 3/15/43; and File No. 61–584, 4/1/43.

33 Neville, 'The Georgia peach who became Lady Haw Haw'.

34 FBI File No. 61–68, 'Baltimore', Summary, pp. 1–38.

35 Jane Anderson, 'Looping the loop over London', in *Flying, Submarining and Mine Sweeping*, by Jane Anderson and Gordon Brice (London: Sir Jospeh Causton, 1916).

36 Retinger, *Memoirs*, pp. 37–39.

37 FBI File No. 61–68, 'Baltimore', Summary, p. 9.

38 There is no reference to Jane Anderson Cienfuegos in the *Daily Mail* in the first year of the war, not even to her arrest. The only female reporter identified was Frances Davis, whose story has already been told in Chapter 2.

39 *New York Times*, 11 October 1936; 15 October 1936; and *Foreign Relations of the United States, Diplomatic Papers, Europe, 1936*, II (Washington: USGPO, 1954) p. 745, 352.1121 Anderson, Jane/12: Telegram, 21 October 1936.

40 Jane Anderson de Ciefuegos, 'Horror in Spain', *Catholic Digest*, 1 (1937), pp. 69–74.

41 FBI File 65–36240, Baltimore, 61–68, Summary Secret.

42 *New York Times*, 28 February 1938. The details are reminiscent of other franquista writings at that time about the Madrid women's prison; see Constantino Bayle, 'La cárcel de mujeres en Madrid', *Razon y Fe*, No. 113 (April 1938), pp. 435–50.

43 *New York Times*, 28 September 1937.

44 FBI File No. 100–2805, 3/16/43.

45 FBI File No. 100–2805, 3/16/43; File No. 61–68, 7/19/45. Summary Secret, pp. 9–11.

46 FBI File No. 65–36240, 7/19/45, Summary Secret, p. 13.

47 An FBI informant had received a letter from Anderson on 14 December 1939, listing the seven medals she claimed to have received from Franco's Spain. See FBI File No. 65–36240.

48 FBI File No. 65–36240, 7/19/45, Summary Secret; *PM*, 16 June 1941; 23 June 1941; 30 June 1941; and *Daily Mirror*, 27 January 1942.

49 Evelyn Waugh married Gabriel Herbert's sister. Cordelia Flyte, the devout younger sister in *Brideshead Revisited*, drove an ambulance for Franco in Spain and presumably is based on Gabriel Herbert.

50 Martin Stannard, *Evelyn Waugh: The Early Years* (London: Dent, 1986), p. 386.

51 Adrian Hastings, 'Some reflections on the English Catholicism of the late 1930s', in his *Bishops and Writers: Aspects of the Evolution of English Catholicism* (Wheathampstead: Anthony Clarke, 1977), pp. 107–25.

52 *Dictionary of National Biography 1931–1940*, p. 454.

53 Pip Scott-Ellis, bemoaning the tattered state of her clothes, her burst shoes and laddered stockings, noted that she had seen Gabriel Herbert, 'very elegant and well soignée', dining with Arnold Lunn at the Grand Hotel in Saragossa on 28 February 1939. See *The Chances of Death: A Diary of the Spanish Civil War*, edited by Raymond Carr (London: Michael Russell, 1995), p. 198.

54 Public Record Office, Kew, FO 371 20544, pp. 94–95, 'Lord Howard of Penrith', 20 October 1936.

55 See Buchanan, *Britain and the Spanish Civil War* (Cambridge: CUP, 1997), p. 119. Jim Fyrth gives the lower figure of £11,000 and emphasizes that the small amount is in contrast with support for the Republican medical volunteers. See *The Signal Was Spain: The Spanish Aid Movement in Britain, 1936–39* (London: Lawrence &

Wishart, 1986), pp. 193–4. Gabriel Herbert, however, considered her medical group well supplied from British donations. See Note 57. For fund-raising see also Public Record Office, Kew, FO 371 20536, 27 August 1937, p. 229.

56 Unless otherwise indicated, the material in this section is based on the following: Gabriel Herbert, interview with Michael Alpert, 15 October 1982, Transcript; MS letter to Michael Alpert, 4 April 1982, Marx Memorial Library, Clerkenwell, Box–8: D/ 1 and 2; and *Daily Sketch*, 26 November 1936; *Universe, 30 October 1936*; 18 December 1936; 2 April 1937.

57 José Felix Lequerica had been educated in England and attended the London School of Economics. See Sir Robert Hodgson, *Spain Resurgent* (London: Hutchinson, 1953), p. 120.

58 *The Universe*, 30 October 1936, p. 10.

59 PRO FO 371 20540, 22 September 1936, pp. 102–3.

60 See Note 56.

61 Tom Burns, *The Use of Memory: Publishing and Further Pursuits* (London: Sheed & Ward, 1993), p. 80.

62 Hilaire Belloc made a four-day visit to Gabriel Herbert in September 1937; see Hilaire Belloc to Lady Phipps, 15 September 1937, in *Letter from Hilaire Belloc* (London: Canter, 1958), p. 265; Arnold Lunn, *Come What May: An Autobiography* (London: Eyre & Spottiswoode, 1940), pp. 298–9. Pip Scott-Ellis records having dinner at the Grand Hotel in Saragossa with Arnold Lunn, 'out here collecting material about "Red Horrors"'; Priscilla Scott-Ellis, *The Chances of Death: A Diary of the Spanish Civil War* (London: Michael Russell, 1995), p. 69. Major-General Sir Walter Maxwell Scott in Nationalist Spain in March 1937 met Gabriel Herbert at a military hospital and on the road. See his 'Report on his Visit to Western Spain' in PRO FO 371/21287/47815 11, pp. 5720–44.

63 *Dictionary of National Biography 1941–1950*, p. 764–765; *The Times*, Obituary, 6 November 1946.

64 See Mary Cadogan, *Women with Wings: Female Flyers in Fact and Fiction* (London: Macmillan, 1992), pp. 67–84.

65 Robert Wohl, *A Passion for Wings: Aviation and the Western Imagination 1908–1918* (New Haven: Yale University Press, 1994), p. 258.

66 See Gaenor Heathcote Amory's foreword in Scott-Ellis, *The Chances of Death*, pp. vii–xiii. Unless indicated otherwise, the page references in the discussion of Pip Scott-Ellis refer to her published Spanish diary.

67 Arnold Lunn, *Come What May*, p. 337.

68 Lunn, *Come What May*, pp. 337–43.

69 José Luis de Vilallonga, Marqués de Castellvell, *Vilallonga: la cruda y tierna verdad: memorias no autorizadas* (Barcelona: Plaza & Janés, 2000), pp. 234–9; *Fiesta* (Paris: Seuil, 1971); and Pierre Boutron, *Fiesta* (1995).

70 José Luis de Vilallonga, *Fiesta* (Paris: Seuil, 1971) and Pierre Boutron's 1995 film of the same name. A more cruel portrayal of Pip appears in Vilallonga's most recent

memoirs though he saves his most scathing descriptions for Pip's family, whom he portrays as extremely cold and quite dotty. On this score, it is probably worth adding that Pip's marriage to a self-confessed roué must have placed both the family and herself under considerable strain. See *Vilallonga: la cruda y tierna verdad*.

71   See Judith Keene, *Last Mile to Huesca: An Australian Nurse in the Spanish Civil War* (Sydney: University of New South Wales Press, 1988).

72   They were sceptical and unhelpful towards families they suspected of being 'Red'. See, for example, *Chances of Death*, 18 April 1939, p. 222.

CHAPTER 8

Conclusions

❧

The Civil War in Spain began as a conflict between Spaniards over competing conceptions about the future of the Spanish state. At issue was whether the country should modernize, or not; and if so, how it should be done, and to whose benefit. These were specifically domestic matters. The various solutions that the parties and interest groups in the 1930s came up with were a function of a range of factors, including demography, class politics and regionalism, all of which were deeply embedded in Spanish history or recent Spanish economic and social events. Although the positions that the competing Spanish interest groups espoused were connected to the broad political developments elsewhere in Europe, their differences, first and foremost, arose from local Spanish conditions.

The foreigners who crossed into Western Spain to support Franco knew very little about Spanish politics. Like most people in Europe between the wars, they probably were aware that Spain had lost the Spanish–American War, had remained outside the Great War and was lagging behind Western Europe, socially and economically. They had come to Spain to fight what they saw as an international war but, paradoxically, one in which the specifics were tied to the personal and political context in the foreign volunteers' own home countries; or, in the case of the White Russians, in the diaspora of exile. The White Russians, the Romanian Iron Guard and, to a large extent, the members of the Joan of Arc Company from France and North Africa, saw Spain as the place in which they could further the struggles to which they were committed at home. Despite an intense individual nationalism, these groups were internationalists in Spain seeing themselves as part of a White International in which a blow struck against their enemies on the Iberian Peninsula would rebound against them somewhere else.

Franco's activists typically explained their objectives in internationalist and universalist terms. They were fighting for Franco to save the Church, to defend tradition or to defeat Communism. They understood the Spanish

Civil War, however, according to frameworks of meaning which were based in their own national historical experiences that had taken place elsewhere. The latter provided the templates into which were fitted Spanish events. The narratives written by many of these foreigners recall nothing so much as dioramas about good and evil. As the tableau is cranked the figures representing good and evil – Catholics versus Freemasons, Christians versus Jews, anti-Communists versus Communists, sexually depraved 'Reds' versus pious Whites – move through their paces in a way that is instantly recognizable and predictable.

Certain Spanish events were easily transformed and universalized into the tableau of good and evil. The figure of the Caudillo in foreign (and local) narratives often replicated the familiar format of the lives of the saints. Franco, the devout and modest Christian and a shy and retiring family man, became an indomitable fighter when confronted with evil wherever he found it. The outstanding example, however, was Moscardó and the siege of the Alcázar. From mid-1936, this became a mythic event for a great many rightists outside Spain. It encapsulated profound interwar anxieties as it appeared to offer an example of Old World morality and virtue standing against new forms of evil and modern technology.

The exception to these formatted narratives of Nationalist Spain by foreigners were the first-person accounts written by members of the international press corps after they had left Franco territory. The stories they filed while they were in Spain were tightly censored by Franco's Press and Propaganda Bureau. Censorship, however, did not blindfold professionals. For the most part, these men, and the few women, were seasoned in a decade of reporting international events. Their writings after they had left Nationalist Spain provided insightful analysis of the Civil War and their own assignments there and were based on careful reflection and reliable evidence.

Among Franco's volunteers, as powerful as their ideological impulses may have been and as overriding their attraction to Franco's New Spain, these factors were not sufficient alone to explain their real-life enlistment. All Franco's foreign supporters in Spain, male and female, were to varying degrees unhooked from the normal moorings that held their peers fast at home. The individuals who crossed the border were moved by a spirit of adventure and at a juncture in their lives at which they were able to head off in search of new experiences. That they were not always welcome when they arrived in Spain and that many of them became casualties of the war was beside the point.

As far as it is possible to ascertain, less than half the volunteers for Franco were veterans of the First World War. The White Russians had been involved in a series of wars and, almost a military caste, were more comfortable in uniform than out. At Nationalist headquarters, however, the Russians' previous experience counted for little. In the Joan of Arc company, except for the under-age enlisted, a good number of the French had also served in the First World War. Many had been recruited through the networks of veterans' groups in France. The young Romanians in Spain had not fought in the First World War, though General Cantacuzino, whose original idea it had been that the Iron Guard travel to Toledo to mark Moscardó's relief, had achieved considerable national fame in the Great War. Overall, the volunteers who had not been part of the generation of the Great War were, like many young men between the wars, longing for military adventure.

Who benefited from the foreign volunteers for Franco? Unequivocally it was the leaders who obtained more advantage than the ordinary volunteers. But this is the case in many enterprises, military or otherwise. Casualties were uneven. For example, the Russians suffered more dead than did the Irish, which may simply reflect the differing lengths of time each spent at the front and the units to which they were assigned. The Irish were in combat for a relatively short time while the Russians, mostly in Carlist units, served out the whole war. Certain leaders like Eoin O'Duffy or the French Réal del Sarte and Charles Maurras derived considerable benefit in recognition and favours bestowed, at least in the first part of their involvement with Franco's Spain. In these three cases, their popularity within Franco's camp fell away as the war dragged on. By way of contrast, the White Russians enjoyed no honeymoon in Nationalist headquarters. From their arrival, when Fok had had to provide a display of Imperial military gymnastics to convince the Spanish recruiters to permit his enlistment, through Shinkarenko's catalogue of real (and imagined) slights, the Russians were never favoured.

From Franco's point of view, what did he gain from the foreign volunteers? Not much in military terms. They probably provided a potential backstop if the Non-Intervention Committee had tried to force the withdrawal of all foreigners fighting on his side. As it transpired, however, the Non-Intervention Committee had neither the teeth nor the will to press the issue. Franco probably obtained some benefit from the amateur writers and travellers who produced narratives of their Spanish trips which faithfully echoed the opinions of the accompanying franquista press officials. These stories provided grist to the pro-Franco mill outside Spain and ensured that the franquista version of the Civil War circulated within pro-Nationalist circles abroad.

The long-term outcome of the history of foreign volunteers with Franco was, perhaps, ironically predictable, in that after the war was over, the historical presence of foreigners, which in any event had always been officially downplayed in Nationalist Spain, was expunged. Although they were on the winning side and the Spanish Republicans were humiliatingly defeated, suppressed at home and driven into exile abroad, the configuration of European politics after 1945 made irrelevant the stories of right-wing volunteers. In postwar Europe, many of those who had been committed pro-fascists before and during the Spanish civil war and the Second World War refashioned their biographies to make them more suitable to democratic times. In Spain they were also rendered invisible, while the official version, at least until Franco's death in 1975, remained that foreigners fought for the 'Reds' and patriotic Spaniards were with Franco.

Select bibliography

Archival sources

Archival sources used in this study are discussed in the Introduction, pp. 9–10 and are cited in detail in the relevant footnotes. Newspapers include the *Advocate*; *Candide*; *Chasovoi*; *Gringoire*; *Humanité*; *Je Suis Partout*; *New York Times*; *Populaire*, and *The Times*.

A selection of the printed sources cited

Aguilar Fernández, Paloma, *La memoria histórica de la Guerra Civil Española (1936–1939): un proceso de aprendizaje político*. Madrid: Centro de Estudios Avanzados en Ciencias Sociales, Instituto Juan March de Estudios e Investigaciones, 1995.

Alexander, Martin and Graham, Helen, *The French and Spanish Popular Fronts: Comparative Perspectives*. Cambridge: Cambridge University Press, 1989.

Alvarez, José E., *The Betrothed of Death: The Spanish Foreign Legion during the Rif Rebellion, 1920–1927*, Westport CT: Greenwood Press, 2001.

Andreyev, Catherine, *Vlasov and the Russian Liberation Movement: Soviet Reality and Emigré Theories*. Cambridge: Cambridge University Press, 1987.

Aparicio, Juan (prologue), *Los legionarios rumanos Ion Motza y Vasile Marin: Caídos por Dios y por España*. Biblioteca Legionaria Rumana, No. 1. Madrid: Editorial 'Ciubul Legionaria', 1941.

Arnal, Oscar L., *Ambivalent Alliance: The Catholic Church and the Action Française, 1899–1939*. Pittsburgh: University of Pittsburgh Press, 1985.

Azcárate, Pablo de, *Mi embajada en Londres durante la Guerra Civil Española*. Barcelona: Esplugues de Llobregat, Editorial Ariel, 1976.

Baldwin, Hanson and Stone, Shepard, (eds), *We Saw It Happen: The News Behind the News That's Fit to Print*, by thirteen correspondents of the *New York Times*, New York: Simon & Schuster, 1939.

Balfour, Sebastian and Preston, Paul, *Spain and the Great Powers in the Twentieth Century*. London: Routledge, 1999.

Bauer, Eddy, *Rouge et or: chroniques de la 'Reconquête' Espagnole, 1937–1938*, Neuchatel: Éditions Victor Attinger, 1938.

Baumann, Gerold Gino F., *Los voluntarios latinoamericanos en la Guerra Civil Española: en las Brigadas Internacionales, las milicias, la retaguardia y en el Ejército Popular*. San José, Costa Rica: Editorial Guayacán, 1997.

Bell, J. Bowyer, 'Ireland and the Spanish Civil War, 1936–1939', *Studia Hibernica*, 9 (1969).

Berberova, Nina Nikolaevna, *The Italics Are Mine*. New York: Alfred A. Knopf, 1992 (translated by Philippe Radley).

Blanco Escolá, Carlos and Aquilar, Miguel Angel, *La incompetencia militar de Franco*. Madrid: Alianza Editorial, 2000.

Blázquez, Luis Fabián, *Riesgo y ventura de los Tercios de Requetés*. Madrid: Actas, 1995.

Blinkhorn, Martin, *Carlism and Crisis in Spain 1931–1939*. Cambridge: Cambridge University Press, 1975.

Blinkhorn, Martin (ed.), *Spain in Conflict 1931–1939: Democracy and its Enemies*. London: Sage Publications, 1986.

Blinkhorn, Martin (ed.), *Fascists and Conservatives: The Radical Right and the Establishment in Twentieth-Century Europe*. London: Unwin Hyman, 1990.

Bolín, Luis A., *Spain: The Vital Years*. London: Cassell, 1967.

Borne, Dominique and Dubief, Henri, *La Crise des années 30: 1929–1938*. Paris: Éditions du Seuil, 1989.

Bourdrel, Philippe, *La Cagoule: histoire d'une société secrète du Front Populaire à la Ve République*. Paris: Albin Michel, 1992.

Bowers, Claude, *My Mission to Spain: Watching the Rehearsal for World War II*. New York: Simon & Schuster, 1954.

Brasillach, Robert, *Une génération dans l'orage, mémoires: notre avant-guerre. Journal d'un homme occupé*. Paris: Plon, 1950.

Brasillach, Robert and Massis, Henri, *Les Cadets de l'Alcázar*. Paris: Plon, 1936.

Brasillach, Robert and Bardèche, Maurice, *Histoire de la guerre d'Espagne*. Paris: Plon, 1939.

Buchanan, Tom, *Britain and the Spanish Civil War*. Cambridge: Cambridge University Press, 1997.

Buchanan, Tom and Conway, Martin (eds), *Political Catholicism in Europe, 1918–1965*. Oxford: Clarendon Press, 1996.

Buckley, Henry W., *Life and Death of the Spanish Republic*. London: Hamish Hamilton, 1940.

Cantacuzino, Alexandru, *Opere Complete, Colectia 'Omul Nou'*. Munich: Traian Golea, 1969.

Cardoza, Harold G., *The March of a Nation: My Year of Spain's Civil War*. New York: Robert M. McBride & Co., 1937.

Carlton, David, 'Eden, Blum and the origins of Non-Intervention', *Journal of Contemporary History*, 6 (3), 1971.

Carr, Raymond (ed.), *The Republic and the Civil War in Spain*. London: Macmillan, 1971.

Catala, Michel, *Les Relations franco-espagnoles pendant la Deuxième Guerre Mondiale: rapprochement nécessaire, réconciliation impossible, 1939–1944*. Paris: L'Harmattan, 1997.

Caute, David, *The Fellow-Travellers: A Postscript to the Enlightenment*. London: Quartet Books, 1977.

Christophe, Paul, *1936: les Catholiques et le Front Populaire*. Paris: Desclée, 1979.

Cierva, Ricardo de la, *Historia esencial de la Guerra Civil Española: todos los problemas resueltos, sesenta años después*. Madridejos, Toledo: Editorial Fénix, 1996.

Codreanu, Corneliu Zelea, *La Garde de Fer: pour les legionnaires*. Paris: Éditions Prométhée, 1938.

Cohn, N. R. C., *Warrant for Genocide: The Myth of the Jewish World-Conspiracy and the Protocols of the Elders of Zion*. Chico, CA: Scholars Press, 1981.

Corbin, John, 'Truth and myth in history: an example from the Spanish Civil War', *Journal of Interdisciplinary History*, **XXV**, (4) (Spring 1995).

Cornwell, John, *Hitler's Pope: The Secret History of Pius XII*. London: Viking, 1999.

Cortada, James W. (ed.), *Historical Dictionary of the Spanish Civil War 1936–1939*, Westport, CT: Greenwood Press, 1982.

Costa, Luis *et al.* (eds), *German and International Perspectives on the Spanish Civil War: The Aesthetics of Partisanship*. Columbia, SC: Camden House, 1992.

Costa Pinto, António, *Salazar's Dictatorship and European Fascism: Problems of Interpretation*. New York: Columbia University Press, 1995.

Cowles, Virginia, *Looking for Trouble*. London: Hamish Hamilton, 1941.

Davey, Owen Anthony, 'The origins of the Légion des Volontaires Français contre le Bolchevisme', *Journal of Contemporary History*, **6** (4) (1971).

Davis, Frances, *My Shadow in the Sun*. New York: Carrick & Evans Inc., 1940.

Dick, Alan, *Inside Story*. London: George Allen & Unwin, 1943.

Drieu la Rochelle, Pierre, *Gilles*. Paris: Gallimard, 1939.

Ducloux, Louis, *From Blackmail to Treason: Political Crime and Corruption in France, 1920–1940*, translated from the French by Ronald Mathews. London: André Deutsch, 1958.

Duroselle, Jean Baptiste, *La Décadence: 1932–1939*. Paris: Imprimerie nationale, 1979.

Edwards, Jill, *The British Government and the Spanish Civil War 1936–1939*. London: Macmillan, 1979.

Eisenwein, George Richard and Shubert, Adrian, *Spain at War: The Spanish Civil War in Context 1931–1939*. London: Longman, 1995.

Enders, Victoria Lorée and Radcliff, Pamela Beth, (eds), *Constructing Spanish Womanhood: Female Identity in Modern Spain*. Albany, NY: State University of New York Press, 1999.

Esch, Patricia A. M. van der, *Prelude to War: The International Repercussions of the Spanish Civil War, 1936–1939*. The Hague: Martinus Nijhoff, 1951.

Farmborough, F., *Life and People in National Spain*. London: Sheed & Ward, 1938.

Fäy, Bernard, *Les Forces de l'Espagne: voyage à Salamanque*. Paris: SGIE, 1937.

Fischer, George (ed.), *Russian Emigré Politics*. New York: Free Russia Fund, 1951.

Flint, James, 'English Catholics and the Bolshevik Revolution: the origins of Catholic anti-Communism', *American Benedictine Review*, **42**, (1) (March 1991).

Flint, James, 'English Catholics and the 'proposed Soviet Alliance, 1939', *Journal of Ecclesiastical History*, **48**, (3) (July 1997).

Foss, W., and Gerahty, C., *The Spanish Arena*. London: Right Book Club, 1939.

Fuller, Major-General J. F. C., *The Conquest of Red Spain*. London: Burns, Oates & Washbourne, 1937.

Fyrth, Jim, *The Signal Was Spain: The Spanish Aid Movement in Britain, 1936–39*, London: Lawrence & Wishart, 1986.

Galey, John H., 'Bridegrooms of Death. A profile study of the Spanish Foreign Legion', *Journal of Contemporary History*, **4**, (2) (April 1969).

Gallagher, M. D., 'Leon Blum and the Spanish Civil War', *Journal of Contemporary History*, **6**, (3), (1971).

Gallego Méndez, María Teresa, *Mujer, falange y franquismo*. Madrid: Taurus, 1983.

Gat, Azar, *Fascist and Liberal Visions of War: Fuller, Liddell Hart, Douhet, and Other Modernists*. Oxford: Clarendon Press, 1998.

Girardet, Raoul, 'Notes sur l'esprit d'un fascisme français, 1934–1940', *Revue française de science politique*, July–September 1955.

Glandy, Anne André, *Maxime Réal del Sarte, sa vie - son oeuvre*, Preface by Henry Bordeaux. Paris: Plon, 1955.

Graham, Helen and Preston, Paul, *The Popular Front in Europe*. London: Macmillan, 1987.

Griffiths, Richard, *Fellow Travellers of the Right: British Enthusiasts for Nazi Germany 1933–39*. London: Constable, 1980.

Gunther, John, *Inside Europe*. London: Hamish Hamilton, 1937.

Gunther, John, *Behind Europe's Curtain*. London: Hamish Hamilton, 1949.

Habeck, Mary, 'The Spanish Civil War and the origins of the Second World War', in Gordon Martel (ed.), *The Origins of the Second World War Reconsidered. Second Edition: A. J. P. Taylor and the Historians*. London: Routledge, 1999.

Hanigen, Frank C. (ed.), *Nothing But Danger: Thrilling Adventures of Ten Newspaper Correspondents in the Civil War*. London: George G. Harrap, 1939.

Hastings, Adrian, *Bishops and Writers: Aspects of the Evolution of English Catholicism*, Wheathampstead: Anthony Clarke, 1977.

Herreros, Isabelo, *Mitología de la Cruz de Franco: El Alcázar de Toledo*. Madrid: Vosa, 1995.

Hindle, Wilfred (ed.), *Foreign Correspondent: Personal Adventures Abroad in Search of the News, by Twelve British Journalists*. London: George G. Harrap, 1939.

Hodgson, Sir Robert McLeod, *Spain Resurgent*, with an introduction by the Earl of Selborne. London: Hutchinson, 1953.

Howson, Gerald, *Arms for Spain: The Untold Story of the Spanish Civil War*. London: John Murray, 1998.

Ion Mota si Vasile Marin: 25 ani dela moarte. Madrid: Editura 'Carpatii', 1962.

Jackson, Gabriel, *The Spanish Republic and the Civil War, 1931–1939*. Princeton: Princeton University Press, 1971.

Jackson, Julian, *The Popular Front in France: Defending Democracy, 1934–38*, Cambridge: Cambridge University Press, 1990.

Jackson, Michael W., *Fallen Sparrows: The International Brigades in the Spanish Civil War*. Philadelphia: American Philosophical Society, 1994.

Jerrold, Douglas, *Georgian Adventure*. London: Right Book Club, 1938.

Johnston, Robert H., *New Mecca, New Babylon: Paris and the Russian Exiles, 1920–1945*. Kingston: McGill-Queen's University Press, 1988.

Jordan, Nicole, *The Popular Front and Central Europe: The Dilemmas of French Impotence, 1918–1940*. Cambridge: Cambridge University Press, 1992.

Joubert, Henri, *L'Espagne de Franco: synthèse de trois conférences données du 17 janvier au 10 février 1938*. Paris: Sorlot, 1938.

Junod, Marcel, *Warrior Without Weapons*. London: Jonathan Cape, 1951.

Keene, Judith, 'An Antipodean Bridegroom of Death: an Australian with Franco's forces in the Spanish Civil War', *Journal of the Royal Australian Historical Society*, 70, part 4 (April 1985).

Keene, Judith, *The Last Mile to Huesca: An Australian Nurse in the Spanish Civil War*. Sydney: University of New South Wales Press, 1988.

Keene, Judith, 'Nor more than brothers and sisters: women in front line combat in the Spanish Civil War', in Peter Monteath and Frederic S. Zuckerman (eds), *Modern Europe: Histories and Identities*. Adelaide: Australian Humanities Press, 1998.

Kemp, Peter, *Mine Were of Trouble*. London: Cassell, 1957.

Kemp, Peter, *No Colours or Crest*. London: Cassell, 1958.

Kershaw, Howard A., *Quaker Service in Modern War*. New York: Prentice Hall, 1950.

Knickerbocker, H. R., *The Siege of Alcázar: A War-Log of the Spanish Revolution*. London: Hutchinson, 1936.

Knightley, Phillip, *Philby: The Life and Views of the KGB Masterspy*. London: André Deutsch, 1988.

Koch, Stephen, *Double Lives: Stalin, Willi Münzenberg and the Seduction of the Intellectuals*. London: HarperCollins, 1995.

Koestler, Arthur, *Spanish Testament*, introduction by the Duchess of Atholl. London: Victor Gollancz Ltd., 1937.

Koestler, Arthur, *The Invisible Writing: The Second Volume of an Autobiography, 1932–40*. New York: Stein & Day, 1984.

Lacouture, Jean, *Léon Blum*, translated by George Holoch. New York: Holmes & Meier, 1982.

Lannon, Frances, *Privilege, Persecution and Prophecy: The Catholic Church in Spain 1875–1975*. Oxford: Clarendon Press, 1987.

Lannon, Frances, 'Women and images of women in the Spanish Civil War', *Transactions of the Royal Historical Society*, Sixth Series, 1 (1991).

Ledeen, Michael, *Universal Fascism: The Theory and Practice of the Fascist International: 1928–36*. New York: Howard Fertig, 1972.

Lerma, José Larios Fernández de Villavicencio, Duke of, *Combat over Spain: Memoirs of a Nationalist Fighter Pilot, 1936–1939*. New York: Macmillan 1966.

Livezeanu, Irina, *Cultural Politics in Greater Romania: Regionalism, Nation Building and Ethnic Struggle, 1918–1930*. Ithaca: Cornell University Press, 1995.

Loveday, Arthur, *World War in Spain*. London: John Murray, 1939.

Lunn, Arnold, *Come What May: An Autobiography*. London: Eyre & Spottiswoode, 1940.

Lunn, Arnold, *Spanish Rehearsal: An Eyewitness in Spain during the Civil War, 1936– 1939*, foreword by William F. Buckley, Jr. Old Greenwich, CT: Devin-Adair, 1937, reprinted 1974.

Lunn, Arnold, *Unkilled for So Long*. London: George Allen & Unwin, 1968.

Lyons, Eugene (ed.), *We Cover the World, by Sixteen Foreign Correspondents*. London: George G. Harrap, 1937.

McCullagh, Francis, *In Franco's Spain: Being the Experiences of an Irish War-Correspondent during the Great Civil War Which Began in 1936*. London: Burns, Oates & Washbourne Ltd., 1937.

McGarry, Fearghal, *Irish Politics and the Spanish Civil War*. Cork: Cork University Press, 1999.

MacKee, Seumas, *I was a Franco Soldier*. London: United Editorial Ltd., 1938.

McNeill Moss, Geoffrey, *The Siege of the Alcázar: A History of the Siege of the Toledo Alcázar, 1936*. New York: Alfred A. Knopf, 1937.

Madariaga, María Rosa de, 'The intervention of Moroccan troops in the Spanish Civil War: a reconsideration', *European History Quarterly*, **22** (1) (1992).

Malefakis, Edward (ed.), *La guerra de España (1936–1939)*. Madrid: Taurus, 1996.

Mangini, Shirley, *Memories of Resistance: Women's Voices from the Spanish Civil War*. New Haven: Yale University Press, 1995.

Marin, Ana, *Poveste de Dincolo...(Amintiri din tara cutropita) [Stories from the Other Side: Memories from the Occupied Country]*. Madrid: Editura Autorului, 1979.

Marty, Albert, *L'Action Française racontée par elle-même*. Paris: Nouvelle Éditions Latines, 1968.

Mathews, Herbert Lionel, *Half of Spain Died: A Reappraisal of the Spanish Civil War*. New York: Scribner, 1973.

Maurras, Charles, *Vers l'Espagne de Franco*. Paris: Éditions du Livre Moderne, 1943.

Mesa, José Luis de, *Los otros internacionales: voluntarios extranjeros desconocidos en el bando nacional durante la guerra civil (1936–1939)* Madrid: Barbarroja, 1998.

Mitchell, Sir Peter Chalmers, *My House in Málaga*. London: Faber and Faber Ltd., 1937.

Mitchell, Timothy, *Betrayal of the Innocents: Desire, Power and the Catholic Church in Spain*. Philadelphia: University of Pennsylvania Press, 1998.

Moloney, Thomas, *Westminster, Whitehall and the Vatican: The Role of Cardinal Hinsley, 1935–43*, Tunbridge Wells: Burns & Oates, 1985.

Monks, Noel, *Eyewitness*. London: Fredrick Muller, 1955.

Monteath, Peter, *Writing the Good Fight: Political Commitment in the International Literature of the Spanish Civil War*. Westport, CT: Greenwood Press, 1994.

Moradiellos, Enrique, 'The origins of the British non-intervention in the Spanish Civil War: Anglo-Spanish relations in early 1936', *European History Quarterly*, XXI (3) (1991).

Moradiellos, Enrique, *La perfidia de Albión: el gobierno británico y la Guerra Civil Española*. Madrid: Siglo Veintiuno Editores, 1996.

Moreno Sardá, Amparo, 'La réplica de las mujeres al franquismo', in Pilar Folgera, María Isabel Cabrera Bosch (eds), *El Feminismo en España: dos siglos de historia*, Madrid: Editorial Pablo Iglesias, 1988.

Las mujeres y la Guerra Civil Española: III, Jornadas de Estudio Monográficos. Salamanca, October 1989, Ministerio de Cultura: Instituto de la Mujer, 1991.

Nabokov, Vladimir Vladimirovich, *Speak, Memory: An Autobiography Revisited*. London: Weidenfeld & Nicolson, 1967.

Nagy-Talavera, Nicholas M., *The Green Shirts and the Others: A History of Fascism in Hungary and Roumania*. Stanford, CA: Hoover Institution Press, 1970.

Nash, Mary, *Defying Male Civilization: Women in the Spanish Civil War*. Denver, CO: Arden Press, 1995.

Nicholson, Helen, *Death in the Morning*. London: Lovat Dickson, 1937.

Noguères, Henri, *La Vie quotidienne en France au temps du Front Populaire 1935–1938*. Paris: Hachette, 1977.

Nolte, Ernst, *The Three Faces of Fascism: Action Française, Italian Fascism and National Socialism*. New York: New American Library, 1963.

O'Duffy, Eoin, *Crusade in Spain*. Clonskeagh: Browne and Nolan, 1938.

Osgood, Samuel M., 'The "Front Populaire": views from the Right,' *International Review of Social History*, 9 (2), (1964).

Osgood, Samuel M., *French Royalism since 1870*. The Hague: Martinus Nijhoff, 1970.

Oudard, Georges, *Chemises noires, brunes, vertes en Espagne*. Paris: Librairie Plon, 1938.

Pachmuss, Temira (ed.), *A Russian Cultural Revival: A Critical Anthology of Émigré Literature before 1939*. Knoxville: University of Tennessee Press, 1981.

Page, Bruce, Leitch, David and Knightley, Phillip, *Philby: The Spy Who Betrayed a Generation*. London: Sphere Books, 1968.

Payne, Stanley G., *Falange: A History of Spanish Fascism*. Stanford: Stanford University Press, 1961.

Payne, Stanley G., *Politics and the Military in Modern Spain*. Stanford: Stanford University Press, 1967.

Payne, Stanley G., *Spain's First Democracy: The Second Republic, 1931–1936*. Madison: University of Wisconsin Press, 1993.

Philby, Kim, *My Silent War*. London: MacGibbon & Kee, 1968.

Pike, David Wingeate, *Les Français et la guerre d'Espagne*. Paris: Presses Universitaires de France, 1975.

Preston, Paul (ed.), *Spain in Crisis: The Evolution and Decline of the Franco Regime*. Hassocks: Harvester Press, 1976.

Preston, Paul, *The Spanish Civil War 1936–39*. London: Weidenfeld & Nicolson, 1986.

Preston, Paul, 'The discreet charm of a dictator', *Times Literary Supplement*, 15 March 1993.

Preston, Paul, 'General Franco as military leader', *Transactions of the Royal Historical Society*, Sixth Series, IV London: Royal Historical Society, 1994.

Preston, Paul, *Franco: A Biography*. London: Fontana, 1995.

Preston, Paul, *The Politics of Revenge: Fascism and the Military in Twentieth-Century Spain*. London: Routledge, 1995.

Preston, Paul, *Comrades!: Portraits from the Spanish Civil War*. London: HarperCollins, 1999.

Preston, Paul and Mackenzie, Ann L. (eds.), *The Republic Besieged: Civil War in Spain 1936–1939*. Edinburgh: Edinburgh University Press, 1996.

Prost, Henri, *Destin de la Roumanie, 1918–1954*, preface by Albert Mousset. Paris: Berger-Levrault, 1954.

Puzzo, Dante Anthony, *Spain and the Great Powers, 1936–1941*. New York: Columbia University Press, 1962.

Raeff, Marc, *Russia Abroad: A Cultural History of the Russian Emigration, 1919–1939*. New York: Oxford University Press, 1990.

Raupach, Hans, 'The impact of the Great Depression in Eastern Europe', *Journal of Contemporary History*, 4 (4), 1969.

Read, Donald, *The Power of News: The History of Reuters 1849–1989*. Oxford: Oxford University Press, 1992.

Réal del Sarte, Maxime, *Au pays de Franco: notre frère Latin*. Paris: Collection la Caravelle, 1937.

Reig Tapia, Alberto, *Franco 'Caudillo': mito y realidad*, 2nd edn. Madrid: Tecnos, 1996.

Rémond, René, *The Right Wing in France from 1815 to de Gaulle*. Philadelphia: University of Pennsylvania Press, 1969.

Rémond, René, *Les Catholiques dans la France des années 30*. Paris: Éditions Cana, 1979.

Ries, Karl and Ring, Hans, *The Legion Condor: A History of the Luftwaffe in the Spanish Civil War, 1936–1939*. West Chester, PA: Schiffer Military History, 1992.

Rodríguez-Moñino Soriano, Rafael, *La misión diplomática de Don Jacobo Stuart Fitz James y Falcó, XVII Duque de Alba, en la Embajada de España en Londres (1937–1945)*. Valencia: Castalia, 1971.

Rodríguez-Puértolas, Julio, *Literatura fascista española*. Madrid: Akal, 1987.

La Rouchefoucauld, Edmée de, *Spanish Women*. New York: Peninsular News Service, 1938.

Roura, Assumpta, *Mujeres para después de una Guerra: informes sobre moralidad y prostitución en la posguerra española*. Barcelona: Flor del Viento, 1998.

Ruiz-Manjón Cabeza, Octavio and Oliver, Miguel Gómez, *Los nuevos historiadores ante la Guerra Civil española*, Vol. 1. Granada: Diputación Provincial de Granada, 1999.

Scott-Ellis, Priscilla, *The Chances of Death: A Diary of the Spanish Civil War*. (ed.) Raymond Carr. London: Michael Russell, 1995.

Seidman, Michael, 'Frentes en calma de la guerra civil', *Historia Social*, 27 (1997), pp. 37–59.

Shubert, Adrian, *The Road to Revolution in Spain: The Coal Miners of Asturias, 1860–1934*. Urbana: University of Illinois Press, 1987.

Shubert, Adrian, *A Social History of Modern Spain*. London: Unwin Hyman, 1990.

Sima, Horia, *Dos movimientos nacionales: José Antonio Primo de Rivera y Corneliu Zelea Codreanu*. Madrid: Ediciones Europa, 1960.

Soucy, Robert, *French Fascism: The Second Wave, 1933–39*. New Haven: Yale University Press, 1995.

Southworth, Herbert Rutledge, *El mito de la cruzada de Franco*. Barcelona: Plaza & Janes, 1964, 1986.

Southworth, Herbert Rutledge, *Le Mythe de la croisade de Franco*. Paris: Ruedo Ibérico, 1964.

Southworth, Herbert Rutledge, *Guernica! Guernica! A Study of Journalism, Diplomacy, Propaganda and History*. Berkeley: University of California Press, 1977.

Stradling, Robert A, 'Franco's Irish Volunteers', *History Today*, 45 (3), (11 March 1995).

Stradling, Robert A., *The Irish and the Spanish Civil War, 1936–39: Crusades in Conflict*. Manchester: Mandolin, 1999.

Sturdza, Michel, *The Suicide of Europe: Memoirs of Prince Michel Sturdza*. Boston: Western Islands Publication, 1968.

Tangye, Nigel, *Red, White and Spain*. London: Rich & Cowan Ltd., 1937.

Templewood, Samuel John Gurney Hoare, 1st Viscount, *Nine Troubled Years*. London: Collins, 1954.

Tennant, Eleonora, *Spanish Journey: Personal Experiences of the Civil War*. London: Eyre & Spottiswoode, 1936.

Tharaud, Jérôme and Tharaud, Jean, *Cruelle Espagne*. Paris: Librairie Plon, 1937.

Tharaud, Jérôme and Tharaud, Jean, *L'Envoyé de l'Archange*. Paris: Librairie Plon, 1939.

Thomas, Frank, *Brother against Brother: Experiences of a British Volunteer in the Spanish Civil War*, (ed.) Robert Stradling. Phoenix Mill: Sutton, 1998.

Thomas, Hugh, *The Spanish Civil War*. New York: Touchstone, 1986.

Thompson, Sir Geoffrey, *Front-Line Diplomat*. London: Hutchinson, 1959.

Thurlow, Richard C., *Fascism in Britain: A History, 1918–1985*. Oxford: Blackwell, 1987.

Tournoux, Jean Raymond, *L'Histoire secrète*. Paris: Plon, 1962.

Trythall, Anthony John, *"Boney" Fuller: The Intellectual General 1878–1966*. London: Cassell, 1977.

Tuñón de Lara, Manuel, *La guerra civil española: 50 años después*. Madrid: Labor, 1985.

Tuñón de Lara, Manuel, *Historia de España, Tomo IX. La crisis del estado: dictadura, república, guerra (1923–1939)*. Barcelona: Labor, 1993.

Tusell, Javier, *Vivir en guerra: España 1936–1939*. Madrid: Sílex, 1996.

Ustinov, Peter, *Dear Me*. London: Heinemann, 1977.

Vago, Bela, *The Shadow of the Swastika: The Rise of Fascism and Anti-Semitism in the Danube Basin, 1936–1939*. London: Saxon House for the Institute of Jewish Affairs, 1975.

Veiga, Francisco, *La mística del ultranacionalismo: historia de la Guardia de Hierro Rumania, 1919–1941*. Bellaterra: Publicaciones de la Universitat Autónoma de Barcelona, 1989.

Vidal Manzanares, César, *La guerra de Franco: historia militar de la Guerra Civil Española*. Barcelona: Planeta, 1996.

Vilallonga, José Luis de, *Fiesta*. Paris: Éditions du Seuil, 1974.

Vilallonga, José Luis de, *Vilallonga: la cruda y tierna verdad: memorias no autorizadas*. Barcelona: Plaza & Janés Editores, 2000.

Viñas, Angel, *La Alemania nazi y el 18 de Julio: antecedentes de la intervención alemana en la guerra civil española*. Madrid: Alianza, 1974.

Vincent, Mary, *Catholicism in the Second Spanish Republic: Religion and Politics in Salamanca, 1930–1936*. Oxford: Clarendon Press, 1996.

Watkins, K. W., *Britain Divided: The Effect of the Spanish Civil War on British Political Opinion*. London: Thomas Nelson, 1963.

Weaver, Denis, *Front Page Europe*. London: The Cresset Press, 1943.

Weber, Eugen Joseph, *Action Française: Royalism and Reaction in Twentieth Century France*. Stanford: Stanford University Press, 1962.

Weber, Eugen Joseph, 'France', in Hans Rogger and Eugen Joseph Weber (eds), *The European Right: A Historical Profile*. Berkeley: University of California Press, 1965.

Weber, Eugen Joseph, 'Men of the Archangel', *Journal of Contemporary History* 1 (April 1966).

Weber, Eugen Joseph, *The Hollow Years: France in the 1930s*. New York: Norton, 1994.

Werth, Alexander, *The Destiny of France*. London: Hamish Hamilton, 1937.

Whitaker, John Thompson, *Fear Came on Europe*, Preface by John Gunther. London: Hamish Hamilton, 1937.

Whitaker, John Thompson, *We Cannot Escape History*. New York: Macmillan, 1943.

Williamson, Philip, *Stanley Baldwin: Conservative Leadership and National Values*. Cambridge: Cambridge University Press, 1999.

Winock, Michel, *Nationalisme, anti-sémitisme et fascisme en France*. Paris: Éditions du Seuil, 1990.

Winock, Michel, *Histoire de l'extrême droite en France*. Paris: Éditions du Seuil, 1993.

Woolf, S. J. (ed.), *Fascism in Europe*. New York: Methuen, 1981.

Yaremchuk, Anton Prokofyevich, *Russkie dobrovol'tsy v Ispanii 1936–1939 [Russian Volunteers in Spain 1936–1939]*. San Francisco: Globus Publishers, 1983.

Index

310 INDEX